FAITH, FORCE, AND REAS

An Armchair History of the Rule of Law

Faith, Force, and Reason follows the evolution of the rule of law from its birth in the marshes of Mesopotamia over 4,000 years ago to its battle against the remnants of apartheid in South Africa in the last twenty-five years. It is recounted through the voices of emperors and kings, judges and jurists, and popes and philosophers who have thought about what the rule of law is all about and how it works.

All of law's most momentous achievements – Justinian's Corpus Juris Civilis, the Magna Carta, and the American Bill of Rights – and most celebrated advocates – Plato and Aristotle, Cicero, Aquinas, Edward Coke, Hugo Grotius, and John Marshall – are featured. So are law's darkest moments: the trial of Socrates, the burning and beheading of witches and heretics, the persecution of Jews, and the proclamation of *lex regia* which legalized the dictatorial powers of Roman emperors and medieval kings.

Faith, Force, and Reason challenges readers to think about the lessons of the history they have read. What does the rule of law mean in our own time? What does it demand of us as well as our political leaders?

DAVID M. BEATTY is Professor Emeritus in the Faculty of Law at the University of Toronto.

FAITH, FORCE, AND REASON

AN ARMCHAIR HISTORY

OF THE RULE OF LAW

DAVID M. BEATTY

UNIVERSITY OF TORONTO PRESS
Toronto Buffalo London

© University of Toronto Press 2022
Toronto Buffalo London
utorontopress.com
Printed in Canada

ISBN 978-1-4875-4079-1 (cloth)   ISBN 978-1-4875-4081-4 (EPUB)
ISBN 978-1-4875-4082-1 (paper)   ISBN 978-1-4875-4080-7 (PDF)

Library and Archives Canada Cataloguing in Publication

Title: Faith, force, and reason : an armchair history of the rule of law / David
  M. Beatty.
Names: Beatty, David M., author.
Description: Includes bibliographical references and index.
Identifiers: Canadiana (print) 20210340460 |
  Canadiana (ebook) 20210340487 |
  ISBN 9781487540791 (cloth) | ISBN 9781487540821 (paper) |
  ISBN 9781487540814 (EPUB) | ISBN 9781487540807 (PDF)
Subjects: LCSH: Rule of law – History.
Classification: LCC K3171.B43 2022 | DDC 340/.11–dc23

We wish to acknowledge the land on which the University of Toronto Press
operates. This land is the traditional territory of the Wendat, the Anishnaabeg,
the Haudenosaunee, the Métis, and the Mississaugas of the Credit First Nation.

University of Toronto Press acknowledges the financial support of the
Government of Canada, the Canada Council for the Arts, and the Ontario Arts
Council, an agency of the Government of Ontario, for its publishing activities.

**Canada Council
for the Arts**

**Conseil des Arts
du Canada**

**ONTARIO ARTS COUNCIL
CONSEIL DES ARTS DE L'ONTARIO**
an Ontario government agency
un organisme du gouvernement de l'Ontario

Funded by the   Financé par le
Government   gouvernement
of Canada   du Canada

Canada

MIX
Paper from
responsible sources
FSC® C016245

To Harry Arthurs, who taught me.
To the scales of justice, which inspired me.
To Ninette, who saved me.

You will study the wisdom of the past, for in a wilderness of conflicting counsels, a trail has there been blazed. You will study the life of mankind, for this is the life you must order and, to order with wisdom, must know. You will study the precepts of justice, for these are the truths that through you will come to their hour of triumph. Here is the high emprise, the fine endeavor, the splendid possibility of achievement to which I summon you and bid you welcome.

Benjamin Cardozo (1925)

Contents

Preface

This is a book about the rule of law. Its purpose is to explain, in a way everyone can understand, what law is and the method and reach of its rule.

There are lots of books on the rule of law but almost all of them are written by and for professionals. Even for those trained in law, they can be heavy lifting.

Currently there is no short introduction that general readers can turn to for the basics. *Faith, Force, and Reason* is meant to fill that gap.

The book is written for anyone with a broad interest in politics and law. My aim has been to tell the story in a way that is easy to read. I have tried to keep the technical jargon, Latin phrases, and Roman numerals to a minimum. Rather than another theoretical analysis of the rationality and coherence of law, I focus on how the rule of law solves real problems.

My primary goal is to provide a pocket history of how the rule of law has come to replace faith and force as the preferred method of conflict resolution. The book follows the way legal thinking has evolved over time and challenges readers to consider what it would mean if the rule of law "governed" how they settled conflicts that occur in their own lives.

Much of the story will sound depressingly familiar. At critical points, the worst stereotypes of self-serving professionals are center stage; we see lawyers looking out for themselves.

But at others, readers will find moments when "thinking like a lawyer" calibrates the scales of justice just right. Best of all, following the history of the rule of law demonstrates that you don't have to be a lawyer to understand how it works.

History teaches that the rule of law is just a way of reasoning that is as pertinent in our personal lives as it is in the public square. As the Greeks understood more than two thousand years ago, when law truly is the king, everyone is "thinking like a lawyer" 24/7.

Anyone who makes a living studying or practicing the law will know all the characters and events that pop up in the story. The book makes no claim to original research. That doesn't mean professionals won't profit from reflecting on the evolution of law's sovereignty over the past four thousand years.

With the benefit of hindsight, it is easy to see the blind spots and missteps of judges and jurists of earlier generations, and the day is not far off when the light of history will reveal our biases and prejudices as well. Even more than the general reader, professionals are vulnerable to a charge of hypocrisy if they hold their presidents and prime ministers to principles and rules they personally ignore.

In truth, all readers should be forewarned. It's not just the professionals who have a personal stake in the story. Anyone who thinks the rule of law is a good idea runs the risk of being branded as an outlaw if they refuse to change some of their most basic daily routines, including their eating habits. As readers will discover in the final pages of the book, the logic of the rule of law leads inescapably to a world that is overwhelmingly vegan.

Anyone who writes a history of anything is indebted to the people who made it. That is especially true in a chronicle of the rule of law, where an idea has been nurtured and defended by a legion of publicly spirited advocates for almost four millennia. Hammurabi and Moses, Aristotle and Plato, Cicero and Justinian, Aquinas and Gratian, Bracton and Coke, de Vitoria and Grotius, Hamilton and Marshall – these are the big names, but they are just the tip of the iceberg. The rule of law would not have the authority and stature it has today without the dedication of countless unsung heroes who dedicated their lives to its utopian ideals.

Even though a history of the rule of law is mostly a recording of the achievements of our ancestors (and so writes its own narrative), mistakes and misscues are bound to happen. Errors of omission and misinterpretation are a constant threat. In saving me from the most egregious, I owe a debt of thanks to family and friends, students and colleagues who have endured countless conversations and offered constructive criticism. Among those who went beyond the call of duty, I owe special thanks to Alex Aleinikoff, Alan Brudner, David Dyzenhaus, Anver Emon, Elizabeth Finne, Jim Gordley, Ninette Kelley, Mathias Kumm, Martin Loughlin, Jim MacPherson, Lorne Sossin, and Russell VerSteeg. I am especially grateful to Daniel Quinlan, Lisa Jemison, Stephanie Mazza, Breanna Muir, Christine Robertson, Sebastian Frye, Jodi Litvin, and Ryan Perks at University of Toronto Press for fine-tuning the text and turning it into a book. It goes without saying that whatever blunders remain are my responsibility.

FAITH, FORCE, AND REASON

An Armchair History of the Rule of Law

Introduction

The rule of law is all the rage. Everybody swears allegiance. China, Russia, and Saudi Arabia all claim to be rule of law states. Economists insist it's an essential condition of successful development. It has become a litmus test of political legitimacy, alongside democracy and human rights.

Despite being part of everyday conversation, precisely what the rule of law means is unclear. The image that comes to mind when we think about the rule of law is fuzzier than our understanding of democracy (popular consent and majority rule) and human rights (freedom and equality).

Even among legal scholars and political philosophers, there is no consensus as to what governments must do to qualify as a rule of law state. Some insist there is no necessary connection between law and justice. Others equate law with oppression and claim the legal order is an instrument of coercion wielded by the ruling class. For many, the rule of law is so overused it has become little more than a slogan. Claimed by so many regimes across such a wide ideological spectrum, it lacks a precise meaning. Being all things to all people, it has no critical edge.

To rescue the rule of law from its current confusion, *Faith, Force, and Reason* offers a retrospective view of where the rule of law has come from and what it has meant in the past. The idea is to search for its identity in its roots. The book follows the rule of law's development from its birth in the marshes of Mesopotamia over four thousand years ago to its ridding South Africa of the remnants of the apartheid state in the last quarter century. It traces law's odyssey, from its call for the protection of widows and orphans in Hammurabi's Code to its denunciation of homophobia and homelessness by South Africa's Constitutional Court some thirty-five hundred years later.

Law's assertion of sovereignty is one of the oldest stories in human history. It reads like a chain novel that has been unfolding for more than four thousand years. Ideas are passed down from father to son and each generation stands on the shoulders of its elders. Mesopotamian law codes provided a template around which the law that Moses gave to the Jewish people was written. Romans studied the methods and ideas of the Greeks, and medieval lawyers mastered both. Americans were children of the Enlightenment, schooled in the classics, who in time became a source of inspiration for jurists in the rest of the world.

The story has all the panache of a classic epic: an eternal struggle for utopia, the ideal, perfectly governed community – a saga marked by ups and downs, highs and lows, victories and defeats. It is recounted through the voices of emperors and kings, judges and jurists, popes and philosophers who have thought about what the rule of law is all about and how it works. It is distinguished by acts of great heroism and inexcusable betrayal.

Reading back into the rule of law's past yields some surprising results. Most notably, unlike our current ambiguity, history shows there has been a basic understanding of what the rule of law is all about for at least twenty-five hundred years. Tracing law's evolution back to its beginning reveals that, ever since the Greeks, the rule of law has been concerned with three principal ideas.

First, rules and commands take on legal force only when they meet basic formal requirements (e.g., they must be general, transparent, and prospective) and are adopted by following certain predetermined procedures. Second, the purpose of law is to encourage people to behave respectfully toward one another and to settle their conflicts peacefully. Finally, the sovereignty of law is universal; it is binding on rulers as much as the people they rule. Since the Greeks, at each stage of history, people have debated all three: what the formalities of law require; what ideals of justice law must serve; and the extent to which rulers and political leaders must obey. We still debate them today.

In order to tell law's story as concisely as possible, a synoptic approach has been adopted. Each of the first nine chapters provides a snapshot of how the rule of law was doing, at different stages of its journey, in the effort to live up to its earliest ambitions. They are not intended to be exhaustive. The goal is to deliver the essentials. They catalog law's most momentous achievements – Justinian's Corpus Juris Civilis, Magna Carta, and the American Bill of Rights – and highlight the lives of such giants as Socrates, Cicero, Aquinas, Edward Coke, Hugo Grotius, and John Marshall.

Two major plotlines dominate the story. First, right from the start, the overarching ambition of the rule of law has been to rid the world of tyranny and injustice, and history shows that bit by bit it's making progress.

Tracing law's journey from Hammurabi to Mandela confirms that the long arc of its history bends unmistakably toward justice.

History also reveals that, in each era, many of law's greatest accomplishments can be traced back to the professionals (especially jurists and judges) and the way they think. *Faith, Force, and Reason* documents how the law on slavery, torture, capital punishment, due process, religious and sexual freedom, dress and speech codes, and the laws of war has evolved over time according to the analytical methods employed by the professionals. It suggests that the evolution in the way lawyers justify their conclusions gives us reason to be optimistic about the future.

If the first lesson of the rule of law's history is that we are moving in the right direction, the second tells a more cautionary tale. Looking across law's four-thousand-year odyssey reminds us how hard-won its victories have been and how fragile its present circumstances really are. Looking back over law's battles on behalf of the victims of tyranny and oppression shows it has failed them as often as it has advanced their cause. The sad but irreducible truth is that for most of human history, slavery, patriarchy, torture, and war have all been legal.

To make matters worse, scrolling through law's defining moments shows that a major cause of its checkered past has been the work of experts and professionals. Aristotle (but not Plato) on women, Aquinas on slavery, and Grotius on war are among the most notorious examples. Cataloging the most egregious injustices carried out in the name of the law explains why the lawyer has been cast as a treacherous character all through history; why Shakespeare spoke for generations when he had Dick the Butcher call for all of them to be killed.

One of the most glaring acts of betrayal committed by the professionals has been their reluctance to embrace the supremacy of law and its authority to hold rulers in check. The idea that law stands above, and acts as a constraint, on the power of rulers is not one judges or jurists have championed enthusiastically. Indeed, all of them – Roman jurists, sharia *fuqaha*, canon and civil law scholars, and English common lawyers – constructed elaborate theories to bend the law to the will of the rulers they served.

The failure of professionals to rigorously defend the sovereignty of law continues in the modern era. The rulings of the United States Supreme Court certifying the legality of slavery, segregation, forced sterilization, the exclusion of women from the legal profession, and the imprisonment of more than one hundred thousand Japanese Americans during the Second World War are among the darkest moments in law's history. The judges could have put a stop to all of these flagrant abuses of power, but they didn't.

Despite the tragedy of the Americans' experience, the record of the rule of law in the modern era, as in every other stage of its odyssey, has not been one of unmitigated failure. Examining how judges in other parts of the world have exercised their powers of review gives us reason for cautious optimism. History shows we are still moving in the right direction. In fact, a series of judgments, rendered by an inspired group of judges who sat on South Africa's highest court at the moment when the country became a constitutional democracy, could mark a new beginning.

The South African decisions are best known for remedying long-standing injustices left over from the apartheid regime. As a group of cases, they are quite remarkable. In little more than a decade, the South Africans outlawed capital punishment, put an end to discrimination against lesbians and gays, and ordered the government to treat the homeless and people infected with HIV/AIDS more humanely. For its inhabitants, these developments closed a dark and disturbing chapter in South African legal history.

The significance of these cases, however, transcends local politics. They are just as notable for the reasons they gave to support their conclusions as for the injustices they remedied. The way the South Africans responded to the iniquities of homophobia, homelessness, and state executions turns out to be part of a shift in legal analysis that has been gaining momentum over the last fifty years.

This new way of thinking has two defining features. First, it builds on a principle of moderation and balance that allows judges to insulate themselves from the influence of those who appointed them and render judgments that are free of political and personal bias. Second, the way the South Africans explained their decisions is easy to understand. You don't have to be a lawyer to see how the process works.

Both characteristics have deep historical roots. Law's accessibility goes back to the very beginning. Hammurabi's Code was intended to speak directly to the citizens of Babylon, and Athenian courts were run by ordinary people, not professionals. As well, the principle (known as proportionality) on which the South Africans based their decisions can be traced back to Aristotle and the Greeks.

The way the principle works, all the focus is on the facts of each case and how the competing interests of those involved can be balanced fairly. Proportionality is the fulcrum on which the scales of justice pivot. It is the only law you need to know and you don't need to be a lawyer to apply it. The principle flourished in all aspects of Greek science and culture long before legal professionals made their debut in Rome.

With the telling of South Africa's engagement with the rule of law, our history is complete. Parts 1 through 3 of the book lay out law's story from its origins till today. Part 4 looks at the lessons learned. It considers what history tells us to do if we want to avoid the injustices and mistakes of the past. Although its orientation is quite different from the rest of the book, it could turn out to be the climax of the story. The alternative, of ignoring the lessons of history, means, as the saying goes, we are doomed to repeat it.

In its concluding chapters, the book considers whether a return to what we might call a "populist" conception of the rule of law could mark the beginning of a new era. The idea is to explore what it would mean if everyone thought about resolving conflict like the South Africans. Using their method as a guide for how to think about the conflicts and controversies that threaten our own peace and security provides a window onto what a state governed by the rule of law might look like in the future.

Readers will have to decide for themselves, but an examination of a range of cases of religious, ethnic, and armed conflict suggests the South African approach has the capacity to settle even the most deeply felt differences in a way that is fair to everyone involved. For our generation, it offers one way to clarify the confusion and uncertainty that currently surrounds the meaning of the rule of law, and suggests how the next chapter in its history might be written.

Because each moment in law's history is so strongly influenced by the thinking of previous generations, *Faith, Force, and Reason* follows a chronological narrative. It tracks law's evolution from its earliest sightings in the ancient world through medieval times and into the modern era.

Each chapter has a common structure. First, the political and social world in which law must operate is described. Then its sources of legitimacy – faith, force, and reason – are examined. Next, its scope, method, and purposes are cataloged and compared. Each chapter highlights the great events and people of their respective eras, both the good and the bad. And in each chapter the force of law is tested by evaluating its treatment of women, minorities, dissidents, and the disadvantaged. How judges and jurists reason is given special scrutiny. The history of law turns out to be vitally affected by the way lawyers think.

The story begins more than four thousand years ago in what was known as the Fertile Crescent or the Hilly Flanks – the place where Africa, Asia, and Europe converge. At this moment in history, this part of the world was (and still is) a violent and dangerous place. Rival empires – Akkadian, Assyrian, Babylonian, Egyptian, Hittite, Persian, Sumerian – took turns fighting deadly wars against each other, and roads and seas were perilous places to travel.

In digging through the ruins of these ancient civilizations, archeologists have turned up lots of evidence that the rulers of these embryonic states all thought that codes of law were an important tool in making their cities safer and more livable places.

Although there were significant variations in the legal regimes that governed these tribal communities, they shared two core features. First, all of them were written by military strongmen who said they had been chosen to lay down the law by the Gods. Second, their stated intention was to do justice and safeguard the righteousness and well-being of their communities.

The most famous of these first law codes was written by a man named Hammurabi, who was one of Babylon's most powerful kings. His code is more than thirty-five hundred years old and is the focus of chapter 1.

If you search for Hammurabi's Code on the Internet, the first thing you will notice is that by modern standards it is incredibly brief. Rather than the dozens of specialized codes (criminal, tax, trade, family, work, school, etc.) that we rely on to organize our affairs, Hammurabi laid down his entire set of laws on the face of a two-meter slab of stone.

As you scroll through the document you will also see that, rather than being written in the language of rules and regulations and commands, Hammurabi's law is presented as a series of simple cases designed to illustrate methods of fair dealing, punishing wrongdoing, alleviating oppression, and providing relief to the poor.

Drawing its legitimacy from the faith of its people and the force of its rulers, the Near Eastern model of the rule of law was able to maintain its authority for more than two thousand years – roughly half of law's entire existence. It was eventually eclipsed by a different conception of the rule of law that was the brainchild of the people who built the city-states of Classical Greece more than twenty-five hundred years ago. Threatened by hostile neighbors and internal strife, the citizens of these ministates, including Athens and Sparta, were forced to rethink how they governed themselves.

In looking for better ways to solve their differences, the Greeks spent a lot of time reflecting on both the theory and practice of law. Although it is most commonly thought of as the world's first democracy, it turns out that Athens was also the world's first rule of law state. The earliest images of law on Achilles's shield, as well as the laws of Lycurgus and Solon, the trial and execution of Socrates, the classics by Plato and Aristotle, are all important moments in the history of law that are featured in chapter 2.

That chapter concentrates on two big changes the Greeks made to the concept of law that almost certainly would not have pleased Hammurabi. First they insisted that law gets its authority from human reason and the consent of the governed, not from the Gods (at least not directly), and then they said that ordinary people had the right to prosecute lawmakers who did not respect it. As well as empowering rulers, law became a way of putting limits on what they could do.

The Greeks had the same goal of good governance as the Babylonians. They intended their law to protect the weak and vulnerable and bring justice to the oppressed. They just thought the way to do this was by everyone using common sense instead of a few people with special powers communing with the Gods.

For the Greeks, law was made by ordinary people doing what comes naturally, from the bottom up. For the Babylonians, it was handed down by religious and military leaders drawing inspiration from a supernatural place on high.

The ways the Babylonians and Greeks thought about law still speak to how we talk about law's purposes and sovereignty today. Indeed, the Greek model has been a reference point for the rest of the world since its inception. The first to recognize its genius were the Romans. Chapter 3 follows the elites of Rome, from their earliest missions to Athens to learn the Greek way, through their nurturing of a professional class of jurists and advocates (like Cicero) who came to monopolize the study and practice of law, to Justinian and the Corpus Juris Civilis and the role law played in organizing the affairs of one of the greatest empires in human history. It reviews the treatises of the jurists and compares their writing about human rights and foreign relations with their approval of slavery and the persecution of Christians and Jews.

In the end, the Romans only bought half the Greek package. Although they loved the idea that the authority and legitimacy of the law was based on human reason, the thought of law being sovereign and binding even the emperor got an emphatic thumbs down. Like Hammurabi, Roman emperors resisted any limitation on their powers. On the authority of his jurists, Justinian famously decreed he was above the law. "Princeps Legibus Solutus," he wrote; the prince is not bound by the laws.

Justinian's Code was written fifty years after the collapse of the western half of the Roman Empire. Less than a hundred years later, at the beginning of the seventh century, in the Arabian Desert, the rule of law experienced another sudden and spectacular revival. Like Hammurabi's Code it was divinely inspired. Chapter 4 provides a synopsis of the revelation and refinement of sharia law by Islamic scholars, including its treatment of women and rival religions.

Islamic jurists read the Greek classics but after a spirited debate, they turned their backs on Plato and Aristotle and headed off in a different direction. Divine authority, they decided, not human logic, is what gave sharia law its legitimacy. Over the course of the next five hundred years they crafted a very elaborate body of law and a sophisticated legal system with judges (*qadis*) and jurists (*fuqaha*) and law schools (*madhahib*) to make it a vibrant part of everyday life in the community of believers (*umma*).

They developed different strategies to decipher the meaning of the revelations reported by Mohammad and gathered in groups of like-minded scholars. Chapter 4 compares the competing approaches of the major schools of law they formed and the trade-offs they made with the sultans. For the most part, the focus of sharia law was on the personal dealings and religious duties of the faithful and, like Roman law, more or less gave rulers a free pass.

Chapter 5 picks up law's adventures in central and western Europe, after the collapse of the Roman Empire, as the continent entered a "dark age." The law codes of the Visigoths and the capitularies of Charlemagne set the stage for the ensuing military battles and legal skirmishes between the pope and the Holy Roman emperor.

The spotlight for much of the chapter is on the revival of law schools and the resurgence of canon (Christian) and Roman (civil) law in Bologna after Justinian's Corpus Juris Civilis conveniently reappeared and the writing of Plato and Aristotle began to circulate again, thanks in large part to the translations of Islamic scholars. When the jurists and scholars of medieval Europe were able to read how Plato and Aristotle thought about the law, they were generally more inspired than their counterparts in North Africa and the Middle East. Canon lawyers in the Catholic Church were especially adept at finding common ground between reason and their faith.

Their scholarship, on the obligation of rulers to obey the law, including basic precepts of due process and laws of war, is examined alongside their thinking about burning witches, forcibly converting Jews, and torturing religious and political dissidents. Measured against the ideals of Plato and Aristotle, the verdict on medieval Europe's embrace of the rule of law is mixed. Critically, although jurists wrote passionately about a ruler's obligation to obey the law, they couldn't bring themselves to say emperors and kings had to answer in court when they misbehaved.

Chapter 6 crosses the Channel to follow the contemporaneous struggles of English common law to hold its kings and queens and the Parliament at Westminster to account. The supernatural rituals (oaths, ordeals) of the shire and hundred courts that predate the Norman Conquest, the Doom Book of King Alfred, the assizes of Henry II, Magna Carta, the writings of Henry de Bracton, and the battle waged by Edward Coke against the Stuart kings all figure prominently in the story. Lord

Mansfield's ruling in Somersett's case, that slavery is not recognized in English common law, still ranks as one of law's most iconic moments.

In the end, the English experiment, like all of its predecessors, came up short. Mirroring the experience of Classical Greece, the rule of law proved to be no match for the power of the people and the sovereignty of their Parliament. As John Selden, a contemporary of Coke and the doyen of English legal history, famously put it, Parliament's sovereignty is so absolute and unfettered it could pass a law sentencing to death everyone who got out of bed before nine o'clock and there would be nothing anyone could do about it.

For most of the English colonists who lived on the eastern coast of North America, the fact Parliament was able to insist that its sovereignty was beyond the reach of the law was a problem, and they decided to do something about it. The American War of Independence, and its victors' decision to spell out the powers and purposes of their new government in a written constitution, marks another watershed in the history of the rule of law.

For the first time since the Greeks, lawmakers were required to follow rules that were set down in a basic law, and if they didn't they could be hauled into court. For the first time ever, legally trained judges took charge of ensuring everyone – rulers and ruled alike – obeyed the law. Entrenching a system of judicial review, the United States became the first country since Classical Greece where, as Thomas Paine famously put it, "law would be king."

Chapter 7 provides an assessment of the American experiment by examining the landmark rulings of its Supreme Court over the course of its first 150 years, a period during which it certified the legality of slavery, racial segregation, forced sterilization, and the internment of Japanese Americans during the Second World War. The different styles of reasoning used by the judges to justify these decisions are analyzed and compared. This review of America's conception of the rule of law concludes with an assessment of how law and politics still wrestle for control of the Court.

Ending tyranny and the oppression of citizens by their governments has always been law's primary mission, but it has also been concerned with relations between states and providing them a way to settle their differences without having to resort to armed force. Chapter 8 traces the evolution of the international law of war from the writings of Cicero, Aquinas, and the Dutch jurist Hugo Grotius, through the adoption of the Geneva and Hague Conventions and the holding of the Nuremberg Trials, to the creation of the International Court of Justice and its judgments on the laws of armed force. Again, the different methods of reasoning employed by the judges are analyzed, and again the results are mixed. Readers will not be surprised to learn that while the Court has drawn the limits of military force very strictly and held the most powerful states to account, it has also ruled that law's sovereignty is not absolute and in some cases has made it more difficult for people who are under attack to defend themselves.

In chapter 9, the final case study of law's battle against dictators and despots examines its most recent triumph over the remnants of the apartheid regime in South Africa. In the four-thousand-year history we have been following, negating the crude legacy of an oligarchy of old white men is unquestionably one of law's most satisfying achievements. The heroes in this most recent chapter of law's adventures turn out to be a dozen unheralded judges who sat on the country's Constitutional Court during its first decade of deliberations. Reading their judgments on capital punishment, gay marriage, homelessness, and health care reveals the full force of the law in overcoming the evils of authoritarian and repressive regimes. They demonstrate why the principle of proportionality has earned its status as the ultimate rule of law.

With the South African take on the rule of law, readers will have been introduced to all of the most important moments and milestones in law's four-thousand-year struggle against dictators and despots. Those who make it through the first nine chapters will have been introduced to each of the major legal systems that have embraced the idea of the rule of law. The basic precepts and analytical tools of Greek and Roman (chapters 2 and 3), Islamic and Christian (chapters 4 and 5), civil and common (chapters 5 and 6), and international and constitutional law (chapters 7 through 9) are summarized and evaluated for their capacity to further law's civilizing mission.

Which brings us to today and the question of how our generation will write the next chapter. In part 4, *Faith, Force, and Reason* considers the lessons we should take away from the history we have just read. What must a government do to establish its credentials as a rule of law state? How can discrimination against women and vulnerable minorities be outlawed? How can the treachery of the lawyers be remedied and the supremacy of law restored?

The last three chapters of the book offer one version of what we might do and what the future of the rule of law might look like. The idea is to map out the next stage of law's journey by applying the reasoning used by the South Africans to a series of ongoing conflicts and disputes that currently threaten peace and harmony around the world. Collisions between cultures, the legalities of war, and the rights and wrongs of disciplining and feeding our children each get a chapter.

Chapter 10 addresses the challenges of multiculturalism and how the "clash of civilizations" might play out in court. Its focus is a series of cases that question the legitimacy of outlawing certain forms of speech (e.g., heresy and hate) and dress (e.g., headscarves and face veils). Chapter 11 examines the international community's responsibility to protect women and children from the villainy of tyrants and the atrocities of war, as well as the legality of the methods of modern warfare, including the use of drones and torture.

Finally, chapter 12 builds on the notion, which was central to the thinking of both Plato and Aristotle, that law is just as pertinent to the way we "govern" our personal lives as it is to how rulers exercise state power. The idea is that instead of just criticizing the ineptitude and ethical failings of our leaders, we should look at what it would mean if each of us approached the conflict and tension in our own lives with the tools of legal reason and the power of rational thought. Spanking, charitable giving, and eating animals provide the case studies.

In the spirit of Thomas More's Utopia, where there were no lawyers and everyone was knowledgeable in the law, this book has been written to appeal as much to those who have not had any legal training as to the professionals. The book's message – that law offers a way to eliminate arbitrariness and inconsistencies from both the public and private dimensions of our lives – is a timeless one that has resonated with people of all cultures and faiths. It suggests that a world like More's Utopia, where everyone is a legal expert, and where people are able to settle their differences on the basis of fairness and reason, doesn't have to be just a figment of our imagination. Counterintuitively, *Faith, Force, and Reason* points to the awkward conclusion that encouraging everyone to "think like a lawyer" may be the way to a brighter future.

PART 1

Ancient History: Warlords, Priests, and Philosophers

Chapter One

Babylon and Jerusalem

Law has controlled the natural evolution of the universe since the beginning of time. Ever since the big bang, some 13.7 billion years ago, the mathematical truths of physics have ruled over everything from the creation of galaxies and the birth of stars to the rise and fall of dinosaurs and the making of you and me. If the laws of energy had not been what they are, we wouldn't be who we are today.

The laws of science have not only determined the formation of matter and the speed of light; they have been the only laws in force for almost all the time the universe has existed. Until humans came along, the forces of nature ruled the world.

And our entrance on the world stage is very recent. We are latecomers. Measured against the billions of years that our planet has existed, our time on it has been incredibly brief. If you compressed the life of the earth into a single day, dinosaurs don't show up until 11:00 p.m., and we don't start farming and building cities until a few minutes before midnight. On the grand timeline of history, the thought that humans might create their own laws alongside the eternal laws of the universe has just occurred.[1] In cosmic time, the whole story in this book takes place in the blink of an eye.

The Long Walk

Paleontologists tell a tale of our evolution out of one branch of the ape family in East Africa sometime between 130,000 and 250,000 years ago. From the fossil record, it appears that roughly 100,000 years ago our ancestors began a slow migration north, out of Africa, across the Arabian peninsula, and on into that part of the world known as the Hilly Flanks or the Fertile Crescent. Today, in what we call the Middle East, the region is comprised of many independent states, including Iraq, Iran, Turkey, Syria, Lebanon, and Jordan.

At the start of the journey we were all hunters and gatherers. Everyone was on the move. Scientists believe they/we traveled in small groups. Even at the dawn of human history the laws of nature were in control. This was a time when Darwin's law of natural selection – "survival of the fittest" – was in full force. For most of the next eighty thousand years everything and everybody on our planet was just trying to get through the last great ice age.

Scientists speculate that when the climate started to warm up again, humans must have lived in groups ranging in size from perhaps a dozen to a hundred people. Conventional wisdom has it that for the next ten thousand years life went on in this way all over the world. In China, India, the Middle East, Europe, and the Americas, pretty well everyone foraged for a living.

We don't know a whole lot about these nomadic people. Precisely because they didn't stay put, they didn't leave much behind to tell us who they were and what they were thinking.

One frequently repeated story line tells of conflicts between families and within tribes being resolved by alpha males and tribal elders. The assumption is that these councils were made up exclusively of men. The idea was to provide a peaceful way to settle disputes as an alternative to private vengeance and fatal "blood feuds."

We also know that as temperatures rose and the possibility of growing food became more viable, more of these nomads decided to settle down and stay in one place. Small, self-sustaining farming communities began to put down roots. Archeologists have uncovered evidence of villages of as many as five hundred people dating back almost fifteen thousand years.

In the ruins of the first human settlements, archeologists have found lots of evidence that suggests these early settlers were both religiously inspired and afraid. Ramparts to fend off predators and ritual spaces to commune with the Gods were common features of these earliest agricultural undertakings. However, in our search for the origins of man-made law, so far no one has turned up any evidence that it was part of the way these first homesteaders organized their lives. There were traditional ways of doing things, and patterns and rhythms of tribal life that everyone was expected to follow, but nothing separate and unique called "law."

Scholars of these earliest villages and towns refer to something called *Me* (pronounced "Meh"), which was the way early Mesopotamians thought about how to coordinate the lives of large numbers of people.

Me was about powers and duties, norms and standards, rules and regulations, wisdom and judgment; the building blocks of what today we would call a civilized state. The evidence uncovered by archeologists suggests the first leaders in these communities were priests and military men, not jurists. It seems most likely that the only laws with any force were the physical imperatives of energy and matter.

The Urban Revolution

The earliest hard evidence that we have of laws made by humans dates back four and a half millennia, a few hundred years after people started to put their thoughts down in writing. (The origins of law almost certainly stretch back further than this, but because it was never written down we don't know what it said.) By this time, the way our ancestors lived in this part of the world had undergone a radical transformation. The tribal, agricultural communities of the late Stone Age had given way to an urban revolution that marks the beginning the Bronze Age.

During this time cities were popping up all over the region. In southern Mesopotamia, known as Sumer, there were more than thirty city-states with populations ranging from 10 to 50,000 people. Most have been long forgotten, but we know of such places as Uruk, Umma, Lagash, Mari, Larsa, Girsu, Nineveh, and Ur, to name a few. It is estimated that at their height the cities of Ur and Uruk each had a population of over 65,000. In its heyday, Babylon had over 100,000 people.

As these cities grew exponentially larger than the earliest agricultural settlements from which they evolved, they doubled down on their investment in the supernatural and in military force. Over time, both the ritual spaces and defensive fortifications became impressive physical structures. The wall that enclosed Jericho (which Joshua famously blew down with his trumpet), dating back more than ten thousand years, was 3 meters high and 2 meters thick. The ziggurat (pyramid) that was built as part of the temple complex of Ur is estimated to have been over 60 meters in length, 50 meters in width, and over 30 meters in height. Towering over everything else, the Great Pyramid of Giza, built forty-five hundred years ago, stands 140 meters high, stretches 203 meters on each side, and weighs almost 6 million tons.

Each city had its own god and militia and the inhabitants of these settlements believed that whether they lived in harmony and abundance or chaos and destitution depended on both. In their creation stories, cities were built as earthly homes for the Gods, and temples were where they lived. Keeping them happy with food and prayers was everybody's first order of business.

These were communities in which everyone believed that the supernatural governed everything that happened in their lives. Their destinies were determined by sun gods and moon gods; gods of earth and water, war and wisdom, fertility and healing. If these divine beings were content, people could expect their cities would flourish. If not, something unpleasant was bound to happen.

All of these cities were quite close to each other and they were constantly fighting over adjacent farmlands and common water resources. The recurring droughts and floods that plagued this part of the world heightened the intensity of these inter-city rivalries. Each appealed to its own rulers and gods to protect them from such natural devastations. The ruler of each city raised an army to ensure its interests were secure. Historians describe this as a time of perpetual war and cross-border raids.[2]

With the introduction of metal weapons, these fights became exponentially more violent, and they could be waged for generations. Massacres and the wholesale enslavement of civilian populations were not uncommon. One of the oldest pieces of literature, the Epic of Gilgamesh, is thought to provide a dramatic account of some of these battles. The first "hundred years war" in human history was fought between Umma and Lagash, two cities of Sumer located only thirty kilometers apart. A visual depiction of the bloodshed and brutality of these clashes can be seen on the Stele of the Vultures on display in the Louvre.

Over the course of the third millennium BCE, different cities dominated the region, and the most powerful rulers called themselves kings. One of the most famous, Sargon of Akkad (who ruled ca. 2350 BCE), reigned over an empire that stretched from the Persian Gulf to the cedars of Lebanon and the banks of the Jordan River.

The safest place for anyone who lived at this time was inside a city's walls – which is not to say these places were free of conflict and strife. Quite the contrary. Disagreements and disputes are part of any city that is home to tens of thousands, and it was no different for the people of Sumer, Mesopotamia, and Assyria.

In addition to having higher population densities, these were more hierarchical and heterogeneous societies than the smaller, simpler settlements from which they had grown. Their populations were divided between different language groups (Semitic and Sumerian), and were comprised of distinct social classes of patricians, plebeians, and slaves. There were religious and military elites, rich and poor, landowners and sharecroppers, employers and workers, as well as traders and visitors from other kingdoms. These city-states were strict patriarchies in which men could sell their wives and children into slavery. The possibilities of people bumping into each other and getting in one another's way were unlimited. Conflict and confrontation were part of everyday life in a big city.

But it was possible to regulate and contain disagreements and anti social behavior, and in the beginning, it seems, the priestly class had most of the power when it came to coordinating the lives of these original urban dwellers. Later, the strong and the wealthy shared and eventually took over the throne. Regardless of the source of the ruler's credentials, these were totalitarian regimes that exercised control and issued commands from behind cloistered walls.

Organizing the lives of thousands of people gathered in one place was as big a job then as it is today. These were large, complex, diverse societies engaged in intensive, year-round agriculture, extensive trade and commerce, and constant fighting with rival clans down the road. In addition to raising an army and leading their cities into battle, rulers were responsible for ensuring fields were irrigated and crops were harvested, people were fed, taxes were collected, temples were built, and conflicts were settled peacefully and with a minimum of private vengeance.

To do it all required a big supporting cast. Central to the effective functioning of these large collective enterprises were scribes whose tablets and scrolls documented the comings and goings of daily living. They wrote a lot. A favorite pastime was compiling lists of the most important features of their lives, such as their medical ailments, religious omens, and laws. The written record of the latter is indelible proof that the ruins of the city-states of the ancient Near East mark the birthplace of law and the administrative state.

Thousands of clay tablets and (many fewer) papyrus scrolls have been found on which are recorded contracts and wills and court proceedings between individuals at every level of these societies. They show that law was an important part of organizing relations in all aspects of city life. Most revealing are bits and pieces of legal codes, the oldest of which were in force more than four thousand years ago.

All of the major Near Eastern empires had their own codes. From the beginning, it was recognized that for their cities to function at their best, the most important of the unwritten traditions and expectations of how people were expected to live together should be written down. Chipping the *Me* into stone was a way for rulers to make sure that the mass of humanity that crowded into their cities knew what their obligations and responsibilities were and what would happen if they failed to meet them.

Each of the legal regimes that governed these incipient states had its own distinctive features, but there were two core characteristics they all shared. First, all of them were written by military strongmen who claimed to be acting by divine command. Some even declared themselves to be gods. In either case, the source of their authority was a combination of physical force and the supernatural.

Second, it was typical of all of the earliest laws in the ancient Near East that their stated intention was to protect the weak, defend the oppressed, and provide relief to the poor. The model they portrayed was of the wise patriarch handing down judgments in everyday disputes that threatened the peace and security of the people.

Over time, codes were written that touched on almost every aspect of daily life in the city. They laid down the law on everything from crime and punishment to professional (doctor, judge, architect) negligence and a man's relations with his wife, children, and slaves. The largest group of laws was focused on family matters, including marriage, divorce, adoption, inheritance, adultery, and incest. There were also rules about doing business and how disputes over property and farming should be resolved. The laws included schedules that fixed compensation for injuries and prices for goods and services, as well as the wages people like farm workers or ox drivers should be paid.[3]

The oldest evidence we have of law structuring the administration of city life in Sumer dates back almost forty-five hundred years. Its author was a man named Urukagina, who became ruler of Lagash sometime after 2400 BCE. No text of his laws has ever been found, but archeologists have uncovered lots of evidence that around that time a person with that name claimed the throne, launched a reform of the city's government, and established a new set of laws.

To the modern eye, the most striking feature of Urukagina's reforms is their overarching, vaulting ambition: first, to clean up the corruption and abuse of power that was routinely practiced at all levels of the bureaucracy, and second, to look after the needs of the weakest and most vulnerable members of society. On the basis of the texts that archeologists have uncovered, Urukagina must go down in history as the first ruler to take power on an anticorruption platform.

The authors of these texts tell of Urukagina's going after officials who had exploited their powers to their own advantage and who squeezed the common people whenever they could. There is evidence he fired officials who misused their powers of transporting people across the river, inspecting cattle, and supervising the fisheries. In a move that presages modern politics, it is said he lightened the load of the Lagashians by reducing their taxes.

Urukagina's reforms were the result of a remarkable initiative. Here we have the first recorded program of legal regulation, and it is dedicated to ideals of justice and fairness and doing the right thing. Urukagina enlists the force of the law to protect the widows and orphans and others who were vulnerable to oppression at the hands of powerful elites. His project is the first attempt we know about to establish a system of good governance through the rule of law.

Although Urukagina was an early advocate of good governance and law reform, it would be wrong to leave the impression he was a perfect ruler. From the evidence that has been collected, it appears he was not above using his powers to advance his own interests. It was said, for example, that his taste for nepotism resulted in family members being appointed to positions of authority. Nor were all his reforms altruistic and benign. Still, for his pioneering example of putting law in the service of justice and good governance, he would have my vote for a place in law's hall of fame.

Hammurabi's Code

By far the most sensational piece of evidence documenting the place of law in the city-states of the ancient Near East was unearthed by a team of French archeologists in southwestern Iran, near the ancient city of Susa. In 1901 they dug up a black, two-meter-tall basalt stele on which an almost complete code of 282 laws had been carved. Today it, too, stands in the Louvre.

Its author was a man named Hammurabi, who might fairly claim to be the first big man of legal history.[4] Hammurabi was one of Babylon's most powerful kings, and he is credited with restoring the greatness of the city after it had experienced a period of decline. His reign, which lasted from 1790 to 1750 BCE, roughly coincided with the midpoint of the almost three thousand years during which the tradition of ancient Near Eastern law flourished. From the list of military conquests that it documents, scholars are pretty certain the code was written near the end of his reign.

Finding Hammurabi's Code was an extraordinary stroke of good fortune. Within the ancient Near Eastern legal tradition, the code had (and still retains) an iconic status. It was viewed as a model of lawmaking for hundreds of years after it was first proclaimed, and its laws continued to be cited for a thousand years after he died. In both content and style it provided a template for other ancient Near Eastern codes, including the law Moses delivered to the Jewish people.

Hammurabi would not have been surprised by his code's influence and durability. In fact, he thought it would last forever. In his mind, its legitimacy and integrity were beyond reproach and could never be bettered. It was, he said, a "righteous law," one that was divinely inspired and that gave voice to the highest wisdom. Spread by conquest, it was a law that was validated by faith, force, and reason simultaneously.

If Hammurabi had been pressed as to why he thought his laws would be ageless and unending, it is almost certain that he would have said it was because his lawmaking powers had been given to him by the Gods. As he explained in the first sentence of the code, the Gods had called him "by name ... Hammurabi, the exalted prince who feared God, to bring about the rule of righteousness in the land, to destroy the wicked and evil doers; so that the strong will not harm the weak." At the top of the stele, his image is drawn receiving the symbols of legal authority (a rod and a ring) from Shamash, the Sun God whose supreme power was to bring injustice to light. And, at the end of the code, Hammurabi called on more than two dozen gods to bring death and destruction down on any ruler who failed to respect his laws or who tried to change them.

Hammurabi would also have said that his laws were destined to retain their force in perpetuity because he had made good on the divine mandate he had been given. His was, he insisted, a "rule of righteousness" under which peace and prosperity had flourished. Virtually the whole of the prologue that introduces the code recounts how he turned himself into an "irresistible warrior" who "conquered and was obeyed by the four corners of the world." He lists two dozen cities he had vanquished and that were now "ruled by law," whose people enjoyed wealth and tranquility and whose gods he had venerated and cared for. He also claimed, at the end of the code, that with the divine wisdom that had been bestowed on him, he had performed the role of a "salvation bearing shepherd" who had settled all disputes, healed all injuries, and provided refuge for the weak from the strong.

And these were not just idle boasts. Hammurabi could point to lots of laws that supported the image he projected of himself. If you look at his code on the Internet,[5] it is not hard to make out the two personalities he describes. As a collection of laws, the code tells a tale of two sovereigns and two different concepts of law. Many laws manifest the mind-set of the warlord – that might makes right – and authorize acts of extreme violence against those who challenged the established order. Others are born of a moral intuition to right a wrong and offer succor and relief to victims of oppression and abuse. For the first Hammurabi, law was an instrument of coercion and obedience; in the hands of his alter ego, it served as a tool of justice and a way to counteract bullying and intimidation.

To maintain peaceful and orderly relations in the city, the military man in Hammurabi looked at law as another weapon. Law was about fighting for the established order, with a vengeance. Indeed, many of the code's provisions read as though they were written by a strongman who was willing to apply whatever force it took to get people to respect and obey them. Although Hammurabi's subjects were better-off than his enemies (who had no access to his courts and who had to resolve their differences on the battlefield), the consequences of challenging his will by breaking the law were not a whole lot different. Brutal and barbaric punishments were central to his idea of law. As he ominously put it in the epilogue to the code, "a disturber was not permitted." Law entailed obedience, and anyone who didn't oblige paid the price.

By the standards of our time, Hammurabi's Code is shocking in the ferocity and cruelty of the punishments it inflicts on people who did something wrong or who made a mistake. Even within the Near Eastern legal tradition, it is perceived to be severe. More than 10 percent of the offenses that are listed are punishable by death, including adultery, incest, kidnapping, and falsely accusing someone else of a capital offense. Depending on the crime, execution could be by burning (law number 25, on arson, and numbers 110 and 157, on incest with one's mother), burying alive (21, break and enter), drowning (129, adultery; 133 and 143, abandoning one's husband; 155, defiling one's daughter-in-law), or impalement (153, murder of their spouses by an adulterous couple).

Hammurabi's Code is also the earliest extant public codification of *lex talionis* – the notion that a given punishment should match the crime: an eye for an eye, a bone for a bone, a tooth for a tooth, and so on (196–7 and 200). In some cases, *lex talionis* could result in the execution of a wrongdoer's children. So, for example, if a man killed a pregnant woman and the fetus dies, his own daughter might be put to death (210). Similarly, if a house collapsed and the owner's son was killed, the son of the builder whose negligence was responsible for the casualty could be executed (230). In Hammurabi's mind, killing a member of the guilty person's family was justified as a way of restoring a balance in the relations of the people who were caught up in such tragedies.

Physical punishments short of execution were also in vogue. Amputation and mutilation were standard punishments for a myriad of crimes. Ears (205, 282), breasts (194), tongues (192), and hands (195, 218, and 226) could be cut off and eyes gouged out (193 and 196). To rub salt in the wounds, the severity of many punishments varied according to a person's class. The rich and powerful got lighter sentences when they were the offenders and more by way of retribution when they were the victims than plebeians and slaves.

As offensive as differential penalties and physical mutilation are to the modern world, Hammurabi would have defended them as necessary to reinforce the hierarchy that structured Babylonian society. Lots of laws in the code were dedicated to this purpose. The amount of compensation that was required to be paid to remedy a wrongful loss, for example, was also determined by social class. In cases in which someone challenged a person above him (or her) in the social hierarchy, Hammurabi was especially severe. Assaulting a superior resulted in a public whipping (202). A son who slapped his father might have his hand amputated (195). A slave who assaulted his master could lose an ear (205). If a woman walked out on her husband without good cause, she could be put to death (143). Indeed, even a suspicion of adultery might result in a wife having to endure the ordeal of being thrown into the river (132).

While laws that inflict horrific punishments and discriminate on the basis of class and gender must have seemed reasonable in Hammurabi's day, as a way of maintaining peaceful relations and social order, they were not destined to last. Far from being the timeless laws that Hammurabi envisaged, history has shown such barbaric and discriminatory enactments had a finite shelf life. Today, they would not count as valid laws; they would be dismissed as extreme and excessive, out of all proportion to the wrongs they seek to rectify. Even retributivists find the talion principle primitive and simpleminded.

After reading the parts of the code that were written by Hammurabi the law and order king, it is tempting to dismiss the whole collection as a relic of another, more primitive world. It has the whiff of victor's justice, where the strong use legal force to maintain their domination of the weak, and it seems to be part and parcel of the biblical depiction of Babylon as a city of false idols, "the mother of whores and abominations."[6] This was a legal system, after all, that also countenanced the use of physical "ordeals" to reveal the truth and was overseen by a ruler who was answerable to no one except the Gods.

Throwing the entire code into the dustbin of legal history would, however, be a mistake. Even though the laws that were proclaimed by "General" Hammurabi have not survived the test of time, those he crafted with the rod of the "salvation-bearing shepherd" have shown themselves to have broad appeal and have therefore proven to be much more resilient. For these parts of his code, Hammurabi could still make a strong case for their immortality. Many of the laws that provided relief to widows and orphans, and those who lived at the bottom of the social hierarchy, still seem as fair and balanced today as they were when they were first enacted 3,700 years ago. Regardless of what standard of justice is applied, lots of these laws still make the grade.

Consider Hammurabi's collection of family laws. Many of these laws were dedicated to protecting the rights of women and children. Even though families were male autocracies, minimum standards of propriety and decency still had to be met. For example, although men had a right to unilaterally terminate a marriage, the law provided that a husband had to make financial provision for the welfare of an ex-wife, and she retained custody of the children (law number 137). Wives who were abused or neglected could go to court and obtain a divorce (142). When a wife became ill, the husband had a duty of care (148). Similarly, with respect to their offspring, Hammurabi told fathers they could only disinherit a child if they had a good reason (168), and even then only after they had shown forgiveness at least once (169). Even within the rigidly hierarchical and patriarchal structure of Babylonian society, there were legal limits on how those in authority could exercise their powers.

Farmworkers, sharecroppers, and tenants benefited from the protection of Hammurabi's laws as well. Farmers got relief from their debts when they suffered a loss of their crops due to bad weather (48). Tenants acquired ownership rights over land they farmed after four years (60). Families that had been sold into slavery to pay off their debts regained their freedom after three years (117). And herdsmen were not responsible for the loss of livestock under their care when they had done nothing wrong (266). However, when fault could be determined, such as when a farmer negligently caused the flooding of a neighbor's fields (53 and 55), or when a shepherd carelessly allowed the animals under his care to graze on another person's land (57), people were held responsible for the losses they caused.

The welfare of workers and war veterans were also advanced in the code. Minimum wages were established for a range of workers, including day laborers, that were adjusted according to the length of the working day and the hardship of the working conditions (271–3). Soldiers who had been prisoners of war could reclaim their lands on their return even if they had been taken over by a third party. They also had a claim against the state to buy out their servile status if they had been captured and enslaved (27 and 32).

Hammurabi's claim for the eternal force of his code is also supported by laws that were designed to ensure that legal proceedings were fair and uncorrupted. Although there were only five of them, these laws, which today we would describe as guaranteeing that everyone received some basic measure of due process, were listed at the very beginning. They imposed severe punishments (including the death penalty) for making false accusations and committing perjury, and judges who made errors of law could be fined and lose their jobs.

Moreover, from the administrative records and accounts of legal proceedings that have been recovered, scholars are able to say that the processes through which conflicts were resolved and the law applied had much to commend them. Overall, it appears enforcement of the codes was pretty informal and user-friendly. Any citizen with a case might petition the king, who could refer it to one of his officials or to a local assembly or who might decide it himself. There were no professional lawyers or jurists, although there is evidence that by Hammurabi's time judges had acquired a special status.

Hammurabi's expectation was that an ordinary person would be able to distinguish right from wrong just by reading his laws. At the end of the code, in the epilogue, he wrote, "Let the oppressed who has a case at law ... read the inscription and it will explain his case to him and he will find out what is just." And it seems they did. Certainly, ordinary citizens were able to participate in deciding cases in small "assemblies" that appear to be the forerunners of the modern jury.

The code's accessibility and ease of comprehension derived in part from the way it was written. Unlike modern codes of law, Hammurabi's did not attempt to be comprehensive and did not lay down absolute proscriptions or general rules. There is nothing that says, "Thou shalt not ...," or that lays down a general principle of criminal responsibility or civil liability. Instead, the code consists of what looks like a compilation of cases – a list of judgments that have been handed down to resolve specific disputes. The form in which the code is expressed is adjudicative rather than legislative. It casts Hammurabi in the role of a wise and just king resolving disputes by rendering judgments rather than by writing pieces of legislation.

The style Hammurabi used for his code is what is commonly referred to as "casuistic." Today, the word has acquired a negative connotation. (It implies unsound and deceptive reasoning; quibbling, making excessive and trivial distinctions.) However, when it is used to describe early Mesopotamian law, it simply means laying out the rights and wrongs of everyday conduct in specific cases. It was a way of educating the public about what they should do in certain situations and what would happen if they didn't. Law was about making good judgments. Judgments were specific, particular expressions of law.

Each law begins with the statement that *if* such and such happens, *then* certain consequences follow. So, for example,

> *if* a man commits incest with his daughter, *then* he is exiled from the city;
> *if* a man commits incest with his mother, *then* both are burned;
> *if* you hire a sailor or a day laborer or an ox driver, *then* the law lays down how much you must pay;
> *if* you are a judge and one of your decisions is reversed on appeal, *then* the law provides you may lose your job and are liable for a large fine.

And so on, for virtually all of the 282 laws.

Hammurabi's Code does not expressly address how it was to be administered and applied. However, from other texts that have been retrieved, scholars now believe that Hammurabi's Code was likely intended more as a teaching tool illustrating proper behavior in specific situations rather than as a binding precedent in future cases. It provided judges and juries with guidance rather than hard-and-fast rules.

Legal scholars think the individual laws that make up the code were treated as paradigm cases. From other evidence archeologists have uncovered, it seems they were never cited in the resolution of actual cases. Litigants were expected to compare their case with the law that it most resembled; no interpretation or textual exegesis was required. Scholars assume judges and juries made their decisions by drawing analogies and inferences and by using common sense. Reasoning was by way of example rather than principles and a priori rules. Understanding law was more about *seeing* the right resolution rather than reading it.

And the code itself, we are told, was written in a style and idiom that would have been easy for ordinary citizens to understand. Presenting the law as a series of judgments in individual cases and then chipping them into pieces of large polished stone to be put on prominent display in the city ensured its intelligibility to as wide an audience as possible. It seems the ruling elites did everything they could to ensure that Babylonians obeyed the code and that ignorance of the law was not a problem. Even people who were illiterate could have the laws read to them and they could picture how their case was likely to be resolved.

The method by which Hammurabi's laws were administered, and their motive of looking out for the least advantaged, are two features that give credence to his claim for the code's immortality. The art of casuistry and the scales of justice are still with us today and give the appearance they can go on forever. Resolving conflicts on a case-by-case basis has been at the heart of Anglo-American common law for hundreds of years, and protecting persecuted minorities against powerful majorities is the primary mission of modern human rights codes. Even if many of Hammurabi's more draconian laws are no longer defensible, the code's method of reasoning and its objective of combatting oppression are still core components of the rule of law today.

No doubt Hammurabi would have been upset to learn that the whole of his code did not last forever. He could, however, take solace from the fact that he is among a select group of lawmakers whose image overlooks both the entrance to the House Chamber in the Capitol Building, where the United States House of Representatives deliberates, and the south wall of the room in which the US Supreme Court hears cases. Even if some of his laws eventually lost their luster, he has been recognized by both the legislative and judicial branches of the US government as one of the greatest lawmakers of all time.

He might also take comfort from that fact that even though his own code was eventually buried in the sands of the Iraqi desert, there is one set of laws that originates in the ancient Near East that adopted some of his judgments almost word for word, and it still governs the lives of millions of people. These laws can be found in the first five books of the Bible and are known to Jews as the Torah. Of all the ancient Near Eastern law codes, Jewish law takes the prize for endurance and longevity.

The Covenant Code

Compared to Mesopotamians and Sumerians, the Jews were relative latecomers to the idea of using law to regulate the life of their community. The origins of how the books of Genesis, Exodus, Leviticus, Numbers, and Deuteronomy came to be central to the Jewish way of life are still shrouded in the sands of the Syrian desert, but there seems to be a consensus that the Ten Commandments and the other laws of Moses could date back as far the late second millennium BCE, which is still more than half a millennium after Hammurabi.[7] Scholars seem pretty confident that they were not set down in writing until some time between the eighth and fifth century BCE. (This is roughly the period when it is believed the Egyptians also embraced the idea of written texts and began etching their laws onto papyrus scrolls.)[8] Whenever they came into force, their influence has been so consequential as to earn Moses a place beside Hammurabi above the gallery doors leading into the House Chamber in Washington.

Although the Torah is embedded in a much longer narrative about the origins and divine mission of the Jewish people, in both substance and style the earliest statements of Jewish law draw heavily on the Near Eastern tradition. Like the laws of their neighbors, they deal, for the most part, with the daily ebb and flow of an ancient Middle Eastern agricultural community, including its religious practices, such as purification rituals and animal sacrifices. It is estimated that as much as three quarters of what is known in Jewish law as the Covenant Code (Ex. 20:22–23:33) covers the same ground as the much older Sumerian texts.[9]

There are laws about family (that are very patriarchal) and doing business (honestly and fairly) and bad behavior (such as murder and theft). Like all Near Eastern codes, punishments under the earliest iterations of Jewish law could be very severe. There was zero toleration of disobedience. The Torah comes down particularly hard on sex crimes, including sex before marriage, adultery, bestiality (Lev. 20:15–16) and sodomy (Lev. 18:22, 20:13).

And they didn't let up for their kids. Children who insulted or disobeyed their parents could be put to death (Ex. 21:15, 17; Deut. 21:18–21). Like virtually all law codes of the time, when the Jews thought about justice and the treatment of those who violated the law, their first instinct was to call for a pretty severe application of *lex talionis.*

In addition to sharing a weakness for strong punishments, Jewish law also expresses "the better angels" of our human nature by looking out for the vulnerable and less fortunate members of the community. For Jews as much as for Mesopotamians, the legitimacy of law is certified by the justice it guarantees. Like Hammurabi, Jews make special mention of their responsibility to look after widows, orphans, and the poor. It is forbidden, for example, to loan money to them and charge interest (Ex. 22:25). In the same spirit of looking out for the downtrodden and oppressed, the law requires Jews who have been sold into indentured servitude to be freed after seven years (Ex. 21:2). It also includes a duty of hospitality toward foreigners.

As well as covering a lot of the same ground as the law of their neighbors, much of Jewish law is written in the same case-centric (casuistic) style favored by Hammurabi. This is especially true of the Covenant Code, which is the second set of laws that Moses received on Mount Sinai from Yahweh (the name Jews gave to their God). When they were put in writing, they were presented as judgments being handed down by God from on high (Ex. 21:1). These laws speak to the members of the tribe and tell them the consequences that follow if certain events like a marriage or a murder come to pass. Again, the focus is on particular events and behaviors rather than laying down all-encompassing principles or absolute rules.

Although Jewish law draws heavily on the Near Eastern legal tradition, like all codes in the region, it developed some unique features of its own. In style, for example, in addition to the law that was expressed as rulings in particular cases, other provisions, most notably the Ten Commandments (Ex. 20:1–17), were written in an apodictic style as hard-and-fast rules. Thou shalt not steal, commit adultery, worship other gods – this was another way of laying down the law that struck a chord with the Jews. In all, the Torah is said to contain 613 commandments of this kind.

In substance, Jewish law also had its own ideas about right and wrong that reflected Jews' collective sense of identity. Like everyone else in this part of the world, the Jewish people were struggling to stay alive in a generally hostile and violent environment. Like their descendants today, they were a small community in a world of imperial powers (Assyrian, Babylonian, Persian, Egyptian, and eventually Greek and Roman) and shifting political ground. In such an unsettled, high-risk world, they used their laws to help forge their own distinct way of life. They had strict dietary laws and codes of cleanliness and they frowned on cross-dressing (Deut. 22:5).

With their belief in one almighty and powerful God, Jews also had little tolerance for heretics and witches (Ex. 22:18) or for people who believed in other deities. In contrast with the ecumenism of Hammurabi, the Torah commanded Jews to destroy the temples and altars of rival faiths (Deut. 7:5, 12:1) and expel those who worshipped false gods from the land Yahweh had promised them (Ex. 23:33). It also outlawed intermarriage with non-Jews (Deut. 7:3). Yahweh may have instructed Jews to deal with one another with justice and fairness, but he commanded them to show no mercy to people who worshipped his rivals.

After Moses's law was written down, Jewish law developed another feature, perhaps its most distinctive. Gradually, as it evolved and became more complex, Jewish law was taken over by those who had become experts in what it said and how it should be applied in situations where the texts were silent or open to competing interpretations. Over time, Jewish law recognized a power of the priests that was separate and even superior to the authority of its political leaders. In Jewish law, the word would become more powerful than the sword. Kings no longer controlled the law – they were subject to it (Deut. 17:18–20).

As in every other tribe and city in the region, the religious and military elites competed for power. Among the Jews, it was the priestly class who prevailed. There were, no doubt, many factors that contributed to their success, but the divine character of Jewish law certainly gave the religious aristocracy a leg up. Because the Torah was understood to be the actual word of God, being masters of its meaning meant more than being the strongest person on the street. Scholars of the text turned Judaism into a religion of words, one that spoke to rulers as much as to those they ruled.

Unlike Hammurabi's law, which consisted of judgments he had made or approved, in Jewish law the judgments in the Torah were the commandments of God. The law that Moses revealed to his people had been dictated directly to him by Yahweh. In Babylon, Hammurabi was the lawmaker who had been chosen by the Gods. In Jewish law, all of the rules were of God's making, and that put a premium on figuring out exactly what they meant and how they should be applied. By the time the Romans marched into the region, roughly fifteen hundred years later, the separation of law and politics in the life of the Jewish community was more or less complete and the religious scholars (rabbis) were firmly in charge.

A big part of the history of Jewish law tells the story of how, once in control, these religious elites took over the exposition and development of the law. Scholars steeped in religious knowledge and traditional wisdom – Ezra, Hillel, Judah, and (much later) Maimonides – led the way. First they built up an oral tradition around the law God gave to Moses. Later (around 220 CE) they committed their collective wisdom to writing (the Mishnah), and several hundred years after that they produced two texts (the Jerusalem and Babylonian Talmuds) of commentaries by religious scholars on what the Torah and Mishnah meant in the world in which they lived. To this day, the Chief Rabbinate dictates Jewish law on a wide range of personal status issues, including marriage and divorce.

It would be hard to exaggerate the significance of the scholars' contribution to the development of Jewish law. The fact that, alone among the ancient Near Eastern religious texts, the Torah has managed to perpetuate its rule to this day is due in large part to the triumph of the high priests and scholars over the military and princely elites. The most unique feature of Jewish law, it turns out, is not so much what it says as who said it.

To follow the path religious scholars traveled in gaining control of Jewish law would take us too close to the present. We would be getting ahead of ourselves. The Mishna was compiled and put in writing when the Romans were at the height of their empire, and there are important threads to the larger story of law's odyssey that we need to stitch in first. The Greek experiment of empowering ordinary people to make their own law and Rome's decision to cede control of the law to a class of professional, secular lawyers (of whom Cicero is unquestionably the best known) take place long before Jewish scholars produced the Talmud.

However, before we leave the land where law was born and move on to the next stop on its journey, let's pause and recap where we are: roughly three thousand years ago, in the Near East, at the end of the second and beginning of the first millennium BCE. Here, for the first time in human history, in the lands of the Sumerians, Babylonians, Assyrians, Egyptians, and Persians, law codes were being written to organize and coordinate the lives of hundreds of thousands of people. The rulers who had them chipped in stone claimed they had been authorized by the Gods to assert their leadership in this way. They painted a picture of themselves as divinely inspired, dispensing justice on a case-by-case basis on every detail of life in their cities.

The law in these codes summarized how the ruler expected his subjects to behave and what duties they were obliged to perform. It was *him* telling *them* how to live a good life and what would happen if they didn't. In the beginning, law was not about imposing limits on what rulers could do. It was rule *by* law – not the rule *of* law that has become the measure of good governance in the modern world. Practically, as we have seen, the barbarity and cruelty of these rulers knew no limits, and their treatment of rival states, as well as women and slaves, is antithetical to what the modern rule of law aspires to be.

The Near Eastern model of the rule of law carried on more or less in this way for the next five hundred years. The idea of law migrated both east, as far as the Indus Valley, and west, to parts of what is now modern Greece, but in substance and style it was pretty much the same as the original. Warlords and high priests were still in charge.

In India, what came to be known as Manu's Law emerged around this time (some think even earlier) as a central core of the Hindu religion.[10] Hindu law has a lot in common with Jewish law. Like the Torah, Manu's laws were said to be the actual words of God (Brahma). For both, law is God-given. And Hindu law, like Jewish law, was taken over early on by a priestly (Brahmin) class whose members used it to consolidate their own authority. According to Hindu tradition, the guardians of the law rank higher than its military defenders (Kshatriyas). In theory, military rulers were subject to the law, but in practice there was no one with the power or authority to hold them to it.

In the West, law seems to have started down a similar path, but sometime during the seventh and sixth centuries (BCE), in the southern part of the Balkan peninsula, it went in a different direction. Led by great statesmen and brilliant scholars, in the late fifth and early fourth centuries, the Greeks developed an idea of law that turned the Near Eastern model on its head. Instead of law being handed down by rulers whose authority was unlimited and came from the Gods, the Greeks insisted that law came from the people, from the bottom up, and that it bound rulers just as much as the people they ruled.

Exactly what the Greeks did, and why it has proven to be so attractive to subsequent generations, has been the subject of endless classroom discussions and scholarly writing. In the next chapter, we will catalog the most important features of law's experience in Classical Greece and contrast it with what had happened in the past and with what was going on in other parts of the world at the same time.

Chapter Two

Athens and Sparta

As the crow flies, the distance between Babylon and Athens is less than two thousand kilometers. You can fly between the two cities in less than five hours. Yet in terms of how these two communities thought about law, the Greeks and the people living in the Near East were light-years apart. Whereas in the Middle East and North Africa, law was understood to be an expression of God's will that powerful rulers relied on to justify their authority, in Athens law was a purely human artifact, and people used it as much to ensure their rulers did not misbehave as to regulate their own conduct.

Although the idea of law evolved in very different directions in Greece and Mesopotamia, the starting point seems to have been the same.[1] For both, law was a way to resolve disputes fairly without having to resort to physical force and personal retaliation. Hesiod, a poet who lived at the end of the eighth century BCE, described law as a way of life that distinguished humans from all other species. Law, he said, was an alternative to "eating each other," which was the default rule in the rest of the world. Hesiod thought humanity's well-being depended on the proper functioning of such legal procedures, but he cautioned that law was a process that could produce "crooked judgments" in the hands of a corrupt judge.

One of the very first images we have of how the Greeks thought about law portrays it in just this way. It appears on the shield of Achilles, which Homer described in his epic the *Iliad*. (Today it can also be seen on the bronze doors that lead into the US Supreme Court.) On it, Homer sketches a scene of village elders rendering judgment in a conflict between two families. The description suggests that, as in Babylon, in the beginning Greek law was about community leaders trying to avert acts of private vengeance (blood feuds) that threatened public order. Their role was to settle cases, in which ordinary people were claiming retribution or compensation for wrongs they believed had been done to them, in a way that both sides would accept as fair. Law was a procedure by which communities could resolve their differences peacefully instead of by brute force.

It is widely believed that the *Iliad* was written sometime in the eighth century BCE, when the art of writing first appeared in ancient Greece, but that Homer was drawing on stories that belonged to an oral tradition that went back as far as the law of Moses, and perhaps even to the time of Hammurabi. On that assumption, scholars have concluded that the process of settling disputes portrayed on Achilles's shield must have originated long before there were written rules for the elders to apply. In other words, it seems likely that law began in ancient Greece as it did in Mesopotamia: as a procedure for settling disputes by respected members of the community who, in rendering their decisions, relied for the most part on their wisdom and common sense. In both, law started as a process for making judgments, not as a catalog of dos and don'ts.

Although it seems safe to assume the Greeks had developed procedures to solve local disputes peacefully by the end of the Bronze Age (roughly 1600 to 1100 BCE), it would be a stretch to say they were living in what we would call rule of law states. When they began using nonviolent procedures for resolving conflict, these would have been strictly voluntary. If one family wanted a fight to the finish, it couldn't be stopped. As in Mesopotamia, this was still a world (known as the Mycenaean era) dominated by warlords and strongmen and characterized by lots of armed aggression. The Mycenaeans were known as a belligerent, bellicose people whose kings, like Hammurabi and Sargon, claimed divine authority for their laws and extended their rule by "eating" their enemies.[2]

Like the ancient empires of the Near East, Mycenaean rule didn't last. The evidence suggests they were overrun by tribes who invaded from the north. Known as Dorians, their descendants gave birth to the Spartans.

Three centuries of chaos (known as the Greek Dark Ages) followed before the first glimmer of Classical Greece begins to emerge in the second half of the eighth century BCE. At some point in the seventh century BCE, the Greeks started putting their laws down in writing and displaying them in public.

This was a time, known as the Archaic period, when hundreds of satellite villages were being built up around larger cities like Sparta and Athens. Most of them were towns of a few thousand inhabitants, but it is estimated that, at its height, Athens had a population of roughly 250,000, of whom roughly half were citizens and almost a third were slaves. Like the perpetual battles that ravaged the Near East, conflict both within and between these early urban communities was an ongoing fact of life.

Tension between peasant farmers and the richest, most powerful land-owners was a constant irritant and recurring flash point. So were soldiers returning from war complaining that even though they had risked their lives in the defense of their cities, they had next to no say in how they were run. In addition to the disputes and disturbances that were part of everyday life inside a city's walls, at any moment a city might find its farms and fields under attack. After hundreds of years of tyranny and bloodshed, the Greeks were ready to try new ways of organizing their affairs.

Sparta

Sparta was one of the first cities in Greece to look to the law to help solve its problems, but it must be recognized that when it comes to the question of Spartan law, much of what we think went on is based on spec-ulation and secondhand information. We don't have any reliable eyewit-ness accounts about the origins or the content of the law the Spartans adopted; nothing like the stele on which Hammurabi's Code is written has ever been found. The circumstances in which they embraced "the Laws of Lycurgus" are as much matters of legend as they are historical facts. Aristotle took the popular account with a grain of salt.

As the story is told (first by Herodotus, a Greek historian living in the fifth century BCE, and later by Plutarch, who wrote in the first cen-tury CE), the Spartans asked Lycurgus, who was a member of one of the leading families, to come up with a set of laws that would put an end to the discord and strife that plagued their city.[3] Depending on whom you believe, some time in the middle of the seventh century BCE, Lycurgus is supposed to have drafted a set of laws (Great Rhetra) and then had them approved by the Gods through the Oracle at Delphi.

However these laws came into being, by strictly adhering to them, Sparta quickly rose to a position of prominence. By the end of the sixth century BCE it had become a major power in the region. It is estimated that by the fifth century BCE there were approximately 250,000 people (of whom only 15,000 were Spartan males) subject to its rule.

To put an end to social conflict and bring the city together, Lycurgus (or those who acted in his name) did two things. First he/they stitched together an eclectic set of institutions and a system of lawmaking that allowed for some participation by all of Sparta's citizens, and then he/they crafted a set of laws that united them as conscripts in a powerful war machine. With laws that turned every Spartan man into a full-time soldier, Sparta punched above its weight. With everyone committed to the same ideal warrior society, Spartans led the heroic defense of Greece against the Persians at Thermopylae and Plataea (480–479 BCE) and ultimately, after a war (Peloponnesian) that lasted more than a quarter century, conquered Athens in 404 BCE.

The system of government under which Sparta operated at the height of its power combined traditional rulers with elected officials and popular assemblies. There were two kings (*archagetai*) and five elected magistrates (*ephors*) who shared executive powers, a popular assembly (the Apella) that voted on legislative proposals and, on the top, an elected council of twenty eight elders (the Gerousia) that screened all proposals that went before the popular assemblies and acted as Sparta's highest court. Thought to be part of Lycurgus's reforms, the Gerousia acted like a modern constitutional court. It had the power to overturn the decisions of the popular assembly and to make judgments about whether one or other of the kings had violated the law and acted illegally. Although the most powerful families controlled all three branches of government, they were elected to the Gerousia and as *ephors* by the popular assembly in which all Spartan male adults were members. Sparta was a plutocracy whose authority was grounded on some measure of popular consent.

Lycurgus's laws are most famous for the austere, militaristic, communal way of life they commanded.[4] Sparta is the first place in recorded history where the whole society was set up as an army camp. The lifestyle was simple and severe. Luxuries were forbidden. Everyone dressed in coarse clothing. Meals, eaten communally, consisted mostly of porridge and black (blood) soup, and everyone was expected to contribute an equal share of the rations that were needed to put the food on the table.

Children who were judged to be weak and vulnerable were exposed at birth and left to die. Those determined to be strong enough were taken from their families at the age of seven, subjected to rigorous physical training, and forced to master the skills of armed combat and embrace traditional Spartan habits and values, including frugality, self-sacrifice, and pederasty. When he graduated at the age of eighteen, it was expected the young warrior would be a courageous, law-biding, citizen-soldier dedicated to putting the interests of the polis ahead of his own. Thermopylae proved that most did.

The constitution Lycurgus drafted for Sparta was a mixture of the old and the new. Like Hammurabi, Lycurgus is supposed to have invoked the authority of the Gods to give legitimacy to his laws, and he was equally determined that they would last forever. The way Plutarch tells it, Lycurgus tried to ensure his laws would govern in perpetuity by extracting a promise from his fellow Spartans that they would abide by his laws and make no attempt to change them until he had consulted the Oracle at Delphi and returned to the city. Then, after receiving the approval of

Apollo, he starved himself to death and had his corpse cremated so that neither he nor his body would ever return and the Spartans would always be bound by their promise.

Although there was nothing original in Lycurgus's claims for the divine and eternal character of his constitution, his concept of law differed from the Near Eastern model in almost every other respect. In contrast to Hammurabi's catalog of 282 individual judgments, Lycurgus's laws were concerned with creating the institutional infrastructure for a city-state that was committed to Spartan values. The most important laws concerned how laws were made and how citizens socialized rather than telling future generations how specific cases should be resolved. The idea was that an intense program of indoctrination and socialization (*agoge*), coupled with an opportunity to review the validity of laws before they took effect (in the Gerousia), would guarantee the integrity of the lawmaking process and the fairness of the rules that were adopted.

Rather than providing solutions to hundreds of different conflicts, the Spartans believed the best way to ensure peace and harmony in their city was by preventing conflict before it happened. Instead of thinking about what justice required when conflicts broke out, the idea was to turn everyone into an ideal citizen by swearing loyalty to a common mind-set. Prevention rather than resolution was the strategy.

Spartans believed the purposes of law were better served by a compulsory system of military training and moral education than by adjudicating between the conflicting interests of its citizens. Apart from the laws that established the system, Lycurgus's instinct seems to have been to downplay the importance of Sparta's legal regime. One of his laws prohibited all future laws from being written so they would be easy to change. Instead of chipping laws into stone and putting them on public display like Hammurabi, he expected Spartan men would memorize the law in their youth as part of their general education.

Although Lycurgus's laws provided the foundation for Sparta's rise to prominence among the city-states of ancient Greece, in the end, Sparta, like Babylon, was unable to sustain its supremacy. By the end of the fourth century BCE, it had been swallowed up by the kingdom of Macedonia, led by Philip and then his son Alexander. Sparta was doomed by its reliance on a brutal system of forced labor, which essentially enslaved the people they conquered (helots) and which posed a constant threat to its stability and security. According to Aristotle, Sparta was also brought down by a political leadership that was able to act with unfettered discretion, was susceptible to corruption, and was vulnerable to the irrational and immoral influence of Spartan women. (It was said that evidence of the depraved and detrimental impact of women on

Spartan society could be seen in their fondness for nudity and adulterous relationships.)

Despite Sparta's eventual defeat on the battlefield, its conception of law retained its appeal over the course of history, and it still has supporters today. Indeed, it seems to resonate with anyone who has a vision of an ideal society and sees law as a legitimate instrument by which the state can direct its citizens to contribute to society's well-being and the values on which it is based. For some, there is something heroic in the idea of navigating a world of violence and armed aggression by emphasizing the security and welfare of the whole community over an individual's personal ambitions and by turning the men of fighting age into the most effective military force in the world. Thinking of a community as a brotherhood of professionally trained soldiers (hoplites) may not be the most lofty or inspiring ambition (neither Plato nor Aristotle thought so), but the idea that law can be instrumental in reducing as well as resolving conflict is still attractive to lots of people.

The Romans, and later the Nazis, especially admired the fierce loyalty and discipline Sparta instilled in its men when it called on them to defend their city. Machiavelli was impressed by the social stability it enjoyed for almost half a millennium. Rousseau loved its simple lifestyle and devotion to the greater good, and Thomas More was so enamored with the Spartan values of community and self-sacrifice that he drew on it as a model for his masterpiece, *Utopia*. Even today, American lawmakers regard Lycurgus's laws to be of such historical significance that his image is another one of the twenty-three lawgivers that overlook the entrance to the United States House of Representatives as inspiration for its deliberations.

Lawyers also recognize Sparta's place in legal history, but their assessment tends to be more equivocal. On the one hand, they recognize Spartans as the first people to write rules about the procedures that must be followed to create a valid law and then take steps to hold their rulers to it. On the other, Sparta's commitment to the idea of law seems hesitant and halfhearted. As we have seen, Spartans looked to the supernatural rather than to law's intrinsic fairness to justify its authority, and they relied much more on their system of education and program of indoctrination to maintain peace and harmony among its citizens than on legal procedures and courts.

When lawyers write about the law in Classical Greece, Athens almost always gets top billing, not Sparta. In the same way that Athens is the poster child for philosophers, scientists, and supporters of the arts, it is the darling of lawyers as well. Its commitment to the rule of law was both less derivative and more robust. It grounded the legitimacy of its law exclusively on the will of the people who wrote it, without any claim of divine approval, and every proposal to introduce a new law was referred to the courts to certify its legality. To ensure it was enforced, every citizen had the right to prosecute magistrates and lawmakers who abused their powers and acted outside the law.

Athens

As in Sparta, the origins of a system of legal regulation in Athens are shrouded in the mists of time.[5] From secondary sources, however, we know that law codes were introduced into Athenian society in the second half of the seventh century BCE, maybe a generation after Lycurgus's laws were adopted in Sparta. Draco was the first in a series of lawgivers who distinguish this period of Athenian legal history. Like Lycurgus, he was chosen by his fellow citizens to compile a set of laws that would put an end to the hostilities and tensions that divided their city. Unlike Lycurgus's, however, Draco's laws were written and displayed publicly on rotating blocks of wood. They are credited with planting the seeds of democracy by widening the franchise and extending the right to vote to anyone who could equip himself militarily, but the governing structure of the city remained in the hands of a few powerful families. We know very little about the substance of Draco's laws except that they established a compulsory procedure to settle cases of homicide, and even in their day they were considered harsh. As in Sparta, even minor offenders could be put to death. Today his name survives primarily as an eponymous adjective: "draconian," meaning cruel or especially severe.

We also know that in the end Draco's laws didn't do the trick. Ordinary Athenians were still dissatisfied with their lot. They didn't have much say in how their city was organized and they were still subject to exploitation by rich and powerful families who owned most of the land. At the beginning of the sixth century BCE, facing rising tensions and threats to the city's stability and security, the Athenians turned to another larger-than-life character to bail them out again.

Solon was a typical polymath of Classical Greece. He was a political and economic reformer, a businessman, and a poet from the city's middle class. His laws, which are believed to have been enacted in 594 BCE, addressed both the social and political grievances of the general population, and they tried to do so in a balanced and evenhanded way. He was neither a radical threat to, nor a fawning apologist for, the ruling class. And, he is another one of the lawgivers who watch over the proceedings of both the United States House of Representatives and the Supreme Court.

To respond to the economic hardships under which Athenians labored, Solon made a number of important changes. He put an end to the practice of enslaving fellow citizens who couldn't pay their debts and he eliminated a property tax small landowners were required to pay to those with larger estates. To launch his reforms he is supposed to have wiped out all existing debts.

On the political side, Solon's laws gave ordinary Athenians a bigger stake in their government but again stopped short of turning the city into a fully democratic state. Even after his reforms, the governing structure of Athens was controlled by the most powerful families and economic elites. Like Sparta, Athens was ruled by councils of magistrates (the Areopagus) and elders (the Council of Four Hundred) that had strict property and wealth qualifications and wielded exclusive authority to propose new laws.

The opportunity for the average Athenian to participate in governing the city was restricted to the assembly, which elected members of the executive councils, and approved new laws when they were proposed, and the "peoples' courts" (Heliaia and dikasteria) where they served as jurors. They clearly had less power than the leading families of the city, but that didn't mean they were without influence.

In fact, according to Aristotle, because Solon's laws were written in broad and general terms and often required interpretation, the masses' domination of the courts gave them considerable political power. It was up to them to decide what the law said and how it would be applied. As Aristotle put it, when democracy is master of the voting power, it is master of the constitution.

In one of his most radical reforms, Solon created a new legal procedure (*ephesis*) that allowed any citizen to appeal the decision of a magistrate to the people's courts. In law as in politics, the people had the final say. Effectively, they controlled both the legislative and judicial branches of government. Over the course of the fifth and fourth centuries BCE, as their jurisdiction expanded, jury courts became the backbone of Athenian democracy.

From a legal perspective, the secular, populist character of Solon's law was its most radical feature. Unlike Hammurabi and Lycurgus, Solon made no attempt to ground the legitimacy of his laws on some higher, divine authority. Where Hammurabi said he was chosen to be Babylon's lawgiver by Marduk, the city's God, and Lycurgus claimed he had received the approval of the Oracle at Delphi, Solon's authority rested on the fact he was chosen by his neighbors.

By any measure, making the people guardians of the law was a bold decision. It was unlike anything that had been tried before. In creating the jury courts and giving them the power to overturn the decisions of the magistrates, the people were able to determine the force of the law and to say what it actually meant. When they sat as jurors, Athenians swore an oath that they would base all their decisions on the law, and when there was no law, or it was unclear, they would do what they thought was just.

In addition to giving the people the final word in defining the substance of the law, Solon made sure it would be rigorously enforced. In another part of his reforms, he instituted a new procedure that allowed any citizen to initiate a lawsuit against anyone, including a magistrate, who had committed a crime against the state. Over time, the power of the people's courts to hold the most powerful officials to account expanded and came to include formal procedures (*euthyna, eisangelia*) in which ordinary Athenians had an opportunity to review the credentials and performance of the magistrates, both before and at the conclusion of their time in office.

Solon's laws marked a watershed in the history of law and democracy and the connection between the two. The emphasis they placed on the courts and legal procedures constituted a major advance over Draco's reforms. It is said Solon thought his laws were so sound that they should last for a hundred years. To demonstrate his confidence in their probity, after delivering them to his fellow citizens he left town for ten years.

Like all the other great rulers and lawgivers who came before him, it turned out his confidence was misplaced. Within his lifetime he saw the authority of his constitution usurped by Pisistratus, who ruled Athens for twenty years as a more or less benign tyrant. His sons proved much less adept at governing, and in 508 BCE the Athenians rallied around another big man to get things back on track.

Although Cleisthenes was a member of one of the leading Athenian families, he carried out a radical realignment of the city's political system in which citizens engaged much more as equals. In addition to their participation in the legislative and judicial branches of government, Cleisthenes opened up the executive to the masses. Solon's Council of Four Hundred was made more democratic by expanding and reorganizing its membership around territorial constituencies rather than traditional family and tribal units, and by limiting tenure to two nonconsecutive one-year terms.

Where Solon had put the people in charge of the judicial branch of government, after Cleisthenes they had control of the executive as well. Where the Areopagus was once the seat of all government power and was controlled by the patrician class, a generation after his reforms practically all of its judicial powers had been taken over by the people's courts, their members chosen by lot and answerable to the popular assembly for the decisions they made. As a result of his reforms, it is estimated that at least one in three Athenian males was directly involved in running the government of their city at some point in their lives. For the sweep of his laws, Cleisthenes earned the title "father of Athenian democracy."

Over the course of the next hundred and fifty years, Athens functioned as the world's "first democracy."[6] In the fifth century BCE and the first half of the fourth, it was probably the most civilized society on earth. Rather than resorting to violence and threats of physical force to solve social conflicts, or to indoctrination and socialization to suppress them, Athenians expected their fellow citizens to find common ground in the law and behave as reasonable people.

Their story has been heralded and retold many times. The image that typically comes to mind when people think about the glory of Classical Greece, at the height of its power, is of popular assemblies (*ecclesia*) of men in white tunics at outdoor meetings engaged in lively debates, passing laws and judging cases. Like the ancient codes of Mesopotamia, the full range of community life was up for discussion. Family law, commercial law, criminal law, property law, even rudimentary ideas of international law were all included.[7]

Rule of Law

However, even when democracy was at its height, there were limits on the powers of the people. Indeed, Athens advertised itself first and foremost as a rule of law state.[8] It was one of their proud boasts that, unlike tyrants in places like Persia, who ruled as they pleased, Athenians decided nothing without the law. By that it was meant that democracy operated within the parameters of traditional customs and ancient laws (*nomoi*), like those that had been written by Draco and Solon. Even Demosthenes, one of the original icons of democratic politics, thought democracy was flawed unless it recognized the supremacy of the law.

At the center of Athenians' legal universe were the codes left to them by Draco and Solon. They functioned much like modern constitutions; they were the bedrock on which everything else was built. They established the governing structure and core commandments that controlled political and social life in the city.

As the foundational laws on which the rest of the Athenian legal regime was constructed, Draco's and Solon's codes had a special status. Like the laws of Hammurabi and Lycurgus, there was a presumption they would last forever. New laws proposing changes had to be passed in the assemblies according to strict procedures, which was not an easy thing to do. Anyone proposing an amendment to the established rules had to show some flaw in the existing law before his fellow lawgivers would give their assent. At the end of the fifth century BCE a special procedure (*graphe paranomon*) was established in which arguments for and against a proposed law were presented in court and a ruling was made on its validity. It was like putting the old law on trial and passing judgment on whether it was guilty of an injustice or mistake.

To qualify as valid law, the decisions of the popular assemblies also had to take a certain form. Laws had to be written and they were supposed to be general enactments that benefited the whole community. Legislation could not be targeted at one segment of the population; nor could it be written retroactively or in secret. Neither could it be inconsistent or administered unfairly.

Constraints were also imposed on the power of the people to punish their fellow citizens. Punishments had to be grounded in and enforced through the law. Athenian law prohibited prosecuting a person twice for the same offence and condemning someone to death without a trial. Part of the judicial oath included a promise to listen to both sides of a case and judge them as fairly as possible.

So, it turns out Athens was not only the "first democracy" the world had ever known, it was also the first rule of law state on the planet. Indeed, the Athenians were clear that of the two – law and democracy – law was the more fundamental. It was, they said, binding on rulers and citizens alike.

In addition to the oath the jurors swore to uphold the law, the supremacy of Athenian law was also acknowledged publicly by the chief magistrates of the city. On taking office, the "archons" swore an oath that they would govern according to the law, and if they didn't they could be prosecuted by any private citizen. So could lawmakers who proposed new laws that did not redress some flaw in the existing law or were not enacted in the proper way.

Making democracy and the rule of law the defining characteristics of their city-state was a remarkable achievement. The Athenians created a system of government in which the coercive powers of the state were exercised by laws that were drafted, debated, and applied by ordinary (male) citizens in public gatherings, binding all of them equally. It was a bold and pathbreaking initiative, but it must be said: like most things in life, it wasn't perfect.

Even the Athenians thought they could do better. Plato (in the *Republic* and the *Laws*) and Aristotle (in the *Politics*) were the most outspoken in their criticisms of their fellow citizens' lawmaking. As they saw it, too often rhetoric replaced reason in the assemblies and the courts. Too much time was spent playing to the passions and prejudices of the crowd.

Too much politics and litigation were marked by factionalism and self-interest. It was not uncommon that laws that failed to meet the required standard of proof were enacted without their promoters being punished.

The popular courts were especially vulnerable to manipulation and abuse.[9] Athenian courts were often used as places where political scores were settled. Malicious prosecutions designed to intimidate and penalize political opponents were a regrettable but recurring feature of the system.

Because Athenians were paid when they sat as jurors, they were typically delighted to do their civic duty. Not surprisingly, that meant juries were much bigger than they are today. Legal proceedings could be large and unruly assemblies. A typical case would have several hundred jurors chosen from a panel of six thousand citizens who were selected annually by lot. The court that tried Socrates had five hundred members. And everyone was an amateur. There were no judges or lawyers to explain the law.

Arguing one's case before such a large audience put a premium on special pleading. For many people, getting up on such a large public stage to present their side of a case (litigants were expected to represent themselves) must have been an intimidating prospect. Responding to that need, a group of professional teachers, known as sophists, who were masters of language and techniques for making winning arguments, offered lessons in speech writing and how to pitch one's case in the most compelling way. Sophists charged a fee for their services, which meant litigants of modest means who could not afford to learn the necessary skills or to hire someone who could write their speech were at a disadvantage. In the service these individuals provided to would-be litigants, some see the genesis of the legal profession.[10]

Sophists and speechwriters who prepared litigants for their day in court were not, however, like lawyers who plead cases today. They had no general expertise or special training in the law and they did not argue cases in court. Their value added was in knowing techniques of persuasion (rhetoric) and the meaning of words. Their critics, including Plato and Aristotle, accused them of being less interested in getting to the truth of a case than in putting their client's position in the best possible light. Plato held them responsible for the verdict to execute Socrates. In time, their notoriety became so scandalous that the word "sophistry" was popularized to refer to the making of arguments that are clever but false.

Because cases might be won on the basis of an emotional pitch or an attack on a person's character, courts could be risky places – especially if you were rich. Seeing an opportunity, another group of Athenians, known as sycophants, began to blackmail wealthy citizens by threatening them with lawsuits. Litigation, in Classical Greece, became an instrument of class war. Because ordinary citizens could claim any magistrate or political leader had violated the law, the risk of being the subject of a frivolous and vexatious lawsuit was very real.

Mob Rule

Of course, on most days and in most cases the courts and assemblies tried to do the right thing. If you could ask their members about their motives, it is almost certain they would say their oath committed them to respect the law and endeavor to do justice in every case. And for the most part they did. The excellence and accomplishments of the Athenian polis have been celebrated down through history.

Still, it is important to remember that at critical moments in Athens' brief history its political and legal institutions could succumb to mob rule. There were notorious cases of wrongful convictions and executions (the Arginusae generals), and mass witch hunts (the Herms and the Mysteries) carried out by the courts. That the Athenians were capable of bending the law to their own (class, tribe, family) purposes, there is no doubt.

The problem stemmed from the fact that, after listening to the evidence and arguments, each juror had an unfettered discretion to do what he personally thought was right. There were no overarching principles or rules that could tell them what the law meant or what justice required in a specific case. The fact that judgments could be biased by a juror's personal prejudices and phobias turned out to be its Achilles' heel. It meant politics could overpower the law.

Undoubtedly, the most notorious verdict in the city's history was the decision in 399 BCE condemning Socrates to death. In terms of violence and loss of life, convicting and killing Socrates for impiety and corrupting the morals of the city's youth was certainly not the most flagrant act of injustice committed by the people of Athens. Still, even though it resulted in the death of only one man, poisoning Socrates is considered one of the darkest moments in the city's history. When they condemned Socrates to death, they took the life of a person subsequent generations have judged to be one of the most important thinkers in human history. They proved Hesiod's prescience when he warned that the law could produce crooked judgments in the hands of judges who were corrupt.

Socrates's story is about as noble as it gets.[11] A short, stocky, scruffy philosopher based in Athens in the last half of the fifth century BCE, he lived the life of a public intellectual who challenged much of what passed as conventional wisdom in the city. He was an opponent of both democracy and sloppy thinking. His whole life was dedicated to searching for ethical and moral truths that would explain how to live a good life. Plato described him as the bravest, wisest, most upright man of his time.

Justice for Socrates was something that was good in and of itself. He rejected the argument of Thrasymachus, a sophist who insisted that justice was all and only about who was strong and clever enough to be able to enforce his will. For Socrates, law was not simply victor's justice by another name. Indeed, as he made clear at the very beginning of Plato's *Republic*, he thought the principles that defined a just life and justice in a city were the same.

His way to discover what justice and a virtuous life entailed was to ask a lot of questions. He didn't believe in providing answers. Truth was uncovered by elimination, not proclamation. Testing for inconsistencies was critical. Questioning the soundness of popular assumptions and conventions was a way to learn how mistakes are made and to distinguish right from wrong. The "Socratic method" is still the model for the instruction of students reading cases in the best law schools in the world.

In a court of five hundred jurors, it is thought he lost by some sixty votes. When it came to sentencing him to death, it is believed an even larger number of people voted against him! Most people consider the judgment to have been politically motivated and of dubious legality. Certainly, after the passage of 2,400 years, it looks like a state execution. Throughout his life Socrates had shown his commitment and loyalty to the polis. He fought in the army and served with distinction in the popular assembly. All of his teaching and indeed his whole being were dedicated to living a just and thoughtful life and serving the best interests of the city. Even if he faked his respect for the city's gods, no one now thinks that meant he deserved to die.

Among philosophers and classical scholars there is a widespread belief that Socrates was convicted as much for the company he kept as for his ideas. He was executed just after the Peloponnesian War had ended in defeat for the Athenians and several of his associates had sided with the Spartans. This looks more like a case of political payback and guilt by association than a conviction based on the facts.

Whatever the motives of those Athenians who voted to put Socrates to death, his execution marks something of a tombstone for the whole city. By any measure, it was a very bad day for democracy. On the question of the life or death of one of their most iconic citizens, they gave in to the tyranny of the majority and the rule of the mob. From that point on it was almost all downhill until 338 BCE, when Philip of Macedon defeated Demosthenes and the Athenians in the Battle of Chaeronea.

The trial and execution of Socrates was a dark day for law and democracy, but it has to be said that the Athenians weren't one hundred percent to blame. Socrates, too, was partly responsible for his fate. He refused to plea for a less severe punishment and after his conviction he passed up a chance to escape. On his view of the law, he had a duty to obey an edict or a judgment, even if it were wrong.

He thought that so long as a piece of legislation or a ruling by a court had followed the proper procedures when it was pronounced, he was obligated to obey. As a citizen of the city, he had had the benefit of living under the rule of law, and so it would be wrong for him to reject its verdict even if he could show it was unjust. Allowing each citizen to choose which rules to obey, he said, would do grievous damage to the force of the law.

The way Socrates understood the law was almost certainly the way most Greeks thought about it at the time. Today we call it a "positivist" conception of law. A law or judgment that passes through the required procedures is a valid law; whether it is good or bad is irrelevant in deciding whether it has legal force.

For positivists, Socrates's decision to accept his punishment was undoubtedly an honorable, even heroic choice. History mostly applauds him for giving his life for an idea – the rule of law – in which he passionately believed. To put the interests of his community ahead of his own, to ensure that the strength of the law would not be weakened, was undoubtedly a noble act. For a lot of people – including me – it would get him into law's hall of fame, even if his understanding of the law allowed it to be used for pernicious purposes as well as good.

And yet, as exemplary as his fidelity to law surely was, his death was a terrible tragedy. It was, in the end, an unnecessary waste of a very big and important life of a husband, father, and public conscience of a great city. It could have been avoided. His absolutist, "positivistic" approach to the assembly's judgment wasn't the only way it might have been understood.

There was at least one other, more nuanced way of thinking about the law he might have latched on to. It had been put forward by Sophocles, one of Athens's great poets, in his play *Antigone*. Had Socrates embraced it he might not have regarded his accepting his friends' offer of escape as an inexcusable act of disloyalty. The real tragedy of his death is that it was as much a suicide as a homicide committed by the state.

The way Sophocles thought about law (like the judgment of the jurors or the rules on piety and corrupting the youth) was that it had to be compatible with "justice ... and the unwritten laws of heaven" or it couldn't qualify as a law and it wouldn't have to be obeyed. This definition of law was given by Sophocles to Antigone (the main character in the play that bears her name), to justify her refusal to obey the king's edict that her slain (and treasonous) brother was not to be given a proper burial. No mortal man, she said, had the power to override the eternal laws of the Gods. Burying one's dead was a divine rule of law and so carried more force than anything the king might command.

We can only speculate why Socrates didn't use Sophocles's argument when discussing with his friend Crito whether to escape before his execution could be carried out. The two were contemporaries, so it seems certain he would have been familiar with her speech. And it appears to speak directly to his situation after he had been sentenced to death. If Antigone was right in disobeying the king, then neither would Socrates have been doing anything wrong if he had paid his guards to look the other way and skipped town. His decision to flee would not have weakened the strength of the law because an unjust verdict cannot qualify as law and his escape couldn't have been condemned as an act of betrayal.

One suggestion is that Socrates saw his execution as an honorable way to bring political harmony to his city, and so he took one for the team. Another possibility is that in drinking the hemlock, he thought he was headed for a paradise where he would find the knowledge and wisdom he had sought all his life. Whatever his motivation, Socrates likely accepted it at least in part because it served his interests as much as those of his fellow citizens who insisted on their right to kill him.

Utopia

The acuteness of Socrates's tragedy is only aggravated when one realizes that the idea that there exists a higher law that binds rulers as much as the people they rule became a subject of serious conversation very soon after his execution. Over the course of the next three generations, the notion that there were higher rules or standards to which humans and their laws had to conform or else lose their legitimacy (and their force) was picked up and developed by a number of people, including Plato and Aristotle. Within years of his execution, the "positive" definition of law Socrates thought demanded his submission was being openly challenged by two of the best minds of all time.[12]

Plato, of course, was Socrates's star student. He is the first person we know about who wrote systematically on the relationship between law and justice and the limits it imposes on a ruler's authority to govern. (Socrates believed the only way to explore ideas was verbally and he never committed anything to writing.) Plato was born around 428 or 427 BCE into one of Athens's leading families. He lived through (and probably served in) the Peloponnesian War with Sparta and witnessed (when he was in his late twenties) the trial of Socrates. He thought these two events demonstrated the failure of Athenian democracy, and they inspired him to dedicate the rest of his life to thinking about how a better polis could be created and greater tragedy avoided.

In his first attempt, the *Republic*, neither law nor democracy figured prominently in the story. In the utopia of his dreams, the rulers are philosopher-kings, the wisest and most thoughtful members of the city. Because of their superior intelligence and education (which continued, more or less uninterrupted, until they were fifty), their judgment is so sound they have no need for any law. In deciding what is in the community's best interest, and what rules its citizens should follow in order to live just lives, the "guardians" do best when their discretion is unfettered and they can do whatever they think is right.

Later in life Plato wrote a more practical guide (the *Laws*) for a new colony he called Magnesia. Scholars still debate the exact nature of the relationship between the *Republic* and the *Laws*. However, there is no doubt that after a very unsuccessful experience advising a father-and-son team of tyrants who ruled Syracuse (a Greek colony on the island of Sicily), he came to the conclusion that, in the real world in which he lived, law was essential if the members of a community were to enjoy peace and justice and live in harmony. If it was unrealistic to think a city might be governed by its best and brightest, the next best alternative was to put limits on those who were in charge.

In the *Laws*, Plato described the best rulers as "servants of the law." He thought the success or failure of a state turned on this precept more than anything else. "Where the law is subject to some other authority," he wrote, "the collapse of the state is not far off; but if law is the master of the government and the government is its slave, then the situation is full of promise and men enjoy all the blessings that the gods shower on a state."[13]

For Plato, the supremacy of law meant the supremacy of reason in how both rulers and private citizens behaved in the city and in their homes. As he saw it, reason dictated that laws could only be adopted if they benefited the whole community. Laws that were passed by particular factions (like the rich or the poor) for their own advantage, he labeled "bogus laws." Like Sophocles, Plato thought such assertions of political power were illegitimate and lacked any force. People who think such laws must be obeyed, he wrote, "are wasting their breath."

For Plato, a rule of law state was the polar opposite of cities like Syracuse or empires like Persia that were ruled by tyrants. Instead of the greed and arbitrary will of the despot, the rule of law promised a polity marked by "peace, respect for others, good laws, justice in full measure, and a state of happiness and harmony among the races of the world." In the *Laws*, Plato was offering his fellow Greeks a practical guide on how to establish a just society and put a stop to the tyranny and turmoil that had dominated politics in his city for virtually the whole of his life.

Plato thought of law first and foremost as an educational tool – a means of teaching people what living a good life entailed and how to achieve it. In Magnesia, laws came with long preambles explaining their logic and rationale. The primary purpose of criminal law was corrective. It was more about reformation and rehabilitation than revenge. *Lex talionis* did not have the prominent place in the laws of Magnesia that it had in the earlier codes of the Near East.

Except in their common ambition to construct a well-ordered society, Plato's ideas about law were as different from codes like Hammurabi's as chalk is to cheese. Plato's law was secular, was based on reason, and it acted as a check on the ruler's authority. It looked very different as well. With preambles explaining what they were about, Magnesia's laws were not just a long list of judgments declaring how specific types of cases should be decided. Rather than the casuistic form ("If this ... then ...) that distinguished the Near Eastern model, in Plato's mind law was made up of broad principles that governed as many cases as possible.

Plato thought law was made up of timeless, universal principles of justice that, like the laws of motion that governed the planets and stars, had an independent existence of their own. Those who were able to exercise their powers of reason rigorously could identify and understand them. At the center of his just society was a principle of specialization that directed each of its members to perform the role for which he or she was naturally predisposed. Those most adept at exercising the power of reason (which included women as well as men) would be streamed into an elite educational program and trained to be rulers. They would never know any other kind of work. The rest would do the jobs for which they were most suited (farmer, soldier, merchant, tradesman) for the whole of their lives and would never bother themselves with politics, except for ensuring their own personal obedience to the law. On the economic front, rather than detailing the wages of specific trades, as was Hammurabi's style, in Magnesia there was a simple rule prohibiting anyone from making more than four times what the lowest wage earner was paid.

In his day Plato was a major player. He was recognized as one of the big thinkers throughout the Greek world. And yet, despite his stature as one of the greatest philosophers of all time, his impact on the society in which he lived seems to have been quite limited. His vision of a utopian society was too close to the oligarchy of Sparta to appeal to the democratically minded Athenians. Even his attempt to sell his ideas to Dionysius and his son in Syracuse didn't end well. (He barely escaped from being sold into slavery.)

Plato's reputation has also suffered in modern times. Although still admired as one of the founding fathers of philosophical inquiry into the most fundamental questions about truth and justice, and about what humans are capable of knowing about ourselves and the world around us, Plato's vision of the ideal political society has been largely discredited. Even with the benefit of the law, Magnesia was a pretty intolerant, elitist, and disagreeable place. Gays, heretics, and religious minorities could be put to death; eugenics and slavery were accepted practices, and an all-powerful and ominously named Nocturnal Council had the authority to interfere in the smallest details of a person's life.

The best of Plato's ideas lived on in the teaching of his students and their descendants. Of these, Aristotle is unquestionably the most distinguished. Another polymath, tutor of Alexander the Great, and founder of his own school (the Lyceum) in Athens, Aristotle embraced a lot of what he learned from Plato, but not everything.

Law and Justice

Like lots of teachers and their students, in many respects Plato and Aristotle were polar opposites. Plato spent most of his time thinking about a purely intellectual world in which eternal, universal, immutable principles of truth and justice and beauty were revealed. He was an idealist, a dreamer. Aristotle, on the other hand, while he understood the importance of abstract thinking, he also thought it was necessary to ground it in the facts of everyday life. Aristotle was the son of a doctor, and like his father, his thinking had an empirical, pragmatic, and scientific bent.

The differences between Plato and Aristotle carried over to their thinking about politics and the law. As we have seen, Plato's ideal republic was ruled by an elite group of philosopher-kings whose wisdom was so superior they had no need of (and were not bound by) the law. Plato also favored the collective, military character of Spartan society over the unruly, democratic methods of governing that prevailed in Athens.

Aristotle, the empiricist, based much of his thinking about politics and law on a study he made of the different constitutional orders that existed among the Greek city-states. From that comparative perspective, he was more comfortable with Athenian democracy and more optimistic about the potential of each individual human being. He was confident ordinary citizens could be trained in the law so that they would be able to resolve cases fairly even when there was no law on point. They didn't need years of training like Plato's guardians. Reason, unaffected by their emotions ("beastly desires"), would tell them what to do. Law, he wrote, was "reason without desire." Contrary to what Plato had written in the *Republic*, Aristotle famously argued that a city was better-off when it was ruled by the best laws than when it is run by its best men.[14]

Philosophers spend a lot of time discussing the differences between Plato and Aristotle, but for lawyers what is more striking is that, when it came to thinking about the rule of law, the two saw eye to eye on the basics. Both thought law was the product of human reason and both insisted that the purpose of law was to ensure justice is done on earth as it is in heaven. Like Plato, Aristotle thought of law as essential to the creation of a well-ordered society, and he also saw it as being man-made. Part of the divine, cosmic order, law's authority was rooted in human nature and the power of rational thought. He also thought reason was the critical agent in directing individuals to do what is just and right, and it bound rulers as much as the people they ruled.

Aristotle and Plato were also agreed that the purpose of law was to create a just society in which everyone aspired to do the right thing, to teach the basic precepts and principles of a virtuous and honorable life. At its simplest, Aristotle defined justice as that which is lawful and fair. His guiding principle was moderation in all things. He described it as a mean between extremes. Like Plato, he regarded justice as the sovereign virtue. It kept the others (wisdom, temperance, piety, and courage) in balance. In addition, and unlike wisdom and courage, it is an aspect of a person's character that anyone can attain. It is a moral imperative for the common person.

At the center of his writing on justice Aristotle embraced broad, formal principles of the kind Plato favored.[15] He distinguished between two different conceptions of political justice and reduced the principles and laws they supported to mathematical formula. One kind of justice was universal and immutable and was based on laws that are embedded in (our human) nature. He likened these laws to the laws of combustion, which were the same in Persia and Athens despite their different cultures and political histories. Natural laws, like fire and justice, governed life in both. For Aristotle, natural law embraced ethical, as well as empirical, truths.

A second form of justice was conventional and more local. It was the foundation on which a state's civil and criminal laws were built. For Aristotle, like his teacher, each community's own local laws were in some sense inferior to the universal, timeless laws of (human) nature. He believed that there was one natural form of government that was best for everyone, no matter where they lived, and it set the standard against which local governments and their laws could be measured. Natural law was prior to local legislation in the same way the capacity to speak is more basic than any of the conventional languages that each of us might use.

Among the principles of natural justice that Aristotle wrote about, two stand out. One was a law of distribution – of rewards and punishments – that was based on what he called a principle of geometric proportion. On this principle, people get what they deserve: those who commit more serious crimes are punished more severely, while those who have contributed more to the well-being of their communities should reap greater honors and rewards.

The second principle of justice Aristotle identified provided the basis for the (natural) law that governs the interactions of individuals acting privately, whether it's rear-ending the car in front of you or buying a cup of coffee. He called this corrective or rectificatory justice, and he claimed it was based on an arithmetic proportion. In this sphere of social relations, Aristotle said, it doesn't matter whether the driver at fault or the party that breaches the contract is good or bad or rich or poor; regardless of a person's circumstances, the law and the outcome of the case is the same. If your bad driving results in a thousand dollars' worth of damage to another person's car, that is the amount you must pay, even if you are the most virtuous and destitute person in town and she is a wealthy, obnoxious bully.

In arguing for the legitimacy of these two different principles of proportionality, Aristotle was appealing to the aristocrats and common folk to see the merits of each other's position. The rich, who were naturally inclined to look at people in terms of their worth, were being told a more basic equality of simple personhood was also an appropriate measure in some circumstances. Aristotle believed that much of the social conflict destroying the quality of life in Athens was based on these competing definitions of equality, and that accepting the authority of both would enhance the well-being of the city as a whole.

He was also speaking a language that would have been familiar to most Athenians. The idea of proportionality, as a standard of harmony and balance, was an important part of the way Greeks thought about their world long before Plato and Aristotle came on the scene. For generations the Greeks had been spotting the symmetry of proportionality in the physical world that surrounded them. In the sixth century BCE, Pythagoras and other mathematicians were using proportionality in their study of astronomy, music (harmonic scales), architecture, and art (the golden mean). According to some, the link between proportionality and justice goes back even further, to Anaximander (610–546 BCE), who considered the balance between the four basic elements of nature (earth, air, fire, and water) to be a matter of proportion and cosmic justice.

Aristotle's contribution was to point out that the force of proportionality was as relevant in the world of social relations as it is in a universe that includes sound waves and moons. (As we shall see in chapter 9, had the jurors applied this principle in the trial of Socrates they would not have condemned him to death.)

Like Socrates and Plato, Aristotle has had more influence on the generations that succeeded him than he did on the people with whom he lived. Although much of his work had an empirical, practical side to it (he compiled a catalog of the different constitutions of the major city-states), no one paid much attention to what he taught, and the fractious rivalries that divided the city continued more or less unabated. During his life, Athens fell to his friend Philip of Macedon and then came under the rule of his son, Alexander, who had been his student. When Alexander died in Babylon in 323 BCE, Aristotle left Athens (some say out of concern that he might meet the same fate as Socrates) and passed away a few months later.

In the Hellenistic age that followed, physical force trumped the force of reason but the idea of law was never totally defeated. Plato's and Aristotle's concept of law as a moral order based on reason was kept alive and enriched by the Stoics, a philosophical school that taught the existence of a universal, natural law of harmony and order that spoke to all human beings. For the Stoics, the law of reason, not the emperor, was the supreme ruling force. With the collapse of democratic politics, however, their focus was more on the life of the individual than on politics and the state.

The Stoics equated law with reason and insisted that it was within the natural capacity of the ordinary person to understand. To live a just life meant following the rational side of human nature. Everything one did had to be justified by reason. Goodness and lawfulness would prevail when everyone governed their behavior by a process of rational thought.

In terms of thinking about how to build a just society, Aristotle's reflections have also stood the test of time, and they still resonate with many people. Unlike Plato, his writing continues to speak to the political as much as the personal dimensions of our lives. The distinction he drew between distributive and corrective justice underlies the separation of public and private law that remains part of all major legal systems to this day. Eminent scholars continue to write in the natural law tradition, and studying comparative constitutional law is in vogue once again.

Sadly, like all of law's heroes who we have encountered so far, it is necessary to put an asterisk beside his name. While Aristotle thought of law in terms of universal, mathematical principles of equality, he also thought some people were less equal than others – women and slaves in particular. He believed that women were an inferior class of being who were best kept in seclusion under the control of their fathers and husbands, and he argued that some people (non-Greeks) were naturally suited to be slaves. No one, it seems, not even Aristotle or Plato, was able to live up to the standards they insisted were an essential part of a virtuous life and the building blocks of a just society.

Even if there weren't any Greeks who were able to practice what they preached, the collective contribution this small crowd of people made to the rule of law in the short space of a few generations was a remarkable achievement. They had turned the original, divinely inspired, top-down idea of law on its head. They insisted law came from the bottom up, from the people exercising their (natural) powers of reason to create societies in which everyone would be treated, and would treat each other, fairly and with respect. Rather than asserting the will of the ruler, law was a process that the people could use to ensure their rulers didn't use their powers to beat up on them. Theirs was a popular, democratic conception of law that ordinary people could understand and control. It would provide a reference point for anyone thinking about drafting a new constitution in the future.

The Golden Mean

The Greeks' reflections on what it means to live under a system of government that adheres to the rule of law ranks alongside their accomplishments in mathematics, philosophy, and the arts, and it still features as one of their most enduring legacies. Their conception of the rule of law was very sophisticated. It was not just a ruler's command (like Hammurabi's); it combined formal requirements and moral imperatives as well. It insisted that the rules governing life in the city be formulated in the proper way, bind everyone, and enhance the life of the community as a whole. The Greeks believed that laws that were the product of human reason were like the laws of nature and would last forever.

Their conception of the rule of law consisted of three parts: (1) Ruling by law, meaning authorized lawmakers issuing commands in the form of general rules that were adopted and applied in the proper way, which required they be transparent, prospective, consistent, and evenhanded. (2) Rulers bound by law, meaning the law is supreme, its scope is universal, and no one (including those who make and apply the law) is above or can escape its authority. And (3) doing justice through law, meaning the substance of any law must promote the well-being of the community as a whole rather than the interests of particular factions. In its ideal form, the rule of law in Athens meant governing by rules that had been debated and adopted according to the proper procedures, that promoted justice, and that were accepted by everyone as the final, ultimate criterion for resolving conflict.

By any measure, the way the Greeks rethought the meaning of law must qualify as one of Thomas Kuhn's earliest "paradigm shifts." The originality and revolutionary sweep of their thinking stands in sharp contrast with what was going on at the same time in the rest of the world. In Asia, North Africa, and the Near East, religion and custom still dominated people's thinking about how they should conduct themselves in their homes and in their dealings with others. No one was trying to imagine new ways of thinking about law. Instead people were being encouraged to look back to a distant past or deep within themselves for how to behave ethically and set the world right.[16]

In India at the time, people were asking questions about the rules of Hindu law, but not in a way that showed any interest in improving the quality of legal regulation. At roughly the same time (or not long before – the dates are still disputed) that Socrates was challenging the conventional wisdom in Athens, the most important voice in the subcontinent on how to live a good life belonged to Siddhartha Gautama, better known today as Buddha. In substance, the ambition of Buddha and Socrates – to figure out how to live a life of virtue, free of suffering and conflict – was the same. And the content of Buddha's message was not that different from the Greeks. In the same way that Aristotle defined justice as a mean between extremes, Buddha said the good life consisted of following the middle path – neither too austere nor too indulgent.

However, although Buddha and the great men of Athens shared similar attachments to virtue and goodness, their ideas of how to achieve them were completely different. For the Greeks, humans are social creatures by nature and need to live in a well-ordered polis if they are to realize their full potential. Buddha, by contrast, thought the path to nirvana was through an intensely spiritual quest and lots and lots of solitary meditation. For Buddha, law consisted of ethical precepts of personal behavior and internal rules of self-control. He rejected the authority of the Brahmin class and recommended each person seek enlightenment on his or her own by looking inward and transcending the material and political world. He also challenged the hierarchical ordering of Hindu society and its law (of Manu), which imposed a rigid system of castes.

In China, before the common era, law had even fewer friends willing to champion its cause. Indeed, for much of Chinese history and until very recently law has had a bad name. For the whole of the time the Athenians were intent on trying to build a rule of law state, the Chinese were killing each other in one of the nastiest eras in their history, known as the Warring States period, from the fifth to the third centuries BCE. For more than five hundred years, beginning in the eighth century, rival warlords slugged it out, basically nonstop, for the title of emperor of all China. Armies numbering in the hundreds of thousands slaughtering enemies in the millions had little interest in, and paid even less attention to, the law. It has been estimated that in the 550 years between 770 and 220 BCE, there were 1,678 wars and only 127 years of peace. It is reported that after one battle, over a hundred thousand prisoners were beheaded.

Within this world of massacres, mayhem, and crumbling social order, scholars emerged who reflected on the chaos and social disintegration that surrounded them and offered different prescriptions for how to get out of the mess. The most famous of these public intellectuals was Confucius, an itinerant teacher in the sixth and fifth centuries BCE whose philosophy of what constituted a good life and a felicitous social order emphasized ideas of harmony and balance (the Doctrine of the Mean) but was hostile to almost all forms of legal regulation.

A generation before Plato and Aristotle were singing law's praises, Confucius and his students were teaching that rulers should have nothing to do with the law and should govern their realms by setting the highest standards of personal behavior in their dealings with their subjects (Analects 2:3). Even starting a lawsuit was considered shameful and something to be avoided (Analects 12:13). Rather than holding rulers legally accountable, like the Greeks, Confucius's way of creating a peaceful and harmonious society was for all social relations to strictly adhere to a set of traditional, hierarchical roles (ruler/subject, parent/child, husband/wife) and the rituals (standing up, bowing down, shaking hands) associated with them. His approach was all about teaching and persuading rather than issuing orders and punishing those who broke the rules. According to Confucius, the only restrictions on what a ruler could or couldn't do were the moral customs and traditions, known as *li*, that governed how people of different social ranks interacted with each other.

Although Confucius's ideas came to dominate the way the Chinese thought about structuring government and organizing their empire, not everyone bought in to the message. Law (*fa*) had its supporters even before Confucius came on the scene, but it only became an important part of the story a couple of hundred years after he died. For a brief period of time, at the end of the third century BCE, law was in vogue under the Qin (pronounced "chin") dynasty (221–206 BCE), but even then it was much closer to the top-down, Near Eastern model of rule by law than the populist conception of the Greeks. Championed by a group known as the "Legalists," law was used by the Qin emperors to consolidate their control and enhance their military strength rather than protect people from despots. Legalists writing at roughly the same time as Plato and Aristotle argued that law be used as an instrument of fear and repression rather than as a way of reforming and rehabilitating delinquent behavior, as Plato and Aristotle envisaged. Wise rulers, they said, would ensure even minor crimes were punished severely.[17]

So even in their own time the Greeks were one of a kind. There was nothing remotely like what they were thinking going on anywhere else in the world. And even if it was as much a thought experiment as a real community of people living under the sovereignty of law, their example was remarkable and unprecedented.

The Greeks stood out and their brilliance was not lost on their neighbors. A few hundred kilometers to the west, one city in particular took notice of what the Greeks had done and over the course of the next thousand years sustained an empire with what is perhaps the most influential legal system ever created. How Rome, a relatively backward provincial city-state, accomplished this astonishing feat is another tale of epic proportions, and so warrants a chapter of its own.

Chapter Three

Rome

First Lawyer

Just about everybody who was anybody when Rome was at its peak knew about, and for the most part admired, the Greeks. If you were part of the smart set, there was a good chance you'd go to Athens to study science, mathematics, philosophy, or the arts. Marcus Tullius Cicero was one of those people. He had the money and the connections to take advantage of such an opportunity, and in 79 BCE he set off with some friends on a "grand tour" of the East. He was twenty-seven and just married. A passionate Hellenophile, he spent six months in Athens studying at Plato's Academy, inhaling the teaching of the Stoics and thinking about the law.

Cicero is another of the larger-than-life characters who have played big roles in the history of law.[1] Born in 106 BCE to a family that was part of the rural gentry in a provincial town south of Rome, he was a member of the wealthy elite but a rank below Rome's patrician class. He lived in the dying days of the Republic, and he despaired its demise. Caught in troubled times like Plato and Aristotle, he also spent much of his life working for and writing about the "ideal republic."

Given his life of privilege, it is not surprising that Cicero's vision of what constituted the best form of government was quite conservative and protective of the interests of the elites. Like Aristotle, he favored a mixed form of government that allowed for the participation of all citizens but functioned more as an oligarchy of old and new money. In the civil wars between Pompey and Julius Caesar, and then between Octavian and Mark Antony, his consuming ambition was to defend Rome's republican constitution. Although he was criticized for being too accommodating to Octavian's imperial ambitions, in his own mind, everything he did was intended to advance the cause of his republican principles, including the rule of law. In the end, like Socrates, his commitment to his ideas and his status as something of an outsider ended up costing him his life.

Cicero spent most of his adult years engaged in politics in one form or another. He was elected consul, the highest position in the government, when he was forty-two, and after that he became a senator. To put bread on the table, he practiced law. In his day, Rome had a very sophisticated legal system that coordinated the lives of almost a million people. Its sheer size and complexity had encouraged some of Rome's traditional elites to dedicate their lives to mastering its operation, and when he came of age Cicero chose to join their profession. He was trained by Q. Mucius Scaevola, one of Rome's leading jurists, and in time he became the most famous advocate in the city's history.

In the latter part of his career, as his and the Republic's fortunes declined, Cicero cut back on his public life and spent more time at one of his half dozen villas putting his ideas down in writing. Taking his cue from Plato, he wrote one book, *On the Republic*, and followed it up with another, *On the Laws*. In addition to embracing the ideas of Plato and Aristotle, Cicero was especially influenced by the Stoics.

Like them, he believed that law was a natural phenomenon, inherent in all men, "constant, unchanging, eternal … binding all peoples and all ages." He described it as "the sole and universal ruler and governor of all things."[2] He thought laws that authorize a person to act in self-defense, or condemn cheating, or require us to help others facing immanent harm were like the laws of physics that give shape to our universe: they are the same everywhere, in Athens as much as Rome, and for all time, yesterday, today, and tomorrow. He argued that to curtail this natural law is unholy, to amend it illicit, to repeal it impossible. Although he didn't say so explicitly, the logic was that neither popular assemblies nor emperors had the power to excuse themselves from its rule.

Like Plato, Aristotle, and the Stoics, Cicero also thought law had a moral center of gravity. For all of them, law's authority depended on its commanding what was right. It had to be for the general well-being of the community or it wasn't a valid law. In his treatise *On the Laws*, he wrote that

law is the highest reason, implanted in nature, which commands what ought to be done and forbids the opposite. This reason, when fully fixed and fully developed in the human mind, is law … [L]aw is prudence, the effect of which is to order persons to act correctly and to forbid them to transgress … The origin of justice is to be found in the law, for law is a natural force; it is the mind and reason of the prudent man, the standard by which Justice and Injustice are measured.[3]

In an ideal republic, according to Cicero, law would be mastered by all educated people as part of their general schooling, and politics would be practiced according to the requirements of natural law. This would set the standard against which all human behavior and the laws of all societies can be evaluated. They distinguish good deeds and good laws from bad.

Like the Greeks, he thought that law, when it was understood in this way, was the best method of resolving conflict because reason held the passions in check. It was an antidote to a politics of selfishness and greed. Law offered the possibility of reaching fair settlements without things getting out of control. A state without law, he said, was like a body without a mind.

Notwithstanding his rhetorical skills as an advocate and the fluency of his writing, in the end Cicero didn't do any better than Plato or Aristotle in persuading his fellow citizens to think of law as a natural, moral idea and to make it the defining character of their politics. Part of the problem, it must be said, was of his own making. Although he was a committed republican, he was anything but a democrat and he was generally unsympathetic to the demands of the lower classes for more political and social equality. As eloquent and engaging as he may have been, he was also very taken with his own accomplishments and he alienated a lot of people. Cicero also suffered a credibility problem on account of his having betrayed the law when, as consul, he put down an attempt to overthrow the government by executing some of the conspirators without respecting their rights to a trial and due process of the law.

To be fair to Cicero, even if he had been a perfect guy the chances of a "new man" being able to persuade his betters to show more respect for the law were at best slim. The idea of law as an eternal, natural force based on reason just wasn't on many people's radar. During the whole of his life, Rome was headed in the opposite direction.

Indeed, the truth is that at no time in their history were the Romans as committed to either democracy or the rule of law as the Athenians. For most of its life, Rome was first and foremost a military state. It was in that sense more like Sparta. Within seventeen years of his signing Cicero's death warrant, Octavian (who was Caesar's great-nephew and adopted son) was made "princeps" (first citizen), took the title of "Augustus," and launched an empire ruled by dictators that would endure for another five hundred years. By the time the Empire collapsed, at the end of the fifth century CE, law was whatever the emperor said it was and democracy was dead.

Might Makes Right

The long arc of Roman history gets its shape from wars and military conquests, class conflicts and family feuds. It is marked by acts of barbaric violence and savage cruelty to friends and foes alike. The Romans and the Qin dynasty, whom we met at the end of the last chapter, had a lot in common.[4] Victories on the battlefield translated into defeated populations who were ruthlessly extorted (taxed) and enslaved. Throughout their history, the Romans fought it out among themselves to determine who would be the city's rulers. At other times, neighbors were the prime targets of their aggression and millions of people were forced to submit. In either context, the way the Romans told their story, might was the ultimate arbiter of what was right.

There is no definitive account of Rome's beginnings.[5] According to the legend the Romans told themselves, the city was founded in 753 BCE and was ruled for its first two hundred years by a series of seven kings. Sometime around 510 BCE, the most powerful families in the city insisted on a piece of the action and staked out the beginnings of a republic that would last almost five hundred years. When the Republic proved inadequate to the task, military leaders claiming the title of emperor took charge and extended Rome's hegemony for another half a millennium.

From the beginning until the end of the Republic, the Romans spent much of their time fighting – a lot of it with each other. From 460 to 360 BCE, they were at peace for fewer than ten years. There were also ongoing struggles between the rich (patricians), who monopolized the institutions of government, and the poor (plebians), who for the most part were forced to do what they were told. Over the last hundred years of its experiment with republicanism, Rome was torn apart by a series of nasty civil wars between the leading families of the city, who fought over how to divide up the spoils of the territories Rome controlled.

At the end of its life, the Republic was at the mercy of warlords (Marius, Sulla, Pompey, Caesar, Antony, and Octavian), their private armies, and numerous street gangs of mercenaries and thugs.[6] Political battles were settled by assassination and armed combat. When the fighting stopped the winners drew up lists of people who could be legally killed by any other citizen, who was then rewarded with a share of the victim's estate. It was because Octavian didn't veto Antony's decision to put Cicero on his list of people who could be killed that Rome's greatest lawyer lost his head.

The first rule of Roman politics throughout its history was that whoever could claim the allegiance of the most powerful legions (by grants of land and buckets of cash) would exercise supreme power, both at home and overseas. During the second and first centuries BCE, Rome went on the march and brought most of Italy, North Africa, Spain, and the Balkans to heel. By the end of the first century, its borders stretched from Britain and Gaul (modern France) in the northwest to Palestine and Persia in the southeast. The strength of its military force allowed the Romans to encircle the Mediterranean, which they referred to as "our sea."

By the time Rome had given up on the Republic and had begun on the second, imperial half of its history, it was a large and powerful military state. At its height it is estimated that it ruled over the lives of fifty million people. It could afford a paid professional army of between three and five hundred thousand soldiers. Its conquests produced huge riches (mostly for the elites) in the form of slaves, taxes, and grain. Defeated nations supplied the food and revenue that fed and paid for the troops as well as the slaves on which the economy was based. Rome was a highly militarized society that depended on armed aggression to sustain its existence and guarantee "la dolce vita."

Not surprisingly, in a city where the army ultimately called the shots, violence was a prominent (some might say preeminent) feature of Roman culture. Millions were slaughtered and enslaved in wars of naked aggression. Polybius, the Greek historian who lived as a hostage in Rome in the second century BCE, was generally an admirer of the Republic, but he had no illusions about the savagery of its ways. He was exaggerating only slightly when he described "the Roman custom" as "exterminating every form of … life they encountered … so when cities are taken by the Romans you may often see not only the corpses of human beings but also dogs cut in half and dismembered limbs of other animals."[7] "They made a desert and called it peace," was how another historian, Tacitus, described the brutality with which the Romans put down the revolts of the Jews, in which it is estimated that more than half a million people were killed.[8]

When it suited the Romans' interests, prisoners might be allowed to live, but only as slaves. More Jews were enslaved than slaughtered over the course of their rebellions against what they perceived to be the intolerance and excesses of Roman rule. At the conclusion of the Punic Wars, before Carthage was burned to the ground, fifty thousand of the city's inhabitants (including women and children) were selected to live out the rest of their lives under the rule of Roman masters. At the height of its powers, the Empire was home to more than five million people who were legally owned by and bound to do the bidding (including providing sexual favors) of their superiors. On conservative estimates, at least a quarter of the population was enslaved.

Even inside the city walls, violence was always just around the corner. Political assassinations, spectacular punishments, and blood sports were the order of the day. At their worst, the Romans fed Christians to the lions for entertainment; watched hundreds of gladiators engage in mortal combat for months at a time; crucified by the thousands slaves who dared challenge their rule; and murdered each other at such a rate that of the twenty six emperors who ruled between 235 and 285 CE, only one died naturally in office. The low point of Roman politics was unquestionably 69 CE, when two emperors were murdered and one committed suicide before a man named Vespasian claimed the throne and ruled for the next decade.

The foundation on which everything in Rome was built was the army. Its support was essential for anyone who aspired to a position of authority. When Rome was still a republic, the most important assembly of citizens (the Comitia Centuriata) that elected the chief magistrates (consul, praetor, aedile, quaestor) was drawn from the ranks of the soldiers. At the height of its powers, the Praetorian Guard had the final say on who would become the emperor and how long he would rule.[9] By the end of the Empire, almost all the emperors were military men whose roots were from outside Rome and frequently of plebian stock. At its demise, military commanders had replaced Rome's patricians as the ruling class.

As you would expect, the system of government the Romans put in place to sustain their war machine was lean and autocratic.[10] It started as a small cabal of plutocrats that morphed into one man rule. Even during the Republic, the most important institutions of government – the magistrates, the Senate, the courts, and assemblies – were controlled by the elites. Membership in the Senate was only open to those who had the proper pedigree or enough money, and voting in the assemblies was weighted heavily in favor of the landed aristocracy and the wealthiest of the business (equestrian) class. Moreover, the popular assemblies had no power to propose new laws, and even when considering whether to give their consent to laws proposed by the magistrates, they were not allowed to engage in a public debate. They could only vote yes or no.

For most of the time that it operated as a republic, Roman government had two distinguishing features. First, its structure was emphatically top down. At its core, there was a powerful executive branch whose senior officials (two consuls) had almost unlimited legal and military authority (imperium) to take whatever action they deemed to be in the city's best interests. Second, and to guard against magistrates abusing their powers (potestas), Rome's constitutional order was organized around a principle of checks and balances. Each magistrate was given the power to veto the decisions of his colleagues who were at the same or a lower rank. A decision of one consul could be vetoed by the other (or by one of the tribunes who represented the common people) and legislative proposals required the approval of the popular assembly before they became law. As well, the consuls' power to inflict corporal punishment, including the death penalty, could be appealed to the Comitia Centuriata. As a final check, once their term (which was limited to one year) was over, magistrates could be prosecuted for any offenses they may have committed while in office. Indeed, this is what happened to Cicero when he was exiled for a year and a half for having condemned some of his political opponents to death without allowing them to plead their case to the Comitia Centuriata.

After Rome switched to an imperial model of government, this system of checks and balances went out the window. As soon as Octavian accepted the title of Augustus, Rome quickly slid into a new reality of one-man rule. At first, the transformation was subtle and discreet. Augustus insisted he was subject to the laws like everyone else and all of the republican institutions and offices were preserved. Over time, however, the magistrates became the emperor's men and the Senate and assemblies did what they were told.

After Augustus died, a law was passed that bestowed all his powers on his successor (and adopted son) Tiberius and exempted him from the constraints of all existing laws. Fifty years later, the Emperor Vespasian had legislation passed that essentially gave him the right to do whatever he pleased. He could issue decrees or have a law passed on any subject, and he could intervene in any lawsuit or criminal proceeding and instruct the court how it should decide the case. From the time of Diocletian (284 CE), the emperor was regarded as ruler of the world with unlimited powers. Eventually, emperors became so intoxicated with their authority they claimed to be descended from the Gods.

At the height of his power, the legal authority of the emperor was absolute and his sovereignty knew no limits. *Princeps legibus solutus* was the phrase they used: the prince is not bound by the laws. When the Emperor Justinian carried out his great codification of Roman law, it was enshrined front and center, along with another: *Quod principi placuit legis habet vigorem* (What pleases the prince has the force of law). Whatever the words, the meaning was clear. The emperor controlled the law, not the other way around. His will, not reason, was supreme. Although it made extensive use of the law, the Roman Empire never recognized it the way the Athenians did, as their king.

Roman Law

Some might find it surprising that a big, aggressive military complex led by warlords and generals had any use for the law. But the fact is, it did. As a practical matter, law was the glue that held the whole enterprise together. It was the great stabilizer providing a measure of peace and harmony to the ordinary people of Rome in their daily lives so that war could be waged abroad. Writing when Augustus was manipulating the Republic's political institutions to suit his imperial ambitions, Livy praised Rome as a city in which men's impulsive and irrational ambitions were subject to the overriding authority of the law. For Cicero, the *ius civile* – the law that governed relations between ordinary citizens – was what ensured the legitimacy and longevity of the Roman state.

The traditional account of the beginnings of Roman law start in the early years of the Republic.[11] After putting an end to the monarchy and one-man rule in 510–509 BCE, the city's patrician class took over the reigns of power, including control of the religious and customary law that organized life in the city. Aristocratic priests (pontiffs) resolved disputes that were submitted to them on the basis of rules and traditions that were not written down and that were known only to them. Moreover, they did not have to back up their decisions with reasons. Rather than explaining and justifying their rulings to the people, their authority included the right to pontificate.

Such an arrangement worked to the obvious disadvantage of the plebians, who eventually demanded change. By 450 BCE, roughly two generations after the Republic's founding, Rome's first written legal code, the Twelve Tables, was on the books. In terms of both its substance and its place in Rome's constitutional order, it was similar to the laws Solon had established in Athens a century and a half years earlier. Legend has it that prior to adopting the Twelve Tables, Rome sent a delegation to Athens to find out how their system worked. Like Solon's laws, the Twelve Tables laid down the basic rules that organized the affairs of a primitive, agricultural community.

The laws dealt with the relationships and things that mattered most in the day-to-day ebb and flow of ordinary life in early Rome. Family laws recognizing the legal authority of a father over his wife and children were front and center. Two tables were devoted to the rights and responsibilities that came with owning, possessing, and/or inheriting property, and another regulated relations between debtors and creditors. There were also sumptuary laws outlawing excessive displays of luxury at funerals, as well as laws assigning responsibility in the case of flooding and the repair of roads.

Like the other codes we've looked at so far, the Twelve Tables put a premium on obedience to the law and treated violent, antisocial behavior, like assault, theft, and arson, very harshly. Like Hammurabi's Code, coercion was the dominant feature of Roman law, retaliation its guiding principle. Arsonists were burned alive and thieves who practiced their trade at night could be legally killed by their victims. In fact, capital punishment awaited a long list of wrongdoers, including people convicted of defaming or falsely accusing another person. Debtors might be executed or, if they were lucky, exiled or enslaved. Even judges who were caught taking a bribe faced public execution.

Like Solon's laws, there seemed to be something in the Twelve Tables for everybody. Debtors were given relief from the worst excesses of their creditors and the patricians were protected by laws that prohibited inter-marriage between plebians and themselves. Women were under the guardianship of their husbands (and before marriage, their fathers) and had no right of divorce, but they could own their own property and were entitled to a husband's support if he terminated the marriage.

One of the most distinctive features of early Roman law was the tre-mendous power it recognized in the senior male of each family. Law was even more patriarchal in Rome than in Athens. The "paterfamilias" was king of his castle, however modest that castle might be. Women were treated as daughters by their husbands, who also had the power of life and death over their children. As in Sparta, a father's *patria potestas* gave him the authority to abandon children who were "deformed" at birth and leave them outside to die.

In its style, the Twelve Tables looked more like Hammurabi's Code than the Ten Commandments or the general, universalizing principles of the Greeks. They made use of the same case-based approach of posing a set of circumstances and events and then describing the consequences that followed. If a tree fell on a neighbor's property, then the owner was obliged to have it removed, but if fruit from his tree fell into someone else's yard, he was entitled to take it back.

The role the Twelve Tables played in Rome's legal regime was similar to the place of Solon's reforms in Athenian law: they were at the center of the city's legal universe and the foundation on which everything else was built. They were designed to put an end to the practice of people relying on self-help and taking the law into their own hands. The first two tables were all about legal process. The very first law gave plaintiffs the authority to haul defendants into court if they refused to appear. Another stipulated that no one could be sentenced to death without a trial. To attract litigants to the courts, judges were bound to render their decisions before sunset on the day they heard the case. As noted above, judges who accepted bribes might be executed.

Like Hammurabi and the Greeks, the Romans thought of their basic law as something that was constant and enduring and not subject to change. They believed it would last forever. They were smart enough to know that the laws that were required to organize an empire were very different from the rules that were appropriate for a modest agricultural settlement, but they liked the illusion of continuity and stability in their legal order.

Until emperors took control of the legal system, legislation ("leges") introducing wholesale changes to the law was relatively rare. Instead, change was brought about in the ordinary course of private litigation. In the later years of the Empire (known as the Dominate), emperors exercised their legislative powers more frequently, but until then adjudication, not legislation, was the primary method of adjusting and keeping law up to date.

To effect the alterations that were necessary to ensure the law remained relevant, and to do it in a way that didn't undermine its foundations, the Romans devised a sophisticated method of law enforcement that allowed for incremental change and relied on a small professional class of jurists and advocates to make it work. The system, known as the "formulary procedure," was adopted in the second half of the second century BCE and lasted until the middle of the third century CE. Essentially, it gave citizens the opportunity to ask the state for permission to redress wrongs that they perceived had been done to them.

At the center of the procedure was the praetor, the second-highest level of magistrate, whose post was created in 367 BCE to take over the administration of justice from the consuls. Initially there was only one, but eventually there were eight who had the power to issue edicts, backed by the force of physical (including capital) punishment, and who acted as gatekeepers to the courts. At the beginning of their terms, praetors would publish an edict outlining what types of cases they would accept as appropriate for a hearing in the courts. (This is another of the seminal events depicted at the entrance of the US Supreme Court.)

The way the process worked was if someone had a complaint against another person, he would approach one of the praetors and lay out the substance of his claim. It could be about almost anything that was part of normal life in the city. He might petition for relief from harassment by creditors, or seek compensation for having been libeled or assaulted by rivals or defrauded in a commercial deal. If the praetor determined there was a law that covered the case, he would refer the matter to a judge who would decide whether, on the facts, the complainant had made out his case. In effect, the praetor determined whether there was an interest that was protected by law and therefore warranted a trial.

If the case was successful, the plaintiff was entitled to use force if the defendant resisted the court's judgment – indeed, he had to if he wanted to remedy the wrong that had been done to him. There were no public prosecutors or police in Rome, so litigants who prevailed in the courts were authorized to secure justice on their own. In effect, the system allowed people who had proven the merits of their claim to exercise a right of self-help.

The formulary procedure was a Roman original; nothing like it had been tried in any of the city states of Mesopotamia or ancient Greece. It was in effect two procedures in one. As just described, it was first and foremost a process for settling private disputes peacefully. It was Rome's updated version of the scene Homer depicted on Achilles's shield.

But it also served a larger, public purpose. In the course of specifying the cases in which a person could expect to find relief in the courts, the procedure became the primary method by which the Romans reconciled the illusion of the immutability of their ancient laws with the need to adapt it to the new world in which they lived. It became the way the Romans practiced constitutional law.

Although radically different, in both substance and style, from the *graphe paranomon* of the Greeks, it served the same purpose. Where the Greeks considered proposals to reform their basic laws during the course of the legislative process, the Romans integrated the new with the old in the course of adjudicating disputes within families and between neighbors. Instead of a general review of whole pieces of proposed legislation – the Greeks' favored approach – the Romans telescoped questions about the scope and legitimacy of their law into the particulars of specific cases. Rather than openly debating whether new laws were compatible with a city's foundational laws, as they did in Athens, in Rome ancient laws like the Twelve Tables were stretched to cover novel sorts of cases without an express acknowledgment of any change taking place.

The formulary procedure was unlike anything in the Greek legal system in one other important respect: it was not nearly as people-friendly. Whereas the jury courts in Athens were popular assemblies controlled by the people, the formulary procedure was a legal proceeding dominated by professionals. Ordinary Romans had little say about changes to the basic laws and typically did not argue their own cases in court. Instead, trained jurists determined the extent to which Rome's foundational laws could be modified to deal with new cases, and people hired advocates like Cicero to represent them in court.

The Jurists

The way in which the law was taken over by a few rich and powerful Romans appears to have been mostly innocent and benign. At least from what they wrote, their motivation seems to have been equal parts altruism and ambition. The idea behind writing their law down in a legal code was that it would make it more accessible to the ordinary people whose lives were most affected by it. It would tell them what their rights were if someone wronged them in some way. The expectation was that making the law public and more transparent would enhance its objectivity and impartiality. It would bring an end to the monopoly the College of Pontiffs had over the development and dissemination of the law.

As history would have it, the best-laid plans don't always happen, and they didn't on this occasion. It didn't take the Romans long to figure out that just writing the law down doesn't achieve the objective if you do it in such a way that people can't agree on what it says. Telling fathers they could leave a newborn child outside to die if it were "deformed" didn't answer the question of whether that included a baby with Down syndrome or a newborn with a broken foot or crooked nose. More often than not, words by themselves weren't enough.

The uncertainty in the meaning of the rules that were written down was compounded by the style in which the Twelve Tables was expressed, which was notoriously enigmatic. To know exactly what their rights were, potential litigants needed help. First they sought the advice of the pontiffs who were most familiar with the law and what it meant. In time, others who were not part of the College of Pontiffs also took up the study of law and began to offer their opinions on what it said.

Initially, these jurists were drawn from the patrician class, and they offered their advice as a public service free of charge. They were apparently much admired for their community spirit. They were knowledgeable in all aspects of the law: statutes, judicial rulings, magisterial edicts, customary rules, and the opinions of their fellow jurists. By the third century BCE, a professional elite had begun to emerge whose business was to advise litigants and judges and even the praetors on the subtleties and obscurities of the law.

In time, students, including Cicero, gathered in the courtyards of the most distinguished and knowledgeable of these jurisconsults to learn their trade. Law teaching, it turns out, began as home schooling (and is yet another of the scenes from law's journey that is commemorated on the front door of the U.S. Supreme Court). The legal education that was imparted in the villas of these legal luminaries was like an apprenticeship in which law was learned by observing and imitating rather than listening to lectures and studying texts. Unlike the formation of Plato's guardians, however, women were not welcome in Rome's first law schools.

The golden era of the jurists coincided with the decline of the Republic and the birth of the Empire and lasted about three hundred years.[12] During this time, legal scholars established schools and wrote hundreds of books, and the opinions of the best of them came to be recognized as having the force of law. Many became praetors and went on to have distinguished public careers. Some, including Q. Mucius Scaevola (who died in 82 BCE), Papinian (142–212 CE), and Ulpian (170–228 CE), gave their lives defending the independence and integrity of the law. Along with Socrates and Cicero, they were among law's earliest martyrs.

If there were a hall of fame for law's greatest advocates, all three would make it in on the first ballot. Scaevola is credited with compiling the first comprehensive treatise on the Twelve Tables and the *lex civile* and was one of the first jurists to open his home to students. Ulpian's brilliant career as a teacher, writer, and adviser to emperors earned him the title of the world's first human rights lawyer from one of Roman law's most distinguished scholars.[13]

Papinian's story is especially compelling. His career as a jurist was brilliant. Toward the end of the Empire, a law was passed that provided that, where his opinion and that of another jurist were in conflict, Papinian's was to prevail. Many scholars regard him as the greatest jurist of all time, and unlike Cicero, his integrity never wavered. Papinian lost his life because he refused to provide the Emperor Caracalla with a legal opinion that would have justified his murdering his brother.

To determine what the law was in any case, jurists were free to form their own opinions. The "pluralist" character of the legal analysis that was practiced in Rome became one of its defining features. It was up to each jurist to decide which approach worked best for him. Jurists were known for their particular style of reasoning. Proculus, it was said, used to highlight the facts of a case. Ulpian was famous for taking a balanced, pragmatic approach that gave equal weight to the interests of each party and looked for support in prior cases and previous authorities. Pomponius typically favored more open-ended arguments based on fairness and good faith. Papinian emphasized considerations of utility.

In the first and second centuries CE, some of these differences were institutionalized and rival schools were established that taught different approaches to the law. The Proculians, it was said, emphasized the certainty and rationality of the law. They were strict constructionists when it came to written texts and looked for unifying principles when applying customary and unwritten law. The Sabinians, by contrast, thought it was important to give effect to the underlying purpose of a statute, and so they were inclined to approach law more flexibly and with the aim of promoting the well-being of the city.

The fact that each jurist was free to develop his own approach to the law enhanced its flexibility and creativity but it did nothing for the efficacy of the system as a whole. Jurists frequently disagreed with one another on basic points of law, and the judges could pick and choose among the available opinions as they pleased. The multiplicity of views that could invariably be found on any question gradually undermined law's coherence and objectivity.

The Romans were alert to the weaknesses of their legal system and they tried to do something about it. For one thing, the system of private legal education was taken over by the state.[14] Teachers were hired and students were required to complete a four- and eventually five-year curriculum and then pass a comprehensive examination. Students were expected to devote themselves full-time to their studies and were exempted from all public duties until age twenty-five, when they were expected to graduate. In the sixth century, the Emperor Justinian designated Beirut, Rome, and Constantinople as the seats of the Empire's official law schools.

In addition, late in the life of the Empire, a law was passed that restricted the number of jurists whose opinions could be cited as authoritative to five and set out rules that judges were to follow when they disagreed. Eventually, Justinian ordered Tribonium, one of the leading jurists of his day, to oversee a commission to sort through all the conflicting opinions and rulings and statutes that had accumulated over hundreds of years and produce a more coherent and manageable compilation.

The result was the Corpus Juris Civilis, regarded by many as Rome's crowning achievement.[15] F.W. Maitland, the British legal historian, called it the best of Roman law. One part of the codification, known as the Digest, was a synthesis of all the jurisprudence that had been written by the jurists over half a millennium. Another, referred to as the Institutes, was a trimmed-down version that served as a student text. Both were proclaimed by Justinian in Constantinople in 533 CE.

Although lots of inconsistencies and ambiguities still remained, Justinian's Code organized, summarized, and analyzed a massive body of overlapping and often conflicting statutes, edicts, plebiscites, rescripts, and legal opinions into a manageable compendium. Incredibly, it synthesized over 3 million lines of legal text into 150,000. To prevent a recurrence of confusion and contradiction in the law, Justinian outlawed all judicial interpretation of the code. Any ambiguity or inconsistency that remained, he said, would be repaired by him. The compilation was so sensible that fifteen hundred years later it still provides the foundation for the legal systems of all the countries of continental Europe, as well as of the Roman Catholic Church.

Of all their accomplishments, the Corpus Juris Civilis was undoubtedly the jurists' crowning achievement (and so, not surprisingly, was also awarded a panel on the doors into the US Supreme Court). It would be another five hundred years before someone (it turned out to be a medieval Catholic jurist named Gratian, whom we'll meet in chapter 5) would try anything as ambitious. But as huge as it was, it wasn't the whole of the jurists' legacy. Almost, if not equally, significant was their discovery of ways to soften and temper the rough edges of the law and their formulation of rules to cover disputes that might arise with foreigners. In the former are the roots of the principles of fairness and equity that permeate all modern legal systems, and in the latter one finds the seeds of international law.

Much of the law that governed relations between individuals in their families and private lives was the work of the jurists acting independently of, but in cooperation with, public officials, including the praetors and judges. From the beginning they demonstrated an interest in the spirit and not just the letter of the law. They favored giving effect to the obvious intent of a contract or a will even if it seemed to conflict with the literal words of the text. Agreements might be enforced even when all the formalities weren't respected. At the margin, they were for substance over form. Ulpian spoke for his fellow jurists when he famously observed that to be learned in the law is to know what is just and that justice is a constant, unfailing disposition to give everyone his due.

With the guidance of the jurists, praetors were able to integrate an inventory of equitable principles in their edicts to ensure justice could be done in each case. These principles formed part of what the Romans came to call the *ius honorarium* and they ensured Roman law had a measure of fairness and reasonableness to it. There were doctrines protecting people against unconscionable bargains and being forced into signing agreements under duress. There was a rule against unjust enrichment and others that punished dishonesty and required litigants to come to court with "clean hands."

In substantive terms, the jurists developed remedies to protect the interests of the most vulnerable members of society, including women, children, the mentally disabled, and even slaves. They thought of themselves as high priests cultivating the virtue of justice, discriminating between equity and iniquity and demonstrating to the ordinary person how to be a good Roman citizen. Over time they modified the power a husband could exert over his wife and children and they put strong limitations on a father's right to sell any of his offspring into slavery or to leave "deformed" infants out to die. They also put a stop to the practice of masters serving up disfavored slaves to wild beasts in the amphitheater, unless they secured the permission of a judge. Although they were not the first to propose a set of principles to ensure legal outcomes were basically reasonable and fair, they were the first to do something about it and to make it actually happen. And, like the Corpus Juris Civilis, echoes of the moral force of their "equitable" analysis are still heard today.

Most of the jurists' attention was focused on relations among their fellow Romans, but they also thought about their dealings and disagreements with strangers and people from the remote corners of the Empire and beyond. As the Empire expanded, Romans interacted with more and more foreigners, and they were forced to think about how to structure legal relations with these people because, at the time, legal systems only applied to those over whom a lawgiver was sovereign. Law, in other words, was ethnocratic; it attached to people rather than geographic territories. In the same way the *ius Torah* only spoke to Jews, only citizens of Rome were governed by Roman law. When in Rome, aliens could not always do as the Romans did because they were not protected by and could not claim the benefit of Roman law.

Although all of the ancient laws we have encountered so far faced the constraint of being attached to people rather than to defined territories, the Romans, being the practical people they were, were the first to do something about it. By the second century BCE, the jurists were adapting local rules to the new circumstances created by their conquests and colonizing habits. Over time they crafted a whole new body of law known as the *ius gentium*, which dealt with marriages and rights of inheritance between Romans and foreigners and included the bare bones of an international commercial code. Although all of its provisions were made in Rome, the jurists advertised it as a universal law of nations. Gaius, who was one of the big names writing in the second century CE, distinguished between the *ius civile*, which he described as the particular law that a people establishes for itself, and the *ius gentium*, which is "the law that natural reason establishes among all mankind, is followed by all peoples alike, and is ... observed by all mankind."[16]

In addition to thinking about rules that would organize peaceful relations with their neighbors, the Romans also recognized the existence of a body of law that governed hostilities and the conduct of war with their enemies. Although not a primary concern of the jurists, there was a *ius fetiale*, which was administered by a special priesthood and governed the declaration of hostilities and the duties to which peace treaties gave rise. Cicero thought the laws of war only permitted armed force to be used to right a wrong, such as rescuing hostages or recovering property, and included basic rules of fair play like keeping promises that were made to an enemy, respecting the inviolability of ambassadors, and refraining from destroying religious temples. However, drawing a distinction that is still recognized today, Cicero did not believe these laws protected pirates or bandits, whom he considered (similar to how we think of modern terrorists) common enemies of the world.

Justice Betrayed

If the Corpus Juris Civilis, *ius honorarium*, *ius gentium*, and *ius fetiale* were the whole story of Roman law, it would be iconic. To have constructed such a sweeping and sophisticated legal system to hold such a huge multiethnic empire together for such a long period of time constitutes one of law's great achievements. The work of the jurists has been heralded as the "flower of Roman civilization." Three of the most celebrated, Gaius, Papinian, and Tribonian, along with Emperor Justinian, have been recognized by the US House of Representatives as among the greatest lawgivers of all time.

At its peak, Roman law provided a stable set of rules, infused with ideas of justice and fairness, to resolve the conflicts and everyday disputes of more than fifty million people. For most of those living within the Empire's borders, law was the preferred method of dispute resolution. For them, solving problems with violence and physical force were relics of a more brutish and distant past.

Unfortunately, there is more to the story of Roman law, and not much of it reflects very well on the jurists. Just as in Babylon and Athens, the legal system they constructed turned out not to be all and only about justice and doing the right thing. The truth is, grotesque injustices and widespread corruption were also part of the system, and the jurists were not perfect people. What they wrote about the law and the way they wrote it favored their own and the emperors' interests. They did, for example, relatively little for those who fell on the wrong side of the law or who were accused of being an enemy of the state. To compound their malpractice, the jurists cast law's legacy in a way that undermined both its supremacy and its accessibility. Critics, like Cicero, thought they had sold out and cashed in.[17]

It should not be surprising that the jurists, as members of the ruling class, focused their attention on the law that governed relations between ordinary people in their families and private lives and had less to say about how citizens interacted with the their governments and public officials. Indeed, as the emperor's authority grew in strength, many jurists gave up their independence and became part of the imperial bureaucracy. They joined the ranks of the judiciary and their opinions were given the force of law. From that point on, law lost its independence. Law was what whatever the emperor willed it to be, and Cicero's idea of law as an expression of natural reason was no more.

By concentrating their attention on private law, the jurists ensured that the emperor essentially had free reign when it came to questions of public law. He could do whatever he wanted. Disfavored groups, like the Jews, could be confined to ghettos and told what occupations they could take up and whom they could marry. Those who were caught up in the criminal justice system received a bare minimum of due process and, if convicted, the most cruel and barbaric punishments imaginable. Witnesses were routinely tortured when they gave evidence, and those (like

Christians) who were found guilty of violating the law could, depending on the severity of their crimes, be crucified, burned, or fed to wild animals.

Not only did the jurists concede the domain of public law to the emperor, they actively participated in the writing of a story about the legal foundation of his powers (*lex regia*) that justified the absolute and unfettered authority of his rule. Even Ulpian, the pioneer of human rights, was a major contributor/conspirator. Collectively, the jurists created a myth about a moment when the Roman people, exhausted by years of fighting and civil war, irrevocably transferred the whole of their lawmaking powers to the emperor. It was pure fiction of course, but it gave credence and popular legitimacy to the idea that the emperor was above the law. *Princeps legibus solutus* was how the jurists defined the rule of law. He had the authority to abrogate his own and his predecessors' laws.

The way the jurists explained the relationship between law and the emperor was a cunning perversion of the Greek idea that the people were the ultimate source of the law. Claiming that the people granted the emperor the power to do whatever he wanted was profoundly undemocratic. And as a result of the jurists' storytelling, the Roman people lost the right to hold their rulers accountable that had been the birthright of their Athenian neighbors. On their interpretation of Rome's constitutional structure, the most powerful person, the first citizen of the city, was sovereign and beyond the reach of the law. By the time of the Empire's collapse, law had come full circle. In the beginning and at the end, the rule of law was just another way rulers could enforce their will. As with Hammurabi, it was rule by, not of, the law.

Writing a false narrative to justify the absolute powers of the emperor was one way the jurists cut the connection between the law and ordinary citizens. Another was by writing about the law in a manner that only the jurists could understand. At the same time they legalized the absolute sovereignty of the emperor, they adopted a method of reasoning that allowed them to maximize their control over the vast expanse of rules and rescripts of private law. They developed a way of analyzing problems that was unlike anything that the Greeks had imagined.

The jurists had no time for the deductive and inductive methods of Plato and Aristotle. They avoided sweeping principles of justice like Aristotle's proportionate and arithmetic equality. They saw no merit in Cicero's model of law as an orderly science of clear-cut doctrines and rules. Instead, they began with practical realities like possession (of property) or harm (to a person) or consent (to a contract) and then fleshed out their meanings by listing cases illustrating what they meant.[18]

For example, to convey the kinds of harms for which one could be held accountable, the jurists compiled lists of cases of negligent behavior whose outcomes turned on their facts. A farmer was liable for the damage caused by a fire he started, in order to burn the stubble in his field, if he did it on a windy day but not if the weather had been calm. A javelin thrower was accountable for injuries caused if the weapon was thrown in an inappropriate place. A mule driver was responsible for damage caused by an animal under his control if he lacked the experience to handle it.

The method of reasoning was austere and opaque. Like Hammurabi's Code, cases were described and conclusions presented with little or no explanation for why the law led to liability in one case but not another. Although the jurists drew distinctions between laws that affected people and those that affected things, and between obligations that were consensual and those that were prescribed, no attempt was made to provide an overarching structure, or a set of first principles governing when, for example, a person would be held responsible for the harm he or she caused. No definitions of negligence or fault were offered to explain the cases.

Nor were reasons provided that explained when considerations of equity and fairness might trump the clear language of an edict or statute and when they wouldn't. There was no discussion of what distinguished good analogies from bad. There was no attempt to deduce the result in a case from an analysis of the concept of negligent behavior, nor did they try to elaborate on the concept of negligence from the way cases were resolved. The cases were intended to speak for themselves. Collectively, they demonstrated what constituted negligent behavior and the limits of people's legal responsibility for their actions.

For most of his career, Cicero was critical of the way the jurists went about their work. He thought that rather than undertaking a serious philosophical inquiry into a concept like negligence, they spent too much time on trivial and inconsequential details, like what to do about rainwater that leaks from the eaves of a neighbor's house. Worse, he accused them of making work for themselves by inventing all kinds of obscure formulations and legal fictions to justify their opinions. He described their representations of the law as "cluttered with complication." In both method and style, this was not a concept of law that could easily be learned as part of a general education.

Whatever can be said about the substance of what they wrote, the way the jurists presented the law unquestionably put it beyond the reach of ordinary citizens. They developed a special vocabulary and method of analysis that only they could fully understand. Without years of study, there was no hope of comprehending how it worked. In Cicero's mind, the jurists had made the law so mysterious and inaccessible that ordinary people were discouraged from trying to learn it.

The result was that in Rome, unlike in Athens, the natural reason of the common man was not good enough. Only those with a comprehensive knowledge of the cases and the other instruments of law (statutes, decrees, edicts, rescripts, responses, opinions) understood how to do legal analysis. Law became a method of settling conflicts that was controlled by a professional elite. Cicero's idea that law was a matter of natural reason that every human can understand was replaced by a special knowledge and a way of thinking that took years of schooling and experience to master.

When the whole body of the jurists' work is examined in its entirety, it is decidedly a mixed bag. It includes the very good and the very bad. If you were asked to make a judgment on their overall contribution to the evolution and development of the rule of law, it would be fair to say that they did as much harm as good. Two steps forward, two steps back.

On the plus side are the first, embryonic structures of private (civil) law, equity, and international law. The way the jurists wrote about private law and equity still shapes how lawyers think about these concepts today. By any measure the magnitude of this accomplishment is huge. On an individual, case-by-case basis, the Roman jurists created a system of dispute resolution for the common people that on most days and in the main was rational, reasonable, and fair. Its achievement is so substantial it is still studied in law schools all over Europe and the core of its structure is still with us today. Better than the laws of Hammurabi, Lycurgus, or Solon, Justinian's Code has stood the test of time. Fifteen hundred years on, it still provides the foundation and basic categories (property, contract, tort, and unjust enrichment) for all the civil law countries of Europe.

On the downside, however, the jurists' legacy is scarred by two regrettable acts of high treason. First, they sacrificed the supremacy of law by saying the absolute authority of the emperor was based on a solid legal foundation. On their account, the emperor, not the law, had the final say. And this is another part of their story that stuck. In fact it ruled, more or less successfully, for the next fifteen hundred years, until a small group of (mostly) English colonists on the eastern coast of North America championed the supremacy of law and raised its flag once again. (The tale of how the Americans restored the sovereignty of law is told in chapter 7.)

The second dimension of the jurists' betrayal – putting an end to the Greek idea that law was for and by the common people – is equally disturbing, and it is still being felt around the world to this day. The jurists demonstrated how a takeover of the law could be effected by a relatively small class of people, and law has been dominated by professional elites ever since. After the Romans, law has never been written in a style that can be easily mastered by the ordinary man or woman on the street. Cicero's ambition, to make law a part of the education of a well-read person, died with him.

After the collapse of the Roman Empire, there was a period, in the West, when law and the legal profession went into a steep decline. As western Europe fell to the invasions of German and Nordic hordes, law lost much of its force and lawyers as a group became extinct. But the flame of justice was never extinguished and eventually (as recounted in chapters 5 and 6), the legal profession reinvented itself and took charge once again.

In the eastern half of the Empire the professionals never lost control. Roman law carried on under the care and custody of the emperor's jurists, but the big news was the proclamation of a new code of religious law in the deserts of Syria, Saudi Arabia, and the Sahara. Although this law, which was told to the Prophet Muhammad by the Archangel Gabriel, did not cast lawyers in major roles, it was monopolized by a group of religious scholars who specialized in the law. The story of the *faqih* (or *fuqaha*, in its plural form) and the development of Islamic (sharia) law is the next big event in the history of law, and is the subject of the chapter that follows.

PART 2

Medieval History: Jurists and Lawyers

Chapter Four

Damascus and Baghdad

Divine Law

In the seventh century, a little more than a hundred years after the collapse of Rome, the rule of law experienced a sudden and spectacular
revival in the Arabian Desert. It was divinely inspired. For twenty years,
beginning around 610 CE, Allah laid down the law to the Prophet
Mohammad through the Archangel Gabriel. The result was the birth of
Islam and a code of laws known as sharia.

That law was born again as part of a religious revelation, and in this
part of the world, should not surprise us. As we read in chapter 1, divine
law was in the region's DNA. The Ten Commandments that God gave
Moses had been central to the life of the Jewish community for more
than two thousand years, and before that religious laws established the
basic rules of right and wrong in Mesopotamia and Egypt.

In Mesopotamia, codes like Hammurabi's were grounded in ideas of
justice that were thought to be a gift from the Gods. Shamash, God of the
Sun, was considered the most important. The idea seems to have been
that with the power of light he could discover the truth and ensure that
justice would always prevail. In Egypt, Ma'at, daughter of the sun god Re,
represented justice as a universal, harmonious order, based on truth and
balance, that acted as a guiding principle for pharaohs and their subjects
alike. In the iconic image of "the weighing of the heart" (on the front
cover of this book), Ma'at's feather of truth is put on the scales of justice
to measure the purity of the dead person's soul.

Initially, the law Mohammad revealed to the people of Mecca emphasized matters of religious practices and rituals like prayers, pilgrimages,
and fasting.[1] After he led his followers to Medina in 622 CE (known
as the migration [*hijra*], it is the year that marks the beginning of the
Islamic calendar), the law spoke more broadly about how to live a good

life and maintain a pious community. The law he reported claimed to be a comprehensive, universal guide to right living. It had a broadly reformist character. It changed the method of solving conflict from blood feuds between tribes to arbitration within the broader community of believers (*umma*). It was made up of both detailed, specific rules and general ethical principles: compassion for the weak; good faith and fair dealing in relations with others; and freedom from corruption and the arbitrary administration of justice.

In its overarching ambition, God's law demanded that Muslims follow a path of social justice. It wasn't good enough just to believe. A practicing Muslim was obliged to act on the law as well. In the Qur'an, God condemned a wide range of exploitive practices, including bribery, usury, and the hoarding of wealth. Divine law included a principle of taxation (*zakat*) that was intended to alleviate the hardships of the needy and the poor. In a world that was governed by and for men, Allah outlawed female infanticide and insisted women were more than just objects of sale. God's law said they had a right to inherit property from their fathers and husbands and to control the dowries they received when they got married. In addition, while the law allowed for the institution of slavery and imposed special taxes on people who belonged to other faiths, it also commanded Muslims to treat their slaves humanely and to respect the religious freedom of their Christian and Jewish neighbors.

A common theme running through the law was the elimination of the extremes and excesses of the traditional ways of tribal life and the establishment of a more even balance between rich and poor, men and women, adherents of different religious faiths, and even between those who broke the law and their victims. Like students of Aristotle and Buddha, Muslims were directed to take "the middle path." Instead of denouncing the established patterns of tribal relations, the law attempted to moderate and soften them. God's law still reflected the patriarchal, retributive character of Arab society, but after He revealed his law to the Prophet, men could no longer marry as many women as they desired. The limit was set at four, and even then stringent conditions of equal treatment made the possibility of polygyny more difficult to establish in practice. In the same spirit, the idea of collective punishment, which was the custom in the desert, was replaced by a strict interpretation of *lex talionis* and its more egalitarian equation of an eye for an eye. In the case of unintentional killing (manslaughter), the death penalty was replaced by the payment of compensation.

The connection between law and justice was part of Islam from the beginning. On this, Mohammad, Plato, and Aristotle (with whom the Arabs were familiar) were of one mind. And, like Roman law, Islamic law was more concerned with the private lives of ordinary people than with relations between rulers and their subjects. Almost all the commands in the sharia were personal and directed to the individual. Islamic law was about the believer's personal life and only derivatively about relations between the citizen and the state. Even murder was treated as a private matter rather than a part of public law. A killing was something to be settled by the families affected rather than by the ruler and the state.

While Mohammad was alive and the Muslim community was centered in Medina, both the declaration and administration of the law remained in his hands. Within his community of believers he controlled all three branches of government. He was both lawgiver and judge. After his death, that had to change. For one thing, no one could make a claim of divine authority for their right to rule. For another, the size of the polity grew exponentially.

Under Muhammad's successors, Islam went on the march and heralded its message. It carried out a series of lightening conquests and its law spread like wildfire all over the Middle East and North Africa, into central Asia as well as the southwestern corner of Europe. Within a hundred years, the character of his community underwent a radical change. In the span of just a couple of generations, Islam went from being the creed of a sleepy agricultural outpost on the western edge of the Arabian Desert to controlling all the lands across the top of Africa up into the southwestern corner of Europe in the west and over to Palestine, Syria, Iraq, and Iran in the east. One hundred years after the Prophet's death, Islam had pushed eastward across Afghanistan and most of the Punjab. To the west, Islam's jihadists crossed North Africa and fought their way to the center of modern France before being stopped in 732 CE by Charles Martel (grandfather of Charlemagne), just over two hundred kilometers from Paris.

In part because it got much bigger and culturally and racially more diverse, the *umma* became more prone to internal conflicts and infighting. Disputes arose and civil wars were fought over who should succeed Mohammad as its leader (caliph). By 661 CE, one of the leading clans in Mecca, the Umayyads, had demonstrated their military superiority, established their headquarters in Damascus, and declared a caliphate that was to last almost a century.

To govern the vast territory they had conquered required a much more sophisticated administrative structure than had been needed in the Prophet's time. From the middle of the seventh century until the middle of the eighth, the Umayyad caliphs gradually built up an infrastructure that could support their empire. They retained many of the institutions and traditions of the people they had conquered. Most importantly, they designated judges (*qadis*) as the primary means of solving conflicts and reconciling local traditions with Islamic law.

The job of the *qadi* was not an easy one, especially in the early years of the empire. Initially, he performed a variety of administrative duties, of which judging cases was only one. Moreover, when he was called on to settle disputes, he had little guidance on how the Qur'an should be interpreted or how its law should be integrated with the different local customs and traditions that governed life on the ground. In effect, the power of each *qadi* to decide a case was unrestricted.

Although the objectivity of the *qadis* has been questioned by some jurists (including Felix Frankfurter and Max Weber), there were lots of good things that could be said about the system of justice they supervised. Compared to what was on offer in Europe at the time, as a method of resolving conflict in the community, it was expeditious, inexpensive, and easy to access. Early on in the medieval era, it was arguably the most sophisticated legal system in the world.

Still, even at the time, there was a feeling that the process allowed too much variation in the law and that the caliphate had lost sight of Islam's central precepts and values. Enforcement of Islamic law was perceived to be haphazard and serendipitous. It depended too much on the whim and the wish of each judge. Critics also took the Umayyads to task for the extravagance and authoritarian nature of their rule.

In the latter years of the caliphate, respected and pious members of the community began to meet in informal groups to discuss how local practices could be brought more in line with the core principles of Islamic law. In time, these groups evolved into a large number of distinct schools of law. The Abbasids (descendants of the Prophet's paternal uncle, Abbas), who succeeded the Umayyads as caliphs in 750 CE, supported these schools (madrassas), and scholars began to work out the practical effects of Islamic law more systematically. They employed the rules of grammar, rhetoric, and logic developed by the Greeks to fill in gaps, resolve ambiguities, and settle contradictions in the Qur'an, and to impose a measure of discipline and order on the subjective, unstructured decision making of the *qadis*.

Like the jurists who rose to prominence in the Roman Empire, leading scholars of Islamic law, the *fuqaha*, were quite pluralistic in their outlook. Initially, relations between the different schools of law were hostile and often violent, but in time they became more tolerant of one another and accepted the idea that a variety of different approaches to revealing God's truth were possible. The prohibition against drinking wine, for example, could be read literally, or purposefully, or by reference to the practice of the first community in Medina, or by what the Prophet

Mohammad did or said. It was also widely accepted that the substance and scope of such commandments could be explored through reasoning by analogy. If wine was outlawed because of its intoxicating effects and its impairment of human reason, then other substances that produce similar chemical reactions might be proscribed as well. In some cases, words could be given an allegorical meaning.

Like the Roman jurists, over time the fuqaha ironed out their major differences and a consensus developed on a standard approach. The master architect of the legal taxonomy on which all jurists came to agree was Mohammed Ibn-Idris al-Shafi'i. In his book the *Risala,* written in Cairo in the middle of the ninth century, he argued for strict limits on the use of reason and analogies and for privileging how the Prophet Mohammed talked about and practiced God's law. The precedents set by the Prophet, his words and deeds (the Sunna), came to be understood as important a source of meaning as the text of the Qur'an itself. By the end of the tenth century, the jurists had gathered themselves into four dominant schools: the Maliki in North and West Africa; the Hanafi in central Asia and the Middle East; the Shafi'i on the coast of East Africa and Southeast Asia; and the Hanbali in the Arabian peninsula. In addition, the Shia, who believed that Mohammad's son-in-law, Ali, should have been his successor, organized their own school, the Ja'fari.

The classical structure of Islamic law was to endure in this form for almost a thousand years. A full-fledged court system with a separate judiciary, a coherent body of positive legal doctrine, a science of legal methodology and interpretation, and the establishment of autonomous schools of law were all in place. Guardianship of the law was under the firm control of independent scholars. *Qadis,* who solicited their opinions when they were uncertain of what rule to apply, and caliphs were both governed by what they said.

Although they depended on the political and financial support of the ruler, the jurists maintained an absolute monopoly over the exposition of the law. The one time a caliph (Al-Ma'mun, 786–833) tried to impose his interpretation by means of a grand inquisition (the Mihna) in the first half of the ninth century, senior jurists (including Ahmad Ibn Hanbali [780–855], after whom one of the four schools of Sunni law is named), resisted, and in the end they prevailed. At its best, Islamic law incorporated all three components of the Greek ideal. Rule by law, rulers bound to respect the law, and justice through law were all established principles of the empire over which the Abbasids ruled.

By the beginning of the eleventh century, Islamic law was living in the glow of its classical age and its future looked robust and bright. In the view of many, this was the most sophisticated legal system on earth.

In the event, however, law's good fortune was not destined to last. Like Roman law, the law of Islam was made to submit to the force of military rule, and thereafter went into a long period of decline. Indeed, it experienced a downward spiral from which it has never fully recovered.

The dominant fact of North African and Middle Eastern legal history is that for more than a thousand years the sovereignty of Islamic law has been held hostage by sultans and emirs and other tribal leaders. So comprehensive has law's subjugation been that, by the second half of the twentieth century, this part of the world had become home to some of the most brutal and abusive rulers in human history. Saddam Hussein, Muammar el-Qaddafi, Hasaf and his son Bashar al-Assad, Omar Al-Bashir, Ali Abdullah Saleh, Hosni Mubarak, and Zine El-Abidine Ben Ali are the legacy of a millennium of mismanagement and misrule.

For historians of North Africa and the Middle East, the complete collapse of the rule of law poses a simple but disturbing question: What went wrong?[2] How, in other words, did it happen that law went from being the dominant force in organizing Arab society to being the means by which strongmen and warlords enforced their rule. The answer, according to most accounts of Arab legal history, is that law was defeated on two fronts.[3] First, foreign powers made a frontal assault on the idea that rulers were subordinate to the law, and second, local jurists contributed to its demise by betraying it from within.

Sultans

The first and most important reason the rule of law lost its sovereignty over this part of the world was that it was simply overpowered, initially by hostile neighbors and then by strangers from farther away. Both were bent on ruling by force the lands Arabs called home.

Students of Arab history will tell you the dark forces of tyranny and oppression were relentless and unforgiving and came, until very recently, from outside. Long before the birth of Islam, armies from Mesopotamia, Persia, Greece, and Rome had the Arabs and their riches in their sights. Later, after the Muslims' own early conquests had spent their force, for a thousand years, from the middle of the tenth century until the middle of the twentieth, the Arab people were victims again and again of subjugation by foreign powers. Initially, these invaders sought control over the international trading routes that cut through the heart of the Arabian peninsula. Today, they demand the oil and gas that lies underground.

First it was the Persians (Buyids) in the middle of the tenth century, followed by the Turks (Seljuks) and then the Europeans (Christians) pursuing a religious jihad (crusade) at the end of the eleventh. The Mongols

captured Baghdad in the thirteenth century and then two more Turk-
ish military sultanates, the Mamluks and the Ottomans, took over. The
Mamluks were masters of Egypt and Syria from the middle of the thirteenth century until the beginning of the sixteenth, when another tribe
of Turks – the Ottomans – laid the foundations of an empire that was to
rule over the Arabs for four hundred years. Allied with the Germans, it
was swept away and replaced again by European powers (principally England and France but also Italy and Spain) at the end of the First World
War. Even when the Arabs gained their independence at the end of the
Second World War, the Europeans selected and/or propped up local
surrogates who could be counted on to protect their interests. In the
case of the Palestinians, Western powers continue to block the creation
of a sovereign state to this day.

The five-hundred-year period following the conquest of the Abbasid
Caliphate by the Persians (roughly 950–1450) is known as the Age of
Sultans. During the whole of this time, the Arab people lived more or
less under the tyranny of strangers whose way of doing business was completely alien to how the rule of law was conceived in Classical Greece.
These were military dynasties whose authority was absolute and applied
with gruesome force. The sultans had complete control of all three
branches of government and exercised their power through members
of their families and the local notables they enlisted in their cause.[4] In
practice, the caliph became a puppet of military strongmen. Judicial
appointments were "farmed" for a fee and/or passed on from father
to son. Selling judicial offices became standard practice. Judges were
expected to do the ruler's bidding to such an extant that pious jurists
often declined appointments when they were offered.

In addition to controlling the selection of judges to sharia courts,
early on rulers began setting up their own courts (*mazalim*) to deal with
complaints against their agents and officials. Over time, these tribunals evolved into an elaborate set of legal institutions with broad jurisdiction and, except for family relations and matters of ritual and faith,
supplanted sharia courts as the primary venue where differences were
settled. Important cases would be heard in the sultan's palace by senior
officials, if not by the sultan himself. As in Rome, law was used as a tool
of state power rather than as a check on its abuse.

For most of this time the sultans had their hands firmly on all the levers
of power. They created their own military class and they dominated the
jurists and religious scholars much more than medieval rulers in Europe
were able to control the church. Ibn Khaldun (1332–1406), the great
Arab historian and jurist, called his fellow scholars "urban weaklings"
who had lost all control of the government and who retained authority

over the religious law only because of its Arabic origins and the desire of the sultans "to make a show of reverence."

During the years of military sultanates and foreign occupation, there were voices calling out for a more rigorous enforcement of the law. Ibn Taymiyya (1263–1328, one of the jurists who never took a judicial appointment) was one of the most famous. In the fourteenth century, he chastised his fellow scholars for their corruption, impiety, and excessive concern for their own welfare. He maintained that rulers were bound to submit to the principles and commandments of sharia law. He famously issued a fatwa (legal ruling) against the Mongols because they insisted on governing according to the code of Genghis Khan rather than the commands of Allah. For the most part, however, Ibn Taymiyya was talking to himself and his fellow jurists, and in his day he had little impact on matters of statecraft and politics. Indeed, he was thrown in jail for his impertinence and the Mongol khans carried on as they pleased.

(Like many of those who played important roles in the history of Greek and Roman law, Ibn Taymiyya has arguably had more influence after his death than he did while he was alive. In the nineteenth century, his ideas resonated with the Wahhabis, a conservative Sunni sect, and the Saudis in the Arabian peninsula and provided the foundation for their legalization of a monarchy whose powers were absolute and comprehensive.)

Over the course of the four hundred years (1517–1919) that the Ottomans dominated the Arabs, the general health of the law was never robust; they were much more interested in waging war. Indeed, between 1450 and 1700, there was hardly a decade when the Ottomans weren't fighting somebody.

Machiavelli saw them as the ultimate absolute monarchs. He thought the sultan in Istanbul was more powerful than the king of France. At times, the jurists had a measure of independence and did control the substance of Islamic law, but by the end of the Ottomans' rule they couldn't even claim that. Over the years, the sultans tightened their grip and increasingly made use of their legislative powers to establish rules and regulations in the areas of commercial, criminal, and administrative law. The sultan's *mazalim* courts were integrated into the bureaucratic structures of his administration and given responsibility for the enforcement of his (*qanun*) laws.

At the same time that the "Sublime Porte" (as the imperial court in Istanbul came to be known) was extending its legislative powers over a wider range of social relations, it began to assert more authority over jurists and religious scholars as well. A hierarchy of positions within the ulema was established and the most important (including the chief mufti) were brought into the ruler's inner circle. Educational qualifications to become a *qadi* (judge) or *faqih* (legal scholar) or a mufti (jurist) were standardized and prestigious schools offering the requisite courses of study were endowed by the sultan.

In the nineteenth century, at the insistence of the Europeans, the Ottomans (and Egyptians) codified their laws and modernized their legal systems to bring them more in line with contemporary norms and modern business practices. A period of reform known as the Tanzimat resulted in the enactment of new criminal, civil, and commercial codes and a new system of secular courts. It also resulted in a further shrinkage in the authority and prestige of the jurists.[5]

Like the earliest Mesopotamian dynasties we encountered in chapter 1, the Ottoman regime ruled by law, but it had no intention of reviving the Greek model of a rule of law state. Law was used to enhance the prestige and power of the empire, not to curb or challenge the sultan's authority. The Ottomans drew a sharp line between the ruling class (*askeris*, ulema) and the people over whom they ruled (*reaya*), and when it suited them they had no inhibition about ignoring some of the most basic precepts of sharia law. They licensed brothels and bars, conscripted child soldiers from Christian communities and forced them to convert to Islam, and brutally put down any call within the Arab community for autonomy and self-rule.

The tyranny and despotism of the Ottomans was stronger at some times and in some places, but it was always there. Even at the end, the last sultan ruled with an iron fist. It was said of Abdul-Hamid II that he laid the foundations of his rule (1876–1909) on a system of espionage, censorship, and repression. George Antonius, a leading Arab nationalist of the day, described his reign as a state of "tyranny and corrupt abuse of power which has scarcely been surpassed in history."[6] Intellectuals, constitutionalists, and nationalists were persecuted, exiled, and/or executed. Even the group known as the Young Turks, who overthrew Abdul-Hamid in the name of constitutional reform, had no time for the niceties of due process and the rule of law when it came to Armenians and Arabs, who were accused of attempting to undermine their authority. The mass murder of more than a million Armenians and the public hangings of Arab leaders that took place in downtown Damascus and Beirut during the First World War are monuments of injustice that mark the tyranny and oppression of their rule.

After the defeat of the Ottomans in the First World War, the Europeans became masters of the region. Having sided with the Germans, the lands of the former Ottoman Empire, and in particular the Middle East and North Africa, became part of the spoils of war. Under mandates approved by the League of Nations, the Europeans carved up the Arab world into five separate states (Syria, Lebanon, Palestine, Iraq, and Transjordan) and either ruled them directly (as the French did in Algeria, Lebanon, and Syria and the British did in Palestine) or (as the British did in Iraq and Transjordan) propped up monarchs they thought they could trust. In Egypt, the British shared sovereignty with King Faruk.

It was not until after the Second World War that the Europeans finally agreed to leave and, except for the Palestinians, Arabs were allowed to govern themselves. Sadly, it didn't make much of a difference. Sooner than later, in Egypt, Syria, Sudan, Libya, Tunisia, and Iraq, local military warlords regained control: Nasser in Egypt, Assad in Syria, Al-Bashir in Sudan, Qaddafi in Libya, Ben Ali in Tunisia, and Saddam Hussein in Iraq. In Jordan, in return for his support during the war, the Allies allowed Amir Abdallah to proclaim himself king. In Saudi Arabia, the House of Saud cut a power-sharing deal with the Wahhabis, a conservative Sunni sect. In Lebanon, tribal chiefs (*za'im*) of sectarian communities played the role of feudal bosses in European suits. Palestinians still have not been given the authority to govern themselves, and their homeland remains a contested arena of armed struggle with the Jewish citizens of Israel.

During the last half of the twentieth century, the rule of law lost its sovereignty and authority everywhere in North Africa and the Middle East. Most people lived under military dictatorships or the rule of absolute monarchs. At their most brutal, these regimes governed by what the *New York Times* columnist Thomas Friedman called "Hama rules," which he described as "no rules at all. You do whatever it takes to stay in power and you don't just defeat your foes. You bomb them in their homes and then you steamroll them so that their children and their children's children will never forget and never dream of challenging you again."[7]

Having lived under the rule of strongmen for more than a millennium, it is hardly surprising that when they finally had a chance to control their own destiny, military leaders took command. With armies having played such a dominant role in the political histories of these countries, it was inevitable that the power that comes from the barrel of a gun would maintain its authority over the region. There was little in their past that encouraged Arabs to think the force of reason could replace physical force as the governing principle of their new sovereign states.

Legal Scholars

In reality, the chance that those who ruled over the Arabs would recognize the supremacy of law was practically nonexistent. Military dictatorships, it turns out, were only half the problem. Not only was the law made to bend to the will of the warlord, it was betrayed by its guardians as well. A double whammy: tyranny from without, treason from within.

Almost from the beginning, legal scholars cooperated with the warlords to ensure both were masters and not servants of the law. In effect, they struck a power-sharing deal. In exchange for conceding the jurists' authority to oversee the evolution and application of sharia law, the sultans would be left in charge of everything else.

Compared to the way the Greeks thought about the rule of law, the jurisprudence that the jurists wrote did not measure up. The law was defined in a way that allowed autocratic regimes to dominate their people and indulge their worst excesses. The Qur'an was stripped of its reformist spirit. By the end of the fourteenth century, Ibn Khaldun had given up on the jurists and told anyone who would listen they couldn't be trusted. At the beginning of the twentieth century, Rashid Rida, a prominent legal reformer in Egypt, was still pressing the same charges of corruption and collusion that Ibn Khaldun and Ibn Taymiyya had leveled more than five hundred years before.[8] Rather than acting as a check on the absolute authority of the sultans and emirs, most jurists played the role of apologists.

The jurists cast their lot with the secular powers early on. Indeed, in the first half of the eleventh century Islamic scholars allied themselves with Muslim warlords who overthrew the Abbasids and grabbed power by force. A doctrine, known as "governorship by seizure," was developed by Abu al-Hasan al-Mawardi (972–1058) in his treatise *The Principles of Government*. Living at a time when the Abbasid Caliphate was under siege by Buyid and Seljuk armies, al-Mawardi's position was that so long as the ruler (sultan, emir) enforced the sharia and recognized the authority of the jurists, he possessed an absolute authority to do as he pleased. In effect, al-Mawardi and the guardians of Islamic law made a deal similar to the one the Roman jurists had struck with the emperor. Like them, the fuqaha were prepared to tolerate a lot of arbitrary and abusive behavior by tyrants and despots so long as their own authority over the law that governed people's spiritual and personal lives was respected.

Part of the problem facing the jurists was that they didn't have a whole lot of law to work with. The sharia is primarily concerned with the personal and private lives of the faithful and only secondarily with how a ruler behaves. Its focus has always been on the relationship between God and the individual rather than the sultan and his subjects, and its emphasis is therefore much more on how a person should conduct him- or herself than on how to navigate the corridors of power. Indeed, it is not, for the most part, a legal code. It is estimated that of the 6,000 verses of the Qur'an, fewer than 500 are of a legal nature and fewer than 100 of these would concern matters of civil or criminal law.[9]

The sharia does address questions of legal procedure and the conduct of judges, but it has very little to say on the dos and don'ts of government regulation. Islamic law did say that the caliph's authority rested on the endorsement of the scholars, but it made no provision for how this mandate should be given. Being bound to rule according to sharia law did imply a duty that the sovereign would promote the public interest, but at the same time it was conceded that his discretion as to how the well-being of his subjects could best be effected was essentially unfettered.

Core subjects like criminal and commercial law are only given superficial treatment. Islamic law doesn't, for example, lay out any general principles of criminal responsibility, nor does it contain anything like a comprehensive criminal code. In fact, it specifies only half a dozen offenses, dealing with illicit sexual relations, theft, apostasy, and drinking wine, as crimes with fixed punishments (*hudud*). Moreover, most crimes that are recognized in Islamic law typically implicate the perpetrator, the victim, and God, and only indirectly involve the state.

Faced with what was mostly a blank slate, it was natural for sharia scholars to give their rulers a free pass. As a practical matter, secular rulers could outlaw whatever they deemed to be a crime, use whatever procedures and methods (including torture) they found effective to prove it, and impose whatever punishment suited their fancy (which often was more severe than what was set out in the sharia).

Sultans also set the rules in the market. Even though Islamic law instructed the faithful in how to conduct their businesses and pay their taxes, like criminal law, its focus is on individual cases and discrete activities. The Qur'an provides for specific taxes (*zakat*) and outlaws particular practices (like charging interest), but it doesn't deal with taxation or trade and commerce comprehensively. As a result, rulers could and did design their business and tax codes pretty much as they pleased. In medieval times, even activities that were proscribed by sharia law, like prostitution and drinking alcohol, were taxed.

In the nineteenth century, after the Europeans arrived, Western commercial and business codes spread throughout the region. Additional taxes beyond those set out in the sharia were imposed and laws were enacted that allowed transactions, like charging interest, that were forbidden by Islamic law. Over the course of the twentieth century, sharia's influence on the economic affairs of the Arab world was for the most part intermittent and superficial.

Not only did the fuqaha not act as a significant check on how sultans exercised their lawmaking powers, but most of them preached a philosophy of submission and "quietism" as well. Especially for Sunni jurists, orthodox doctrine declared that it was the duty of all Muslims to obey their rulers regardless of how corrupt and oppressive their regimes.[10] So long as the ruler enforced the sharia everyone had a duty to do whatever else he might command. Following the position taken by al-Mawardi, Islamic jurists insisted that Muslims were obligated to obey their rulers regardless of how they seized the throne. Instead of holding the sultans and emirs to the highest standards of justice and good government, they preached a mind-set of passivism and submission.

The legal elites opted for the absolute authority of secular rulers for a reason. In the years following Mohammad's death, the community of believers had been racked by violence and civil war. Three of the first four caliphs who succeeded him were murdered; in less than 150 years Muslims fought three bloody civil wars. From the jurists' perspective, the killing of Muslims by other Muslims was a grave moral failing, something the Qur'an condemned in the strongest terms.

To stop the fighting, all four Sunni schools of law made political "quietism" their mantra. Their message to the umma was to concentrate on living up to their personal and religious obligations in their daily lives and not concern themselves with the tyranny and corruption of their rulers. Al-Ghazali (1058–1111), considered one of the greatest Islamic jurists of all time, summed up the feeling of most of his colleagues when he famously declared that a hundred years of living under a tyrant was better than a year of internal strife. The desire to avoid conflict between believers trumped all other considerations. Might made right and unless a person was ordered to violate God's law, he or she had a duty to accept whatever the sultan or emir said or did. As a practical matter, the only limits that constrained the authority of the ruler were those he imposed on himself.

The scholars of Islamic law did little to protect the faithful from the corruption and oppression of despots and tyrants, and they didn't do a whole lot more to make sure the sovereignty of law governed the daily lives of ordinary people. Although the jurists took control of matters of family and faith, the way they thought about private law did not match the classical conception of law imagined by Plato, Aristotle, and Cicero. Under the guidance and supervision of the fuqaha, sharia law became riddled with complexity, contradiction, and rules that disadvantaged more than half the community.

The failure of the sharia to live up to the ideals of the rule of law can be traced back to the early years when the central precepts of classical Islamic law were debated. At the center of these discussions, Islamic scholars argued about the role that reason and revelation should play in the elaboration and evolution of divine law. Initially, at the beginning of the Abbasid Caliphate, reason and logic were considered important sources for the development of the sharia. Those who said that reason had a vital role to play were known as Mu'tazilites. Two of the greatest scholars of Islamic law and philosophy, Ibn Sina (Avicenna, 980–1037) and Ibn Rushd (Averroes, 1126–1198), taught that the logic of Plato and Aristotle were important tools in the deduction and application of rules that governed relations among the faithful.

Others, however, were opposed. Al-Ghazali, who wrote a book entitled *The Incoherence of the Philosophers*, was one of them. Known as Ash'arites, these scholars argued that only divine sources, the Qur'an, the Hadith (the recorded sayings of Mohammad), and the Sunna (traditional social and legal practices of the Islamic community), could reveal the true meaning of God's law. Ultimately, the Ash'arites prevailed and a strict interpretation of the revealed sources became the principal way of finding out how Allah expected people to behave.

By the eleventh century, the major features of the law were fixed. The scholars had organized themselves into five principal schools of law. After al-Shafi'i, everyone was agreed that the words of the Qu'ran and the Hadith of the Prophet were the primary sources from which the rules of Islamic law were to be derived and that reason and principles of logic could only be used as secondary resources. Gradually, and especially for the Sunnis, there was a metaphorical "closing of the gate" after which the ability of the jurists to try new approaches was curtailed. Although reasoning by analogy (*qiyas*) was permitted in a limited range of circumstances, more open-ended forms of analysis (*istihsan, istislah*) that relied on principles of reasonableness and common sense were discouraged. Ibn Rushd wrote a rejoinder to al-Ghazali (entitled *The Incoherence of Incoherence*), but all that got him was the animosity of the more traditional scholars, who condemned him as a heretic, sent him into exile, and ordered that his texts be burned.

As the opportunities for independent reasoning underwent a relentless shrinkage over time, jurists increasingly looked to the past for guidance. Like their Jewish cousins, their orientation became introspective, idealistic, and very bookish. They devoted endless hours to studying and applying rules of rhetoric, grammar, and logic to the basic texts. They looked for guidance from the treatises that had been written by earlier generations of scholars. The idea took hold that the work of finding the true meaning of God's commandments had already been accomplished and that the answers to questions about new problems were to be found in the seminal texts of the past rather than by subjecting them to a fresh analysis.

The result was that each new generation of jurists spent years studying the writings of those who came before them rather than pursue independent thinking on their own. In working through the rules of sharia law, the authority of reason (*ijtihad*) was replaced by a ritual of imitation (*taqlid*) that effectively gave jurists a monopoly over its development and made it next to impossible for anyone else to engage. Islamic law became so complex that, like Plato's guardians, only a tiny elite who had completed years of study were in a position to say what God's law meant. The jurists alone were masters of the rules of grammar, rhetoric, disputation, and jurisprudence (*usul al-fiqh*), which gave them access to God's mind. Thinking about what the sharia requires was not for the uneducated or simpleminded. To master all the twists and turns of a divine text and scholarly writing could take a student twenty years.

Sharia and the Rule of Law

Once the connection between reason and the law had been severed, it was inevitable that the rules that were passed down from the classical scholars would lose touch with reality and stop making sense. As formulated by the medieval jurists, the sharia failed to meet all three of the central precepts of the rule of law that were followed by the Greeks. In terms of law's formal requirements, many of the sharia's commandments did not provide clear direction and some didn't even qualify as rules. As for law's supremacy, except for matters of ritual and faith, rulers were free to do pretty much as they pleased. As a code of how to live a virtuous life, the law the jurists wrote was riddled with injustice, especially against women and adherents of different faiths.

Many of the commandments contained in the sharia don't meet the formal qualities of law. In important cases, there is no finality or conclusive meaning in what the sharia says. There are no definitive answers. Central questions about how relations within the family should be structured were, and remain, matters of serious disagreement. Rights and obligations between spouses and children, for example, have been interpreted by the legal scholars in conflicting and contradictory ways. Instead of clear and certain direction, God's lists of dos and don'ts are often inconsistent and imprecise.

As already noted, the jurists in all five schools agreed on the basic framework to be used in deriving the rules of divine law.[11] The Qur'an, the Hadith, and the Sunna of the earliest Muslim communities are the primary sources of Islamic law, which can be supplemented by analogical reasoning (*qiyas*) and points of agreement (*ijma*) among the jurists. But they disagreed on how these sources should be used and the extent to which other methods of reasoning should be permitted.

Each school emphasized different tools of analysis to determine what the law requires. The Ja'faris make the most use of reason and rationality.

Among the Sunnis, the Hanafi school is considered the most liberal. It has allowed more freedom and flexibility of reasoning than the others. It endorses a principle (*istihsan*) that permits jurists to employ considerations of fairness and common sense in fashioning solutions to problems that are not directly addressed in the Qur'an or the Sunna. The Hanbalis, by contrast, have generally opposed such forms of independent reasoning and have favored a more literalist approach. In between, the Malikis, whose influence has been exerted primarily in North and West Africa, developed principles (*istislah/ maslaha*) that allowed them to take account of the public interest and well-being of the community and gave special weight to the practices and precedents of the first community of believers who gathered with Mohammad in Medina.

Differences among the jurists were compounded by the fact that most of sharia law is based on the Sunna and Hadith rather than the words recorded in the Qur'an. Because Mohammad's words and deeds were often not recorded until generations after he died, the most important source of God's will was shrouded in ambiguity and uncertainty. To minimize the chance of forgeries and false reports degrading the integrity of the law, elaborate rules to certify the authenticity of practices and commandments attributed to the Prophet were formulated by the jurists. In the end, they were not successful. Like participants in the game of "broken telephone" (or *le téléphone arabe*, as it is known to the French), jurists came to radically different understandings of what the law said.

Because the Qur'an and the words of the Prophet were open to multiple interpretations, it did not take long for significant differences to develop. Depending on where they lived, Muslims could be told they were permitted or prohibited from doing the same thing. Islam has no pope whose word is final and who could settle the jurists' disputes. Even matters as fundamental as the duration and consensual nature of marriage were up for grabs.

Temporary marriages (*mut'a*), for example, were recognized as legitimate by Shia jurists but the four Sunni schools said they were just a crude cover for prostitution. Similarly, against the majority of jurists, who said that God's will gave fathers the right to choose whom their daughters would marry, Hanafi jurists gave the final say to the woman. Under Hanafi law, women had the right to repudiate a father's choice when they came of age.

In addition to their treatment of forced and temporary marriages, each of the schools of law formulated its own rules on divorce, inheritance, and the custody of children. On all these issues, the jurists agreed to disagree. They have come to a common conclusion that Allah may say one thing to people who live in Iran or Iraq and something different to believers who live in Egypt or Saudi Arabia.

The practice of recognizing multiple opinions on points of law has the virtue of being flexible and respectful of the views of others. However, as we have seen in the evolution of Roman law prior to its consolidation in Justinian's Corpus Juris Civilis, it undercuts everything the rule of law is about. Not only does it compromise the law's certainty and intelligibility, it undermines its supremacy and leaves a trail of injustice in its wake. Instead of a community that is governed by law, it produces a society that is ruled by professional elites who are free to privilege their own sense of right and wrong.

Pluralism in and supremacy of the law are mutually exclusive. By the very act of asserting the authority of formulating the rules of piety, Islamic jurists put themselves above the law and made themselves sovereign over the private lives of the faithful. Rather than being bound by law, they made it. In effect, the muftis and fuqaha substituted their will for Allah's. Instead of a divine law that is universal and immutable, they created a God who speaks in many tongues and a law that sends conflicting messages.

The diversity in Islamic law has been exploited by all segments of the ruling classes. The differences between the schools of law is not just a turf war between legal elites – they can and are used by judges and rulers, who draw on them to justify whatever law or regulation suits their purposes. Where the schools adopt different rules, judges can pick the one that produces the result they favour. Like their brothers in Classical Rome, judges in North Africa and the Middle East are able to use the diversity in the law to decide cases based on their personal preferences. Rather than being restricted to one school or method of analyzing the law, sharia judges can invoke a doctrine known as *talfiq* that allows them to pick and choose from among different jurists more or less as they please.

It is not only judges and jurists who have gained from the pluralist character of Islamic law; politicians have as well, and sometimes for the good. As a result of the differences of opinion among the jurists, progressive politicians have, for example, been able to promote the cause of women's rights. By embracing the jurisprudence of the school with the most egalitarian interpretation of the law, politicians have been able to limit a father's right to marry his daughters without their consent, restrict the practice of female circumcision, broaden the grounds on which a woman can claim a divorce, and, in the case of Tunisia, outlaw polygamy altogether. In 2004, Morocco carried out major reforms of its family law to reduce its bias against women, including the abolition of compulsory guardianship of women and the establishment of joint and equal responsibility between husband and wife in the home.

While the malleable character of sharia law has proven to be a useful feature for reform-minded politicians, it comes with a catch. The consensus among scholars that all schools are free to follow their own method of reasoning cuts both ways. It allows politicians of all stripes to wrap their preferred policies in the Prophet's mantle. Conservative politicians can justify draconian punishments and discriminatory laws against minorities and women by invoking the legal authority of the school with the most orthodox approach.

The most notorious case of a ruler favoring a traditional and conservative interpretation of the law in the modern era is the crown prince of Saudi Arabia. Under Saudi law, women are still treated like children. They are told how they must dress and they have virtually no say in government. They do not even have the right to vote. Nor may they leave home or take a job without the permission of their fathers or husbands. Until 2018, it was illegal for a woman to drive a car, and those who dared defy the law might be sentenced to 150 lashes and months in jail.

And women aren't the only people who have suffered the Saudis' disfavor. Christians are not allowed to build houses of worship and gays, apostates, and adulterers can be stoned to death. And no one can say exercising the power of the state in such ways is unjust or inhuman. Because Saudi law is based on the jurisprudence of the Wahhabi jurists, the crown prince and his brothers can defend their decrees as having the blessing of Allah.

To justify their acceptance of the many variations that can be found in the law, the jurists quote the sayings of the Prophet. According to one, Mohammad is reported to have proclaimed that "difference of opinion within my community is a sign of the bounty of Allah." On another occasion, he was heard to say that "My community will never agree on an error." The jurists claim that in making such statements, the Prophet must have meant that the jurisprudential approach of all five schools is equally valid. It implies that in deciding whether something like a temporary marriage or a punishment like stoning should be permitted or prohibited, there can be no right or wrong.

Exactly what Mohammad meant by his observations is impossible to prove conclusively, one way or another. The will of God is not something that is amenable to scientific explanation. What is certain is that claiming divine authority for the diversity of Islamic law can't be the end of the conversation. The Hadith and Sunna quoted by the jurists can't literally mean that each interpretation of every rule of the sharia by all five schools is an accurate description of God's will.

The conflicting positions of the Shias and Sunnis on the legality of temporary marriages, for example, can't both be right. Both can't be what God intends. Temporary marriages can't be permitted and proscribed at the same time. One contradicts the other; therefore one of them must be wrong. So, too, on the question whether women can marry without the consent of their male guardian – either they can or they can't. It can't be both.

That jurists have made mistakes in their interpretation of divine law is undeniable. They are, after all, only human. Indeed, most recognize their own fallibility. Another of the Prophet's sayings that jurists like to quote is that on the Day of Judgment they will receive a single reward if their interpretation is wrong and a double reward if it is correct.

Some errors may not matter a whole lot, but others certainly do. Undoubtedly the most glaring relate to the treatment of women. As it has been interpreted by the jurists, sharia law is universally hostile to the autonomy of women. Without exception, all schools of law, whether Sunni and Shia, have embraced an interpretation of the Qur'an, the Sunna, and the Hadith of the Prophet that denies women the equal benefit and protection of the law. They have formulated the law in a way that grants important privileges to men.

According to all mainstream jurists, God has commanded that men are uniquely entitled to have more than one spouse; marry someone who is not a Muslim; end a marriage by unilateral proclamation; and insist on obedience from the person (or persons) to whom they are married. Women can't do any of these things, and to compound the injustice, they generally only inherit half as much as their brothers.

Islamic law discriminates against women not because that was the only way the Qur'an, the Sunna, and the Hadith of the Prophet could be understood. The jurists had to choose between taking the words of the Qur'an and the Prophet literally or reading them in terms of the purposes they were intended to serve. From the very beginning they have been predisposed to the former. They put the emphasis on the particular words in which specific commands were written rather than the general principles and values that underlie and explain them.

Sometimes the jurists do look for deeper meanings.[12] As noted earlier, jurists interpreted the specific prohibition of wine to cover all intoxicating substances. They have also acknowledged that some things that might have been justified in the past can no longer be considered legitimate today. Some practices, like slavery, that once seemed natural and appropriate are now universally recognized to be wrong. Just because Islamic law permitted the enslavement of people in Muhammad's time doesn't make it good law today.

In the context of the era in which he lived, Muhammad's position on slavery might be defended as a rational way for Muslims to provide for their collective security and as another of his attempts at gradual reform, this time of the laws of war. In some ways, Islamic law put more restrictions on the practice of slavery than Roman and Greek jurisprudence. For example, sharia law contemplates the enslavement of prisoners of war, but never of other Muslims. Nor does it tolerate parents selling their children into slavery, as was allowed by Roman law, and it encourages those who did own slaves to emancipate them.

Still, no matter how justified Islam's take on slavery was at its inception, no reputable scholar would say it is still a permissible way of ordering human relations. Even if Islam's treatment of the subject marked an improvement over what came before, it constitutes a flagrant violation of the principle of equality and an intolerable denial of human freedom. Today, virtually all Muslims accept that any assertion of ownership of one person by another is illegitimate, unjust, and a defilement of God's law.

The same is true of punishment. In most parts of the Arab world, it is widely accepted that the extreme punishments attached to *hudud* offenses are out of place in the modern world. Cutting off the hands of thieves and stoning adulterers and apostates hearken back to a time when police and prisons were practically nonexistent. In such a world, one could argue for the need for punishment to shock and awe. It made sense to enhance law's deterrent function to scare people into obedience by making the penalties for the worst offenders extremely nasty. Today, with more effective law enforcement and the proliferation of prisons, the majority of Muslims recognize punishments like stoning and amputation to be excessive and illegitimate.

When it comes to slavery and punishment, most jurists have been alert to the historical context of the law and the reasons why strict enforcement of the traditional rules can no longer be justified. Suspiciously, the great majority of them have failed to follow this insight in their pronouncements on the status of women. Instead, they have focused their attention on the literal meaning of the words in the text and have lost sight of the underlying purposes and values they were meant to serve.

Permitting men to have multiple wives is a striking example. The jurists have read the words of the Qur'an literally, as part of an eternal tale of male privilege, rather than seeing polygyny as a temporary expedient to alleviate the shortage of marriageable men that was caused by the loss of male life in Islam's early wars. In the world in which the Qur'an was written, allowing men to have four wives was a way of furthering the equality of the sexes. When there weren't enough men to go around it ensured more women would have the chance to have a husband and be part of raising a family. Today, when the number of men and women in the world is more evenly balanced, the reasons for permitting men to have more than one spouse no longer govern.

In defense of their position, it is sometimes said that God did not formulate the law the way He did because it is just; rather, it is just because He made it the law. But that just begs the question of whether the law is just the words on the page (a man can have up to four wives) or whether it should be understood to include the underlining values and principles (ensuring women have equal opportunities in raising a family) as well.

The way the jurists have interpreted the law to favor their own (male) interests is fundamentally at odds with the precepts of justice that underpin the rule of law and with Islam's affirmation that all pious believers are equal. In the words of one of Islam's most respected female voices, what the legal scholars have done is "to convince us that their egotistic, highly subjective, and mediocre view of culture and society has a sacred basis."[13] They have taken a law that was originally strongly egalitarian and committed to protecting the rights of women and turned it into a mandate for a patriarchy that is inclined to promote its own agenda.

The ways in which Islam's legal scholars rejected the core ideals of the rule of law bears a strong resemblance to how the Roman jurists behaved. Inventing processes of reasoning that were not transparent or easily accessible to ordinary people, both groups manipulated the substantive rules to favor their own interests and those of the rulers they served. The formula was so successful, it should come as no surprise that when legal professionals in other parts of the world and in other religions had the chance, they took advantage of the same opportunity. We have already noticed how the rabbis took charge of the development of Jewish law, and a thousand years later, legal scholars in the Roman Catholic Church and civil lawyers who revived Roman law did the same. The triumphs and tragedies of the jurists of medieval Europe are the next major landmarks on law's quest to bring peace and justice to the world, and their story is taken up in the two chapters that follow.

Chapter Five

Bologna and Rome (Again)

The Dark Ages

Because law's promise has always been to solve conflict peacefully, it is perhaps its fate that whenever and wherever it seeks to establish its rule, it has had to do so in surroundings that are harsh and unfriendly. Sharia, Roman, Greek, and Mesopotamian law were all born in worlds where war was an ever-present danger and violence was a fact of daily life. Medieval law in western Europe was no different. Indeed, for more than five hundred years following the collapse of Rome, law struggled to stay alive in a part of the planet that was overrun by paid mercenaries and armed thugs.

After Rome was sacked by Germanic hordes, the light of the law grew dim. The political sophistication of the various tribes (Franks, Saxons, Burgundians, Visigoths and Ostrogoths, Vandals and Lombards) that ruled central and western Europe over the succeeding centuries has been described by one scholar as being at the level of "marauding street gangs."[1] Compared to the Greeks, Romans, and Arabs, their ideas about law and politics were, on the whole, quite primitive.

The illumination of law came closest to being extinguished in western Europe in the centuries immediately after the Germans plundered Rome. That is one of the reasons the years between 476 CE, when Odovacar deposed the last Roman emperor, and the end of the eleventh century, when the Crusades were first launched, are often referred to as the "Dark Ages." The tribes invading from the north and east of Rome were a crude and unforgiving crowd. These were not societies with long philosophical traditions. Like Sparta, they were little more than war machines.

This was a time of private armies and armed terrorists (known in the later Middle Ages as knights) who only respected the law when it suited them. The system of government under which the Merovingian kings ruled France from roughly 500 to 750 CE has been characterized as "despotism tempered by assassination." Brawn and brute force were the sources of authority that mattered most.[2]

Even Charlemagne (747?–814), who is considered the most enlightened of the early medieval rulers, (his education included reading Cicero and studying rhetoric and dialectics), was more a military commander than a servant of the law. He was almost always on the march (at one stretch for almost thirty years) and he ruled with an iron fist. In one of his laws he required all of his male subjects, at the age of twelve, to swear an oath of loyalty that for most of them meant signing up for compulsory military service. In another, he insisted that all the Saxons he had defeated after thirty years of war convert to Christianity or be killed. After one battle, at Verden in 782, he didn't offer his prisoners the choice. Instead, he beheaded forty-five hundred of them in an attempt to encourage the rest to see the light. His idea of showing mercy to his enemies was to blind them rather than having them put to death.

As a practical matter, for a period of more than five hundred years following the fall of Rome, Europe reverted to the law of the jungle.[3] In addition to fighting among themselves, the German tribes had to hold off raids by Islamic fighters from the south in the seventh and eighth centuries and invasions by Vikings from the north and Magyrs (Hungarians) from the east in the nineth and tenth. The ferocity and inhumanity of the violence knew no limits. No one was spared – women and children included. Rape and pillage were part of the victors' spoils. Between 720 and 804, the Continent experienced less than ten years of peace.

Even within the German tribes, physical force was pervasive. Fights were settled by rituals of trial by battle, blood feud, and collective punishment. If someone was murdered, it was the duty of his or her kin to hunt down and kill the murderer and a suitable number of his family as a message to future offenders. It was a world in which warlords with titles like duke or count could burn their wives for committing adultery.

For the ordinary person, such a hostile environment made for a precarious existence. The feudal Europe that started to emerge in the sixth and seventh centuries was a world of peasants living in small agriculture towns and villages. They were isolated and exposed. At the end of the first millennium, only London and Venice had populations of more than ten thousand people. There was little commerce or long-distance travel. Most people never ventured more than a few kilometers from their village. More than half the population was tied to the land of some wealthy landlord. Although they were classed as serfs rather than slaves, they were not free to leave the land and their daily existence was not a whole lot better than the beasts they herded.

To guard against the constant threat of being attacked, those who were weakest and most vulnerable did the only thing they could: they pledged allegiance to those powerful enough to defend them. As early as the seventh century, relationships of lords and vassals began to supplant purely tribal associations, and by the second half of the ninth what is commonly (though controversially) referred to as feudalism was in full swing. In a world where might made right, swearing an oath of fidelity to a big man was like taking out insurance against terrorism.

When the system was fully developed (in the eleventh and twelfth centuries), feudal relations came to cover the whole of medieval society from top to bottom. Everyone was linked, from king to peasant, with a range of different ranks of greater and lesser nobility in between. The connection was based on promises of protection that were given in exchange for military, agricultural, and personal services. Typically, by swearing an oath of fealty, a man became a vassal to his lord and received a parcel of land (fief) that he was entitled to work for as long as he fulfilled the obligations he had undertaken to perform.

Medieval Law

As violent and cruel as feudal life could be, it was never a completely lawless world. Although Rome's law schools and its lawyers vanished from the scene, in a few places, including Ireland and Iceland, customary and ecclesiastical law continued to be taught by clerics to students in local monasteries. Depending on their education and clientele, Irish lawyers might be included in the ranks of the nobility and could command substantial fees.

Even the barbarians who conquered Rome understood the virtues of law and had basic rules and procedures to settle their differences. When the German tribes first thought about law, they equated it with the traditional ways of doing things. Like the earliest law in Babylon, it didn't have a separate, formal existence. It was mixed up with customs and rituals that organized the rhythms and patterns of daily living. The foundation of Germanic law was an accumulation of unwritten customary rules, not codified laws like Draco's and Solon's in Athens or the Twelve Tables in Rome. Over time, they adopted large parts of the law they learned from the Romans and from the teaching and rules (canons) of the Catholic Church.

In the beginning, German folk law was both simpler and less rational than the Roman law of the emperor and the jurists. It was concerned for the most part with controlling violence and putting an end to private "blood feuds" by establishing schedules of payments (wergild, bot) that varied with the extent of the injuries sustained (so much for the loss of an eye or an arm or a leg) and with the status of the perpetrator and his victim. Trials were conducted before public assemblies (moots) and in many cases proof of a person's guilt or innocence was established by undergoing physical ordeals like walking on coals or holding burning metal objects or putting one's arm in scalding water. The idea was that if the wounds healed properly, that was a sign of God's blessing.

Following the example of the Romans, in many of these barbarian kingdoms, the rulers put the customary law of their communities down in writing. In their organization and classification of the law, these codes were cruder than Justinian's Corpus Juris Civilis, but they were also capable of professing allegiance to law's highest ideals. One of the most famous was the code the Visigoths wrote in the middle of the seventh century.

Known as the Forum Judicum, the Visigoth Code followed Rome's example of organizing the law into twelve chapters covering everything from family and business relations to property, defamation, and crime. The overarching objective was to encourage people to settle their differences peacefully rather than by fighting each other. Judges were given the power to summon parties to court, and ignorance of the law was not accepted as an excuse.

To ensure law proved to be a better way to resolve disputes than relying on physical force, the code included rules intended to secure the integrity and efficacy of the legal process. Some focused on the honesty and impartiality of the judiciary. Others laid out rules for gathering evidence and giving testimony that were necessary to prove one's case.

The Visigoths' Code shows law at its best and its worst. Much like Hammurabi's Code, it was a juxtaposition of extremes: ringing declarations of justice and equity set down alongside physical punishments (blinding, branding, burning, scalping, stoning, enslavement, castration, and decapitation) of appalling brutality. In one passage, the law is described as "the guardian and promoter of good morals; the rudder of the state; the messenger of justice; the mistress of life; the soul of the body politic." In the next, the code says anyone accused of a crime could be tortured and a woman who had an abortion or committed adultery could be blinded or put to death.

A whole chapter at the end of the code is devoted to the oppression and forced conversion of Jews. Jews who persisted in following the laws of their faith in what they ate, when they worked, what they read, and what rituals (like circumcision) they performed could be whipped, scalped, mutilated, exiled, and enslaved. Overall, the code leaves no doubt of its being the work of people who believed less in the power of reason than in the supernatural powers of a supreme deity and in raw physical force.

In one respect, the Germanic tribes did better than the Romans in that their rulers were more constrained by the law than the emperors in Rome. Law may have been rougher and less sophisticated for the Germans than it was for the Romans, but the law they had was considered to be more stable and enduring and bound everyone in the tribe. Like the Greeks, the Germans thought of law as something that remained fixed and unaltered through the ages and that governed the behavior of rulers and ruled alike.

German military leaders who conquered Rome never had the pretensions of Justinian. They never claimed the power to introduce new laws unilaterally nor the status of being above the law. They were expected to respect the traditional laws and customs of their forefathers. They weren't free to do whatever they wanted.

It was possible for a ruler to change the law, but he couldn't do it by himself. On the most important issues, Germanic rulers, including Charlemagne, had to assemble the most powerful members of the tribe and get them to agree. Consent of the nobility was a precondition for the legitimacy of their rule.

Even the most powerful warlords whose military conquests made them kings, and whose rule extended over rival tribes, didn't legislate like Roman emperors. Early medieval rulers exercised their authority by traveling with their "courts" through their realms settling cases and dispensing justice according to the traditional laws of the land. Law's method was mostly about resolving disputes and adjudicating cases rather than formulating new rules for the whole kingdom. As a practical matter, law meant handing down judgments in actual cases rather than issuing new commands. Germanic law was more in the mold of the decisions that Hammurabi listed in his code than of the edicts and decrees of the Roman emperors.

The practice of issuing imperial legislation was revived by Charlemagne after he was crowned Holy Roman emperor by Pope Leo III in St. Peter's Basilica on Christmas Day in the year 800. The story of Charlemagne's assumption of the imperial lawmaking powers of the Roman emperors is hidden behind a shroud of religious smoke and mirrors. The origins of the story date back to the fourth century, when the Emperor Constantine converted to Christianity. In the course of his rule, it was said he delegated his lawmaking powers in the western (Roman) half of the empire to the pope (Sylvestor I) in gratitude of having been cured of leprosy. This transfer of sovereignty was known as the Donation of Constantine, and until the fifteenth century few people knew it was fake.

It is now generally accepted that the Donation of Constantine was actually written sometime during the eighth century, at a time when popes had come to rely on the Carolingian kings to protect them. In the waning years of the century, when Pope Leo III was attacked by his enemies in Rome, he sought refuge with Charlemagne. For reasons that are still debated, shortly thereafter Leo cemented the papal-Carolingian alliance by returning the symbols of imperial power to Charlemagne and declaring him to be the first "Holy" Roman emperor. With the imperial crown on his head, Roman law became part of the legal landscape in western Europe once again and the lawmaking powers of the emperor were back in vogue.

As a man of great faith and a believer in the righteousness of physical force, Charlemagne embraced law as a way of establishing a Christian empire and keeping the peace.[4] He and his sons issued hundreds of wide-ranging "capitularies" aimed at establishing harmonious, peaceful kingdoms built on Christian values. Like the Visigoths' Code, there were declarations of protection for widows and orphans, condemnations of unfair and dishonest dealings, brutal and unforgiving punishments for criminal and sacrilegious (e.g., eating meat during Lent) behavior, as well as schedules of payments for harms and injuries that were intended to replace the customary practices of trials by battle and blood feuds.

In addition to the substantive laws that established the rights and wrongs of proper relations among his subjects, Charlemagne's capitularies also included directives that were intended to upgrade the justice system by ensuring peasants and serfs had access to the courts. Royal officials (*missi*) were appointed to oversee local courts and instruct them as to how they should enforce the law and perform their duties. Bishops were cautioned not to abuse their authority over those who lived on their property and worshipped in their church.

Royal and imperial laws like Charlemagne's typically built on the foundations of the traditional rules of customary law, and together they provided the broad framework of medieval law. They were not, however, the whole story. Alongside the traditional rules of tribal law and the edicts and orders of emperors and kings, local communities developed their own laws and everyone bowed, in varying degrees, to the laws of the church. Both secular laws, whose jurisdiction was restricted to a specific property controlled by a member of the nobility, and divine laws that claimed universal, eternal authority, were also defining features of the legal landscape. They operated side by side, often overlapping, sometimes pulling in opposite directions.

For most people, feudal law and the law of the manor had the most immediate impact on their day-to-day existence. Lords had ultimate authority over everything that happened on their property. They fixed the number of days a person was obligated to work for them, what dues and taxes he owed, and what use he could make of communal pastures and forests. They also wrote the rules that legally bound the serf to a specific piece of land and claimed a veto over whom he and other members of his family might marry.

In regulating relations between a lord and the people living on his land, feudal law amounted to a privatization of the legal system. It was built on the practice of kings granting their closest associates the authority to establish their own legal regimes over the lands they controlled. It amounted to the delegation of the sovereign's power to private fiefdoms. Even though the law was enforced in assemblies in which all classes were represented, the lord controlled the proceedings. As a practical matter, manor courts were a means by which nobles were able to exact services and payments from their serfs. At the beginning of the medieval period, the highest-ranking dukes and counts were recognized as having jurisdiction over questions of "high justice," which included the right to execute anyone convicted of a capital offence.

By the middle of the eleventh century, when city life began to revive, local municipal and mercantile laws were added to the mix. Like feudal laws regulating life on the manor, municipal laws drew their authority from charters granted by the king addressing the everyday events and activities of urban living. Rules of mutual aid, policing and protection, regulation of rents, guilds, and commerce, the rights of citizens and strangers – all were common features of medieval municipal law. Like their country cousins, city folk also created their own courts and auxiliary legal institutions to enforce the law that they wrote.

On top of all the secular law that set limits on what constituted acceptable behavior in medieval Europe, church law added its own long list of dos and don'ts that people ignored at their peril.[5] Indeed, of all the different sets of laws regulating life in medieval Europe, canon law – the law of the Roman Catholic Church – undoubtedly had the broadest reach. It transcended the feudal manors and cities in which people lived and the tribes to which they belonged, and its roots went very deep. In fact, the laws of the Catholic Church became part of Europe's legal order (and that of parts of Asia, North Africa, and the Middle East) even before the medieval period began. The tipping point occurred in 312, when Constantine converted to Christianity. At that moment, church law came to be imbued with the coercive power of the state and the scope of its jurisdiction grew exponentially.

When Christianity became the official religion of the Roman Empire, the focus of its law expanded beyond matters of ritual and ceremony. Like the sharia, canon law was especially concerned with marriage and family relations, sexual behavior, economic activities, and relations with people of other faiths. Bishops were given the responsibility of enforcing the law in ecclesiastical courts. In less than a hundred years, canon law went from the rules that governed the religious practices and beliefs of a persecuted minority to a complex legal system that worked alongside the empire's civil and criminal laws.

Law and Revolution

The recognition of Christianity as the official religion of the Roman Empire infused canon law with the power of the state, but it also meant church law came within the orbit of the secular authorities. In the five hundred years following the collapse of Rome, the church and its law were under the thumb of the emperor and princes who ruled over medieval Europe. The Emperor Justinian (482–565) asserted absolute control over both church and state and all of his successors, including Charlemagne, continued to claim broad ecclesiastical authority.

None of the Germanic kingdoms that carved up Rome's former territories were predisposed to cede much independence to the church. Medieval rulers claimed the right to veto any attempt by the clerics to interfere with their administration. They also typically chose the bishops and senior church officials in their realms, and the German kings who, following Charlemagne, succeeded to the title of Holy Roman emperor, regularly chose the pope. From the middle of the tenth century to the middle of the eleventh, more than three-quarters of them were the emperor's personal picks. Even knights and nobles selected the priests who ministered to the faithful in their fiefdoms and routinely taxed and (mis)appropriated church property. Except when a very forceful pope sat on Saint Peter's throne, or a ruler (like Charlemagne) was amenable, the scope and authority of canon law over early medieval rulers was limited and did not pack much of a punch.

By the start of the second millennium, the state of the law in medieval Europe could be described as crowded, chaotic, and confused. There were lots of overlapping and sometimes competing sets of laws but no formal, overarching legal system. Customary law, royal law, church law, feudal law, mercantile law, municipal law – all operated more or less as distinct legal orders. So while law's presence was pervasive, there was nobody like the Roman jurists trying to coordinate all the different parts into an integrated system – no one like Cicero thinking about the meaning of law and its role in making sure reason and justice reigned supreme in the society in which they lived.

In the second half of the eleventh century, that changed. All of a sudden (it happened so fast some refer to it as law's big bang) the stars were aligned in law's favor. Both the economics and politics of medieval Europe were susceptible to a vigorous program of law reform. Trade and commerce were on the rise while the secular and clerical elites were sparring over the scope of their sovereignty and the force of their lawmaking authority. In both the palace and the marketplace there were strong incentives to develop a more coherent and coordinated legal system. By the beginning of the twelfth century, the ambitions of both merchants and monarchs were being frustrated by the confusion of so many different legal orders that had taken hold. For the first time in a long time it was in everyone's interest – military and spiritual leaders, international traders, even serfs seeking the freedom that came with living in a city – to start thinking about revitalizing the rule of law.

The economic motivator for a more rational legal order was precipitated by a warming period in western Europe, which stimulated substantial population growth, an uptick in agricultural production, and the development of cities. By the end of the thirteenth century, there were roughly fifty cities with populations ranging from 15,000 to 30,000, half a dozen (including London, Barcelona, and Milan) with more than 50,000, and one megacity, Paris, with more than 200,000 inhabitants. As more people escaped the bonds of feudal living and sought their freedom and fortune in the city, international and regional commerce revived and the inefficiencies and inequities of the diffused legal order became more costly.

The political push came from the popes.[6] Beginning in the middle of the eleventh century, German emperors, inspired by Charlemagne's vision of an ideal Christian empire, chose a series of smart and ambitious clerics, who were committed to an agenda of reform, to lead the church. Their goal was to wrest control of their religion from Rome's ruling classes, who treated the papacy as a personal fiefdom and who, in their opinion, were responsible for the corruption and moral debasement of the clergy and the church. They wanted to put an end to the practice of selling clerical offices (simony), the marriage of priests, and the life of privilege and excess enjoyed by many church leaders.

In the second half of the century, the pope and the church went on the offensive. In 1059, in what has been described as the church's declaration of independence, Pope Nicholas II decreed that a group of papal advisers known as the College of Cardinals would be given the power to choose future popes. Then, in 1075, in a document entitled *Dictatus papae*, Gregory VII, who has been called the greatest churchman of the Middle Ages, made the claim that, when push came to shove, it was the pope, not the emperor, who had the final say. His judgment on church law was declared to be infallible and beyond question by any other human being. He insisted that he alone had the power to make new laws and annul those that were incompatible with the laws of the church. In addition, he said he had the power, unlike the caliph, to hear complaints against rulers and to depose those who transgressed church law. His claims were so far-reaching that his papacy has been described as the first revolution in Western political history. From that point on, in their power struggles with emperors and kings, popes routinely claimed supreme lawmaking authority over all of western Europe.

The issue that sparked Gregory's assertions of divine authority was the so-called investiture struggle over who controlled the appointments in and property of the church (a battle the church is still fighting, almost a thousand years later, in China). These were issues of fundamental political importance; huge amounts of wealth and power were at stake. Gregory, who was well versed in canon law, insisted that affairs of the church were his jurisdiction, not the emperor's, and that church law was supreme. When Henry IV, the German king, challenged him, he was deposed.

To regain his crown, Henry was forced, on pain of excommunication, to concede his limited involvement in the selection of bishops and other church officials and in the administration of the properties they managed. Legend has it that, to rub salt in the wound, Gregory made Henry stand outside the castle of Canossa in the Apennines, in northern Italy, in the middle of winter. For three days, he was made to do penance before he was allowed to have his title back. Gregory's message was clear: The pope was the supreme lawmaker. Kings and emperors, no less than their subjects, were bound by his will and his interpretation of the laws of the church.

Of which there were many. After hundreds of years of uneven but unrelenting growth, canon law was breathtaking in its scope. It had rules on just about everything, from strategic relations between popes and princes to personal intimacies between husbands and wives. The vast majority of people living in Europe at the time were governed by its rules. It controlled what and when they ate, what they could say, who they might marry, when they worked, how they carried on business, how much they gave to the poor, the quality of their sexual life on earth, and their spiritual life after death.

Despite being a large and unwieldy body of often conflicting and ambiguous rules, Gregory saw church law as a way of doing battle with his secular rivals. Lacking an army of their own, he and his successors launched a sweeping study of canon law in a search for legal authorities that would provide support for their claims. In the middle of the twelfth century, a canon lawyer from Bologna named Gratian organized thousands of texts of canon law into a single, comprehensive legal treatise. His *Decretum* did for canon law what Justinian's Corpus Juris Civilis had done for the Romans and al-Shafi'i's *Risala* had done for Islam: it marked the birth of canon law as a full-fledged legal system. Following the dialectal methods of the classical scholars, it resolved ambiguities and inconsistencies and established the rules to be followed in interpreting canonical texts. It's publication, in 1140, marks the beginning of what is considered to be the classical period of canon law, which lasted for almost 250 years. It remained a standard text of canon law until the twentieth century and became one of the most widely read books in Western history.

The *Decretum* brought order and a system of classification to canon law in a way that broadened the jurisdiction of the church and the power of the pope. In addition to absolute control over the appointment of priests and bishops, it claimed the exclusive right to deal with any church official who committed a crime. Moreover, because its rules on marriage and divorce had important implications for questions of inheritance and succession, popes exercised considerable influence in the world of secular politics as well. By the end of the twelfth century the papal Curia was receiving thousands of appeals every year from all over Europe on everything from family quarrels and feudal obligations to heresy and the disciplinary powers of the church.

Jurists

At the same time that popes were looking to the law to support their assertions of sovereignty, at the end of the eleventh century, law caught the attention of a small group of scholars in Bologna whose lives were devoted to studying classical Roman texts. Their interest in jurisprudence was sparked by the reappearance of Justinian's Code, the Corpus Juris Civilis. After five hundred years of being out of circulation, a copy of the Digest turned up in northern Italy. Those who read it were impressed by the sophisticated legal arguments it contained, and in due course they began to make notes (glosses) and write commentaries on what it said.

Justinian's Code was a piece of writing unlike anything these scholars had seen. Finding an original copy of the Digest was like a long lost ancestor coming back from the dead. Because it was connected, by the coronation of Charlemagne and the Donation of Constantine, back to a time when Roman emperors still ruled the world, the newly discovered code was understood by those who studied it to be a body of law whose pedigree was perfect and whose legal authority was still intact.

As a practical matter, it was obvious that, in the pluralist legal world in which these scholars lived, the force of the Corpus Juris Civilis was not what it once had been. Their reality was a continent divided up among competing power centers – kings, popes, lords, and civic magistrates – who insisted on their independent sovereignty and the power to make their own laws. In the realpolitik of medieval Europe, the authority of the Holy Roman emperor to impose his will was, in contrast with those who first claimed the title, hemmed in on all sides.

It didn't take long for the scholars in Bologna to conclude that basic legal concepts like the *lex regia*, and the rules of property that were part of the Corpus Juris Civilis, had to be adapted to fit the multipolar world in which they lived. Law, as Bartolus de Sassoferrato (an outstanding fourteenth-century jurist) astutely observed, had to face the facts. Kings were insisting they had the same powers as the emperor in their own kingdoms, and where they had the military power to back it up, medieval jurists gave these claims their stamp of approval. All "princes," they said, could claim the benefit of the *lex regia*. Like the Romans of classical times, the French, German, English, and Spanish people were deemed to have delegated their lawmaking powers to their kings.

In such a world, where the sovereignty to enact and enforce rules and regulations that touched virtually every aspect of daily life was claimed by multiple rulers and church officials, law quickly became an important subject of scholarly study. For the first time since the Roman jurists, lots of people dedicated their lives to thinking about law. A man named Irnerius has traditionally been recognized as the first professor of Roman law; he taught at Bologna toward the end of the eleventh century. Within a generation, Irnerius and his colleagues would lay the foundations for what would become Europe's first university. By the end of the twelfth century, a select group of jurists in Bologna (two of the most famous being Azo [1150–1230] and Accursius [1182–1263]) had established themselves as preeminent scholars of the law. They attracted thousands of students of both civil and canon law from all over Europe. Thomas Beckett (1118–1170) was one of them. In the thirteenth century, more universities, including Paris and Oxford, established themselves as important centers of legal studies. By the middle of the century, a standard curriculum had been recognized in both Roman and church law.

Within a period of a hundred years, lawyers established themselves as an independent profession whose members were highly sought-after by monarchs and popes and independent city-states.[7] During the twelfth century, regents all over Europe came to see the advantages of maintaining their rule by law. Frederick Barbarossa (1122–1190), the great-grandson of Henry IV, was a big fan. He was an early patron of the law school in Bologna and among the first to appreciate the significance of Justinian's Corpus Juris Civilis.

The kings of Spain, France, and England were not far behind. They all brought lawyers to their courts and pursued a strategy of establishing their authority to render justice and maintain peace through a vigorous enforcement of the law. So did the Italian city-states. All of them conscripted lawyers to defend their assertions of sovereignty and counter the precepts of canon law on which the popes based their claims of supremacy.

As law replaced force as the primary method of solving disputes, the prestige of legal education grew exponentially. From the middle of the twelfth century until the end of the thirteenth every pope but one was trained in law. Most of the cardinals were lawyers. Indeed, by the end of the twelfth century, lawyers and jurists had become central players in the administration of both the church and state. They regained their authority as a professional and intellectual elite. As advisers, counselors, judges, and ambassadors, legal professionals dominated all three branches of government.

The impact of their collective effort was enormous. Some say it is hard to exaggerate their contribution in reviving the idea of the rule of law and laying the foundations for the role it plays in the modern world.[8] The social utility of their work has been compared to the discoveries of atomic scientists in the last hundred years. At their best, jurists took an unruly legal landscape and reordered it in ways that made it more coherent and just.

In the beginning, the jurists set out to adapt a legal code that had been designed for an empire that had collapsed seven hundred years earlier and to make it work in a totally different environment. The primary focus of the jurists in the twelfth and thirteenth centuries was to write glosses, comments, and critical analysis of the whole of Justinian's Corpus Juris Civilis so it could be applied in a world and to a set of cases it never imagined. Their aim was to eliminate the ambiguities and inconsistencies. They tried to reconcile and coordinate each of its parts in terms of its other provisions.

One of the central questions the jurists addressed was whether the sovereignty of European monarchs was absolute or conditional. Was it made on the understanding that "the people" could demand their sovereignty be returned to them if they were unhappy with how their king was exercising the authority he had been given?

They also debated what limits, if any, constrained the powers of the emperor and medieval kings. They asked such questions as: If a ruler was *legibus solutus*, like the Roman emperor, was he bound by his own laws?

Could he, for example, seize property of his vassals or break a contract? What about canon law or the traditional feudal laws that were beyond his control – what constraints did they impose?

In their quest to enhance the law's coherence and clarity, the jurists got a big break in the late twelfth and early thirteenth centuries, when many of Aristotle's works found their way back to Europe. The major route was through Spain, where his writing was passed on by Islamic scholars to their Catholic counterparts (known as "scholastics"), who then dedicated their lives to reconciling and integrating them with the established law and doctrines of the church. Using the classical techniques of dialectics (resolving differences by rational argument) to overcome apparent inconsistencies and contradictions, they worked out the common commandments of reason and their faith.

Aristotle's biggest fan in the Middle Ages was the Dominican priest Thomas Aquinas (1225–1274). Although he was a theologian and philosopher rather than a jurist, he put forward a theory of law that drew heavily on Aristotle; in fact, the connection was so close that some said Aquinas had baptized him. He also read Plato, Cicero, the Stoics, and Augustine, as well as Avicenna and Averroes, whom we met in the last chapter. With their writings in mind, Aquinas sat down and wrote what is considered to be one of the most powerful arguments for the idea of an unchanging, timeless, natural law ever constructed.[9]

Aquinas agreed with Aristotle that humans are naturally social beings and that there are eternal, universal laws that are appropriate for organizing how we live together. As a Christian he believed these laws were divinely inspired: the state and the rules that should govern it were part of God's grand design. As an Aristotelian, he thought they could be understood and followed by everyone as a guide to a full and virtuous life.

Aquinas believed humans were capable of understanding God's law in two ways: reason and revelation. Although a few great men received this higher law directly from God (e.g., Moses and Mohammad), for most of us it is by the force of reason that we learn the rules that spell out how to live a good life. According to Aquinas, the law that is naturally suited to the organization of human affairs is the law of right reason that is discoverable by every person exercising their natural powers of rational thinking. Beginning with the first and most fundamental principle of doing good and avoiding evil, humans can derive secondary rules – like the Golden Rule – that tell us how to behave at work, on the street, and at home.

Like Cicero and the Greeks, Aquinas thought of law as being both rational and moral in character. And like them, he viewed prudence and justice as two of the cardinal virtues of a proper human life. Given the natural sociability of humans, law must have as its purpose the well-being of those governed by its rules. Law places reason in the service of peace, harmony, and the common good. Reason identifies principles of law that are embedded in our (human) nature, and those principles provide an infallible guide of right and wrong.

In the sixteenth century, lots of jurists hitched their wagons to Aquinas and Aristotle and took the rule of law to a whole new level. Known as "the late Scholastics," the genius of these late-medieval jurists was to combine the best of both Roman law and Greek philosophy. They adopted Aristotle's theory of corrective justice to organize the law of interpersonal relations and provide a common foundation for all the rules of property, contract, tort, and unjust enrichment. In essence, they explained and refined the Roman classification of cases using the general principles and dialectical methods of the Greeks. In so doing, they brought a logic and structure to the practice of deciding cases that it had never had in the past.

In the course of reorienting and revising basic concepts and principles of Roman law, the jurists created a new, independent system of common law for the whole of Europe. Known as the *ius commune*, it fused Roman, cannon, and feudal law into a universal, supranational legal regime. It filled in gaps and omissions in the laws of kings, lords, merchants, and independent city-states and became a standard against which all other laws could be judged.

Like the *ius gentium* of Roman law, the *ius commune* offered solutions to cases in which the parties pointed to different laws (royal, feudal, church, municipal) to settle their disputes. It offered judges an independent basis on which to rule in such cases without having to choose the legal regime of one party over another. It served as a kind of peacemaker's law in cases that crossed territorial and legal borders.

Of course, medieval jurists had no illusions that the laws they devised for the settlement of disputes between monarchs and military rivals would be effective in all or even most cases. Indeed, at the same time that they were working out the scope and substance of the *ius commune*, jurists thought about when it was legitimate to go to war and how it should be conducted. And so, in addition to scripting a regime of international law to govern relations between people from different kingdoms in times of peace, they also developed doctrines on the legitimate use of armed force.

Drawing on the writings of Augustine, the Greek philosophers, and Cicero, medieval jurists derived a set of basic principles that justified the use of force in exceptional circumstances. Natural law – right reason – might require the use of force to enforce the law, defend oneself and others from attack, or protect property from being invaded or stolen.

Over the course of the Middle Ages, jurists and theologians settled on basic parameters that differentiated lawful from illegal wars. Their view, essentially, was that wars could only be fought for the purpose of enforcing legal rights and resisting evil. For a war to be just, a decision had to be taken by a ruler, with the requisite political authority, to right a wrong or punish a wrongdoer when there was no other way to defend the legal order. There was a principle of proportionality that required the good that would be done by going to war to outweigh the death and destruction it would cause. There were rules of conduct governing what was permissible in the course of doing battle, including prohibitions against the deliberate killing of civilians, the enslavement of prisoners, and the use of weapons of mass destruction (such as the crossbow). There were even rules imposing duties of fairness and moderation in fixing the terms of peace.

When they were analyzing the contours of a body of law like the rules of armed force or the *ius commune*, medieval legal scholars, like the jurists of Classical Rome and the *fuqaha* of Islamic law, were rarely of one mind. Although there was widespread agreement on the most general and basic principles of law, in the details and secondary rules there was lots of room for people to come to different conclusions. The prevailing spirit of the profession was that progress in legal science was enhanced by the encouragement of opposing points of view

On occasion, a whole generation of scholars might develop a completely new way of thinking about the law. In the fifteenth century, for example, a group known as the "humanists" turned their backs on the "glossators" and "commentators" and their mission of adapting the Corpus Juris Civilis to suit the circumstances of the medieval era. The humanists rejected such reinterpretations on the ground they gave the law a meaning that those who wrote it never intended. They insisted jurists were obliged to remain faithful to the way the law was understood when it was first written. Their approach still appeals to many modern legal scholars, including a majority of the judges who currently sit on the United States Supreme Court. Today they are known as "originalists."

Regardless of the period in which they wrote or the method of analysis they employed, there was a natural orientation among all jurists to ground their lectures and treatises in actual cases. Alongside their commitment to universal principles of justice and reason, they were pragmatists and casuists at heart.[10] Their first concern was to provide solutions to the ordinary conflicts of everyday living. They used their expertise to figure out what the legal rights and wrongs were when, for example, smoke from a person's fireplace billowed into the apartment above; or when a consumer paid a price that was more than what the goods were worth; or when a landowner built a mill on his property that interfered with the flow of water to a mill downstream.

In searching for solutions to such ordinary (one could say "run-of-the-mill") disputes that disrupted the peace and harmony of medieval Europe, the jurists expected that the universal principles of natural law would be applied flexibly to take account of the circumstances of each case. Their principles allowed for lots of exceptions; it all depended on the facts. Even rules as basic as keeping a promise or respecting the property of others might have to give way if enforcing it would result in an even greater injustice.

Combining the logic of Aristotle and the casuistry of the Roman jurists led them to conclude that promises that were induced by fraud or force or based on a mistake or made with a person suffering a disability were not binding. Nor would a person be held liable for taking another person's property (like a loaf of bread) if he needed it to survive. An example they liked to cite from Cicero was a promise to return a sword to its owner, who wanted it back so he could kill an innocent person. Everyone was agreed: once the owner's motives were known, this was a promise that had to be broken.

Facts also determined the outcome of the cases in which the activities of property owners adversely affected the well-being of their neighbors. In the case of smoke from a person's fireplace polluting the apartment upstairs, it mattered to the medieval jurists if the fumes came from a hearth that heated a home rather than from an oven that was in the business of making cheese. For Bartolus de Sassoferrato, the rights and wrongs in the two cases differed because of the amount of the smoke involved and the function of the fire that produced it. In the case of mill owners fighting over a common water resource, jurists (including Bartolus) generally thought the first person to build should be protected against latecomers, but for some, the results might be different if the second mill was built on the property where the source of the water was located.

Law's Renaissance

By proposing solutions, based on the force of reason, in thousands of cases from across Europe, the jurists gradually brought the rule of law back to life. Disputes were settled in ways that were expected to promote the well-being of the community and affirm the sovereignty of the law. By the time the medieval period came to a close, law had regained much of the moral and legal authority that it had when Athens was establishing itself as the world's first rule of law state.

The impulse to look out for the welfare of the weakest and most vulnerable members of their communities was a cast of mind most jurists shared. They wove broad principles of equity throughout the jurisprudence they wrote. Canon lawyers developed specific rules for taxing income (tithes) that were aimed at providing relief for the poor. Civil lawyers expanded the law of the marketplace to protect consumers against exploitative practices and the unethical manipulation of prices. Some jurists challenged the legality of slavery. Others, including the Spanish philosopher and jurist Francisco de Vitoria, disputed the legality of forcible conversion and the subjugation of Indigenous tribes in the Americas to European rule.

Inspired by the ideals of Classical Greece, jurists looked for ways to inject rationality and fairness into the legal process. In Classical Rome, we saw that due process for those opposing the will of the emperor was not a high priority for the jurists. But it was for their medieval descendants; due process was an important focus of their work and one of the most enduring parts of their legacy.

Indeed, medieval jurists were the first to formulate some of the most basic precepts of our modern criminal justice system. Canon lawyers led the way. They pushed for a presumption of innocence when a person was accused of violating the law. They introduced the notion of mens rea – that criminal intent was an essential component of a criminal act. They insisted everyone was entitled to a fair trial, restricted the circumstances in which torture might be used, and (early in the thirteenth century) effectively put an end to the barbaric and irrational practice of deciding cases based on how a person responded to an assortment of physical ordeals.

In the procedures they constructed for the conduct of trials, judges were expected to interrogate witnesses according to principles of reason and rational proof. Rules of relevance were introduced to exclude prejudicial facts that did not bear directly on the guilt or innocence of an accused. In his investigation of the facts of a case, the judge was supposed to put himself in the position of the parties who were before the court. It was an overarching principle of canon law that judges and others charged with the interpretation and enforcement of the law should always maintain a fair equilibrium between the parties.

In addition to raising the profile of law, both in the courtroom and on the battlefield, medieval jurists discussed ways in which its authority permeated the palaces of princes and popes.[11] Here again, the jurisprudence medieval scholars wrote on the supremacy of law was more nuanced and balanced than the rules and doctrines, like the *lex regia* and *princeps legibus solutus*, that were the brainchild of their Roman ancestors.

In ways that would have been unimaginable to Roman jurists, both canon and civilian lawyers thought of law as a limit on a ruler's authority to act arbitrarily. To be considered a valid law, a ruler's command had to serve the common good. Medieval jurists thought of law as protecting individuals and communities from the autocratic rule of the despot. For them, the difference between a legitimate sovereign and a tyrant was that the first respected the law, the second didn't.

The distinction was fundamental for Aquinas. He taught that a community's rules had the quality of law only if they conformed to right reason. Laws contrary to reason were unjust and unjust laws were not really laws at all. As a practical matter, he argued that laws were unjust if they (1) failed to enhance the common prosperity of the community; (2) exceeded the powers of the ruler; or (3) distributed the burdens necessary to enhance the general welfare unfairly.

In addition to the constraints of natural law, jurists argued that medieval rulers were bound by the strictures of divine (canon) law, customary (feudal) law, and the *ius commune*. Like natural law, they were beyond the ruler's jurisdiction. They also said the prince was bound by his own laws until he amended them in the proper fashion. In their opinion, rulers could not tear up a contract they had signed or unilaterally seize the property of their subjects.

The logic of their position – that the prince was bound by the law – led some jurists (including Aquinas) to the conclusion that subjects/citizens had no duty to obey the "laws" of a tyrant. They recognized the rights of resistance and civil disobedience and described laws that couldn't meet the tests of justice and reason as acts of violence – no different than victor's justice or the raw use of force. In the sixteenth century, advocates for French Protestants (Huguenots) known as Monarchomachs wrote tracts defending the right of persecuted minorities to depose and even kill a king who abused his powers and acted outside the law.

Justice Betrayed

By any measure, the jurisprudence the jurists wrote over the course of the medieval era is impressive. Combining their mastery of Greek philosophy and Roman law, the jurists of medieval Europe explained how law's moral and legal authority could be revived. Law was pledged to serve the highest ideals of Aristotelian justice and its sovereignty was stretched to include the deliberations of rulers in addition to those they ruled.

Like the accomplishments of so many of law's heroes, however, the achievements of the medieval jurists look better on paper than in the hurly-burly of real life. The hard reality was that, despite their best intentions, medieval Europe was a place run by a few very powerful and violent men and, in the event, lots of innocent people got crushed. Advocates for the rule of law were no match against the power of a willful monarch.

For the greater part of the medieval period, political and religious conflicts were settled on the basis of military prowess rather than on principles of rationality and justice. Together, emperors, kings, dukes, and knights created a world of extreme cruelty and violence characterized by mass killing, rape, pillage, and wanton destruction. In the eleventh and twelfth centuries, physical force was still the primary means of attaining and maintaining power. Armies of paid mercenaries were hired to wage war. Force – the power to command and coerce – was the most important metric according to which members of the nobility were ranked.

In 1066, William, Duke of Normandy, conquered England and crowned himself king, and in a little over a century – between 1096 and 1204 – the Catholic Church launched three massive crusades against the followers of Islam and one against their Greek Orthodox rivals. On 20 August 1191 – during the Third Crusade – Richard the Lionheart, William the Conqueror's great-great-grandson and the golden boy of medieval chivalry, took a page from Charlemagne's book and executed more than twenty-five hundred Muslim prisoners in front of their families outside the city of Acre.

And the bloodshed never really stopped. Although the thirteenth century is commonly portrayed as a more peaceful time (there were no major wars between 1214 and 1296), the pope was still able to mobilize two more crusades against the Muslims and another against the Albigensian (Cathar) heretics in the South of France. Politics inevitably heated up again, and the fourteenth and fifteenth centuries were plagued by armed conflict, social disorder, and wars between political rivals. The 115 years between 1337 and 1453 were dominated by a prolonged struggle (known as the Hundred Years' War) between the Valois and Plantagenet families over who would rule over the French. Prompted by Luther and the Protestant Reformation, religious wars tore Europe apart for the better part of the sixteenth and seventeenth centuries.[12] If that weren't enough, when they weren't fighting each other, one or other of the European powers was doing battle with Islam and the Ottomans.

Every country felt the effects of these conflicts. Northern Italy during this period has been described as a morass of alliances, wars, and intrigues between various city-states, a place where lawlessness was a constant fact of life and armed mercenaries paid heed to the law only when it advanced their purposes. France was racked by thirty years of religious war at the end of the sixteenth century. In 1572, Catholics slaughtered ten thousand Huguenots in what is known as the St. Bartholomew's Day Massacre. In Spain, Ferdinand (1452–1516) and Isabella (1451–1504) joined forces with the pope to set up the Inquisition and force Jews to convert or leave the country. Run for the most part by church lawyers, these courts held that anyone suspected of not being a true Christian could be tortured and burned at the stake. Germany's turn to succumb to sectarian violence came during the first thirty years of the seventeenth century. At the same time, Protestants in the Netherlands needed eighty years to fight for their independence from Spanish (Catholic) rule.

In response to years of political unrest and sectarian strife, authoritarian monarchs who ruled their kingdoms like the emperor in Rome came to dominate the political landscape. The sixteenth century saw the dawn of an era of "absolute" monarchs. Henry VIII of England, Francis I of France, and Charles V of Spain (who was also the Holy Roman emperor) dominated their kingdoms almost as much as Caesar Augustus did Rome. All of them claimed a "divine right" to rule and a space in which they were not bound by the law. Sadly, when push came to shove, they usually got their way; the king's wish, when it was strongly held, was the subject's command. On one occasion, this even resulted in the emperor (Charles V) imprisoning the pope.

To justify their assertions of absolute authority, kings and queens surrounded themselves with jurists and lawyers who were paid to provide them with the legal advice they wanted to hear. In the monarchs' power struggles with the church, civilian lawyers were recruited as hired guns. At the same time that canon lawyers were developing legal arguments in favor of the universal authority of the pope, a long list of medieval Europe's most famous jurists were defending the lawmaking powers of emperors and kings.

Irnerius, the father of law teaching, made his home at the court of Emperor Henry IV. Two of his students, Bulgarus and Martinus, advised Frederick Barbarossa on the strength of his claim that, as Holy Roman emperor, he was Europe's supreme ruler, with precedence over all other princes. Bartolus de Sassoferrato (1313–1357) and Baldus de Ubaldis (1327–1408), who were among law's staunchest defenders, recognized a sovereign's right to dispense with due process whenever he said he had acted out of "certain knowledge." French jurists were notorious for using every legal subterfuge available to defend the idea that the French monarch was the absolute ruler of the territories he controlled. The legal system they devised has been described as "an invincible agency of despotism." Even canon lawyers had a vested interest in supporting a top-down approach to the law that gave legitimacy to claims of a "divine right of kings."

Like Plato and Aristotle, medieval jurists gave a real-world account of the law alongside their advocacy of the ideal. At the same time they were defending the supremacy and integrity of the law, they were creating doctrines and devices that could be used by their patrons to get around it. Among other claims, they said a prince's will was law whenever he claimed to be acting for the general welfare of the community or when he insisted it was "necessary" to act in a certain way. According to one school of thought (which found favor in Canada five hundred years later), a ruler could do whatever he wanted so long as he said he was acting "notwithstanding the law." To compound their complicity, the jurists also reworked the Roman law of "lèse-majesté" to provide sweeping grounds on which anyone not prepared to play by the king's rules might be convicted of treason and then flogged, flayed, and drawn and quartered before eventually being put to death.

To top it off, all of them, including Aquinas, were agreed that even if a ruler broke the law, not much could be done about it. No one had the temerity to write a narrative in which rulers could be taken to court. Except for citizens of the cities in northern Italy, who could prosecute the chief magistrate (podesta) when he failed to respect the law (in a process known as "syndication"), victims of rulers who acted illegally could only defend themselves by physical force. Resistance was their only recourse.

Unlike the Athenians, there were no legal remedies for medieval Europeans to pursue, no official procedures by which a ruler's unlawful acts could be challenged. The best they could do was write "advice books" (generically known as "mirrors for princes") about the moral virtues of exemplary rulers and their responsibility for ensuring the flourishing and justness of their realms. Machiavelli's *The Prince* is the best-known work of this tradition.

The partiality of the legal professionals toward those whom they served is also reflected in the jurisprudence they wrote on questions of public law, including their treatises on criminal justice and the rules of war. As a practical matter, most people who were accused of violating the law were in for a rough ride.

Despite the jurists' commitment to the Aristotelian ideals of justice and reason, on the logic they followed, a fair trial still allowed for torturing the accused. In their minds, the purpose of due process was to ensure that innocent people were not wrongly convicted, and the torture of suspects was carried out to make sure that didn't happen. Extracting confessions meant that only those who admitted their guilt would be punished. Although jurists were generally cautious in spelling out the circumstances when torture could be used (nobles, professors, and pregnant women were exempted), due process meant little for Cathars who lived in southern France in the thirteenth century or to Muslims and Jews in fifteenth-century Spain. An accusation of heresy raised a presumption of guilt and a very high probability of being tortured and eventually killed.

A conviction of any serious crime made matters worse. It set off a chain of events in which the dignity of the offender was targeted. Public spectacles involving gruesome pain and death in front of thousands of spectators were acted out as rituals of repentance and celebrated as the most effective way of deterring antisocial behavior.[13]

From the twelfth century through to the sixteenth, there was a dramatic increase in the severity and spectacularity of criminal punishment. Depending on the offence, a person might be burned (heretics and homosexuals), boiled (counterfeiters), branded (thieves), beheaded (nobility), even buried alive (women). And, in many cases, spectators could be treated to a series of warm-up acts in which the convicted person might be flogged, flayed, mutilated, and dismembered before he was put to death. Even those who were convicted of noncapital crimes might have their hands or feet chopped off, their eyes gouged out, their tongues bored, or their face branded. Just for begging, a person could be pilloried and whipped.

As with the medieval conception of due process, so, too, with its laws of war.[14] The gap between theory and practice was huge. In the course of pursuing their holy wars, Christian armies were capable of horrific atrocities. With the blessings of popes, crusaders engaged in orgies of violence, including the wholesale slaughter of innocent women and children. First it was Muslims and Jews, who felt the fury of the crusaders' faith when they captured Jerusalem in 1099; a hundred years later, between fifteen and twenty thousand Cathars were wiped out in the town of Béziers.

At the same time the jurists declared wars of aggression to be unlawful and unjust, they assured the popes that their crusades against infidels and heretics were legal. Under their watch, Christianity was transformed from a pacifist faith, in which adherents were told to love their neighbors and turn the other cheek, into a "warrior religion" used to defend occupied territory thousands of miles from home. An order of monks, known as the Templars, whose members took an oath to defend the faith with the sword alongside a vow of chastity, served as the pope's personal militia.

Many of the rules of engagement the jurists recognized were very one-sided and tolerant of behaviors that even on their own standards were transparently unjust. The prohibition against weapons of mass destruction (the crossbow), for example, did not apply in wars against infidels. Similarly, as the atrocities in Jerusalem and Béziers attest, the way they interpreted the prohibition against killing civilians left most of them at risk. Even de Vitoria, the champion of Indigenous Peoples, thought the laws of war allowed European nations to attack if they were denied their rights to proselytize and trade. Most shocking of all, Aquinas, the author of the most powerful analysis of natural law ever written, defended the enslavement of a defeated enemy (including women and children) not just as a necessary evil (which was the position Aristotle took), but as a just practice in which the lives of the conquered were spared and the victor secured the services of the defeated population.

At the end of the day, in spite of the sophisticated jurisprudence they wrote, the license rulers derived from the law to exert their will was practically unrestricted. The fact is, beginning in the thirteenth century, at the height of the age of chivalry, medieval Europe launched a five-hundred-year-long campaign of violence and repression against every conceivable minority group who might be considered an enemy of the state. Discrimination against heretics, Jews, homosexuals, women, witches, and lepers was intensified and sanctified in law.

Women in particular did not do well by medieval law. Medieval Europe was intensely patriarchal.[15] As in Athens, Rome, and Baghdad, women on the Continent were treated like children. Women knew their place, which didn't include being a lawyer or a priest. Medieval law did not recognize their capacity to enter contracts or terminate bad marriages. Those who stepped out of line could be chastised (beaten) by their husbands for domestic faults and killed if they committed adultery. Starting in the second half of the fifteenth century, thousands who were found to be witches (often after being tortured) were burned at the stake.

Religious minorities suffered even more. Jews were singled out for the worst abuse. Systematic discrimination against Jews became part of European culture after the Roman Empire embraced Christianity as the state religion.[16] As we saw at the beginning of this chapter, in the seventh century the Visigoths legalized antisemitism in their law codes. In the middle of the eleventh century, Europe experienced a wave of Judophobia and thousands were senselessly slaughtered by the crusaders on their way to do battle with the Muslims.

By the thirteenth century, most Jews were treated as outcasts, like lepers. Canon law decreed they couldn't marry, eat with, or frequent the same public baths as Christians. In 1215, the same Lateran Council that permitted the use of crossbows against non-Christians forced Jews to wear yellow labels as an emblem of their pariah status. At end of the thirteenth century, they were expelled from England and France. In the fourteenth, they were blamed for the Plague, attacked by mobs, and burned at the stake. In the fifteenth, those living in Spain were forced to convert and eventually expelled once again. In the sixteenth, Pope

Paul IV cut the Jewish population in Rome by half and then rounded up the rest into ghettos, restricted their freedom to trade except in food and secondhand clothing, compelled them to speak Latin or Italian, and forced them to wear yellow hats.

As allies of and advisers to such repressive regimes, it comes as no surprise that by the end of the medieval period (indeed long before), legal professionals were viewed by ordinary people with suspicion, distrust, and active hostility. They were accused of hypocrisy, dishonesty, and lining their own pockets. It was said that students who went to Bologna to learn the law were instructed in the art of duplicity and how to get rich. When the butcher in Shakespeare's *Henry VI, Part 2*, called out to "kill all the lawyers," he was expressing a feeling that many in the audience would have shared.

The wariness and mistrust that ordinary people had for lawyers and the law was exacerbated by its inaccessibility and incomprehensibility. The dialectical methods the jurists employed were complex and confusing and took years of professional training to master. In its mode of analysis, medieval law was more like Roman and Islamic law than the populist version of the Babylonians and the Greeks. Rather than being part of a general education, as Cicero had advocated, law took years to master and became the exclusive property and private monopoly of paid professionals.

When we compare the impact of the medieval jurists and their Roman predecessors on the rule of law, we discover many differences. The role that faith played in the development and enforcement of the law was no doubt the most significant. But there were also similarities. Overall, jurists in both eras were capable of making great strides in advancing the sovereignty and integrity of law while simultaneously acting in ways that compromised its authority and reputation. On balance, it seems fair to say that, notwithstanding all of the injustice and oppression it sanctioned, the rule of law was still moving in the right direction. It is no coincidence that, not long after law's intellectual flowering in the capitals of Europe, a renaissance in the arts and science would follow.

The generally positive path of law's development in medieval Europe was more or less the same throughout the western and central parts of the continent. This was very much a transnational experience. No country set up a legal system that was radically different from the others. There was, however, one nation that marched to a different drummer in its search for the promised land that warrants our attention before we leave the medieval period for the modern era. English legal history includes some moments of such high drama that our portrait of the rule of law in the Middle Ages would be distorted if we didn't pause to sketch them in.

Chapter Six

London

After Rome

The first five hundred years of English political history after the fall of Rome were pretty similar to what happened on the Continent.[1] If anything, the deterioration and collapse of legal order after the Romans left was even more precipitous and pervasive. Over the course of the fifth century, cities and government virtually disappeared. Strongmen came to dominate tribal communities and micro kingdoms emerged that fought each other over land and other resources, including humans. In the early post-Roman years, the country was also subject to raiding parties and the incursions of German tribes (mainly Angles and Saxons) and in the ninth and tenth centuries to full-blown invasions (and ultimately conquest) by the Danes. This was the world of King Arthur and the Knights of the Round Table. It was a time and place where life for just about everybody was, as Thomas Hobbes would describe it five hundred years later, "nasty, brutish, and short."

The Germans brought with them their ways of organizing their communities and their ideas about law. Kings were chosen by the most powerful military leaders in a region and were only able to change the traditional ways of doing things with their approval. Like their cousins on the Continent, by the seventh century English kings were setting their laws down in written legal codes that were intended to bind the ruler and the ruled alike. By the end of the seventh century, England had been carved up into four rival Anglo-Saxon kingdoms: Northumbria, Mercia, Wessex, and East Anglia.

Like early monarchies all over Europe, Anglo-Saxon government was at first mostly about resolving conflicts and settling disputes, doing justice and keeping the peace. It was conducted in local assemblies (moots) made up of free men in the village or county (shire). Slaves and serfs were not invited. In effect, conflicts were settled and judgments were rendered by a person's neighbors. As in Greece, ordinary people were expected to understand and be able to enforce the traditional (customary) rules of their communities. Unlike Roman, sharia, and canon law, early English law had no use for experts or professionals.

English kings knew about and generally admired the way Charlemagne exercised his feudal authority and thought about the law. In the tenth century, they began to make more use of their powers to issue charters and proclamations that applied throughout their realms and to call for meetings of the richest and most influential of their subjects to discuss and approve them. To cement their alliances, they granted vast estates and titles to their favorites, which included giving them the authority ("jurisdiction") to set up their own courts to enforce the feudal obligations of their serfs and to punish those who misbehaved. Knights and nobles – beneficiaries of the king's largesse – were also expected to make sure royal laws were enforced and the "king's peace" maintained.

English kings also followed the Carolingian practice of generally respecting the customary laws and procedures of local communities. By the tenth century, a political structure that organized villages and the surrounding countryside into shires (counties) and smaller administrative units called hundreds (representing a territory capable of supporting a hundred families) was in place.[2] At both levels, courts were established in which decisions were made by the local freemen.

The primary purpose of these people's courts was to ensure conflicts were settled peacefully. The goal was to deflect the instinct for revenge and retaliation and put an end to the carnage of blood feuds. The hundred courts dealt with cases of petty theft and common assault as well as neighborly disputes, such as who had the best claim to a piece of property or who should be held responsible for the flooding of a common field. The shire courts handled bigger cases and more serious crimes. These courts were also the places where new royal laws would be read to the local populations by the king's officials.

Like their cousins on the Continent, these local assemblies thought of themselves as dispensing divine justice, which called for some very unscientific procedures; indeed, they were capable of inflicting the most barbaric punishments imaginable. To the modern eye, their mode of operation was perverse. The way they worked, proof came after, not before, the judgment. Judgments determined who had the burden of proof and what form the proof had to take. Oaths and ordeals were the primary ways guilt and innocence were established, and something as minor as a conviction of petty theft could result in a public execution. Compared to Roman law, early English law was pretty crude.

Compared to the rest of Europe, however, by the start of the new millennium England was doing as well as anyone – in fact better than most. Alfred the Great (849–899) and his West Saxon (Wessex) descendants had unified the country and carried on the values and traditions of the Carolingian Empire long after they had died on the Continent. Starting with Alfred's Doom Book, law codes became an important part of early English government. In addition to reaffirming the traditional system of fines and compensation (wergild and bot) for almost every injury and wound imaginable, these codes had a strong moralizing and reformist character. Alfred's Doom Book set the standard by highlighting numerous principles of Jewish law, including the Ten Commandments, before itemizing his own laws and those of his Anglo-Saxon ancestors.

In declaring their codes to be the law of the land, English kings ruled with the counsel and consent of the richest and most powerful men in the realm. Although assemblies were characteristic of the way German tribes governed themselves from the beginning, under the reign of Alfred's grandson Athelstan (924–939) they became a more prominent feature of the way English kings managed their kingdoms. From this time on, in formulating new laws and enforcing the old, these gatherings took the title of "the witan [wise men] of the English people." Although, to the modern eye, this looks like a bunch strongmen imposing their will, these meetings are seen by historians as laying the foundation for what would become the English Parliament at Westminster. By the beginning of the eleventh century, the witan had become powerful enough to insist that Alfred's great-great-grandson, Athelred, meet its demands before it would recognize him as king.

Over the course of the five hundred years after the Romans left Britain, England experienced a gradual recovery, such that by the tenth century it had become one of the wealthier and better-governed kingdoms in Europe. Royal, feudal, church, and customary law worked (more or less) in tandem and assemblies of national and local elites were instrumental in the enactment and enforcement of each. Together they created a legal system that enlisted the cooperation of the freemen in the country and that, with all its rough edges, more or less kept the peace. As a result, in 1066, when the English king died without any natural heirs, it was seen by various contenders, including William, Duke of Normandy, to be a prize worth fighting for.

The Common Law [3]

The date 14 October 1066 stands out in British political history. On that day, in the Battle of Hastings, William defeated Harold Godwinson, who had been elected king nine months earlier by the witan after the previous monarch, Edward the Confessor, died without any successors. The event marked the end of the Saxon era of English history and the beginning of Norman rule.[4] It has been described as the single greatest political change England ever experienced. The Anglo-Saxons lost their land and were forced to work for their Norman conquerors. One of the first jobs they were given was embroidering what has come to be known as the Bayeux Tapestry, a seventy-meter-long piece of Norman propaganda meant to justify the invasion. (The original is still intact and on public display in Bayeux, in Normandy.) Overnight, they went from being rulers to being ruled.

The date also marks a watershed in English legal history. William the Conqueror became king of England at roughly the same time that Pope Gregory VII was doing battle on the Continent with Henry IV, the German emperor, over who would have control of the church. As we read in the last chapter, that struggle was carried on by both sides enlisting legal experts to advance their cause.

When William the Conqueror claimed the English throne, the revival of legal studies that would blossom in Bologna in the first half of the twelfth century was still two generations in the future. When he set about pacifying his new kingdom, none of the commentaries and treatises the jurists would later write were available. He had to make do with the legal order his Anglo-Saxon predecessors had left behind, and for the most part that is what he did. At his coronation, he confirmed the validity of the laws of Edward the Confessor and embraced the system of shire and hundred courts to enforce the feudal laws of the local communities.

William made the shire and hundred courts part of his administration and used them to enhance the legitimacy of his rule. Royal officials (sheriffs) were appointed to watch over and report on the courts' work. To reinforce his control, he separated them from church courts and excluded clerics from any involvement in their deliberations. By the time the jurists on the Continent were pouring new life into the Corpus Juris Civilis and Gratian was producing the *Decretum* (ca. 1140), William's descendants were busy melding the ancient codes and the local laws of the shire and hundred courts into what would become a common law for the whole country.

The most important person in the early development of what has come to be known as English common law was William's great-grandson, Henry II (1133–1189).[5] Henry succeeded to the throne in 1154 after the country had experienced fifteen years of a very nasty civil war between his family and that of Stephen of Blois, whose mother (Adela) was William the Conqueror's daughter. Known as "the Anarchy," this period was marked by an almost complete breakdown of law and order. Basically, anyone who could built a castle and terrorized the people in the neighborhood. Not surprisingly, when the fighting stopped there were lots of disputes and hard feelings between those who sided with Henry and ended up with the castles and those who backed Stephen and were dispossessed.

There were courts in which such conflicts could be settled. In fact, as was the case in medieval Europe, there were lots of them. In addition to the shire and hundred courts, there were manor (feudal) courts, borough (urban) courts, and ecclesiastical courts where litigants could plead their cases. Standing above all of them was the king's personal court: the *curia regis.*

The problem wasn't the availability of courts – it was that they all suffered serious limitations. Critically, all still used methods to establish guilt and innocence that were based on divine intervention, and the conclusions they reached were, as often as not, arbitrary and unjust. Most decisions were made without any consideration of what had or hadn't actually happened. Typically, the outcome was determined by supernatural forces (oaths and ordeals) or physical combat (trial by battle). In addition, partiality and bias always loomed in the background, especially in feudal courts, which were part of a lord's private domain.

The reality was that the legal system Henry inherited was broken. Irrational, biased, and overly formalistic, it could be fundamentally unfair. Henry's response was a series of reforms that built on the existing system as much as possible and moved forward incrementally. Instead of attempting a wholesale change in the rules, his goal was to centralize, rationalize, and professionalize what was already in place. His strategy was to create a set of alternative procedures (writs) by which the conflicts between and among his and Stephen's supporters could be resolved. His method was more like that of the Roman praetor than Caesar Augustus.

Henry produced little new legislation; he never drafted a comprehensive code like Justinian. Instead, he tried to attract litigants to his courts by offering to solve their conflicts faster, more fairly, and with less regard for formalities. Because land was a major source of conflict, many of the new procedures were tailored to resolve disputes over rights of ownership and possession. Others dealt with antisocial behavior. His hope was that offering better ways to settle everyday conflicts would bring peace to his kingdom, enhance the scope and legitimacy of his own sovereignty, and make him lots of money (from court fees and fines) along the way.

Henry's reforms were distinctive in the way they coordinated the roles of judge and jury. His system was simultaneously more populist and more professional than anything that had been attempted before.

It made more use of local juries to find out what actually happened in a case and it enlisted a small number of his councillors (typically those who had been involved in the development of the new procedures) to help the local courts do their job. His initiatives were so successful that within 150 years (roughly 1150–1300) the English system of common law, which combined the expertise of a learned group of judges with the local knowledge of popular juries, was flourishing.

Juries reinforced the legitimacy of the law by acknowledging a measure of sovereignty in local communities. In rendering judgment, the operation of the law was in the hands of the people whose lives it controlled. In the course of his reign, Henry created more opportunities in which inquests and juries could be used to make findings of fact and determine whether a law had been broken and a charge should be laid. By the time of his great-grandson (Edward I, 1272–1307), juries had replaced oaths, ordeals, and trials by battle when it came to determining what the outcome of a case would be.

Many factors contributed to the central role juries came to play in the operation of the common law. In addition to their obvious attraction as a more rational way of making findings of fact and distinguishing right from wrong, juries got a big boost in 1215 when Pope Innocent III outlawed ordeals at the Fourth Lateran Council. The inevitable triumph of the jury over the traditional alternatives of fighting and fate came when litigants who were reluctant to face a judgment of their peers were told they would be crushed to death (*peine forte et dure*) if they didn't.

The rise of the judiciary as experts in the law followed naturally once the decision was made to integrate juries into the proceedings opened up by the new writs. As critical as the jury was to the integrity of the system, there was never any thought it could do the job on its own. Local juries needed instruction in the methods and procedures of the new writs, and so Henry sent his officials to guide them in their deliberations.

Within the lifetime of his grandson (Henry III, 1207–1272), itinerant justices who crisscrossed the kingdom on "eyres" and "assizes," and full-time judges who ran the royal courts at Westminster, were keeping records (plea rolls) of their decisions and writing texts on what the collective output of their rulings meant. The first big books on the English legal system were written by judges: Glanvil's *Treatise on English Law* (ca. 1188) and Bracton's *On the Laws and Customs Of England* (ca. 1250). Law reports cataloging the leading cases, known as Year Books, and abridgements grouping them by subject, followed shortly after.

In making judges the center of gravity of the legal system, the English took a different path from those followed by the Romans and the Greeks. Whereas in Athens and Rome, judges were people who had no special expertise in the law, English judges were professionals. Judges became custodians of the law rather than (as in Rome) the jurists or (as in Greece) the people. This meant that the basic principles of English law were debated in court rather than in lecture halls and private studios, as they were on the Continent.

The way English judges thought about the law was quite unlike how continental jurists went about their work. Jurists on the Continent, it will be recalled, spent their time figuring out how to adapt a code designed for a world that had ceased to exist to the cities and towns in which they lived. It was all about interpretation and figuring out the meaning of words that were embedded in an ancient, iconic text.

English judges, by contrast, worked out the basic rules of English common law, as they searched for solutions to the disputes they were empowered to resolve, by rummaging through the decisions of their predecessors on the bench. Their instinct was to focus on past practice. Before they came to any conclusion, they wanted to know how judges had thought about the law in the past. Rather than look for answers in the words of a code, common law judges assumed the relevant legal principles would be found in prior cases.

Henry de Bracton (1210–1268), who has been celebrated as "the crown and flower of English medieval jurisprudence," exemplified the difference. Although he was familiar with Roman law and included lots of citations to Azo when he was discussing issues that had not been the subject of litigation in English courts, what is most original in his approach is his reference to and reliance on the rulings of his fellow judges. His focus was on finding out how the judges who proceeded him on the bench thought about the sorts of cases that he and his colleagues were being asked to decide. Working from plea rolls going back a generation, Bracton drew on more than five hundred cases in describing the English legal landscape. In the course of writing his treatise, he compiled a notebook with references to more than two thousand of his colleagues' decisions.

In his discussion of these decisions, Bracton's attitude was pragmatic, flexible, and modest. Implicitly, in the way he writes about the decisions he collected, there is a recognition of the value of consistency in how judges approach the cases they are asked to decide. Impartiality requires that similar cases be resolved according to the same set of rules.

However, there is in Bracton's treatise no sense that cases represent binding precedents; earlier decisions had no inherent governing authority on their own. The principle of stare decisis, which would become a hallmark of British jurisprudence, was still hundreds of years in the future. Instead, in a casuistic style that resembles the way Hammurabi and the Romans codified their law, Bracton highlighted the decisions he thought demonstrated legal reasoning at its best. His heroes were two judges, Pateschull and (his student) Raleigh, who in turn was Bracton's mentor. He despaired about the legal knowledge of some of his contemporaries and the conventional wisdom is that his book was written to tell them how they could do their jobs better.

Bracton was the first to promote a case-based approach to the development of the law, but he was not alone in favoring a flexible and pragmatic way of thinking. From the beginning, it seems to have been the practice of royal justices to overcome rigidities and technicalities in the law whenever justice and equity required it. William Bereford, who was chief justice of the Court of Common Pleas from 1309 until 1326 and who was considered one of the leading jurists in the fourteenth century, was especially inclined to approach earlier cases with an open mind. A strong believer in the new methods of making findings of fact, he was prepared to order parties to accept a jury verdict even when the law allowed the litigants to proceed by swearing oaths or choosing trial by battle. For Bereford, as for Bracton, in appropriate cases, truth and justice trumped tradition.

When Henry II died in 1189 he left behind the foundations of a common law of property and crime that, while far from perfect, had much that could be said in its favor. Although it catered to the needs of the gentry and large landowners, and could render verdicts that were arbitrary, unjust, and extremely harsh, it greatly expanded the number of conflicts and disputes that could be settled peacefully and more or less impartially in the courts. It also provided procedures by which officials who were corrupt or abused their powers could be held to account. And, in expanding the role of local juries doing justice and keeping the peace in their communities, it strengthened the popular foundations of English law and its nascent political institutions.

By the time his great-grandson (Edward I) died in 1307, this judge-made law had evolved to become the constitutional order of the kingdom. Property and criminal law not only provided the rules on which disputes between neighbors would be settled, it spoke to the rights and obligations of the king and his subjects as well. Instead of the rules (like the *lex regia*) governing the distribution of power being entrenched in a basic code (like the Corpus Juris Civilis), the rights and the duties of the king and his vassals were settled in judgments about property claims and disorderly behavior. When they chose to govern by adjudication rather than legislation, Henry and his descendants bequeathed to the country a judge-made ("unwritten") constitution the likes of which had never been seen before or since.

English government is still exceptional in never having had a defining moment when a basic law comes into force and a new constitutional order is born. In England, constitutional principles emerged over time from inductions and generalizations that judges drew from the decisions of their forefathers. From its inception, the English constitution was embedded in the ordinary, common law rules of the kingdom. There was no separation of constitutional and private law. Property and criminal law were both. As one of the country's most famous legal scholars (A.V. Dicey) once explained, the English constitution is not the source but the consequence of the rights of individual Englishmen as defined by the courts. England's constitution is the product of judicial rulings rather than serving as their premise.

Magna Carta (1215)

Henry II was succeeded first by his son Richard the Lionheart (r. 1189–1199), who we met in the last chapter slaughtering Muslims in the Crusades, and then, when Richard was killed fighting the French, by his youngest (legitimate) son John (r. 1199–1216), who is known in popular history as the villain in the legend of Robin Hood. John's Hollywood persona – that of a rapist, murderer, and thief – is more or less the picture that is painted of "bad King John" by professional historians. Although he is given credit as an able administrator, he is portrayed as a monarch who was paranoid, oppressive, and given to grasp, by any means, for as much wealth and power as he could get his hands on. To counter the nobles who opposed him, he turned the system of royal justice he inherited from his father into a tyranny of judicial absolutism that was committed to doing his bidding. To raise money for his wars, he exploited his position at the top of the feudal order and enlisted his judges to exact punitive levies and keep his nobles in line.

After John lost Normandy to Philip Augustus, the king of France, at the Battle of Bouvines, relations with his barons deteriorated even further and by 1215 the country was on the verge of another civil war. The magnates' list of grievances with the king was a long one. They wanted an end to his unrelenting efforts to fleece them. They objected to his imposition of new taxes to pay for his wars without their consent, and they chafed under vicious forest laws that allowed him to rule over vast tracts of land in the style of a Roman emperor. Most of all, they resented the way he could circumvent feudal obligations they had to meet and frustrate their ability to obtain justice in the courts. To secure their continued allegiance they insisted he sign a Great Charter (Magna Carta) recognizing their legal rights, and on

15 June 1215, in a meadow thirty kilometers west of London known as Runnymede, he did.

The signing of the Magna Carta eight hundred years ago remains one of the most celebrated moments in legal history.[6] (And as such, not surprisingly, it was selected as another one of the great events in the history of law to appear at the entrance to the US Supreme Court.) Although it did nothing to relieve the oppression of the serfs who made up almost half the population, and parts of it were overtly antisemitic (restricting the freedom of Jews to collect interest on loans), it still is one of the most iconic statements in favor of the rule of law ever written. More than anything else, Magna Carta was an attempt by the richest and most powerful people in the country to restore the legitimacy and force of the common law and to secure the king's promise to respect it. Rather than enforce their rights on the battlefield, they persuaded the king to remedy their complaints of injustice and oppression in accordance with the time-honored law of his kingdom.

Much of the charter is concerned with confirming John's agreement that he would respect the law and ancient customs when he sought to enforce his feudal rights against his nobles and that he would not raise taxes without their consent. But Magna Carta also recognized important rights to a fair trial and due process of law "to all the free men" in his realm. In a major concession, he acknowledged that his subjects could only be punished for proven violations of the law (clause 39). In effect, he made his powers of coercion subject to review by the courts. In one of the great triumphs of the law, he promised that from that time on no one would be penalized or jailed or have his property seized unless it could be proven that a law had been broken. In the same spirit, his officials were forbidden from putting anyone on trial without evidence from credible witnesses. To show good faith, John added that justice could not be bought or sold and that he would only appoint judges who were knowledgeable in the law.

To rectify past wrongdoings, John promised that fines that had been imposed or goods that had been taken without legal justification would be restored. In the future, he agreed, property would be seized only if compensation were paid. In another clause, he promised punishments would be proportional to the seriousness of the offence and never so extreme as to deprive a person of his livelihood.

In addition to extending the reach of the law, he also agreed to the barons' demand that he make it more accessible. Instead of having to catch up with his court as it traveled around the kingdom, the Court of Common Pleas was given a permanent home in the Palace of Westminster. He also agreed to send his justices to preside over the shire courts four times a year instead of two.

In all of these ways Magna Carta marked a major advance in the evolution of the rule of law. By its terms, significant limitations were imposed on the sovereignty of one of the most powerful rulers in Europe. After Runnymede, English kings had no authority to throw people in jail, take their property, or levy a tax unless they followed rules, including the common law, that were not all of their own making.

Of course, in the real world of medieval politics, Magna Carta was not an instant panacea. In fact, it failed to achieve a lasting peace and John and his nobles were locked in battle again within the year. Like so many of law's great moments, the story Magna Carta told on parchment was an idealistic version of what was going on in the village. The hard reality was that, because it lacked an effective enforcement clause, the full force of its power would not be felt for another four hundred years.

In the original version that John signed, Magna Carta did contain a clause (61) designating a committee of twenty-five barons to monitor his compliance and authorizing the seizure of his lands and possessions if he didn't live up to its terms. But it was never put into effect. Almost before the wax of his seal had hardened, John appealed to the pope for help, and he was more than willing to oblige. Trained in law at Bologna, Innocent III regarded Magna Carta as a violation of Roman law, a feudal coup d'état, and he declared it "illegal, unjust … null and void of all validity forever." A year later John was dead, and when the charter was reissued on 12 November 1216 in the name of his son, Henry III, the enforcement clause had disappeared and nothing was put in its place.

The idea that Magna Carta might be enforced in the courts never crossed anyone's mind. As we saw in the last chapter, in the thirteenth century the conventional wisdom of all the leading jurists on the Continent was that no earthly power could pass judgment on a king. Although they argued that European rulers were bound to respect the *ius commune*, canon law, and their feudal obligations, they were very clear that nothing could be done (at least in this world) if they didn't.

Experts in English law, including Bracton, were of the same opinion. Like his European colleagues, Bracton believed that the law was all about doing justice and promoting the common good and as such was higher than, and therefore binding on, the king. In one famous passage, he wrote that law made the king and that one who rules by will rather than by *lex* is not a *rex*. But, like them, he was also firmly of the opinion that judges did not have the authority or power to hold him to it. Like Aquinas, Bracton thought that the only way a king who ruled as a tyrant could be challenged was by force. If a king "is without a bridle, that is without law," he wrote, "they [the earls and the barons] ought to put a bridle on him." Political power and military force, not the law, were the way to hold rulers to account.

Building on the tradition of English kings seeking the advice and approval of the most important nobles, Bracton also drew a distinction between the king acting on his own authority and acting in partnership with the most powerful nobles in the realm. His position was that although no one was equal or superior to the king, the combined authority of a monarch acting with the consent of "the witan of the English people" trumped the will of a sovereign who acted on his own. The supreme lawmaking authority in the country was the "king in council" not the king issuing personal commands.

Bracton's idea that enforcement of the rule of law depended on the leading magnates using their power to hold the king to his legal/feudal obligations took root over time and gradually became the first principle in how England governs itself. Kings who challenged this orthodoxy and claimed a capacity to rule on their own – as was the case with Edward II, who reigned from 1307 to 1327, and Richard II, who reigned from 1377 to 1399 – were deposed. Four hundred years after Bracton wrote, his characterization of the higher lawmaking authority of the king, when he acted in consultation and with the consent of the leading families in the kingdom, provided the foundation for Parliament's challenge to the sovereignty of the Stuart kings. The idea that Parliament's lawmaking powers are supreme and know no limit, which is the bedrock on which constitutional government in the United Kingdom was built, can trace its roots back to him.

Edward Coke (1552–1634)

In the four hundred years from the thirteenth to the seventeenth centuries, the involvement of the nobility in the affairs of state continued to grow. The meetings of the king's nobles became more regular, more inclusive, and produced increasingly insistent demands that he secure the nobles' consent before levying new taxes. They routinely cited Magna Carta and presented him with petitions to refer cases of alleged injustice to his courts. Unlike the French parlements, the English Parliament saw its role as not only defending the constitutional order established by the common law but also advising the monarch in the formulation of new legislation.

In the minds of some people, including John Fortescue (1394–1480), the difference in the English and continental systems was as stark as night and day. Fortescue, like Bracton, was a lawyer, legal scholar, and ultimately chief justice of the Court of Common Pleas. He also wrote a big book on the political and constitutional dimensions of the common law and on the difference between an absolute and limited monarchy.

As he saw it, rulers in Germany and France, who based their authority on the imperial precepts of Roman law, were examples of the first model, while the kings of England, whose authority was exercised with the consent of their subjects, and who were bound to respect the "common" law like everyone else, exercised their powers in a more responsible and legitimate way.

For the ordinary Englishman, it must be said, the difference in the two structures of kingship would have been hard to discern. Certainly for those at the bottom of the heap, England's legal and political system could be as arbitrary, corrupt, and oppressive as anything on the Continent. Law was written and judgments pronounced in languages (Latin and French) and constructed with a complexity (of a multitude of writs) that made it impossible for ordinary people to understand. When it came to exploitation and injustice, the English were not inclined to take a back seat to any of their continental cousins.

Part of the problem was that during the course of the fourteenth century the common law began to lose much of its reformist spirit. Around this time, lawyers emerged as a distinct profession with control over who gained admittance to their guild and a strong interest in preserving a system that made them rich. They established Inns of Court where they could pass on to their children and friends their mastery of the legal labyrinth by which access to the courts was controlled. Within a hundred years they were completely in charge. By the end of the century, lawyers had replaced clerics as the group from which future judges were chosen.

The Inns of Court, which remain in existence to this day, were run by the judges and the most senior lawyers in the kingdom. The students were all young men (women were excluded) from affluent families who could afford the fees. The education they received was long (it could take up to ten years); practical rather than theoretical (much of a student's time was spent apprenticing with an established lawyer observing proceedings in the courts); and very parochial (lectures focused on the exceedingly complex procedural rules that were followed in the king's courts and on the judgments and rulings they produced). Rather than the classical education lawyers received on the Continent, English law students were trained as litigators whose skill was in being able to manipulate the maze of procedures that confronted (and confounded) would-be litigants and the mountain of precedents that determined how a case would be resolved.

When they were selected as judges, lawyers typically brought with them the mind-set they learned as students and had honed in practice. When they took their seat on the bench, they were naturally inclined to concentrate on the procedural technicalities that governed execution of the writs. They abandoned the pragmatic, flexible approach of Bracton and Bereford in favor of a rigid application of stare decisis. Rather than assessing the quality of reason used to reach a decision, cases were organized in a strict hierarchy. Lower courts were bound to adhere to the decisions of higher courts and even judges who sat on the highest courts were reluctant to set aside decisions of those who preceded them on the bench. (The principle became so central to English legal thinking that it was only in 1966 that the House of Lords, then England's highest court, acknowledged that, when it was "right to do so," it had the authority to disregard its own earlier rulings.)

With elites in control of the legal system, it is no surprise the disfavored and downtrodden didn't do particularly well. Religious minorities were subject to vicious and unrelenting persecution. As we noted in the last chapter, at the urging of the people and with the approval of the canon lawyers, Jews were disadvantaged and disrespected in multiple ways and ultimately expelled from the country at the end of the thirteenth century. In the sixteenth century, the powers that be directed their coercive instincts at women, thousands of whom were burned as heretics and witches. Catholics and gays were persecuted from the time of Henry VIII (1491–1547), and through the whole period anyone who dared to challenge the country's laws or displease its rulers was liable to be charged with treason and punished with a severity and cruelty that matched anything the continental jurists could imagine. On one estimate, when there were roughly 3 million people living in the country, Henry executed over 70,000 of his subjects during his thirty-six year reign – an average of roughly 2,000 people a year, or 6 every day. The fact English kings sought the guidance and approval of their nobility before they asserted their royal powers, and professed loyalty to an indigenous legal system, didn't noticeably enhance the quality of justice in their kingdom.

The climax of the story of the common law and the participation of the rich and powerful in the governance of England can be told in the life of a single man: Edward Coke (pronounced variously "Cook" or "Kuke"), born in 1552 into a middle-class family six years before Elizabeth I inherited the throne.[7] The fact that his father had been a lawyer no doubt encouraged him to join the profession. Elizabeth chose him to be Speaker of the House of Commons and her attorney general, and her successor, James I, made him chief justice of the Court of Common Pleas and later chief justice of England. With Cicero as his model of the advocate exercising his talents on the political stage, Coke was reelected to the House of Commons when he was sixty-eight years of age. In the twilight of his career, he became one of the leaders of the

Opposition who lectured the king about his obligations under Magna Carta and championed the next great check on the powers of the monarch, known as the Petition of Right.

Coke's devotion to the common law is legendary. As the source of individual liberty, there was, he said, no jewel in the world so excellent as the common laws of England. He regarded the ancient rules of common law as a constitutional brake on the powers of the king. As he told the story, indigenous Anglo-Saxon law defended the freedom of the English people against the arbitrary practices of their Norman rulers. In his opinion, the traditional rules of the common law were the best safeguard anyone could have to protect not only his person, possessions, and property, but also his wife, children, and reputation. It was, he said, "the strongest fortress to protect the weakest of all."

For Coke, "right reason and the common law" were one and the same, and he dedicated his life to preserving its most important rulings and explaining what they meant. During his career he found time to produce a new set of annual "Reports" in which he collected the leading cases (the Year Books had ceased publication) and a four-volume treatise that some regard as the greatest study of the common law ever written. Sharing Justinian's purpose of instructing, arranging, and giving order to the law, he called his treatise the *Institutes*. To make it more accessible, he wrote it in English.

There were few in Coke's day who shared his unrestrained enthusiasm for the common law. The one group that did – his fellow lawyers – considered him their champion. They identified with his dedication to the medieval origins, intricate procedures, and unique style of reasoning of the common law, not least because it strengthened their ability to maintain their monopoly over the third branch of government and their profession. During the Puritan Revolution (1642–51) they resisted the efforts of the most radical of the parliamentary forces (known as Levellers and Diggers) to effect any serious legal reform. Little wonder lawyers were distrusted as much in England as on the Continent.

The experience of many people, rich and poor, made them leery of the law. At the bottom of the social hierarchy, the dissidents and the downtrodden regarded it as oppressive and corrupt. The law was stacked against them in everything they did. Execution awaited anyone who challenged the established order; prison was the destination of anyone who didn't pay his debts.

At the top of the hierarchy, kings and their supporters were equally suspicious. They saw in the common law an unwelcome limit on their rule. Before he became King of England, James I (1566–1625) had ruled Scotland (as James VI), where the continental system of Roman law was in force and kings were considered to have the power of emperors. Five years before he took the English Crown, he wrote a book defending the absolute rule and divine right of kings. In it he claimed to be the sole source of all law with the power to dismiss any assembly he called to advise him. Like his Tudor ancestors, he also claimed a special power (royal prerogative) to issue proclamations and act outside the law when, in his opinion, the well-being of the kingdom demanded it.

James I's and Coke's attitudes toward the law were so at odds that the two were bound to come into in conflict, and they did. Often the fight was over whether the king's prerogative allowed him to intervene in cases that were already before the common law courts. When he was a judge, Coke was continually issuing writs of prohibition to stop the king's prerogative courts (the Chancery and the Star Chamber) involving themselves in cases that were already under consideration of the common law judges. On several occasions, he told the king to his face he had no authority to settle jurisdictional disputes between the common law judges and his courts.

Coke pushed for the independence and supremacy of judge-made law even when it ran the risk of infuriating the king. A constant irritant in his relations with James concerned the competing jurisdictions of canon and common law. In England, as on the Continent, the battles between secular lawyers and church lawyers over where different cases should be litigated had been going on for years. James I, who as king was also head of the Church of England, said he would listen to arguments from both sides and decide where the line should be drawn.

On a cold Sunday morning, 13 November 1608, in the Palace of Whitehall, in another of those dramatic scenes that illuminate the history of law (and so occupies another of the panels on the doors into the United States Supreme Court), Coke told James he didn't have the authority or the knowledge to intervene. He explained that the king could only exercise his royal prerogative within the limits of the common law and that he had no right to decide cases in which he was personally involved. Moreover, he added, cases concerning the life, property, or welfare of his subjects could only be decided by "the artificial reason … of the law," which required years of study and experience to acquire. Only judges, the legal professionals, Coke said, could determine law's content and the jurisdiction of the courts.

Fights between kings and their subjects (no matter how talented) rarely went well for the latter, and so it was no surprise when James fired Coke ten years after he had made him chief justice of the Common Pleas. He had had enough, and even Coke conceded he had the authority to let him go. No one disputed that the king's prerogative included the right to select the judges who would enforce the law.

Coke, however, was far from being ready to give up the battle, and five years later he was elected to a Parliament, half of whose members were trained in the law. With their support, he took up the cause of the rule of law once again. In a matter of months he was thrown in jail for challenging the king's attempt to silence Parliament. Years later, Coke stood up to James's son, Charles I, to explain the meaning of Magna Carta's prohibition against unlawful arrests and detentions and to insist it be recognized in law. This time Coke prevailed. Grudgingly, Charles accepted Parliament's Petition of Right and renounced his prerogative to arrest or detain or seize the property of his subjects without the authority and due process of the law.

The conflict between Coke and the Stuarts was one of the most dramatic episodes in English constitutional history.[8] However, within fifteen years their struggles were overtaken by events and rendered moot by the Puritan Revolution, the execution of Charles I (on 30 January 1649) and the claim by subsequent Parliaments of the absolute sovereignty of their rule. At first, Oliver Cromwell governed as a military dictator (with the title lord protector) for five years (1653–8) and then the Stuarts were restored to the throne for a brief period of time. However, after the "Glorious Revolution" of 1688, and the invitation of the leading parliamentarians to William III to take the English Crown, no one doubted that of all the actors and institutions that comprised the English government, Parliament was on top. It passed the Bill of Rights on 16 December 1689, which confirmed its sovereignty and denied the king the power to suspend laws on his own.

In Coke's time, the issue of how parliamentary sovereignty and the supremacy of the common law were connected was not nearly as pressing as the extent to which the law limited the king's prerogative to act in whatever way he considered to be in the best interests of the nation. But it was a question in which senior members of the judiciary took an interest and, as might be expected, Coke took an aggressive position in favor of the common law. The occasion that prompted Coke's reflections was a complaint by Thomas Bonham, a Cambridge-educated doctor, about the validity of a statute that allowed the Royal College of Physicians to prosecute anyone practicing medicine without being certified by them and to pocket half of any fine they levied.

In one of the most famous decisions in English common law, Coke struck down the statute.[9] It was a fundamental maxim of common law, he said, that no man can be a judge in his own case. Acts of Parliament that were "against common right and reason, or repugnant, or impossible to be performed," he wrote, would be judged by the courts to be void. Like the monarchs with whom it shared power, Parliament was also subordinate to the common law and subject to its rule. In a judgment Bracton could never have conceived of writing, Coke allowed a victim of a clear injustice to take the sovereign to court.

The reaction to Coke's judgment was swift and mostly negative. It was challenged by the country's leading legal luminaries almost before the ink was dry. Sir Francis Bacon, Lord Chancellor Ellesmere, and John Selden (considered by many to be the leading lawyer in the kingdom) all disputed its validity. Indeed, it was such a radical position for the time that some historians claim even Coke didn't mean what it appeared he had said.[10]

While Coke's feelings on the subject remain a matter of conjecture (all his papers were confiscated by the Stuarts after he died, never to resurface), what is certain is that at the time no one took them seriously. Parliamentary sovereignty, not the supremacy of law, was the rage. In *Leviathan* (1651), Thomas Hobbes argued that all sovereigns had absolute powers that couldn't be challenged, regardless of whether they ruled as a single person or an elected assembly. He rejected Coke's claim that the king's prerogative powers were subject to the law. The will of all sovereigns, parliaments no less than kings, knew no limits. Philip Herbert, the 4th Earl of Pembroke, agreed with Hobbes. In 1648 he told his countrymen, "Parliament can do anything but make a man a woman and a woman a man." (His intellectual heirs can point to transsexual and transgender legislation and say that, as a matter of British law, Parliament can now do even that.)

Over the course of the seventeenth and eighteenth centuries, the force of politics and the power of the people gained momentum. The idea that the surest way to put an end to arbitrary rule was for the people to govern themselves came into fashion. Giving more people (initially just male property owners) a stake in government and separating the powers (legislative, executive, and judicial) of governing was seen to be the best way of countering political abuse and holding it in check. Rather than finding ways to subordinate the sovereign to the rule of law, the people demanded they be recognized as the source of all sovereign authority.

In 1690, Locke published his *Two Treatises on Government*, in which he defended the overthrow of the Stuarts. A ruler's authority, he argued, was based on the people's consent. The coercive power of the state was justified as a matter of contract between the ruler and the ruled. If the ruler broke the contract, the people had a right to resist. Sovereign power ultimately resided in them.

In Locke's theory of government, the people had the right to decide when a ruler crossed the line. Revolution was the logical response to arbitrary rule. The sovereignty of the people meant that, of the three branches of government, the legislature is supreme. Legislatures fix the limits of their own authority. Courts can't tell the people what they can do. Majorities rule; judges serve. Magistrates derive their power from the legislature. For Locke, the will of the people, not the writ of the judge, established the legitimate reach of the law.

The celebration of popular sovereignty in England did not go unnoticed on the Continent – indeed, it soon became one of the dominant stories of the Enlightenment. The argument that government is created by a social contract, agreed to by the people, was picked up and promoted by powerful advocates. Rousseau (1712–1778) and Kant (1724–1804) both used the idea to argue that the collective will of the people was the sovereign and supreme lawmaking power. In England, Blackstone (1723–1780) and Bentham (1748–1832), who disagreed fundamentally about the nature of law, were both champions of the supremacy of Parliament. In his *Commentaries on the Laws of England* (1765), Blackstone wrote about the rationality, justice, and accessibility of the common law in a way that echoed Cicero's thinking, but he also described Parliament's powers as "absolute," "despotic," and "without control."

In the two hundred years following his death, Coke and the idea of the supremacy of law had some victories but not many. In 1765, the Court of King's Bench handed down a judgment outlawing searches and seizures in private homes without the prior authorization of a judge.[11] Twenty five years later, this common law principle found its way across the Atlantic, where it was entrenched as the Fourth Amendment to the United States Constitution, which marked that nation's founding as the world's second rule of law state. For many, its most celebrated achievement was Lord Mansfield's judgment in Somersett's case (1772) that granted slaves who made it to England their freedom.[12] While Greek and Roman, canon and sharia law all tolerated some humans owning fellow human beings as personal property, English judges were the first to say that it had no place in the common law. Sadly, it would take another sixty years before Parliament and the people signed on and outlawed the slave trade.

The fact that Coke's message never really struck a chord with his own countrymen was certainly a setback for the rule of law, but it wasn't the end of his story. As history would have it, his advocacy for the supremacy of law would eventually resonate with a group of revolutionaries, living on the eastern coast of North America in the second half of the eighteenth century, who objected to the way they were being treated by Parliament and their king.

While no one found him easy reading, Thomas Jefferson, John Adams, John Jay, and Patrick Henry all cited him as authority for their right to nullify statutes passed at Westminster that didn't meet the standards of the common law. Jefferson thought it was because Coke's *Institutes* went out of fashion in his own country that England slid into "Toryism" and treated its colonists with disdain and disrespect.

To ensure their countrymen didn't fall to the same temptation, the founding fathers of the United States entrenched Coke's logic, of subordinating the power of the sovereign (people) to the rule of law, into their Constitution, where it has been a beacon to the world ever since. How they transformed a medieval idea about the supremacy of law into one of the most radical attempts to tame the excesses and abuses of politics is yet another of the remarkable moments that recur again and again in the history of law. The highs and lows of their efforts are recounted in the chapter that follows.

PART 3

Modern History: The Judges

Chapter Seven

Washington

The next great moment in the history of law inspired the birth of a nation. By the end of the eighteenth century, roughly four million (mostly) English colonists had come to live along the Atlantic coast of North America. Even though they were surrounded by Native Americans who had lived in the region for thousands of years, they thought of themselves as being on their own, more or less cut off from the rest of the world. After defeating the British in their War of Independence (1775–83), the circumstances in which the Americans found themselves were unique – and they knew it. They (or more precisely, the approximately four hundred thousand white males who were eligible to vote) were free to create whatever system of government they wanted.[1]

The Americans were aware of all the highs and lows the rule of law had experienced in the previous four thousand years. They were familiar with all the people and places we have visited in previous chapters. They knew about Classical Greece and Rome and law's flowering in England from medieval times, through Coke and on into the era in which they lived. Over half of those who signed the Declaration of Independence and were delegates to the Constitutional Convention were lawyers. Many of the most influential of the founding fathers – John Adams, Alexander Hamilton, John Jay, Thomas Jefferson, James Madison, John Marshall, James Monroe, and James Wilson – had studied law.

After suffering what they considered to have been decades of corrupt and arbitrary governance by the Parliament at Westminster and their king (George III), most Americans had had enough of English rule. They were determined to govern themselves, especially when it came to deciding whether and how much they should be taxed. They saw themselves as republicans. Many were also members of dissenting religious communities, and so it was a high priority that their government respected people's liberty to decide for themselves what their relationship with God would be.

With the benefit of hindsight, we know that, like the Greeks, the Americans could not live up to their own ambitions. Despite their keen sense of the injustices that had been done to them, they couldn't see the terrible wrongs they were doing to others. Their racism and sexism blinded them to thinking that a slave republic, in which less than 10 percent of the population had the right to vote, was the best they could do. In their utopia, African Americans only counted as three-fifths of a white person in calculating the population of a state. Women were considered whole persons for the purpose of conducting a census, but they counted for nothing when it came to the vote. Native Americans were regarded as lesser beings to be treated either as wards of the state or as the enemy.

A Government of Laws

Within the world in which they lived, however, the aspirations of these well-off white men were truly revolutionary. Leaving aside their racist and sexist instincts, their standard of good governance was exceptional. With his typically evocative turns of phrase, Thomas Jefferson laid out the vision in the preamble to the Declaration of Independence in a single sentence: "We hold these truths to be self-evident, that all men are created equal, that they are endowed by their Creator with certain unalienable Rights, that among these are Life, Liberty and the pursuit of Happiness." In their republic, he went on, governments were bound to respect and protect these universal truths and, as Aquinas and Bracton had taught, if a government betrayed them, the people had the right to get rid of it.

Everyone started from the premise that the rule of law was a precondition of good governance; the basic idea that governments must rule by law was taken for granted. The English legal system that we read about in the last chapter was embraced more or less lock, stock, and barrel. Like the English, the Americans used a combination of legislation and common law adjudication to regulate the private lives of their people. Codes were passed, common law rules established, and county courts constructed all over the country to resolve the normal, everyday conflicts over property, inheritances, commerce, and crime that arise whenever humans form families, make friends, and build communities of like-minded people.

The Americans made some changes in the law to take account of the vast, wide-open spaces and pioneering spirit that characterized life in their republic, but nothing revolutionary. One of the most noticeable differences was the American's preference for a more accessible legal profession. There were no Inns of Court. A small number of elite universities (including Harvard, Yale, Princeton, and Columbia) offered courses in law but they were available only to the few who could afford them. To become a lawyer most students "read the law" (typically home-grown treatises and texts), either on their own or under the tutelage of an experienced practitioner, and watched what went on in court. To be "called to the bar," and certified to practice, one only needed to pass an oral exam in front of another lawyer, who might just happen to be your friend.

Where the Americans were true revolutionaries was in how fervently they believed in the supremacy of law. Their claim for independence was fueled by the conviction that rulers were bound by the rule of law as much as the people they ruled. They believed their grievances against Parliament and the king were grounded in the ancient precepts and tra-ditions of English common law.

In thinking through the scope of law's sovereignty, the leaders of the revolution read all the great works in law and political philosophy.[2] With their roots in the soil of English political history, it is not surprising John Locke had a big influence on their thinking. It was his defense of the principle that the legitimacy of all government is grounded in the con-sent of the governed that justified the revolution. In the Declaration of Independence, they told the world of their grievances with George III and why they no longer felt bound by his rule.

From Locke and Montesquieu, the Americans borrowed the idea of separating the powers of the sovereign and assigning them to differ-ent people rather than fusing them in a single, all-powerful ruler, like Napoleon, as the French would soon do after their own revolution. The new federal government they created to unite the colonies was divided into three independent branches: the executive (president); the legis-lative (Congress, comprising a Senate and House of Representatives); and the judicial (Supreme Court). The government in Washington was also made to share its lawmaking authority with the governments of the founding colonies, which were called states in the new republic.

Within this system of checks and balances, the Americans debated a novel and radical method of preventing future rulers from behaving as arbitrarily as George III and Parliament had treated them. Building on another great Lockean theme, the proposal was to entrench a bill of rights in the new constitution that would mark off definitive boundar-ies beyond which no government writ could run. Some of the original colonies already had bills of rights, and many citizens believed the new federal government should be constrained by one as well.

The debate on whether to adopt a constitutional bill of rights was lively and robust. Generally, those who worried that the new national government might be too powerful were in favor, while supporters of a strong central government were opposed. James Madison was initially cool to the idea but ended up being its most important advocate.[3]

At first, the debate went against putting a bill of rights in the new constitution, and on 17 September 1787 it was adopted without one. Two arguments, made by Alexander Hamilton in the *Federalist Papers* (no. 84), seemed to carry the day. First, it was said a bill of rights was unnecessary. Second, he warned it could be dangerous – it could backfire and be counterproductive.

Hamilton thought a bill of rights was unnecessary because, traditionally, legal rights were aimed at limiting the prerogative powers of monarchs. Earlier proclamations like Magna Carta (1215) and the English Bill of Rights (1689) were "reservation[s] of rights not surrendered to the prince." In the new United States of America, where the people were sovereign, such proclamations had no application. Because the people retained all the rights and privileges they did not explicitly relinquish to the new government, there was no need to make additional, specific reservations.

The argument that adopting a bill of rights might serve to actually increase the powers of the new government followed a similar logic. The danger, Hamilton cautioned, was that someone might ask why the Constitution would say certain things shall not be done when there was no power to do them in the first place. If the Constitution said the federal government shall not do something, like restrict the freedom of the press, the fear was there would be a temptation to imply a residual, "constructive power" in the government to regulate anything that wasn't specifically mentioned. Otherwise, the document would appear incoherent. It would be guarding against the abuse of an authority that was never given. By explicitly protecting a list of particular rights, the implication was that everything else was up for grabs.

Although the sceptics initially carried the day, those who wanted a bill of rights ultimately prevailed. As the Constitution was ratified in each state, it was tacitly agreed that attaching a bill of rights would be at the top of the first Congress's agenda. In due course, on 25 September 1789, the Senate adopted the Bill of Rights as the first ten amendments to the Constitution, and by 15 December 1791 a sufficient number of states had ratified them that they became part of the "supreme law" of the new republic.

The amendments entrenched a full catalog of basic rights. Congress was barred from passing laws that denied people the right to practice their religion or that abridged their freedom of assembly or speech.

No person could be deprived of his or her life, liberty, or property without due process of law. Trial by jury, protection against unreasonable searches and seizures, and the right to a speedy and public trial of anyone accused of a crime were guaranteed. And, mindful of Hamilton's concerns, it was explicitly stated (in the Ninth Amendment) that the enumeration of these specific rights was "not to be construed to deny or disparage others retained by the people."

In putting the fundamental principles and structure of their government in a written constitution and attaching a bill of rights, the Americans were truly pioneers. Although proclamations of human rights were well-known to legal history, the idea of judges enforcing them was not. Never before had the judiciary been given such responsibility. As we have seen, jurists and lawyers played important roles in the governance of Rome and medieval Europe, but nothing like this. Not since Coke's judgment in Dr. Bonham's case had the third branch of government assumed the power to invalidate the acts of the other two.

True to its character as a country of merchants and homesteaders, America's upgrade of the rule of law was more practical than conceptual. No one claimed they were making a philosophical breakthrough. They didn't try to redefine the rule of law. Medieval jurists had been telling Europe's rulers they were bound by the law for hundreds of years. America's genius was to put in place a legal procedure to ensure they actually obeyed.

What the Americans did was organize the three branches of government so that the judiciary was on top. Politicians were made to answer to the judges. Where there was a conflict, the Supreme Court would have the last word. Only the courts, Hamilton argued, had the capacity to protect individuals and minorities from hostile majorities, motivated by "ill humours," exercising their powers arbitrarily. By incorporating a process of "judicial review" into the lawmaking process, the United States put itself in the position of becoming the first fully functioning rule of law state since Athens. By enlisting judges to certify the legality of all the decisions made in Washington (and the state capitals) in the name of the people, the full force of the rule of law, as it had been imagined by the Greeks, was revived. As Thomas Paine famously remarked, rather than submit to the English monarch, Americans had decided to make law their king.

The official announcement was made on 24 February 1803. On that day, the Supreme Court handed down its judgment in the landmark case of *Marbury v. Madison*.[4] The case is considered one of the Court's most important rulings not so much for averting a great injustice (which it didn't) as for the principle of constitutional supremacy that was used to decide the case. That affirmation earned it a place in the last panel on the doors you pass through to enter the Court.

The case was grounded in old fashioned pork barrel politics and grew out of Thomas Jefferson's frustration with John Adams's attempt to fill a large number of judicial vacancies with his own people before he vacated the presidency and Jefferson took over as his successor. In the course of working through what was a political minefield, the judges had to address the question of whether Congress could pass a law that gave the Supreme Court the power to act as a trial court ("original jurisdiction") in cases that challenged the legitimacy of such appointments. Chief Justice John Marshall and his colleagues said Congress couldn't.

His reasoning was simple: For an act or regulation of government to qualify as a valid law, it must be able to trace its authorization back to the Constitution. If it can't, it isn't a law the courts will enforce. In this case, the Constitution was very specific in listing the types of cases in which the Supreme Court did not have to wait until a lower court had made an initial ruling, and questions about the legitimacy of judicial appointments was not one of them.

Marshall was very clear that whenever a court was asked to apply a law that conflicted with the Constitution, it must always side with the latter. Its status as the supreme law meant that the Constitution must govern. In a rule of law state, governments – even governments of "We the People" – are subordinate to a higher (constitutional) law.

In the course of explaining his thinking, Marshall famously characterized the American model as "a government of laws not of men" before announcing that the judges accepted the mandate they had been given. They embraced their role as guardians of the Constitution. "It is emphatically the province and the duty of the judicial department," he wrote, "to say what the law is."

At that moment in history, it could have been said that the prospects for the rule of law never looked brighter. A new era appeared to be dawning. The Americans had finally found a way of preventing those who controlled the powers of the state from enacting laws that were arbitrary and unjust. The wisdom of the founding fathers seemed about to bear fruit. The gap between the idea and the reality of law would finally be bridged.

And then, as had happened in law's history so often before, there was another failure of will. As in Rome and medieval Europe and the Middle East, political power corrupted the moral authority of the country's rulers, judges proved to be inadequate defenders of the law, and, in its historic pattern of rise and fall, law spiraled down through another period of steep decline.

The First 150 Years

In their earliest decisions, the judges concentrated on laying the legal foundation and superstructure for the nation. In addition to defending the supremacy of the Constitution, it marked out the boundaries between the national and state governments and solidified its own independence. It also handed down major rulings fleshing out the law on America's relations with foreign nations and its own Aboriginal peoples.

Despite the fact that his formal education consisted of one year of grammar school and six weeks studying law, John Marshall was the Court's dominant personality. Marshall was chief justice of the United States from 1801 to 1835. His greatness is told in the titles ("Expounder of the Constitution" and "Definer of a Nation") with which he has been honored. He was an exceptionally prolific jurist and from all reports a good guy. Most people (a notable exception was Jefferson, to whom he was distantly related) found him to be affable and fair-minded.[5]

As important as the rules of constitutional law that the Court laid down was the way it went about its business. After listening to the lawyers argue a case, the judges typically retired to the hotel where they lived and over dinner and a good bottle (or two) of wine debated the pros and cons of the submissions they had heard that day. With the force of his personality and intellect, Marshall persuaded his colleagues that they should endeavor to speak in a single voice.

In working out the basic principles of federalism and the separate powers of the three branches of government, the Marshall Court was remarkably united. In the more than one thousand cases the Court heard during his tenure, its decisions were almost always unanimous. Unlike the Roman, Islamic, and medieval jurists, Marshall and his colleagues acted collectively rather than as individuals and came to their decisions by consensus. There were exceptions, of course, but not many. Even when there were differences of opinion, it was agreed those in the minority would follow a protocol of "silent acquiescence."

John Marshall would certainly be a first-ballot candidate for law's hall of fame but, like all of law's heroes that we have met thus far, he was human and was complicit in two of the worst injustices of his time. He was a slave owner who once ruled (in the *Antelope* case of 1825) that the law and the Court were powerless to stop the slave trade and the international trafficking of other human beings. On two other occasions (*Johnson v. M'Intosh* [1823] and *Cherokee Nation v. Georgia* [1831]) he ignored de Vitoria's defense of Aboriginal sovereignty and upheld the government's claims of legal authority over all of North America on the basis of crude and racist stereotypes. Depending on his purposes, he might refer to Native Americans as "fierce savages" or "pupils and wards." He also embraced the so-called doctrine of discovery that allowed European powers to trump Native Americans' claim of prior occupancy, either by purchase or military conquest.

After Marshall, however, things got much worse and the Court's fortunes suffered a sharp decline. In the hundred years following his death, the Court lost its unity and the jurisprudence it wrote was a disaster. It wasn't until the middle of the twentieth century that it started to defend the rule of law and the rights of women and racial minorities against the "ill humours" of the people.

In fact, between the middle of the nineteenth century and the middle of the twentieth, the Court gave its blessing to laws that imposed slavery, segregation, sterilization, and sexual and racial discrimination on the American people. It systematically tolerated American politicians abusing the rights of African Americans, women, people who suffered disabilities, and citizens of Japanese ancestry. To make matters worse, when the Court did stand up to Congress and state legislatures and insisted the Constitution be respected, it often did so in a way that prejudiced the interests of those who needed its protection most.[6]

The first big sign that things weren't right occurred in 1856 when the Court told Dred Scott that no African slaves who had been brought to America, or their descendants – including those who had been freed – could ever become American citizens.[7] Sixteen years later, in 1872, the judges advised Myra Bradwell – who was not allowed to practice law in the state of Illinois because she was a woman – there was nothing they could do for her.[8] In 1896, they ruled that the people of Louisiana had the right to enforce a system of apartheid in public transportation against African Americans and others of mixed race, including Homer Plessy, who was genetically seven-eighths white.[9] In 1927, the Court ruled the state of Virginia could forcibly sterilize Carrie Buck, whom it described as "a feeble minded white woman … the daughter of a feeble minded mother … and the mother of an illegitimate feeble minded child."[10] In 1944, the Court could find no fault in the internment of over one hundred thousand persons of Japanese ancestry (seventy thousand of whom were American citizens) living on the West Coast.[11] In between, it handed down a series of rulings in which it struck down various laws designed to improve the conditions of working people, including one that guaranteed minimum wages for women.[12]

As a body of jurisprudence, the Court's rulings on race and gender over the course of the first 150 years of its existence are appalling. They make a mockery of the idea that justice is an essential attribute of the rule of law that goes back, as we have seen, to the beginning. When victims of such arbitrary and abusive acts of lawmaking asked for their help, the judges demurred. Instead of doing their duty as guardians of the Constitution, they gave the legal stamp of approval to laws that were overtly racist and sexist.

The Court's performance is so shocking and so shameful it is difficult to comprehend how it could all have gone so terribly wrong. Why did the country's highest court certify the legitimacy of so many horrible acts of state-sponsored injustice? Why did the elite of the legal profession betray the law as frequently and brutally as they did?

If you could ask the judges who decided these cases, they would tell you it wasn't their fault. It would be wrong, they would say, to blame them. They were only doing what the Constitution required. They were just enforcing the law. And if you took the time to read their decisions, you would almost certainly think, at least initially, that there was something in what they said. Examined on its own, one at a time, each judgment does seem to make some sense.

Take the case of Dred Scott. Scott was a slave who sued his master for assault and for his freedom. Citing Mansfield's judgment in Somersett's case, he argued that because he and his family had once been taken from Missouri, which was a slave state, to Illinois, where slavery was outlawed, he had become a free man and so could no longer be legally beaten or sold by his owners.

John Sanford, who had acquired legal ownership of Scott, defended the rights of slave owners by denying Scott had ever won his freedom and claimed that, as a slave, Scott had no right to complain about how he was treated. Even more fundamentally, he said Scott had no right to sue in court. The Constitution was clear that only "citizens" had that right, and Scott was certainly not a citizen of the United States or of any of its individual states.

So the first issue the Supreme Court had to address was whether Scott in particular, and descendants of African slaves in general, could be considered American citizens. To answer that question the Court examined what the status of slaves was perceived to have been at the time the Constitution was adopted. For seven of the nine judges who sat on the case, the evidence was unequivocal: slaves who had been brought to America from Africa, as well as their descendants, were generally "considered as a subordinate and inferior class of beings" and were not intended to be part of the sovereign people or citizens of the new United States.

The Court cited a lot of evidence in support of its opinion. The facts of slavery were not pretty. Roger Taney, who succeeded Marshall as chief justice and who wrote the opinion, was certainly on solid ground when he said that, at the time when Americans claimed their independence, slaves were widely regarded as "ordinary articles of merchandise," not as fellow human beings. That was the prevailing point of view. Four of the first five presidents of the United States owned slaves while in office; this included Jefferson, who wrote the greater part of the Declaration of Independence, and Madison, who had the same claim to authorship of the Bill of Rights. (So, as we have seen, did John Marshall.) Even the northern states that were largely opposed to slavery had laws prohibiting marriages between Blacks and whites and excluding Blacks from state militias. For Taney, such enactments were irrefutable proof of the general belief that Blacks were "beings of an inferior order, and altogether unfit to associate with the white race, either in social or political relations."

The Court's duty, Taney said, was to interpret the Constitution according to "its true intent and meaning when it was adopted." Its job was to identify the original, historical understanding of the status of citizenship, not to decide on its own perception of the justice or injustice of Scott's plight. If, with the hindsight of more than half a century, the result seemed arbitrary and unfair, he pointed out that the Constitution contained provisions spelling out how it could be amended. If the Constitution needed changing, that was for the people, not the judges, to make happen. As far as Taney was concerned, he didn't have the power to do what Scott requested.

Taney's explanation for his failure to remedy the injustice about which Dred Scott had complained was that the latter was looking for something – citizenship for African Americans – in the Constitution that just wasn't there. Myra Bradwell heard more or less the same thing when the judges dismissed her plea to be admitted to their ancient and noble profession. However, the way they explained their decision to her was quite different. In her case, the answer appeared to be so clear-cut that the judges felt no need to resort to history to clarify what the Constitution meant.

Bradwell based her claim on the "privileges and immunities of citizens" in the Fourteenth Amendment, which had been passed after the Civil War to overrule the Court's decision in *Dred Scott.* Bradwell demanded the privilege of being able to practice law like everyone else who had acquired the necessary knowledge and mastered the requisite skills. In her case, as a white woman, there was no doubt she was a citizen. Her problem was that the privilege she claimed – to be admitted to the bar – was not one the Constitution guaranteed.

According to the Court, her fate had been sealed by a decision it had made the day before. In that case it had ruled that state laws that severely restricted who could take up the trade of being a butcher were constitutional. In its reasons, the Court explained that the "privileges and immunities" that were protected in the Fourteenth Amendment only included those that attached to a person's national citizenship; they did not extend to rights and liberties, like practicing a trade or a profession, that took place entirely within a state.

The Court told Myra Bradwell that its interpretation of the "privileges and immunities" clause in the butchers' case governed the rights of lawyers as well. There was no need to review the historical record to discover the meaning of the words because that job had already been done. The logic was so straightforward that the Court needed only two pages to explain its decision. (Dred Scott, by comparison, had to read nine judgments totaling almost 250 pages to find out why he lost.)

Homer Plessy got the same story when he complained about a Louisiana law that required railway companies to provide separate facilities for the two races on their trains. Like Scott and Bradwell, he was told he was asking for something that the Constitution simply didn't provide. Even though (as Taney had suggested) it had been amended (by the Fourteenth Amendment) after the Civil War to recognize the right of African Americans to become citizens of the United States and to guarantee them "life, liberty ... and the equal protection of the laws," it did not, the Court said, require "social" as opposed to "political" equality, or "a comingling of the races on terms unsatisfactory to either." It only outlawed distinctions that implied legal inferiority.

In explaining to Plessy why his rights had not been violated, the Court combined the analyses it had used with Dred Scott and Myra Bradwell. There was no basis for his complaint, Plessy was told, both as a matter of original intent and the Court's own precedents. In its reasons for judgment, the Court offered both historical evidence of the original intention behind the amendments and its own prior decisions to defend its reading of the text.

The distinction between social and political equality could be seen in the separate schools that existed in states that had recognized the political rights of Blacks as well as in laws that prohibited interracial marriages. It was also implicit in an earlier decision of the Court that had invalidated a state law that only allowed white persons to sit on juries. The difference, the Court said, was that the law excluding Blacks from juries implied a legal inferiority that went beyond social stigmatization.

The basic fallacy of his argument, the Court told Plessy, was that enforced separation of the races did not "stamp the colored race with a badge of inferiority." If he felt demeaned or diminished by being excluded from places where whites were present, it was not because of anything in the law but only because he "chose to put that construction on it."

In other words, it was his own fault. To drive the point home, the Court asked Plessy to consider how whites would feel if their roles were reversed: if Blacks became the dominant power in the legislature and passed a similar law, there was no doubt in the Court's mind that whites wouldn't think of themselves as having been put in an inferior position.

To soften the blow, the Court told Plessy that even though he had no right to complain about segregation in public transportation, there were limits on what he might be required to endure. Laws that commanded whites and Blacks to walk on opposite sides of streets, or paint their houses the color of their skin, for example, went too far. In exercising their "constructive powers," governments had to meet an overarching standard of reasonableness.

Seeing something in the Constitution that wasn't there was Scott's and Bradwell's and Plessy's problem, and it turned out to be Carrie Buck's mistake as well. Buck was an eighteen-year-old "feeble-minded white woman" who asked the Court to stop the state of Virginia from forcibly sterilizing her.

Her interlocutor was Oliver Wendell Holmes Jr., the "Brahmin from Boston" and one of the Herculean figures in America's pantheon of law. As was his style, Holmes was direct and to the point. In a three-page judgment, he told Buck her right not to be deprived of her "life, liberty or property without due process of law" and her right to the "equal protection of the laws" had not been infringed because the Constitution allowed the government to pass laws that sacrificed people's rights when it was in the best interests of the country or a state to do so.

Holmes's reasoning followed the same logic as the doctrine of constructive powers that Hamilton had warned about in the debates over the pros and cons of adopting a bill of rights. In Holmes's view, no right or freedom, not even the right to life, was absolute and unconditional. In extreme circumstances, the welfare of the community might trump even the most vital interests of the individual. To help her understand why she lost, he offered a couple of analogies and another of the Court's earlier decisions.

Holmes's first analogy was to the country, in a time of war, calling on its "best citizens for their lives." His logic was that if government can ask people to make the ultimate sacrifice, "it would be strange if it could not call upon those who already sap the strength of the State for these lesser sacrifices, often not felt to be such by those concerned, in order to prevent our being swamped with incompetence." Carrie Buck was only being asked to make a contribution to the well-being of the community like everyone else. As he put it, "three generations of imbeciles were enough."

Holmes's second analogy was to an order of compulsory vaccination. Holmes pointed out that in one of the Court's earlier rulings, it had held that a program of compulsory vaccination did not constitute an infringement of people's rights. As he saw it, the principle in the two cases was the same. Governments can claim sovereignty over the physical body of a person when and to the extent it is essential to the interests of the larger community in which he or she lives.

Carrie Buck, Homer Plessy, Myra Bradwell, and Dred Scott all lost their cases because the judges didn't think the rights they claimed were protected in the Constitution. In the case of Fred Korematsu, one of the tens of thousands of Japanese Americans interned during the Second World War, the judges' explanation for why the government was permitted to deny his presumption of innocence was different. He didn't lose because what he was asking – to have his loyalty judged on the basis of his individual circumstances instead of his race – was not protected in the Constitution. No one doubted that the Bill of Rights guaranteed the determination of guilt and innocence based on one's personal rather racial status. The issue for the judges was one of prudence and caution in the face of a lack of expertise.

As a practical matter, Korematsu ended up in an internment camp because the judges didn't think they had the power to second-guess the generals. They were unwilling to challenge the judgment of the military authorities that it was impossible to set up a system to test the loyalty of each person individually and that the only way to protect the country against enemy spies was by rounding up the whole group. Nor were the judges willing to question the generals' conclusion that there weren't any milder forms of restraint that could provide adequate security.

Deference to military orders was a principle that the Court had already embraced when it upheld an earlier curfew that the military had imposed. Even though the judges recognized that the restriction of Korematsu's liberty was much greater, they said the principle was the same. They saw no reason for the Court to abandon the posture of restraint it had adopted in the previous case.

When you read the Court's decision in *Korematsu*, it has an aura of legitimacy about it like all the others. If ever it is appropriate for judges to act with caution and deference this must surely be the case when it comes to questioning military orders in times of war. For many it seems counterintuitive that generals should design their military strategies on the basis of legal opinions from their lawyers. However, when the wrong that was done to Japanese Americans is added to those suffered by Blacks, women, and the disabled, every justification that is offered by the Court for its rulings begins to look suspicious.

Indeed, as the cases keep piling up, the judges' plea – that the Court had no power to stop politicians and government officials treating so many vulnerable people so badly – seems wildly implausible. It seems highly improbable that a constitution that was written, in the words of its preamble, "in order to form a more perfect union, establish justice ... promote the general welfare, and secure the blessings of liberty" would be so tolerant of such arbitrariness and abuse. How could someone as thoughtful and eloquent as Madison compose such an insidious text?

Law and Legal Reasoning

The short answer is that he didn't. The failure was not in the founding fathers' powers of expression, although there is no doubt they could have been clearer in some places. The real culprits were the judges who followed Marshall on the bench. The reasons they gave for their decisions, it turns out, were entirely self-serving. The truth is they deliberately chose to turn the promise of *Marbury v. Madison* into a mandate for legalizing a racist and sexist state.

If one goes back and rereads the cases, it becomes apparent that the Court's explanations for failing to protect women, the disabled, and racial minorities from governments bent on abusing their powers just don't stand up. The fact of the matter is that in no case were the hands of any of the judges tied in the ways that they claimed.

Without Marshall's leadership, the Court became a much more fractured and divided institution. Judges increasingly disagreed with one another and began to write separate opinions, even when they agreed on the result. It became accepted that each judge had a lot of choice as to how they interpreted individual cases. They were free to make use of whichever method of analysis (original intent, precedent, analogy, reasonableness, judicial restraint, etc.) most appealed to them, and they had almost unfettered discretion when it came to deciding how any one of them might be applied.

With multiple ways to approach a case, it was possible for each judge to provide reasons to justify a decision either way and to back it up with credible legal authority. In every case, each judge had the option of writing a judgment upholding the rights of the victims or defending the power of government to do what it did. So long as they used one of the accepted modes of legal analysis, judges had the power to practice politics and do whatever they personally thought was right.

And they did. In all of the cases we have considered, at least one of the judges took issue with the Court's decision and told his colleagues they were making a mistake. Someone dissented in every case. Although the dissenters were not successful in persuading their brethren of the force of their analysis, they did demonstrate that a choice had to be made. Sometimes a dissenting opinion provided a different way of analyzing a case. Other times, judges might agree that they should give effect to the original meaning of the Constitution, or follow one of their own prior rulings but disagree on what that meaning was or what that precedent said.

In *Dred Scott,* for example, the Court said its ruling – that no descendant of an African slave, not even those who had been freed, could become a citizen of the United States – was based on the original understanding of those who wrote and ratified the Constitution. But the truth is that the thinking that lay behind America's highest law was not nearly so definitive or clear-cut.

As Benjamin Curtis, one of the judges who dissented from the Court's ruling, pointed out, in the years immediately preceding the adoption of the Constitution, everyone who was descended from African slaves and was born or became a free person in New Hampshire, New York, New Jersey, Massachusetts, North Carolina, and Pennsylvania was considered to be a citizen of those states and, so long as they met the other (age, sex, property) qualifications, were entitled to vote. Even if Taney was right in saying that whites generally thought of Blacks as their intellectual and social inferiors, and treated them as ordinary articles of commercial property, the fact remained that, in almost half of the country that became the United States, free African Americans had the same right to seek justice in federal and state courts as whites.

The historical reality was that, like a lot of things that went into the Constitution, the northern and southern states thought about the meaning of citizenship and the status of whites and Blacks very differently. For this reason, both constituencies shared the belief that, the less said about race and slavery in the Constitution, the better. Both sides knew the other's position and there was a tacit understanding that they would each do their own thing.

When Chief Justice Taney told Dred Scott he couldn't help him because the Constitution never intended for African Americans to become American citizens, he was not telling the whole truth. Taney chose to focus on one part of the historical record and ignore the part that Curtis and John McLean, the other judge who dissented, thought was most pertinent.

Nor was the Court completely forthright with Bradwell, Plessy, Buck, or Korematsu when it told them the resolution of their cases was settled by one of its earlier precedents. In truth, the Court's earlier judgments are even more open to competing interpretations than the Constitution.

When judges who sit on their country's highest court are told that one of their own prior rulings governs how a subsequent case should be resolved, they must answer two separate questions. First, they must decide whether they agree with the precedent that is said to be controlling. Second, if they answer the first question in the affirmative, they must then determine if the earlier judgment really governs their case.

Judges on the US Supreme Court must always ask themselves what they personally think of previous cases that are cited to them because, for them, no precedent can ever be automatically binding. If a prior ruling is wrong or mistaken in some way, it ought to be overruled. And they have in numerous cases, including *Plessy* and *Korematsu*. If a Supreme Court judge disagrees with the reasoning that has been followed in an earlier decision, it can have no authority over him. That is the inescapable logic of Marshall's declaration of constitutional supremacy in *Marbury v. Madison*.

A judicial decision has the same legal status as an act of Congress – both are subordinate brands of law. When either conflicts with the Constitution, they have no legitimacy or legal force. As the supreme law, the Constitution always prevails. As guardians of that supreme law, judges have a duty to invalidate any of the past decisions of the Court that, on further reflection, don't measure up.

All of the judges who sat on these cases understood this hierarchy in the American legal system. In *Dred Scott*, Taney was quite explicit that the authority of the Court's earlier rulings depended entirely on the force of their reasoning.

In *Bradwell*, three of the judges completely ignored the Court's earlier ruling in the butchers' case. They had sat on that case and they thought it had been wrongly decided. They didn't agree with the Court's narrow interpretation of the Fourteenth Amendment then, and they saw no reason to change their minds when Myra Bradwell pleaded for their help. So, even though they agreed with their colleagues that there was nothing they could do for her, rather than sign on to the Court's judgment, Joseph Bradley took the time to produce a separate concurring opinion for himself and his colleagues.

As Bradley saw it, the Illinois legislature had the authority to deny women the right to practice law, but his reason was very different. Rather than the narrow interpretation the Court had adopted in the butchers' case, he read the words "privileges and immunities" in the Fourteenth Amendment in the spirit of Cicero and Aquinas and looked to the basic precepts of natural law to tell him what they meant. It would be contrary to the "nature of things," he argued, to include the practice of law or any other occupation in the "privileges and immunities" that could be claimed by women. "The paramount destiny and mission of woman," he wrote, "are to fulfill the noble and benign offices of wife and mother. This is the law of the Creator."

When it comes to arguments based on the Court's own precedents, judges have the power not only to reject and ignore them; they also have a lot of freedom to interpret them as they please. Even when a judge agrees with a ruling in a prior case, he or she still has a large measure of discretion in deciding how far its authority should reach. First, the principle for which an earlier case stands must be extracted from the judgment. Then a decision must be made about the scope and force of the reasoning on which the principle is based.

In Carrie Buck's case, for example, Holmes thought forced steriliza- tion fell within the same principle as compulsory vaccinations to which the Court had already given its approval. One of his colleagues, Pierce Butler, disagreed. In Homer Plessy's case, a majority of the Court felt that its earlier ruling outlawing the exclusion of Blacks from jury service did not apply to their forced segregation on trains. John Harlan read the case differently and told his colleagues that in principle the cases were the same. In *Korematsu*, three judges disagreed with the Court that his treatment fell within the same principle that governed the legitimacy of the curfew. For them, the impact of each varied too much to justify the same result.

So in fact, in none of these cases did either of the traditional sources of legal reasoning point definitively to one answer over another. The politi- cal history surrounding the original understanding of the Constitution, as well as the Court's own prior decisions, raised more questions than answers. They could be and were read to justify whichever outcome each judge personally favored. No surprise, then, that in all of these cases at least one judge filed a dissenting opinion.

The inability of judges to find definitive answers in the law and politics of the past was compounded by similar flaws in each of the other methods of reasoning they employed. It turned out that the indeterminacy that is inherent in the traditional sources of legal analysis is endemic to all of the analytical tools the judges used to justify the conclusions they reached.

Analogies, like the ones Holmes used with Carrie Buck, are a lot like prior cases. With every analogy there is a threshold question of whether it even applies. Is serving in the military and risking one's life in a time of war really comparable to being singled out and sterilized against one's will? Is a vaccination as invasive as a surgical procedure that cuts off the possibility of having children? Neither analogy worked for Justice But- ler, who dissented in the case, and the fact that most people now think Holmes got it wrong suggests Butler was right.

The doctrine of constructive powers and the principle of reasonableness that allow governments to restrict rights and freedoms that are not explicitly guaranteed in the Constitution both suffer the same weakness. Unfettered and on their own, they are too indeterminate and open-ended. Depending on one's moral values and worldview, they can be manipulated to uphold or deny a person's claim that their constitutional rights have been violated.

In *Plessy*, for example, Harlan took issue with the way his colleagues had applied the reasonableness test. (He even questioned whether using a principle of reasonableness was a proper tool for judges to use at all.) As he saw it, whatever evil might result from the forced integration of public transportation, it was less than what would transpire from allowing governments to regulate the enjoyment of civil rights on the basis of a person's race. Conceding governments that power, Harlan warned, was a prescription for racial hatred and would make peace between Blacks and whites precarious. If the test was one of reasonableness, he thought Plessy, not the Government of Louisiana, had the stronger case.

The malleability of a principle of reasonableness and the doctrine of constructive powers is especially evident in the Court's treatment of Korematsu. In his case, there was a fundamental difference of opinion between the six judges who formed the majority and their three colleagues who dissented regarding the extent to which it was reasonable for the Court to defer to the generals. How much restraint should be shown was up to each judge. Characteristically, Felix Frankfurter wrote a separate concurring opinion to emphasize the Court's limited supervisory role over the military. Even among the dissenting judges, two of them took diametrically opposed positions on whether reasonableness was an appropriate standard for judges to apply in deciding where the line should be drawn.

Doctrines of constructive powers, reasonableness, and judicial restraint suited the judges because, like the other modes of reasoning they favored, these gave them a lot of flexibility to rule according to their own sense of right and wrong. In deciding whether the individual's interest or the community's welfare was more important, they were able to assign each the weight they personally thought was appropriate. On the scales of justice, it was the judges who determined how seriously a law impacted on the lives it affected rather than those who claimed their rights had been violated. Plessy was told his personal feelings didn't count and he should think more like a white! Carrie Buck was admonished by Holmes for inflating her sense of loss. The balance of interests was governed by the judges' own sense of the relative importance of the two sides of a case even before it had been argued in court.

When all the judgments that were written in these cases are read in their entirety, the judges' claim that they were faithful servants of the law just doesn't hold up. The reality is that in every case the judges had a choice in deciding whose interest would prevail. There was always more than one tool a judge might use to analyze a case, each of which was capable of producing conflicting results. What rights people had could be defined on the basis of how the Bill of Rights was originally understood, or according to one of the Court's own prior rulings, or on the basis of an analogy or a principle of reasonableness, or even by the dictates of divine (natural) law.

And it is because each of them claimed the freedom to craft their own judgment, in any way they saw fit, that the judges must shoulder much of the blame for the discrimination that Blacks, women, the disabled, and people of Japanese ancestry were made to suffer in the first century and a half of the country's history. They didn't start any of it, but they could have stopped it and they didn't. On five separate occasions they had the opportunity to call out the country's political leaders for their racist and sexist attitudes, but each time they took a pass. In each case the judges had a choice how they would rule, and the great majority of them got it wrong every time.

Because the judges' conception of legal reasoning tolerated so many different ways of thinking, judges were free to rule according to their own sense of right and wrong. Legal reasoning became a way to justify decisions arrived at independently on personal (political, philosophical, religious) grounds rather than a way of determining which outcome was mandated by law. If, like Holmes, you were from Beacon Hill and believed in eugenics, then poor uneducated women didn't have the final say over their reproductive organs. If, like Butler, you were the Court's only Catholic and believed in the moral foundations of natural law and the sanctity of human life, they did. On either view, how Carrie Buck was treated by the state had nothing to do with the law.

By the end of the Second World War, even the strongest supporters of judicial review believed the experiment was a failure. Respected professors of law wrote scathing indictments of the Court. By any measure, America's great contribution to the rule of law had been a huge disappointment. The way the Supreme Court had come to understand its powers of review was perverse. Not only did it authorize governments to beat up on women and vulnerable minorities, it destroyed the integrity of the judiciary in the process. It had transformed the rule of law into the moral preferences and political whims of nine middle-aged and elderly white males. It permitted the racism and sexism of American politics to contaminate the law.

As the list of pernicious rulings grew longer, the Court's moral authority kept sinking lower. It hit rock bottom in 1937. After a series of judgments invalidating laws aimed at alleviating the worst effects of the Great Depression, its reputation was so bad President Roosevelt considered doubling its size so he could appoint judges who would counter the conservative bias that had come to infect the Court's thinking over the previous thirty years. Although Roosevelt's "court-packing" plan was widely criticized and never put into effect, no one doubted that his concerns about the judges' impartiality were well-founded.[13]

Indeed, in addition to its dreadful record on race and gender, the Court had shown a strong class bias against the interests of workers. The favoritism the judges showed toward capitalists and corporations, especially in the early years of the twentieth century, was blatant and unrepentant. Under the banner of personal liberty, it struck down numerous pieces of labor legislation establishing maximum hours of work and minimum wages for women and children as well as protections for unions and worker organizations. One of the cases, in which the Court invalidated a law that regulated the working hours of bakers in New York, gave its name to what became known as the "Lochner Era."

Hiding behind the facade of precedent, these decisions were also transparently political and had little to do with law. Earlier judgments were cited on both sides of a case but no one was fooled by the way they were manipulated to serve the political agenda of the judges. Louis Brandeis, one of the Court's most progressive judges, was relentless in his criticism of his colleagues' failure to give adequate consideration to the social problems that drove the plaintiffs to look to the judges for help.

Brown v. Board of Education

The rule of law was in this profound state of malaise when, on 17 May 1954, there occurred another of those moments of high drama that mark law's journey through time. On that day the Supreme Court handed down its decision in *Brown v. Board of Education of Topeka*.[14] In a unanimous judgment that was reprinted in full in the country's leading newspapers, it ruled that segregating white and Black children in separate schools denied the latter equal protection of the laws.

Separate schools were not equal schools, the Court said, even if the physical facilities, teaching resources, budgets, and all other tangible factors were identical. With the stroke of a pen, the Court turned its back on its past and reestablished its own and law's integrity simultaneously. In a single judgment, the Court's reputation was restored overnight.

In what was and remains the most celebrated ruling it has ever made, the Court turned everything it had been doing on its head. Not only did it reverse the legacy of *Plessy* and *Dred Scott* and give an important boost to the civil rights movement in bringing overt racial discrimination to an end, it adopted a different style of reasoning as well. It changed the nature of its review from a focus on the words of the constitutional text to a closer attention to the facts.

In explaining its decision to an unsuspecting public, the Court abandoned its traditional approach. Historical sources went out the window. It was recognized that the origins of the Fourteenth Amendment were murky and contested; governments had not been in the business of providing public education in 1868, when the amendment was adopted and the ambitions of those who wrote and ratified it were various and often conflicting. Northern states typically intended that the guarantee of the equal protection of the laws would mean the end of all legal distinctions based on the color of one's skin. People who lived in the South expected it to have a much more limited effect.

Legal precedents didn't fair any better. The doctrine of "separate but equal" announced in *Plessy* was finally overruled. Although the Court had declined to disavow it in the past, in *Brown* Taney's judgment was declared to be bad law and without any precedential value. This time the Court was firmly of the opinion that the clock could not be turned back to 1868, or even 1896, when *Plessy* was written.

The decision to outlaw segregation in schools was justified exclusively on the basis of the effects that separating the races had on students' education. This time the Court took the views of the victims seriously, and from what they told the Court, the impact was profound. Psychological studies showed that Blacks perceived laws that excluded them from places occupied by whites as a public branding of inferiority and that internalizing such feelings directly affected a child's motivation to learn. Even in schools that were equal in amenities and resources, the education could not be the same. On the scales of justice, the treatment of the two races was badly out of balance.

Brown v. Board of Education's place in the legal history of the United States is based on its ruling outlawing racial segregation. It was a huge victory for basic human rights over the forces of invidious discrimination. But the way the judges came to their decision was equally pathbreaking and deserves our attention. In *Brown*, the Court offered a radically different way for judges to decide cases. Findings of fact, not definitions of words, were what mattered.

To appreciate the significance of the Court focusing more on the actual impact of a law and less on the words of the Constitution, imagine what would have happened if the Court had adopted this style of reasoning from the beginning. Had the Court assessed the facts of cases impartially, from the perspective of the parties, it could have dealt a fatal blow to slavery and shut apartheid down before it got off the ground. It could also have heralded the emancipation of women and the rights of the disabled. Dred Scott would have been able to sue his master for assault. Homer Plessy could have sat wherever he wanted. Carrie Buck would not have been sterilized and Fred Korematsu would never have been kicked out of his home.

In fact, the Court did exactly the opposite. In all these cases it adamantly refused to consider the impact of the laws on their victims, and said so explicitly. Plessy, it will be recalled, was told that the "underlying fallacy" of his case was that he, not the law, placed the badge of inferiority that he saw stamped on his person. The fact he personally felt degraded and abused didn't count. On the scales of justice it was given no weight.

Holmes did the same thing to Carrie Buck. In one of his arrogant asides, he depreciated the trauma and violence she was forced to endure. Compared to the ultimate price the country's best gave in defending their country, he thought Buck was being asked for a "lesser sacrifice," even though he acknowledged that it was unlikely she would see it in those terms.

In *Korematsu*, the Court avoided facing the extreme deprivation of liberty imposed on Americans of Japanese ancestry on the basis of a legal technicality. The majority ruled that the only law before them was the order excluding people from their homes and that the fact that the exclusion order was part of a larger set of military regulations that resulted in their being (in the words of one of the dissenting judges) "locked up in concentration camps" was of no concern to the Court.

In all of these cases, the injustice that the Court refused to remedy was the same it rectified in *Brown*: majorities indulging themselves at the expense of vulnerable minorities, enacting laws that favored their interests even when it imposed burdens that profoundly affected how others could go about their daily routines. Severe restrictions were put on peoples' most basic liberties – where they lived, where they went to school, how they traveled, what they did for a living – for only very modest, if any, improvement in the welfare of others.

Dred Scott could be beaten by his master so that he could better enjoy a life of leisure. Homer Plessy was chained by laws that denied him the freedom to move about New Orleans so that the mental space whites claimed for themselves would not be disturbed. Carrie Buck was surgically assaulted and Myra Bradwell was physically barred from practicing law in the courts for reasons that no one today thinks had anything to do with the quality of life in Virginia or Illinois. In Korematsu's case, the Court's assessment of both his and the country's interests was partial and unbalanced. Not only did it refuse to consider the deprivation Japanese Americans suffered by being indefinitely confined in detention camps, it also failed to examine the extent to which national security was enhanced by imprisoning the entire group.

A single fault line runs through all of these cases. The Court avoided confronting the gross imbalance in the laws it was reviewing by refusing to accept the victims' account of how prejudicial these laws were for them. Judges compromised their impartiality by substituting their own evaluation of how burdensome these laws really were. In each case, the Court understated the law's harmful effects. Instead of being bound by the facts, it made them up.

That changed in *Brown*. For the first time, the Court handed down a major ruling on the Constitution that was based almost exclusively on the facts that were reported to them by the people involved in the case. It listened to the individuals who were prejudiced by these laws and accepted their evidence of the burdens they were forced to bear. Their feelings were taken as legitimate and genuine and given the weight they deserved. It looked like the blaming and belittling that Plessy and Buck had to put up with was over.

Politicians in Robes

In the history of judicial review in America, *Brown* will always be a landmark decision. If nothing else, it marked the beginning of the end of apartheid in the United States. Regrettably, it didn't turn out to be a watershed for the law itself. A change occurred in the Court's thinking, but it did not fundamentally alter how judges went about their work. Instead, over time this fact-driven, pragmatic way of judging became just one more technique of legal reasoning that was available to the judges when it suited their purposes.

Indeed, in the years following *Brown*, the Court continued to expand the sources of legal reasoning that were considered legitimate for judges to use. Most notably, in deciding what constitutes "cruel and unusual" punishment (which is outlawed in the Eighth Amendment), the Court said that in addition to the understanding of punishment that prevailed at the end of the eighteenth century and the Court's own prior rulings, regard should be had to "the evolving standards of decency that mark the progress of a maturing society." So, for example, Antonin Scalia, a judge who passionately believed that the Constitution should be interpreted according to its original understanding, acknowledged that if a state passed a law that brought back public lashings or branding, he would declare it to be unconstitutional even though punishments of this kind were normal and acceptable in the world in which the Bill of Rights was written.

More controversially, toward the end of the century, judges began to make reference to foreign cases to help them canvass the different ways a conflict might be resolved. For example, the Court looked at how the death penalty was handled in other countries, and on the issue of gay rights it made reference to a decision of the European Court of Human Rights to support its striking down a law that made oral and anal sex between consenting gays a crime. It noted that the judges in Strasbourg had explicitly rejected the reasoning the Americans had used in an earlier case in which they had ruled sodomy laws were constitutional. The European Court's analysis was accepted and was one of the reasons the Court gave for overruling its earlier decision.

The continuing enlargement of the sources of reasoning in the fifty years since the Court's judgment in *Brown* has meant judges now have virtually unlimited choice in how they exercise their powers of review. Political and social history, legal precedents, analogies, natural law, principles of reasonableness, standards of decency, judicial restraint, comparative jurisprudence, even God's law – all can play a part. How much and to what end is entirely up to each judge. On the American model, legal reasoning is a matter of personal preference for each judge. In practice, America's law has become more pluralistic than its politics.

As you would expect, with such unfettered freedom, the judges have been sharply divided on all the big political questions that were put to the Court in the second half of the twentieth century, including the death penalty, ownership of guns, affirmative action, gay rights, abortion, and the way elections are conducted. On all these controversial, high-profile issues, it was common for six or seven opinions to be written. No definition was conclusive. Judges were free to give their preferred interpretations the force of law.

Today, virtually no one takes seriously the idea that there is a single right answer for every case. Richard Posner, one of the country's leading jurists and an appellate court judge for more than a quarter of a century, spoke for most constitutional lawyers when he insisted that "constitutional cases ... cannot be called right or wrong by reference to legal norms."[15] Among the professional elites, the Court's practice is accepted as a legitimate way for the judges to go about their work. There is a general acquiescence in the fact that, in the final analysis, what governments are allowed to do depends on the political and legal philosophies of those who are sitting on the bench.

Now, in the early decades of the third millennium (of the Common Era), the American model of judicial review looks a lot like the conception of law that Edward Coke defended in front of James I. With its toleration and accommodation of so many different ways of thinking, it operates on the kind of "artificial reason" that he claimed was characteristic of the common law. It doesn't work logically, like a syllogism. This isn't the sort of analysis that Plato, Aristotle, Cicero, or Aquinas thought was at the center of law. It lacks a logic that distinguishes law from other rules and its method is ultimately hostage to the political preferences of each judge.

A related consequence of judges being able to use different analytical methods to evaluate a case is that the Court's judgments become longer and more complex. They can go on as long as short novels. Concise, fact-focused rulings, like *Brown*, that can be published in the newspaper and read by the public are unheard of. Even standard cases routinely elicit three or four separate opinions in which the judges debate with each other which form of analysis is most appropriate and where each leads. Decisions run for dozens of pages in a jargon-filled style that makes it difficult for the ordinary citizen to comprehend. The American conception of law is not people-friendly.

The personal, pluralistic way American judges think about the cases they are asked to decide maximizes the power of each individual judge and privileges the position of lawyers generally. Only those trained in the law are able to understand the way the game is played. America has become a republic, like Plato's, controlled by elites. The only difference is that, instead of drawing its guardians from the academy, America has opted for an oligarchy of jurists.

The elite status of lawyers in the United States has a long history. As already noted, most of those responsible for writing the Constitution and organizing the structure of the government had some legal training. Alexis de Tocqueville noticed their prominence in his travels in America in 1831–2. He called the legal profession America's aristocracy, "the political upper class and the most intellectual section of society." In contrast with French lawyers, whom he described as "only men of learning," he thought American (and English) lawyers "resemble somewhat Egyptian priests and are, like them, the sole interpreters of an obscure science."

The way the US Supreme Court oversees the work of the two elected branches of government is plainly not good for democracy. The language and method it uses to settle the most basic conflicts over race and gender denies most people their voice on the issues they care about most. Indeed, because of the size of the courtroom and the Court's refusal to allow its proceedings to be televised, only very few of them are even allowed to observe the judges hear a case and announce their rulings.

At the same time that the American model of judicial review weakens the country's ability to govern itself in a truly democratic way, it also undermines the integrity of the law. It turns out America's conception of the rule of law is doubly flawed. The Court's highly personal, pluralistic mode of operation simultaneously diminishes the power of ordinary people to participate in the resolution of the big hot-button issues in their communities and allows politics to intrude deeply into the inner workings of the Court. It happens in the following way.

Faced with the many ways it is permissible to analyze a case, judges are typically quick to develop their own personal styles and preferred sources, such that early in their legal careers, if not before, they come to be identified with a particular mode of reasoning. Like the Roman jurists and medieval lawyers before them, they establish a legal persona as originalists or pragmatists or as jurists who look to moral philosophy or natural law to tell them what the Constitution means: Holmes the pragmatist; Frankfurter the advocate of judicial restraint; Hugo Black (who wrote the Court's judgment in *Korematsu*) a strong exponent of textualism and original intent.[16] Most remain wedded to their own way of doing things throughout their careers, although a few do grow and learn on the job.

With a person's ideas about law being a matter of public record, it is natural for a president to nominate people to the Court who share his political and legal philosophy. In the United States, the president effectively decides who gets appointed to the Supreme Court, though his choice must be confirmed by the Senate. The senators have rejected a few nominations, but typically presidents get the person they want. In the modern era, Republican presidents have generally favored judges who were inclined to read the Constitution strictly and with an eye to its literal and historic meaning, while Democrats look for jurists who will give the Constitution and the Bill of Rights a broader and more philosophical read.

In effect, the appointment process allows presidents to pick judicial proxies to represent them in the debates on all the big moral issues that come before the Court. Whether women have a right to have an abortion, for example, is decided more or less on party lines. Judges appointed by Democrats tend to give more weight to the interests of the woman, while Republicans typically give priority to fetal life. It has become a mantra for Republican presidential candidates to promise they will favor jurists who are committed to reversing or rolling back a woman's right to have an abortion that the Court established almost fifty years ago.[17] Indeed, so closely are the judges allied with the presidents who appoint them, many law teachers tell their students that, when they are reading judgments of the Court, they should think of them as "politicians in black robes."

The corrosive power of partisan politics continues to eat away at the integrity of American law to this day. Recent rulings on election laws, gun control, and health-care policy (like abortion) have split along party lines. When lesbians and gays come before the Court, the judges divide into their liberal and conservative wings. As often as not, decisions come down to the opinion of a single judge. Since John Roberts became chief justice in 2005, there have been more than 100 decisions in which the Court split 5–4, and it was almost always the same four on each side. For a long time, Anthony Kennedy, a moderate conservative who was appointed by Ronald Regan, cast the deciding vote. The fact that gays are able to marry and African Americans benefit from affirmative action programs is mostly because that is what Kennedy believed was right.[18]

At the dawn of a new millennium, there is little reason to be optimistic about the future of the rule of law in the United States. The politics of judging is deliberate and overt and no effort is made to do anything about it. The Senate has the power to reject a president's nominee, but except in extreme cases, it almost never does. Its confirmation hearings have become mostly a media event – more a slice of reality TV than a serious inquiry into the way a person thinks as a jurist and a judge.

Sometimes probing questions are asked about a nominee's understanding of the law, but these are easy to evade – typically on the grounds that it is not appropriate to comment on issues that might come before the Court. Even Elena Kagan, the second justice nominated by Barack Obama, who rejected the argument when she was a law professor, offered this excuse when she refused to answer questions about the Court's jurisprudence during her own confirmation hearing.

If those who aspired to be judges were obliged to be forthcoming about their understanding of the law, the senators would have no difficulty getting an accurate picture of their legal philosophy. All they would have to do is question the person about some of the landmark cases the Court has already decided. To find out what someone thinks about the supremacy and moral character of the law, the senators need only engage them on any of the judgments we have looked at in this chapter.

They might explore what a nominee thinks about the Court telling Plessy that the feelings he experienced in a system of enforced segregation weren't legally relevant. Alternatively, they might have a discussion about Holmes lecturing Carrie Buck that her sterilization was nothing compared to the sacrifice the country asks of its citizens in times of war and to think of it like a vaccination. Or ask which (if any) of the six judgments that were written in *Roe v. Wade* (recognizing the right to have an abortion) or in *Gregg v. Georgia*[19] (upholding the death penalty), the candidate thinks got it right, and why.

These are not questions that compromise the impartiality of a prospective justice. There is nothing unethical or inappropriate about conversations of this sort. In the case of someone like Amy Coney Barrett (Donald Trump's last appointment to the Court), who taught constitutional law at an elite law school, it would be just a matter of repeating what she said in class.

As ethical and informative as such a conversation would be, the reality is that there is no chance one will be struck anytime soon. Neither senators nor nominees have an incentive to engage in an open and honest discussion about the Court's early history on racism and sexism and what could have been done to repair it. Rating the force of a precedent is considered taboo. Nor is there any pressure for change within the profession. Indeed, before Kagan gave her testimony to the Senate Judiciary Committee, Ronald Dworkin, one of the country's leading legal scholars, counseled her to stonewall her inquisitors when any questions about her approach to the law were raised.

Some lawyers and legal academics have tried to sound the alarm, but to little effect. Mainstream legal scholarship in the United States generally accepts the legitimacy of the Court's pluralist approach and defends the current system of filling seats on the bench. Giving judges so much discretion is not seen as a threat to their impartiality or the integrity of law.

Barack Obama, who was a law teacher at one of the best law schools in the country before he became president, once likened controversial court decisions to a marathon. The first twenty-five miles, he said, are determined by precedent and other traditional forms of legal argument. The last mile, however, is decided by a judge's own values, concerns, perspectives on the world, and "the breadth and depth of one's empathy." In close cases that could go either way, Obama assumes America's highest judges are in the same position as the jurors in Athens; free to decide on their own sense of right and wrong.

Obama's characterization of the judges' reasoning process is widely shared on both the left and the right. On the same assumption, Ronald Dworkin dismissed as simplistic and wrongheaded anyone who thinks judges can fix the limits of legitimate government without relying on their own sense of justice. Richard Posner says it is ideology that determines the outcome of a case. At the end of his career, William Rehnquist, the sixteenth chief justice of the Supreme Court, also embraced this truth when he advised a colleague that it was only the result of a case, not the principles and analysis on which it was based, that mattered.

The way judicial review has evolved in the United States is a terrible tragedy. The gap between the aspiration and the reality of the rule of law remains as wide as ever. The way the judges in Washington have gone about resolving conflict is the antithesis of the Greek ideal. In all three of its dimensions, the American conception of the rule of law comes up short. It lacks certainty and legitimacy and can be distorted by judges to the prejudice of minorities who have few friends in high places.

The jurisprudence that was written by the US Supreme Court in its first 150 years will go down as one of the darker chapters in the history of the rule of law. Fortunately, it wasn't the last. In the twentieth century, the idea of judges resolving major social conflict and acting as a check on the powers of political leaders gained ground on two other fronts. At the beginning of the century, international lawyers pushed the idea of using judges instead of generals to solve disputes between sovereign states, and by the middle of the century legal professionals all over the world were advocating for their countries to embrace the idea of judicial review. In the next two chapters, we will follow the fate of law's most recent adventures.

Chapter Eight

The Hague

The Origins of International Law

The history of the rule of law that we have followed so far has been mostly about relations between rulers and the people they govern. From its earliest days, law's overarching ambition has been to promote justice and protect people against the whim and the will of the despot. Law's primary purpose has been to foster human welfare by providing a check on arbitrariness and abuse of power in government. However, for almost all of its history, the rule of law has also been concerned with relations between rulers, including the question of when, if ever, armed aggression and the use of physical force is a legitimate way to settle conflicts between rival sovereigns and independent states.[1]

It will come as no surprise that when lawyers and jurists first thought about war they came at it from a legal perspective. Right from the beginning, their instinct was to see armed force as a powerful, but exceptional, way of enforcing the rule of law. In a world with no courts or tribunals in which to resolve disputes between sovereign rulers, war was often the only way to ensure princes and predators did not profit from or go unpunished for bad behavior. In writing to his son on the requirements for a good life, Cicero made the point in his typically cogent way. There are only two ways to settle disputes, he said: talking it through or imposing one's will; the force of reason or brute force.[2]

Cicero believed rulers should only resort to the latter when further dialogue became pointless. Only when all nonviolent methods had been tried and failed could war be waged to defend one's community, right a wrong, or punish a wrongdoer. Armed force was a legitimate way to punish wrongdoing and defend oneself, but only as a last resort. Wars were fought to defend the law when law couldn't defend itself.

Cicero also thought that whenever circumstances did justify going to war, there were basic rules of proper conduct that ought to be respected. War was lawful only after a demand for justice, such as the recovery of property or the return of hostages, had gone unheeded, and only on condition that it was pursued without engaging in acts of barbarity or cruelty. He argued that ambassadors and religious temples were inviolable. He also insisted enemies should be given clear warning of an impending attack and the conquered should be treated with compassion.[3]

Like everything he wrote about the law, Cicero's theory of armed conflict drew on the natural law tradition of the Stoics. Applied to the question of when it is legitimate to start a war, the logic of natural law is compellingly simple. As we read in chapter 3, the Stoics started from the premise that universal laws of nature govern the evolution of everything in the world, including human behavior. For them, the primary attribute that makes humans unique is our natural capacity for reason and self-reflection. The power of reason is the natural way humans settle disputes; physical force, by contrast, is the method of the brute. With the power of rational thought, the Stoics believed, "natural" laws governing when and how armed force should be used could be identified – universal, timeless rules that bound all people in all ages. If adhered to, they would facilitate a world living naturally in harmony and in peace.

It is worth noting that, while Cicero's ideas about the legitimacy of war as tool of law enforcement drew on the natural law tradition of the Stoics, similar ideas flourished in other parts of the world, including in China (even though, as we noted in chapter 1, Confucian thought was not well-disposed to legal regulation). On the issue of war, however, the Chinese and Greeks thought a lot alike. For both, peace was the natural, preferred state of the world, war a last resort to defend against foreign invasions, counter rebellions, and maintain harmony in foreign relations. Like Cicero and the Greeks, the Chinese believed war should only be fought according to basic rules of moderation and fair play.

Although the idea that war is only legitimate as a way to enforce the law when used as a means of last resort, and that no more force should be used than is necessary, has a natural logic to it, not everyone signed on. Of the different legal traditions we have examined, Islamic law is a notable exception. Although sharia law insists that peaceful relations are the norm among the faithful, regardless of race or ethnicity, when it comes to the infidel, the Qur'an envisages a perpetual state of war. Islamic law divides the world into lands in which the faithful live – called the *Dar al-Islam* – and those inhabited by the infidel – the *Dar al-Harb*, or the house of war. Islamic law gives its blessing to the former attacking the latter whenever it suits their purposes. No threat or act of wrongdoing is required.[4]

Cicero's understanding of the relationship between law and war received a more welcoming reception from theologians in the Catholic Church. Like him, they argued wars were consistent with canon law when they were waged for the purpose of defending the faith, avenging wrongs, and exacting reparations.[5]

The idea of war being a legitimate tool of law enforcement in a limited set of circumstances got strong support in the sixteenth century from Francisco de Vitoria and his colleagues in what has come to be known as the Salamanca school. De Vitoria and his contemporaries were looking for answers to the questions that were raised by the voyages of discovery that European monarchs were sending to the New World. What were the rights and wrongs of the Spanish conquistadores colonizing lands that millions of Inca and Aztec, Iroquois and Apache called home? De Vitoria and his fellow jurists, known as the late scholastics, took up the challenge and crafted a sophisticated account of when it was legitimate for armed force to be used to pacify native rulers and their people.

Like the Stoics, these Dominican and Jesuit jurists thought of war as an exceptional method of law enforcement. They argued that a war of conquest over Indigenous Peoples could only be justified when (1) it was necessary to vindicate a valid legal claim; (2) all nonviolent means of settlement had been tried and failed; (3) there were no ulterior motives; (4) there was a reasonable probability of success; and (5) the military means that were employed were proportional to the ends they were intended to achieve.

Another part of their theory was that sovereign rulers had a monopoly on the legitimate use of armed force. Like Cicero, they said warlords and bandits, pirates and rebels might launch insurrections and organize raids, but they could never legally wage war. War was the sport of kings.

From the premise that not all armed conflict qualified as a "just war," it also followed that in such cases the conquerors had no legal claim to the territory and property they seized. The principles of natural law offered a strong counterargument to the traditional understanding that at the end of a war, victors were entitled to the spoils. Again, following Cicero, they insisted that whoever prevailed on the battlefield had an obligation to show a measure of moderation and compassion in settling the terms of peace.

To ensure wars were only fought when all the prerequisites had been met, de Vitoria and his successors encouraged rulers to consult with legal experts. The way they understood the world, lawyers had as much to say in deciding when and how a war should be fought as the generals.

Especially when passions were inflamed, the cool voice of reason needed to be heard.

However compelling these arguments may have been, the reality was that none of the royal courts of Europe paid much attention. Regardless of the force of the jurists' words on paper, their treatises did little to improve interstate relations in either the Old or New World. As we read in chapter 5, terrible wars of horrific brutality were a pervasive, ongoing feature of the medieval era.

At the time the Salamanca school was thinking through the logic of when and how just wars might be fought, Europe was plagued by political and sectarian hostilities and Native populations were being massacred all over the New World. Despite the force of their tracts, Catholics continued to fight Protestants and Protestants fought each other, and all the while French, English, Spanish, and German monarchs battled over competing territorial and dynastic pretensions.

To compound the tragedy of such wanton violence, it turned out that the natural law story that the jurists were promoting was itself part of the problem. Because its method of evaluating the justice of war was organized around general principles like "just cause" and "necessity," rulers were able to manipulate them to justify their territorial and strategic ambitions. Everyone insisted their wars were just and exaggerated the necessity of their chosen means.

The Crusades were defended as legitimate invasions of Palestine to regain control over Christianity's holiest sites, which the crusaders insisted had been wrongfully seized by Islamic warriors. The conquest and colonization of Africa, Asia, and the Americas were defended as lawful engagements to ensure the natural rights of Europeans to travel, trade, and promote their faith in the face of native resistance. Miraculously, canon lawyers were able to transform a religion that taught its adherents to turn the other cheek and love their neighbors into a "Church Militant" led by military-religious orders like the Templars and Hospitaliers.

The truth was that even law's most ardent defenders could be selective and strategic in their thinking. Like the Greeks when they were fighting barbarians, and Muslims in their battles with infidels, Christians typically had one set of rules for settling disputes among themselves and another for fighting people of other faiths. Pope Innocent II banned the crossbow and other missile-firing weapons (the medieval equivalent of weapons of mass destruction), but only in wars between Christians. Aquinas thought enslavement of defeated populations, including women and children, could be justified, but not if they were Christian. At the same time de Vitoria was defending the rights of Indigenous Peoples in the

New World against wars of naked aggression, he recognized the legitimacy of Europeans using armed force to defend their rights to trade, proselytize, and rescue innocent victims from rituals of human sacrifice and other gross human rights violations. On the facts as he knew them, the Spanish conquest of Central and South America was a justifiable case of humanitarian intervention.

Such was the state of the legal universe when law's next hall of famer, an astonishingly precocious child named Hugo de Groot (better known as Grotius), stepped onto the world stage. Widely recognized as the "Father of International Law," he is another of the twenty-three lawmakers whose images watch over the deliberations of the US House of Representatives.[6] He was born in Delft in 1583 into a family that was part of the ruling elite (his uncle was a law professor and head of the University of Leiden). His brilliance showed itself immediately. He was enrolled in the law faculty at age eleven, and at fifteen he was part of a diplomatic mission to France, where he was dubbed the "Miracle of Holland" by the French king.

A humanist and a deeply religious person committed to tolerance between different faiths, he lived in a time and place in which war and sectarian conflict raged all around him. For the whole of his life (Protestant) Holland was fighting a war of independence against (Catholic) Spain, and for his last twenty-seven years he lived through the Thirty Years' War, which has gone down in history as one of the bloodiest periods of European history. When he cast his eye over the state of international relations in Europe, he was appalled by the trivial causes for which men went to war and by the "frenzy ... it let loose for the committing of all crimes."

Jailed for his religious ideas, he used his incarceration to think about the failed state of the law between nations and concluded he could do better. After escaping prison with the help of his wife, he fled to France and wrote a book, *On the Laws of War and Peace*, which to this day is still considered the starting point of the rights and wrongs of armed conflict.

The book is an exhaustive (and at times exhausting) piece of work. Translated into English, it runs to over seven hundred pages. It purports to build a universal system of law to govern relations between states on the natural capacity of humans for rational intelligence and the customs and practices that have been followed by rulers in the past. Its unstated ambition was to construct the entire edifice of international law on the twin pillars of reason and consent.

Grotius was an ardent advocate of natural law. The core of his thinking about the laws of war and peace drew heavily on the just war literature of the classical and medieval scholars. References to Cicero, Augustine,

Aquinas, and de Vitoria appear all through the text. Like them, Grotius thought physical force was a legitimate way to right wrongs when there was no other peaceful way of defending the universal norms of natural law. Where the methods of justice cease, he wrote, war begins. On the other hand, if either side offered to settle a dispute by having an independent, impartial third party arbitrate, his position was that it would be unlawful for the other side to go to war.

He identified three legal causes that legitimized the use of armed force: (1) self-defense; (2) recovery of property (including debts); and (3) punishment for past transgressions. Following the natural law tradition, in each case he cautioned that resort to armed force should be exercised with moderation and restraint and that those who had been conquered should be treated with clemency. He cautioned rulers to resist the siren calls of imperialism and told them wars of religious conversion and claims of discovery of previously occupied land were unlawful.

Despite being a champion of natural law, Grotius was alert to its limitations. He understood that, as a practical matter, neither the principle of just cause nor necessity had imposed any meaningful constraint on when and how wars were to be fought. He knew from experience that, in every war, both sides claimed everything they did was an essential operation undertaken for a just (legal) cause and that there was no way the validity of either claim could be challenged. Even the worst atrocities of sectarian violence were defended as being unavoidable by those who committed them.

Grotius worried that the difficulty of determining who were the good guys, and how much force was necessary to secure their rights, meant it was next to impossible to know who was entitled to the legal protections and entitlements that came from waging a just war and who had legitimate title to the spoils when the fighting stopped. To shore up the broad principles of natural law, Grotius looked for rules of good behavior in the ways wars had been fought in the past. To better connect the logic of natural law with the brutality of the real world, he proposed adding to the laws of war practices and standards that nations had adhered to in the past. The idea was that established norms and customs of military conduct that had been respected by rulers throughout history demonstrated a measure of consensus and consent among those authorized to wage war. As he envisaged the legal regime that governed relations between sovereign rulers, it consisted of a "volitional" law of nations operating alongside a "natural" law of reason.

To identify patterns and common threads that governed behavior in times of war, Grotius read everything the Greeks and Romans, Christians and Jews had to say about military conflict. In some cases, his research paid off. For example, his review of military tactics showed that using poison (first-generation chemical weapons) and committing rape had never been acceptable to the most enlightened rulers, no matter what the reason. In terms of the international legal order he envisaged, both were illegitimate behaviors that were outlawed by the law of nations. They were what today we call war crimes.

Not all the customs and practices Grotius uncovered, however, proved to be compatible with the moderating principles of natural law. Some, like the long-standing practice of recognizing the right of soldiers to kill the enemy and keep whatever property they plundered, regardless of whether the war they were fighting was just, threatened rather than strengthened the moral authority of natural law. Grotius realized this was not an ideal solution, but he didn't think he had a choice.

As he saw it, the legal enforcement of practices that made might right, and that gave unjust warriors a license to kill and steal, was a case of choosing the lesser evil. Because there was no way to challenge the claim that a military operation was a necessary tactic to enforce a valid legal claim, it had to be assumed that soldiers on both sides were telling the truth. Both sides had to be treated equally in order to ensure that those fighters who really were waging a just war received the benefit and protection of the law.

Even though the agnosticism of this "law of nations," on the question of which side in a conflict was fighting for a just cause, had a certain logic to it, the conclusions to which it led resulted in the legalization of horrendous behavior. Including plundering and killing as part of the laws of war meant that no soldier had to answer for behaviors that would be treated as murder and armed robbery if committed in peacetime. In Grotius's legal universe, unarmed civilians and prisoners of war could be killed or enslaved and the victors were entitled to keep all the loot (including women and children) they could grab.

With the benefit of hindsight, there can be no doubt that Grotius's idea of joining an empirical law of customs and practices to a natural law of reason begat a legal regime that was extremely tolerant of a whole lot of violence and horrendous brutality. Offensive wars, preemptive wars, and wars to defend the rights of others all got the green light. Wars could be launched to counter present violations of a ruler's sovereignty; punish legal transgressions committed in the past; and avert threats of unlawful conduct in the future. Any breach of natural law provided a legal basis to start a war. Rulers who interfered with travel or trade or who committed gross human rights violations were liable to be attacked.

The key to understanding how Grotius could have written a treatise that legalized so much barbaric behavior is his faith. The legal universe he constructed was the work of a devout Christian. He believed Europe's monarchs would be governed by their consciences and that the principles of natural law would rein them in. Even if emperors and kings couldn't be put in the dock, he assumed the knowledge that in the next world they would face divine judgment would temper their aggression. Writing to believers of the same God, Grotius expected rulers to pay heed to the universal laws of reason in all things, including war.

Even when a ruler had just cause to go to war, Grotius warned against making such decisions rashly. He told rulers they shouldn't strike back if the aggression they suffered was of a minor nature or if the good that could be accomplished by an armed response was insignificant. Invoking Cicero, he advised the monarchs of seventeenth-century Europe to think like physicians: use light treatments for less serious conditions and save the most powerful remedies for the gravest threats. It was all a question of balance. The force used to respond to an attack should be roughly of the same weight and character as the initial act of aggression.

Grotius insisted that natural law required rulers to take a "prudent" approach in deciding whether to go to war. If, for example, the odds that an armed conflict would produce a good or evil outcome were about equal, he said it should be chosen "only if the good has somewhat more of good than evil has of evil." He encouraged rulers to think about the decision in terms of ends and means. First the good and evil consequences of engaging in hostilities must be considered, and then the means that are available to pursue the objectives that have been chosen should be examined. In Grotius's mind, it was also important for rulers to assess the effectiveness of different strategies. Entering armed conflicts that had little chance of success defied human reason and therefore natural law.

Balance and restraint were central to Grotius's understanding of the laws of war. He thought of law as a moderating force – an antidote to extremism and excess. Even though he recognized that the law of nations licensed the killing of innocent civilians, he insisted that the natural law of reason condemned such attacks because they did nothing to enhance the safety and security of the killers. Although he thought killing a few women and children, if they were trapped inside a "house of brigands" or on a "ship full of pirates," might be justifiable, the indiscriminate loss of many innocent lives was not.

In the end, despite the monumental character of the legal order he constructed, Grotius's message didn't resonate with many people. Indeed, over time his ideas came under attack from both the Left and the Right. Rousseau was dismissive of his attempt to derive an international law of nations from the customs and practices that rulers had followed in the past. He regarded it as an irrational effort to derive an "ought" from an "is"; to turn a fact into proof of what is morally or legally right. As well, he didn't think Grotius did enough to distinguish civilians from the states in which they lived and provide them the protection to which, as noncombatants, they were entitled. Kant was even more blunt. He pointed out that Grotius's statement of the law had never stopped anyone from going to war, and in fact could be used as cover and cited as justification in cases of clearly hostile aggression.

In the nineteenth century, his influence sank even further. Carl von Clausewitz, a Prussian military officer, dismissed Grotius's law of nations as "certain self-imposed, imperceptible limitations hardly worth mentioning." He expressed the dominant view of the time when he characterized war as just "the continuation of politics by other means." The authority to settle conflicts by the use of force was accepted as the sovereign right of every state. Rather than a tool of law enforcement, war became just another way of doing business.

In the new age of empires, the law of war became whatever the victor declared it to be. There were no limits. Rather than the dualistic character that Grotius envisaged, the law of war was reduced to the rules that nations agreed on and the logic of brute force. The principles of natural law that were central to Grotius's conception of international law were ignored. The legality of war no longer had anything to do with either justice or reason. Theories of just war were treated as utopias of moral philosophy, not as meaningful rules of law. Lawyers' opinions were not required reading for Napoleon or his generals.

That changed in the second half of the nineteenth century, when interest in the legal regulation of armed conflict revived. The period between 1850 and 1900 has been called the law of war's "epoch of highest repute." At first the emphasis was on the who and how of waging war rather than on the when or why. In 1863, Abraham Lincoln commissioned a code of conduct, known as the Lieber Code, setting out instructions on how Union soldiers were to conduct themselves in the American Civil War. A year later, a dozen European states took the first tentative steps toward laying down rules regulating how people behaved in war. Known today as the First Geneva Convention, it was the brainchild of Henri Dunant, a Swiss banker who witnessed the horrific carnage of one of the major battles (Solferino) in the wars for Italian unification and vowed to do something about it.

One of the first things he did was write a book (*A Memory of Solferino*) about what he had seen. In it he described "piles of bleeding corpses, the crushing of skulls, ripping bellies open, brains spurt under wheels." These were the brutal facts of "sheer butchery; a struggle between savage beasts, maddened with blood and fury." Inspired by

Dunant's writing, the Swiss government organized a meeting of European nations to work out a set of principles for the care of the sick and wounded. It was this gathering that led to the formation of the International Committee of the Red Cross. Although rules of military engagement go back at least as far as Hammurabi's time, this multinational agreement marks the beginning of what is known today as international humanitarian law.

The First Geneva Convention was a modest beginning. The obligations it imposed were purely humanitarian; it was all about taking care of the sick and wounded. Apart from outlawing attacks on medical personnel and facilities, it did not limit when wars could be waged nor the way they were fought. Moreover, the convention did not contain any mechanism to ensure that the rules it did lay down were enforced.

Four years later, in 1868, twenty countries, again mostly from Europe, but also including Persia, the Ottomans, and Brazil, met in St. Petersburg and issued a declaration that the only legitimate objective in fighting a war is "to weaken the military forces of the enemy." That meant weapons "that uselessly aggravate the suffering of disabled men or render their death inevitable" exceeded the lawful purposes of war and so were "contrary to the laws of humanity." On that logic they were able to renounce the use of a type of exploding bullet that had just been developed by the Russians.

International Law in the Twentieth Century

Following the successes of Geneva and St. Petersburg, Europe's jurists raised their profile. They established an institute of international law, started a journal to facilitate an exchange of views, and supported Tsar Alexander II's initiative to organize a conference to discuss codifying the laws of war. At the dawn of the twentieth century, as lawyers assumed a more prominent role, the skeleton of a legal code of armed conflict began to take shape.

Again at the urging of the Russians, and with the goal of "extending the empire of law and strengthening the appreciation of international justice," all the major world powers gathered in The Hague in the final days of the nineteenth century to hammer out rules for "the Pacific Settlement of International Disputes" and to establish "Laws and Customs of War on Land." The result, known as The Hague Convention of 1899, was eventually signed by forty-nine countries, including China, the United States, Russia, Japan, the Austro-Hungarian Empire, and most of South America. It came into force on 4 September 1900 and was revised in 1907 to cover naval warfare.

The Hague Convention incorporated the Geneva Convention of 1864, the St. Petersburg Declaration, and more. First, it extended the duty of humanitarian treatment beyond the sick and wounded to include prisoners of war and soldiers who had surrendered. Next, it declared that the means of war were not unlimited and added to the list of proscribed tactics bombardment from balloons, poisonous and chemical weapons, and all "arms, projectiles or material of a nature to cause superfluous injury." As well, it encouraged states to make use of peaceful processes of resolving conflict, including mediation, fact-finding commissions of inquiry, and a newly created Permanent Court of Arbitration. Finally, conscious of the limited scope of the rules on which they were able to agree, and with a nod to Grotius, the delegates and their governments pledged that both soldiers and civilians would "remain under the protection and empire of the principles of international law as they result from the usages established between civilized nations, from the laws of humanity and the requirements of the public conscience."

The recognition of an unwritten, residual component of the international law of armed force was the brainchild of Foydor (or Friedrich) Martens, who represented Russia at The Hague and was the meeting's unofficial host. Martens held the chair of international law at the University of St. Petersburg and had written a big book on the history of international law. He was one of the leaders of the international law community who championed the "empire of law" in the last quarter of the nineteenth century. A strong believer in the force of natural law to settle conflicts between sovereign states, he was nominated for the Nobel Peace Prize more than once.

The Hague Convention was undoubtedly the capstone in Martens's distinguished career. In the clause he wrote, the natural law tradition that had been a part of international law from Cicero to Grotius was brought back to life. The creation of the Permanent Court of Arbitration was another first that would mark the beginning of an era in which judges were authorized to review the decisions of the generals and their political masters.

The idea that principles of law exist to regulate and resolve international conflicts, and that independent, impartial jurists can be found throughout the world's different legal systems to enforce them, runs through the whole of the twentieth century. Breaking with a tradition that went back to the dawn of legal history, the international community turned its back on the practice of relying on war to enforce the law and began to advocate for the use of courts instead. Initially, resolving the rights and wrongs of interstate conflicts through judicial proceedings, rather than on the battlefield, was purely voluntary; judges could only replace generals if both sides agreed. By the dawn of the new millennium, however, rulers who were suspected of having committed crimes in war could be arrested and, if convicted, sent to jail.

The initial push for the legal enforcement of international law came after the First World War. In article 12 of the Treaty of Versailles, the members of the international community promised to submit their conflicts to arbitration, or the Council of the League of Nations, and not to resort to war until three months after such peaceful attempts to resolve the conflict had passed. They also agreed to establish a Permanent Court of International Justice to facilitate the peaceful resolution of disputes arising out of the Treaty of Versailles and the various conventions and agreements that followed in its wake. Opening its doors in the Peace Palace in The Hague in 1922, planet earth had its first ever world court.

Although its rulings were binding only on countries that agreed to its jurisdiction, it could issue advisory opinions when asked to do so by either the Council or General Assembly of the League of Nations. In answering questions submitted to it, the Court was expected to adopt the broad structure of Grotius's legal framework. It was authorized to apply both "international custom, as evidence of a general practice accepted as law," and "general principles of law recognized by civilized nations." In its short life between the two world wars, it heard some sixty cases on everything from border disputes and the rights of minorities to be educated in their own language to the legal status of Greenland.

Afflicted with the league's failure to concern itself with armed conflicts short of all-out war, and limited to cases in which the parties agreed to its jurisdiction, the Court's role in resolving international conflict turned out to be marginal. After Germany, Japan, and Italy quit the league and Stalin's Russia was expelled, the Court stood by helplessly as wars broke out in Africa, Asia, and Europe. No one was willing, in John Lennon's words, to give peace a chance. The Second World War followed soon after.

The War of the World, as the historian Niall Ferguson has described it, was a wasteland like no other. Here is proof, if it were needed, of Cicero's truth that in times of war, law remains silent. From 1939 until 1945, physical force, as the ultimate arbiter of international conflict, reigned supreme. Law was nowhere in sight. If the history of the rule of law is a story of rise and fall and rise and fall, this was arguably law's darkest moment.

For the first time in military history, death and destruction rained down from on high. When aerial bombardment became a critical part of waging war, civilians came into the line of fire. Dozens of cities on all sides, including Stalingrad, London, Tokyo, and Berlin, all suffered immense loss of life. When the Americans firebombed more than sixty Japanese cities, over 500,000 civilians lost their lives. Roughly 200,000 people (almost all of them civilians) were instantly killed in Hiroshima and Nagasaki when the US military carried out Harry Truman's order to drop two nuclear bombs. The Second World War was by far the deadliest conflict in human history. It is estimated that over 70 million lives were lost, more than half of them civilians.

In the wake of such horrific slaughter and unconscionable destruction, the international community declared its commitment to a fundamental, root-and-branch reformation of the law. The when, why, who, and how of war all needed a fix. Encouraging the peaceful resolution of disputes and postponing the start of war for a few months were no longer good enough.

The centerpiece of these efforts was the United Nations Charter, a new constitution for the planet. In the preamble, "the peoples of the United Nations" declared their determination "to save succeeding generations from the scourge of war, which twice in our lifetime has brought untold sorrow to mankind." To achieve their ambition, they began (in article 2) by reaffirming the principle of the peaceful settlement of all disputes between member states and renouncing the use of force as a method of conflict resolution. Armed force was only permitted in two specific circumstances.

First, the UN Security Council was empowered to use military force when it is "necessary to maintain or restore international peace and security" (article 42). Second, individual states were entitled to resort to force in "self-defence" when they come under an "armed attack" (article 51). Even a state's right to defend itself is made conditional on notifying the Security Council and lasts only until the Security Council has taken whatever measures are necessary to restore peace. In effect, on 26 June 1945, the day the charter came into effect, the international community declared that war was no longer a legitimate way to enforce the law.

In addition to limiting the circumstances when force could be used, after the Second World War the international community continued to concern itself with the ways – the who and the how – legitimate wars could be fought. In 1949, the rules governing the treatment of the sick and wounded, prisoners of war, and civilian populations were updated and revised in four new Geneva Conventions. In what is known as common article 3, noncombatants in all conflicts were guaranteed the right to be treated humanely, without violence or attacks on their personal dignity. In 1977, protocols were adopted in which new protections for civilians were added, wars against colonial and racist regimes were legalized, and the Martens clause was reaffirmed.

Over the course of the second half of the twentieth century, new ways of killing (including land mines and lasers) were added to the proscribed list of weapons and international humanitarian law was extended to provide more extensive protection for civilians. In the 1970s and '80s, international conventions outlawing weapons that are "excessively injurious" and attacks that result in "excessive" loss of civilian life were adopted. Weapons and methods of warfare that "cause superfluous injury or unnecessary suffering" were proscribed. Genocide and torture were declared to be illegal (in 1951 and 1987, respectively), and in 1998 the Statute of Rome identified a long list of the gravest violations of the laws of armed conflict as crimes against humanity and war crimes.[7]

By the dawn of the new millennium, the laws of war and peace were immeasurably stronger than what Grotius had envisaged almost four hundred years earlier. Now, the only reason a state can use force is in self-defense and the range of legitimate behavior in the conduct of war is much more restricted. Military force can no longer be used as an instrument of punishment or to recover territory that has been wrongfully taken by another state. Civilians can no longer be targeted and, critically, there are now judicial institutions to which injured parties and innocent victims can turn for help.

The Second World War precipitated major changes in the rules of when and how wars could be fought, and it resulted in the enhanced enforceability of the law as well. Within a year of the war's conclusion, the Nazis most responsible for the atrocities committed in the name of the German Reich were put on trial at Nuremburg before an International Military Tribunal.[8] Six months later, Japan's political and military leaders faced similar trials in Tokyo. For the first time, those who launched unjustified acts of armed aggression were charged and convicted of war crimes and crimes against humanity that were part of The Hague Conventions and the principles of customary international law.

Prosecuting German and Japanese political and military leaders at the end of the Second World War was an extraordinary and controversial decision, but it set a precedent. Although no other rulers would be prosecuted for another fifty years, by the end of the century trials of war criminals were becoming part of the international legal order. In the 1990s, special tribunals were established to deal with allegations of war crimes and crimes against humanity committed in Rwanda, Cambodia, and the former Yugoslavia. With the enactment of the Statute of Rome in 1998, an International Criminal Court with an independent prosecutor was created to hold anyone who violated the laws of war and armed aggression to account. In contrast with the world as it was when Grotius lived, there are now rules of international criminal law that bind rulers and ruled alike.

The Rule of Law in The Hague

At the same time that the German and Japanese leaderships were being held accountable for their legal transgressions, the international community reaffirmed its commitment to the idea of an independent world court. Taking over from where the Permanent Court of International Justice had left off, the International Court of Justice was created to act as the judicial arm of the United Nations and provide a peaceful method of resolving future conflicts. Everyone had high hopes. Drawing its members from the best and brightest jurists in international law, the Court was empowered to give advisory opinions on any legal question that was put to it by the Security Council and/or the General Assembly. Like its predecessor, it was also authorized to adjudicate international conflicts when the parties agreed to its jurisdiction.

Although cases were slow in coming, over the course of a twenty-year period beginning in 1986, the Court was asked for its opinion on the use of armed force on five separate occasions. The importance of the cases transcended the specific conflicts they addressed. They provided the most distinguished practitioners and scholars of international law from around the world with the opportunity to lay down the rules, once and for all, on how states must resolve their differences.

As might be anticipated from everything we have encountered in law's history so far, the jurisprudence they wrote turns out to be a mixed blessing. On the one hand, the moderating force of natural law, which was so central to Grotius's way of thinking, was revived and given new precision. On the other, the message was conveyed in a way that is almost impossible for most people to understand, and so has virtually no significance in the real world.

The Court's first major ruling on the law of armed conflict grew out of a dispute between Nicaragua and the United States.[9] The focus of the Court's attention was on Washington's involvement in a nasty civil war that plagued El Salvador for most of the 1980s. The Americans were worried that Marxist insurgents would overthrow the Salvadoran government, just as they had in Nicaragua. Claiming a right to act for the collective self-defense of El Salvador, Honduras, and Costa Rica, the Americans gave the Salvadoran government financial and logistical support and attempted, by military means, to cut off the supply of arms that passed through Nicaragua to the insurgents. Nicaragua took exception to the Americans' intervention and asked the Court to condemn it.

The legality of the Americans' military strikes turned on whether they could prove they were acting in self-defense. In addressing this question, all fifteen judges who heard the case shared a common understanding that states warding off attacks should have to meet the same legal standards as an ordinary citizen who faces a common assault. In international law, as in domestic systems of criminal law, the fundamental rule is that force used in self-defense must never be excessive. Just as you and I can slap, but not shoot, someone who violates us with an unwanted grope, neither can states engage in overkill when their sovereignty and security are threatened.

Although the UN Charter doesn't say so explicitly, the Court declared (in paragraph 176) that it was a well-established rule of customary international law that acting in self-defense only permits "measures which are proportional to the armed attack and necessary to respond to it." Echoing Grotius more than 350 years after he lived, the Court laid down the law that force can only be used as a last resort, when all other less drastic means have failed, and only so long as it is similar in kind to the act of aggression it aims to repel.

In the Nicaragua case, the Court found against the Americans on both counts. First, it said that at the time the Americans attacked Nicaragua there was no need to resort to force. On the evidence before them, by the time the Americans launched their assault, the insurgents in El Salvador had been defeated and the threat they posed no longer justified taking action against Nicaragua. The danger had passed. The use of force could not be justified as an act of self-defense because it came too late.

In addition to finding the Americans could have accomplished their purposes by means that respected the sovereignty and territorial integrity of Nicaragua, the Court also ruled that the extent of the force they directed against Nicaragua's Sandinista government was out of all proportion to the arms and other support the Nicaraguans had given the insurgents. The Americans had mined and attacked Nicaraguan ports, blown up oil pipelines and storage facilities, fired rockets at a naval base, and extended financial and logistical support to the "Contras," an opposition group committed to the violent overthrow of the Sandinista government.

In the Court's opinion, although American support for the Contras by itself might have been proportional to the armed assistance and logistical support the Nicaraguans gave to the Salvadoran rebels, the collective force of all the military strikes was not. Even the Court's American judge thought that the United States had violated international law when it failed to notify neutral countries that maintained normal relations with Nicaragua of the danger they faced if they entered Nicaraguan ports.

The rules the Court laid down in the Nicaragua case have established the limits on the legitimate use of force ever since. Subsequently, on each occasion when it was asked to judge whether the use of force was lawful or not, necessity and proportionality were two of the lenses through which the Court examined the facts of the case. Regardless of the size and status of the states involved, the laws of war were equally binding.

In 1996, ten years after its ruling in the Nicaragua case, the Court was asked by the UN General Assembly whether "the threat or use of nuclear weapons in any circumstances (is) permitted under international law."[10] Most of the judges didn't think the question could be answered with a simple yes or no. Like guerrilla wars in Central America, the legality of nuclear weapons called for a delicate balancing of the competing interests at stake.

Everyone was agreed that the circumstances in which nuclear weapons would be legal would be exceedingly rare. No one doubted that, because of their unique and catastrophic effects, the use of such weapons would almost always be a violation of the protection extended to civilians by the Martens clause (paragraph 78). However, the Court also recognized that, as a principle of customary international law, proportionality did not rule out the possibility that, "in an extreme circumstance of self-defence, in which the very survival of a State would be at stake," nuclear weapons might be lawfully used. Without the facts of a concrete case before them, that was all they were able to say.

In the new millennium, the Court was asked to sort out the rights and wrongs of armed force three more times, and in each case it confirmed that the principles of necessity and proportionality fix the outer limits on when states can legitimately have resort to military power and how much force can be used.

In 2003, it found that the United States had acted illegally a second time by using unnecessary and disproportionate force against Iran.[11] The case grew out of what was known as the Tanker War, which broke out in the Persian Gulf in the 1980s during a brutal eight-year struggle between Iran and Iraq. In the course of the conflict, both sides engaged in aggressive acts that threatened commercial shipping in the Gulf.

The spark that triggered US involvement consisted of two attacks: one against a Kuwaiti tanker flagged to the United States and a second against an American warship that was escorting commercial shipping in the Gulf. In response to the first, the Americans blew up an Iranian oil platform that was defended by military personnel and that the Americans claimed had been involved in coordinating the initial attack. In response to the mining of one of their navy vessels, the Americans hit back even harder. Code-named Operation Praying Mantis, their attack included the destruction of Iranian aircraft and navy vessels in addition to the bombing of two more oil platforms.

Like its ruling in the Nicaragua case, the Court found that the use of force by the Americans was both unnecessary and, at least in the second incident, excessive. Destroying the oil platforms was unnecessary because the Americans had never said anything about these structures when they complained to the Iranians about the effects of the Tanker War on shipping in the Gulf.

Before the Americans could consider the platforms to be serious threats and legitimate targets, the Court said it was necessary to warn the Iranians of what would happen if the platforms continued to be used for military purposes and the attacks didn't stop. Not saying anything to the Iranians about the oil platforms suggested to the judges that the Americans didn't really think they had any strategic importance. Until diplomatic efforts had been tried and failed, it was impossible to say armed force was the only way the conflict could be resolved.

The judges added that, even if the platforms had been a legitimate military target, they didn't think their destruction, as part of larger and more extensive counterattack, was proportional to the material damage that the Americans had suffered. Although they allowed that the destruction of the oil platforms might have been proportional if they had played a role in the attacks and if that was all the Americans had done, being part of a much larger military operation against Iranian forces was not. As a response to the mining of a single American warship that was damaged but not sunk and did not result in any loss of life, Operation Praying Mantis was not a proportionate response.

The measure of proportionality the Court used in the Nicaraguan and Iranian cases was the same. Compared to the hostile acts of aggression it was reacting to, the force Americans used to defend their interests was excessive. They overreacted. America's response was out of proportion to what the Nicaraguans and Iranians had done to them. Nor were they proportional to the military objectives they sought to achieve. In Iran they came too early, in Nicaragua they came too late.

In comparing the amount of force used by the Nicaraguans and Iranians with the American response, the Court focused on the facts. To ensure the principle of proportionality was applied objectively and free of their own biases, the judges looked for evidence of the parties' own evaluation of the events. In the Iranian case, they relied on the Americans' failure to mention the oil platforms when they complained to the government in Tehran as evidence that Washington didn't think they were of much military consequence. From where the judges sat, it looked more like the Americans were intent on punishing the Iranians and teaching them a lesson.

In the Nicaragua case, the Court took note of the fact that the Americans had not reported the action they took against Nicaragua to the Security Council, as the UN Charter requires. The Americans' failure to follow the rules allowed the Court to draw the inference that the Americans themselves didn't think Nicaragua's support of the insurgents amounted to an armed attack justifying a military response. In addition, the Court noted that, at the time the Americans took action against Nicaragua, none of the states they claimed to be defending had declared themselves victims of an armed attack.

In 2004, the year after its ruling in the oil platforms case, the General Assembly was at the Court's door asking for another advisory opinion. This time the question was whether a security wall Israel constructed on Palestinian territory that it occupied was legal.[12] The Court said emphatically that it wasn't. Even though they recognized Israel's right of self-defense, the judges were of the opinion that the route the Israelis chose for the wall constituted a grave infringement of Palestinian interests and was not the least intrusive means by which the security of its citizens could be guaranteed. In several locations, the wall caused serious hardship and dislocation in the lives of ordinary Palestinians without significantly enhancing the safety of those it was meant to protect.

The Court's most recent opinion on the use of armed force was handed down at the end of 2005. With the violence that has devastated so much of Africa for so long, it was inevitable that the Court would eventually get involved here as well. The conflict it was asked to adjudicate was between the Democratic Republic of the Congo and Uganda.[13] Like the conflicts in Central America, it was typical of the low-grade, proxy wars that are common in the world today. Rather than the traditional engagements in which national armies do battle, today wars are waged by rival political groups fighting insurgencies to control territory and overthrow governments with the clandestine backing of other states.

The conflict between Uganda and the Congo grew out of the political instability and armed rebel activity that plagued the Great Lakes region after the 1994 genocide in Rwanda. The Congolese government petitioned the Court to find that its Ugandan counterpart had participated in unjustified acts of armed aggression against its people and to order appropriate reparations. Uganda said it was acting in self-defense against Ugandan rebels (the Lord's Resistance Army) operating freely across the border in the Congo.

The Court ruled against the Ugandans. Once again it couldn't reconcile a claim of self-defense with the facts. For all of the judges – except the one nominated by the Ugandans – the fatal contradiction in the Ugandans' position was their taking control of airports and towns 1,800 kilometers from their common border. The Court found it impossible to describe military interventions so far from its territory as credible acts of self-defense.

The further from their borders the Ugandans advanced, the less proportionate and less necessary their response was to the attacks they said justified their taking military action. Proportionality and necessity required that defensive force be limited to the border areas where the attacks and the threat to Ugandan security had occurred. As in the Nicaraguan case, the Court took note of the fact that the Ugandans never reported the events they said justified their acting in self-defense to the Security Council.

In its ruling in favor of the case of the Congolese, the Court affirmed that the rules of war were the same in Africa as in Central America and the Middle East; they applied equally to African headmen and American presidents. When all five of the Court's judgments on the use of armed force are read together, this much of the modern law of war is clear: Wherever it occurs, armed force is only legal when it is necessary and proportional to the threat it is trying to repel. The bottom line is simple. The rule is, as the saying goes, "tit for tat." Nothing more, nothing less.

From where we were a hundred years ago, that's progress. The laws of war are immeasurably more humane now than they have ever been. Necessity implies there are no alternative, less drastic means that can settle the conflict, while proportionality requires a rough equivalence between the act of aggression that has taken place (or is threatened) and the force that is used to defend against it. Rulers are no longer able to stretch claims of necessity to suit their own purposes, as they could when Grotius wrote. In requiring force to approximate what it is trying to repel, judges have established an objective standard against which combatants' claims can be measured. At a minimum, it means no more indiscriminately bombing civilian populations and no more raping women.

The Politicization of Law

If necessity and proportionality were the whole story of the rights and wrongs of war and peace, it would mark a major milestone in the history of law. In war as in peace, rulers would be bound by law and acts of wanton violence would be punished. If the Statute of Rome were rigorously enforced, all serious breaches of the principle of proportionality would be prosecuted as war crimes.

But as the history we have been following has taught us to expect, in law as in life, moments of great inspiration are not common and when they do occur they often have little lasting effect. The truth is that necessity and proportionality don't tell the whole story. At least not in The Hague. In fact, notwithstanding the impression the last few pages will have left, in the rulings of the Court, they actually played quite a peripheral role. Although the Court recognized these principles as part of the established rules of international law, it didn't embrace them as emphatically or as enthusiastically as it could have. As with so many phases in the history of law, for every two steps the jurists took forward, they took one (some might say more than one) back.

As a practical matter, the Court limited the application of the principles of necessity and proportionality to cases in which one state has been attacked by another state with a definitive act of armed force. In all other cases – for example, when the attack was by a group of insurgents, or where it was not possible to prove another state was involved – no force of any kind, even if it is proportional, is lawful. As well, proportional responses to acts of aggression that didn't rise to the level of an armed attack were considered not to be protected by section 51 of the UN Charter and so were also outlawed.

Restricting the application of the principles of proportionality and necessity in these ways constituted a serious limitation on the rights of states to defend themselves against hostile acts of aggression. In all of the cases the Court heard, it meant that neither principle was applicable. The conflicts in Uganda and Palestine weren't covered because the attacks were not initiated in either case by an internationally recognized state. In the Iranian case, the Court ruled that the Americans could not prove the attack was directed by Tehran. In Nicaragua, the problem was that the assistance that country provided to the insurgents in El Salvador was not of a sufficient scale to constitute an armed attack. Whatever the reason, the consequence of the Court's rulings was that states that were subject to attacks by terrorists, insurgents, and/or private militias could not legally take proportionate action to defend themselves.

In all of these cases, once the Court ruled that no "armed attack" had occurred, concerns about necessity and proportionality were beside the point. In the absence of an armed attack, there was no right of self-defense, period. Any force would be illegal. Indeed, in its judgment in the Nicaragua case, the Court said that even if the American assault on Nicaragua had met the tests of necessity and proportionality, it still would have been a violation of international law because there had been no armed attack to defend against.

In effect, because of the priority the Court put on defining what constituted an "armed attack," everything it said about proportionality and necessity was gratuitous. Even though its discussion of the principles was an accurate statement of the law, and supported the conclusions that it reached, it was not an essential part of any of its decisions. Those passages in their judgments that dealt with the necessity and proportionality of the armed force they were reviewing were superfluous; what lawyers call "obiter dicta."

Rather than taking Grotius as their inspiration, and turning proportionality into an overarching obligation of moderation in all cases of military conflict, the judges chose to emphasize the distinctiveness of a slew of discrete legal categories and the importance of drawing bright lines. "Armed attacks" were distinguished from "frontier incidents," "reprisals," and other acts of wrongful "intervention," with different rights of response for each. International humanitarian law, international human rights law, and customary international law were treated as distinct legal categories. The separation of the rules of when force can be used (*jus ad bellum*) and what amount of force is legal once the combat begins (*jus in bello*) was maintained. Individual and collective self-defense were governed by different rules. Armed conflicts between independent states were distinguished from civil wars and insurgencies that remain inside a country's borders.

The result was a complex legal framework that serves no one's interest except the jurists. For ordinary members of the general public, the multiplicity of categories and doctrines makes the judgments almost impossible to understand. Like the jurisprudence written by the American Supreme Court and the sharia jurists, it is as if they were written in a foreign language.

It is one of the most regrettable aspects of the Court's jurisprudence on armed conflict that it has become a labyrinth of legalese that is intimidating to anyone not trained in the intricacies of international law. Each judgment has the appearance of a heavy book. The shortest (the Palestinian wall) is over 130 pages; the longest (Nicaragua) required more than 500 pages for the judges collectively to explain to the Americans what they had done wrong. To compound their complexity, all are written in a legal jargon (international lawyers love to drop the Latin names for their principles) that is not easy to follow, even for someone trained in the law. As a practical matter, generals and ordinary soldiers can reasonably plead ambiguity and uncertainty as to the practical, nitty-gritty meaning of the law without fear of contradiction.

Where the Court's judgments strike members of the general public as opaque and impenetrable, for professional jurists they represent an opportunity to play the role of Plato's philosopher-king. The more categories and classifications, the better. Like the pluralist concept of law that prevails in Washington, the jurisprudence the judges have written in The Hague guarantees each of them a broad discretion to organize and synthesize a kaleidoscope of categories and rules as they see fit.

The end product is neither pretty nor polite. With the freedom to express their own take on the law, judges openly disagree on whether, for example, supplying weapons and logistical support constitutes an armed attack; or whether there is a right of self-defense against armed attacks by non-state actors; or even whether the principle of proportionality requires a rough measure of equivalence between the attack that gives rise to the right of self-defense and the response. Like their counterparts in Washington, it is accepted that every judge has the authority to come to his or her own conclusion about what the rules of law actually say and how they should be applied.

With such unfettered discretion on conflicts of such raw intensity, it is not surprising that it is the political affiliations of the judge that determines almost without exception how he or she votes. Everyone is guilty of putting politics above the law. The American judge dissented in every case in which the Court narrowed the legal limits of armed force except the ruling against Uganda. In that case, the judge nominated by Uganda was the only member of the Court to vote against the Congolese. Political allegiances also proved too seductive for the French and British judges, who, along with the American, dissented from the Court's general condemnation of nuclear weapons.

The judges themselves have not been shy about airing their differences. In their judgments they are very open and animated in expressing their views. When they disagree with each other about which rule or principle is to be applied, they don't pull any punches. Their exchanges, though superficially courteous, are sharp and unsparing. Everyone is too formal and diplomatic to lay a charge of bias, but the implication of their remarks is unavoidable.

In his dissent in the Nicaraguan case, in words he recognized as being "uncommonly critical," the American judge, Stephen Schwebel, challenged the Court's opinion because it "misperceives and misconstrues essential facts" and "misconceives and misapplies the law." In the Iranian case, his successor, Thomas Buergenthal, described the Court's judgment as "seriously flawed" and accused his colleagues of engaging in a questionable fact-finding process and citing passages from previous cases to create a false impression of the law. Subsequently, he refused to sign the Court's judgment finding Israel in violation of international law for the construction of a security wall in the Palestinian territories because, he said, it "never seriously examined" the armed attacks it was meant to stop. In the nuclear weapons case, Rosalyn Higgins, the English judge, dismissed the Court's opinion as omitting "an essential step in the legal process – that of legal reasoning." In the Congolese case, the judge nominated by Uganda justified his refusal to go along with his colleagues on the basis of there having been a "persistent uneven treatment of the parties."

When members of the same Court are so publicly critical of each other's work, the big loser is the law. The fact the judges can have such radically different perceptions of the law and how it works means the concept of international law as an objective, impartial method of resolving interstate conflict is an illusion. Everything in the hundreds of pages of explanation is a charade. Each judge demonstrates a mastery of the complexity and intricacies of the relevant legal categories, but in the end it's his or her nationality and political loyalties that determines how he or she votes.

When judges on the world's highest international court lose their credibility, so does the law they have been entrusted to defend. Governments that have no faith in the objectivity and impartiality of those responsible for the enforcement of the law don't look to them for solutions. It is no accident that none of the major powers thinks of The Hague as a viable place to settle their differences. The Security Council has never asked the Court for its opinion. Only in the Peace Palace, where the Court sits, and in small seminar rooms in law schools around the world, is there much interest in what the elite of international jurists have to say.

For everyone who believes that the force of reason is a better way to solve conflicts between hostile states than physical force, the Court's jurisprudence is doubly depressing. Not only have the judges undermined the idea that there are universal rules of reason capable of resolving conflicts in a way that is fair to all sides, their betrayal was entirely gratuitous. As we have seen, it would have been just as easy for them to settle these disputes in a way that reinforced the sovereignty and integrity of law. The judges could have resolved all of these cases using the principles of necessity and proportionality and come to exactly the same conclusions. All they needed was two words instead of two hundred pages.

The failure of the judges in The Hague to make the rule of law a meaningful force on the international stage was a blow to peace and justice in the world but, after the history we have followed, it was not unexpected. Fortunately, it didn't do collateral damage to law's reputation for being able to resolve local conflicts among people who are citizens of the same state.

Despite the failure of international lawyers to displace diplomats and generals as the lead players on the international stage, in the last half of the twentieth century jurists were able to claim considerable success when they focused on disputes closer to home. Especially after the US Supreme Court ordered an end to racial segregation in its ruling in *Brown*, the idea of using a system of judicial review in domestic disputes became much more attractive. Countries all over the world began to study the American model. At the same time that judges were losing their authority to tell sovereign states how they must treat each other, numerous courts were being given the power to put limits on what governments could do to their own people.

Happily, and in sharp contrast with the International Court of Justice in The Hague, judges in many countries have been quite successful enforcing a set of restrictions on the scope of governmental authority that are both objective and fair. Where the tale of international law is one of missed opportunities and failed expectations, the next chapter, which tells the story of comparative constitutional law at the dawn of the new millennium, is much more positive and upbeat.

Chapter Nine

Johannesburg

Judicial Review

Until the middle of the twentieth century, the Americans were the only people who relied on judges to keep an eye on the other two branches of government. Everywhere else, those who cared about establishing good governance in their communities looked for ways to improve politics rather than search for solutions in the law. Making politics more democratic by extending the franchise, reforming the electoral process, and improving transparency and accountability were widely believed to be the best ways to keep arbitrariness in government to a minimum. The emphasis was on increasing the number of people who could contribute to the conversation and making sure their voices could be heard.

During the nineteenth century and the first half of the twentieth, few people anywhere agreed with Thomas Paine that making law the king was a good idea. Even the jurists did little to advance its cause. In legal circles, most of the believers in the idea that law and justice were synonymous belonged to the Catholic Church. Debates about the rule of law were dominated by "positivists," who insisted on a clear distinction between law and morality; "realists," who denied the objectivity and determinacy of law; and "historicists," who emphasized the local roots and cultural diversity of all things legal.

That changed after the Second World War. The genocide carried out by the Nazis showed that democracy's dark side knew no limits. The danger – that once in power, "the people" could abuse their sovereignty as easily as emperors and monarchs – had been evident from the start. The Athenians' slaughter of the Melians and the Reign of Terror during the French Revolution showed how passionately people could indulge in excess. But the inhumanity of the Holocaust was so horrific that the idea of a pure, unbridled sovereignty of the people could never be trusted again. Certainly not if you were Jewish.

As part of the postwar settlement, the defeated powers – Germany, Italy, and Japan – were made to adopt the American model of including a bill of rights in their constitutions and making judges responsible for ensuring it was respected. In the case of Japan, the Americans essentially wrote the whole constitution. As victors, they claimed the right to define the role of law and justice in the countries they had defeated.

In the second half of the twentieth century, bills of rights and judicial review spread as never before. India, with its staggering diversity of religious, linguistic, and ethnic communities, led the way when it gained its independence from Great Britain. Other countries with histories of ethnic and religious conflict, including Ireland, Canada, and Spain, followed suit. Even in the international arena, despite all of law's failures in the last fifty years, bills of rights and international tribunals have come to play a much more active role in settling conflicts between sovereign states.

After the fall of the Berlin Wall in 1989 and the subsequent collapse of the "people's democracies" of the former Eastern Bloc, American law teachers promoted the idea of using judges to review the legality of legislation all over the world. By the new millennium, judicial review was being practiced in Africa, Asia, the Americas, Europe, and the Middle East. Assigning judges the responsibility of guaranteeing the supremacy and justice of law became one of the litmus tests of good governance.

The story of how important judges and bills of rights have become in the way governments operate has been, for the most part, positive and full of promise. Unlike the first 150 years in the United States, judicial supervision of the elected branches of government over the last quarter century has advanced the cause of justice and generally done lots of good. More often than not, when those who have been victims of arbitrary treatment by their governments have come to court, the judges have been there for them. The faith that people put in the judiciary has proven to have been, by and large, well-placed.

As would be expected, there are variations in the records of the world's judicial elites.[1] Some courts are stronger than others. Some are vigorous defenders of the connection between law and justice. German jurists have been thinking hard about the role of judges in marking out the limits of legitimate government for a long time, and the Federal Constitutional Court that was established in Karlsruhe at the end of the Second World War quickly earned a reputation for the clarity and rigour of its analysis. Others are more deferential to their country's political leaders and the will of the people to fix the rules in the societies in which they live. This has been especially true in Japan. Reflecting a culture that emphasizes harmony and respect, in the seventy years it has been responsible for maintaining the integrity of the country's system of government, Japan's Supreme Court has only challenged the authority of the politicians a handful of times.

If you had to choose the jurists who should be awarded the gold medal for best overall performance, the dozen who oversaw the birth of a democratic South Africa would be at or near the top of many people's list. Charged with determining the legality of the legislative legacy of the apartheid regime, these judges operated in a political context that was positively electric. From a magnificent courthouse built on Constitution Hill in Johannesburg, adjacent to the prison that held, at different times, Mohandas Gandhi and Nelson Mandela, a small group of men and women, young and old, Black and white, Christian, Muslim, and Jew, rendered a series of judgments on some of the country's most politically charged issues that did more for justice and human rights in a little more than 10 years than the US Supreme Court accomplished in its first 150.

The South Africans committed themselves to the supremacy of law without reservation. They insisted that the scope and sovereignty of the law was absolute and all-encompassing; everyone who exercised the powers of the state was bound. Early on they expressly acknowledged their own duty to adhere to the requirements of the Constitution in their development of the common law. As one of the three branches of government, they, no less than the politicians, were bound to submit to the sovereignty of law.

Their commitment to the rule of law was apparent from the first day they showed up for work. In the first case they heard they outlawed capital punishment. Three years later, they decriminalized sodomy, which turned out to be the first in a series of cases involving gays and lesbians in which the Court also recognized their right to marry and adopt children. The year after that the judges issued their first ruling that the government had to do more to protect women against domestic violence, and within another five years they were insisting the rights of women to inherit property and assume leadership roles had to be recognized in the customary law of South Africa's Indigenous people. In the year 2000, barely five years after they had heard their first case, they issued a landmark ruling spelling out what obligations the state had to people who were homeless, and in 2002 they did the same for those infected with HIV/AIDS.

On any scale, the performance warrants high praise. Not perfect, but almost certainly one of the most impressive collections of jurisprudence ever written in such a short space of time. With only the force of reason to support them, they stood up to the authorities and powers that be

for the benefit of the country's misfits and outcasts – murderers, homosexuals, the homeless, and people infected with HIV/AIDS. The contrast
with what the Americans had done over a century and a half couldn't
have been greater.

In working its way through each of these political minefields, the
Court showed itself to be remarkably unified and independent-minded.
The judges read widely on how these issues had been handled by other
courts around the world but were agreed that, in the end, they had to
work out solutions for South Africa on their own. Indeed, one of the
most striking features of the Court's judgments in these early cases is
how emphatic the judges were in distancing themselves from the way
the US Supreme Court had approached questions about punishment,
discrimination, and the responsibility of government to be proactive in
a rule of law state.

In the death penalty case, the Court explicitly referred to and rejected
the reasoning the judges in Washington had used to support their conclusion that state executions could be justified in some circumstances.
In legalizing gay sex, the South Africans said the way the Americans had
defended making sodomy a criminal offense was unhelpful. In spelling
out the state's obligation to protect women from violence, the judges in
Johannesburg refused to follow the Americans in thinking that governments cannot be held liable for a violation of the Constitution when they
fail to act. In all of these cases, the American and South African understandings of the rule of law were polar opposites.

Capital Punishment

The difference in the ways the two Courts went about writing their judgments was evident from the beginning. The approach the Americans
took in deciding whether the death penalty is a "cruel and unusual punishment" is what you would expect.[2] The judges came at the question
exactly the same way they analyzed issues of race and gender: it was all
a matter of interpretation and the meaning of words. They probed the
Constitution and its prohibition of "cruel and unusual punishments"
from different angles. As in all of the cases we examined in chapter 7
(except *Brown*), in the Court's mind, the solution to the case involved
their formulating an authoritative definition for punishments that were
"cruel and unusual."

In this case, as in the others, the Court followed its practice of using
different lines of reasoning and multiple sources of meaning to get the
answer. Once again, the dictionaries of choice were the original understandings of those who made the decision to include these words in the

Eighth Amendment and the way the Court itself had interpreted them in
the past. In each case the evidence was loud and clear. Neither the founding fathers nor their predecessors on the bench thought capital punishment was either unusual or cruel. The Constitution itself recognized the
legality of state executions in the Fifth and Fourteenth Amendments and
the Court had ratified different ways of killing, including firing squads
and electrocution.

After the Court examined the original understanding of the words
"cruel and unusual punishment" and reviewed its own prior rulings, it
turned to two more contemporary sources to make sure their meaning
hadn't changed. First, it tested capital punishment against "the evolving
standards of decency that mark the progress of a maturing society" and
concluded that, even against this more modern benchmark, it couldn't
be characterized as unusual or cruel. Then, it examined whether the
death penalty was compatible with the "dignity of man," which the Court
said was "the basic concept" underlying the Eighth Amendment. On this
question, too, it came to the same result.

The Court based its conclusion – that even on contemporary standards of decency, capital punishment isn't unusual or cruel – on the
fact that a large majority of states had retained the death penalty in the
course of recent revisions of their criminal laws. The Court treated this
legislative history as "objective evidence" that many Americans continued to believe capital punishment is the right way to treat people who
are convicted of having intentionally taken the life of another human
being. Its logic was that, because the death penalty was consistent with
contemporary standards of decency in America, it could be called neither unusual nor cruel.

The Court's final reason for ruling that the death penalty is a lawful
form of punishment was its finding that it did not deny the dignity of
convicted murderers who are executed. "The dignity of man," which the
Court identified as the moral bedrock of the Eighth Amendment, meant
that punishments could not be "excessive." In particular, punishments
that inflicted "unnecessary and wanton ... pain" or were "grossly out of
proportion to the severity of the crime" were banned.

Seven of the nine judges who sat on the case didn't think that the
standard methods of executing people who deliberately killed another
person were "excessive" in either sense of the word. Death could be
administered in a relatively painless way and, though severe, it was not
excessive "for the most extreme of crimes." *Lex talionis* may still be a
legitimate principle of law in a limited number of cases.

It must be said, however, that the Court did not press this inquiry very
far. Insofar as much of the evidence of the contemporary standards of

decency was legislative in character, the Court felt an obligation to defer to the judgment of the elected representatives of the people. As in *Korematsu*, the judges didn't feel this was a matter they should push very hard.

The Court was not prepared to second-guess the judgments of state legislatures that the death penalty was a necessary punishment because it deterred the commission of future acts of murder – and so saved innocent lives – better than any other, less severe sentence. Unless it could be shown that such a conclusion was clearly wrong, the judges said they would respect it.

It was not the Court's job, the majority insisted, to determine "the value of capital punishment as a deterrent of crime"; that was "a complex factual issue the resolution of which properly rests with the legislature." So long as the method of execution is not needlessly painful and the penalty is proportional to the severity of the crime, the Court insisted it had no power to order the state to use less severe punishments, even where alternatives were available.

The legalization of state executions fits the pattern of rulings we considered in chapter 7 in both reasoning and result. Here again, the interpretive model of judicial review shows itself to be exceedingly tolerant of very violent behavior by the state: forced segregation, sterilization, internment – and now executions of those found guilty of murder. It is not surprising, then, that when the South African judges were asked for their opinion on the death penalty, they didn't see the American approach as a model to follow. Instead, they opted for a completely different line of thought.[3]

To begin with, to give meaning to the words outlawing "cruel, inhuman and degrading punishment," they said neither of the traditional dictionaries American judges rely on when they are interpreting the Constitution could provide any guidance. No historical reviews of the original understanding of the words; no parsing of precedent. In fact, none of the resources the Americans used were of any help.

Original understandings were of no use because there weren't any. When the politicians were hammering out the terms of the country's new constitution, they couldn't agree on whether there was a place for the death penalty in the new South Africa, and so they decided to leave that question to the Court. They called this the "Solomonic solution."

Nor could precedent provide any guidance to the South Africans, for the simple reason that none existed. The death penalty was the Court's first case. In searching for the right answer, there could be no looking back.

The South Africans were especially adamant that public opinion could not be of any assistance in deciding whether or not capital punishment was constitutional. The question they had to answer, they said, was not whether the majority of South Africans believed the death penalty was a proper sentence for murder. It was whether the Constitution allowed it. Echoing John Marshall, they insisted it was their job, not the people's, to say what the Constitution authorized politicians to do. The logic of entrenching a bill of rights in the Constitution called for a reasoned opinion from the Court, not a roar from the crowd.

The only part of the Americans' thinking that the South Africans agreed with was that the moral foundation of the prohibition against cruel and unusual punishments was their degradation and denial of human dignity. But even here the South Africans disagreed with the Americans on precisely what that meant.

The Americans, as we have just seen, thought the concept of human dignity proscribed punishments that were excessive in relation either to the pain they inflicted or the seriousness of the crime. The South Africans were more demanding. They thought that the severity of punishments had to be tailored to their purposes of deterrence and retribution as well.

They insisted that for a punishment to respect the dignity of a person, it must display a measure of proportionality between its ends and its means. It had to be the least severe sanction that was required to bring about the desired results. Not only that, the South Africans said governments would have to prove the punishments they chose met the test. They said the American position of deferring to the political branches unless it could be shown they were clearly wrong was too soft.

In rejecting the American method of evaluating the legality of the death penalty, the South Africans weren't just being anti-American. The jurists of Johannesburg didn't think the analysis of any court could tell them what to do. They studied the opinions of Canadian, German, Hungarian, Indian, and Tanzanian judges, as well of international tribunals and courts, but concluded that they had to figure out the right way to think about the issue on their own.

The South Africans were also clear that the legality of capital punishment was the only issue before them and that other instances of killing by the state could not help them reach a decision. Like Hammurabi and the Roman jurists, they displayed the mind-set of the casuist and focused all their attention on the facts surrounding state executions. They dismissed as irrelevant other cases in which the state was authorized to kill, like war and rebellions and police shootings. It also distinguished cases of self-defense on the ground that they involve situations of exceptional urgency when there is no other way for the person attacked to save his or her life.

In the end, to decide whether the death penalty was a cruel, inhuman, or degrading punishment, the South Africans adopted a balancing approach in which the lives and dignity of convicted murderers were weighed against the lives of innocent victims of future homicides that would be saved by the execution of recidivists and others who would be deterred from killing in the future by the possibility of their being put to death. Instead of looking in legal dictionaries for the answer, they relied on the scales of justice to show them how the two sets of interests compared.

From the perspective of the condemned man, the stakes were obviously enormous. In the words of the Court, for him the death penalty was "the most extreme form of punishment to which (a person) can be subjected. Its execution is final and irrevocable. It puts an end not only to the right to life itself, but to all other personal rights." In the course of its judgment, the Court endorsed the views of three Canadian jurists who described state executions as "the supreme indignity to the individual, the ultimate corporal punishment, the final and complete lobotomy, and the absolute and irrevocable castration."

The Court also pointed out that the enormity of the penalty for the convicted murderer was aggravated by the fact that it could only be carried out in the most arbitrary and pernicious way. In this respect, South Africa's legal system suffered the same flaws that threaten all criminal justice systems. As a practical matter, whether a sentence of death is handed down in a case is strongly correlated with race and poverty and in the final analysis is largely a matter of chance. Who lives or dies depends on a long list of factors, including the way the police carried out their investigation and the prosecutor presented the case, how effectively the accused was defended, and the personality of the judge. Indeed, not only could the state not guarantee that people who were charged with capital crimes would be treated fairly, it also couldn't ensure that no one would be falsely convicted and wrongly executed.

On the other side of the scales were the lives of victims of future murders who would be saved by the preventative and deterrent effects of executing those convicted of the most violent crimes. After reviewing the evidence on how infrequently the death penalty had actually been carried out, the Court concluded that the government's interest in deterring future murders and saving lives did not carry a lot of weight. The judges questioned whether anyone would be deterred by the possibility of being executed when, over the course of the previous five years, fewer than 150 out of 100,000 murders committed in the country resulted in the imposition of a death sentence.

The way the judges saw it, the practice of such isolated, intermittent executions showed that even if more innocent people would be murdered if the death penalty were abolished, this wasn't something that bothered the government very much. This was a price South Africans had indicated they were willing to pay. The rarity of executions showed that deterring homicides and saving the lives of future victims was not one of the state's highest priorities. The execution of so few murderers showed the government was quite comfortable putting the lives of future victims at risk.

In this, it should be said the South Africans were acting pretty normally. The lives of future victims are statistical lives that, however irrationally, for most people don't have as much weight as the lives of identifiable people. They are like road fatalities. Governments deliberately set speed limits at levels they know will result in more deaths than if motorists were forced to drive more slowly. When death is anonymous, sometimes we value convenience over loss of life.

Moreover, even if it were accepted as a matter of common sense that some people would be deterred from committing a violent crime by the threat of being executed, the Court questioned whether less severe forms of punishment like life or long-term imprisonment would be just as effective in saving lives. Given how rarely a death sentence was carried out, the judges doubted whether the marginal deterrence of capital punishment could be that much higher. They suggested that more lives might be saved by the state setting an example of respecting rather than taking the life of the convicted murderer.

At the end of its judgment, the Court concluded that those defending capital punishment had failed to prove that the death penalty would prevent and deter more murders and save more lives than long-term prison sentences. If deterrence and prevention were the goals, the Court's advice was that a better law enforcement and criminal justice system was the way to get it. The slight possibility that a small number of lives might be saved was not enough to outweigh the magnitude of the loss the convicted murderer (who on some occasions will be innocent) is forced to bear.

At this point, some defenders of capital punishment will want to say that the death penalty isn't just about prevention and deterrence and saving lives – it's also about retribution and giving convicted murderers what they deserve; doing to them what they did to the people they killed. As we have seen, an eye for an eye and a life for a life is the guiding principle of the ancient *lex talionis* that goes back at least as far as Hammurabi.

The Court considered this argument in the course of its judgment and dealt with it the same way it handled the claims about the preventive and deterrent effects of capital punishment. It accepted the legitimacy of the state seeking retribution on behalf of the community but questioned whether executing people was necessary to secure it. Once again, the Court took its standard from the state's own behavior, which showed that there were less drastic alternatives available that didn't impose on criminals the same suffering they had inflicted on their victims.

Punishment must be commensurate with the crime, the Court said, but that doesn't mean it has to be the exact equivalent. The Court pointed out that the South African state did not do to rapists or criminals who wounded someone in the course of their unlawful activity, what they had done to their victims. In these and other cases (e.g., arson), the state's own practice showed that a long prison sentence was a sufficient way for the community to express its outrage and visit retribution on the wrongdoer.

At the end of the day, all eleven judges were of the same opinion. For all of them, executing convicted murderers was excessive in precisely the way the Americans had refused to consider. Capital punishment lacks a measure of proportionality between its ends and its means; it is more than is necessary to get the desired results. Even if it could be proven that it was slightly more effective as a deterrent, because it was carried out so infrequently, the value added was too small to warrant deliberately extinguishing the life of another person who is unlikely to reoffend. The death penalty was unconstitutional because it was out of proportion to whatever good it could do.

To underscore its commitment to the principle of proportionality as the critical lens through which it would assess the balance of competing interests in a case, three days after it outlawed capital punishment, the Court used the same logic to explain to the South African government that it no longer had the authority to inflict corporal punishment on young offenders. Hours after it had pitched capital punishment into the dustbin of South African legal history, it told the country that a state that adheres to the rule of law doesn't strike its children.[4]

As in the death penalty case, the Court spent a good deal of its time talking about the right to dignity and immunity from cruel, inhuman, and degrading punishments. Again it examined the status of corporal punishment in other parts of the world. On any definition of the word, it concluded, the deliberate infliction of physical and mental pain was inhuman and cruel.

Once again, the cruelty and inhumanity of corporal punishment lay in the lack of proportionality between ends and means when adults whip and cane their children. On the scales of justice, the brutality, humiliation, and degradation of deliberately inflicting pain on a young person is out of all proportion to whatever good it might do. As a way of teaching young offenders how to behave, forcing them to endure physical and psychological pain is excessive.

In the old apartheid state of South Africa, corporal punishment of juveniles had been justified as being less brutal than incarceration in a prison for adult offenders, which at the time was the only other alternative. The thinking was that the short, sharp infliction of pain would be less harmful in the long run than locking them up in the violent world of penitentiaries.

Whatever its original justification, the Court insisted that was not the choice facing politicians today. Alternative systems of juvenile justice, with proven records of success, were now available to rehabilitate young offenders. Physical force was no longer the least drastic way of reforming delinquent behavior, and so the Court had no hesitation adding corporal punishment of juveniles to the list of penal sanctions that were beyond the lawmaking powers of the new South African state. Indeed, five years later it upheld the authority of the state to outlaw physical punishment of students by their teachers even when it had the approval of their church.[5]

The way the Court addressed the question of how severely a state can punish its citizens was hugely symbolic. From day one the principle of proportionality was made the litmus test in defining what kinds of force and coercion can be justified in a rule of law state. In terms of the moral character of the new South Africa, criminal law was made more just and less cruel overnight.

Lesbians and Gays

Many individuals and groups benefited from the way the judges in Johannesburg chose to think about their work, but none more than lesbians and gays. Same-sex couples were "a discreet and insular minority" in the old South Africa who had had no success persuading politicians to stop punishing them because of their sexual orientation. The rulers in the racist, apartheid South Africa discriminated on the basis of people's sexual preferences as well as on the color of their skin. Indeed, anyone who had sexual relations with someone of the same sex was treated by the state as a common criminal.

In a political world ruled by a white, male, Christian elite, gays and lesbians were powerless to do anything about their situation. Governments didn't listen when gays and lesbians said a person's sexual preferences were not a matter of legitimate concern to the state and insisted on being treated the same as heterosexuals. Lots of laws from the apartheid era, including the refusal to recognize gay marriages, remained on the books even after the entrenchment of the new constitution. As a result, as soon as the Bill of Rights came into force, same-sex couples were among the first who climbed Constitution Hill to seek relief from the Court.

Three years after it outlawed the death penalty and corporal punishment of juveniles, the judges were asked to evaluate the way the South African state treated gays and lesbians. In that case, the question was whether the state had the authority to make sodomy between two consenting males a crime.[6] In quick succession there followed claims by gay and lesbian couples to spousal benefits and to register as parents and adopt children.[7] Ten years after they put an end to capital punishment, they had to decide whether gays and lesbians had the right to marry.[8]

Much more than their rulings on capital and corporal punishment, on gay rights the South Africans were pioneers. In less than a decade, the judges in Johannesburg did more to bring discrimination against gays and lesbians to an end than had been done anywhere before in such a short space of time. On one of the most controversial and hotly contested moral issues of our time, they never faltered in sustaining a principled defense of minority rights. On eight separate occasions gays and lesbians came to the Court, and never once were they disappointed. Moreover, and in another point of sharp contrast with the Americans, every one of the judges' decisions were unanimous. Much more than the judges in Washington, the South Africans were Marshall's true heirs.

In all of these cases, the Court followed the same pattern of reasoning that organized its thinking on capital and corporal punishment. First, the judges identified the constitutional rights that were threatened by laws that denied people benefits or imposed special burdens because of their sexual orientation.

Here again, the interpretive part of the judgment was largely a pro forma exercise. There were lots of rights – to equality, dignity, and privacy – that could do the trick. In the Court's opinion, treating gays and lesbians differently from heterosexual couples was a flagrant violation of their rights to the equal benefit of the law and to being shown proper respect.

On its face, the choice to deny same-sex couples the opportunity to marry was demonstrably discriminatory: heterosexuals could marry, homosexuals couldn't. The state provided an opportunity and bestowed an aura of legal legitimacy on heterosexual unions that gay and lesbian relationships were denied. Heterosexuals were given preferential treatment.

Supporters of the traditional understanding of marriage as a relationship between a man and a woman tried to persuade the Court that the
charge of unequal treatment was misplaced. Treating people differently,
they argued, is not always discriminatory. Where there are relevant differences between individuals, you must differentiate between them in
order to treat them equally. For example, laws that prohibit children
under a certain age from marrying do not deny them equal benefit and
protection of the law. For traditionalists, the fact that it is legitimate for
the state to outlaw child marriages shows that not all restrictions on who
can get married are a bad thing.

The Court didn't find the analogy convincing. It rejected the idea
that a person's sexual orientation could be a legitimate criterion of distinction like his or her age. The reason minors were prohibited from
marrying didn't justify excluding lesbians and gays from the country's
marriage and family laws. The decision of a gay or lesbian person to
marry someone of the same sex is made by a mature human being. No
other adults were prohibited from getting married because of their
erotic preferences. Gays and lesbians were treated like children in spite
of the fact they weren't.

The Court also rejected the argument that it was legitimate to exclude
gays and lesbians from the legal status of marriage because they can't
procreate. Again, the judges pointed out that the state didn't make that
a disqualifying condition for anyone else. Many heterosexual couples,
including the elderly and people who are infertile, are in the same situation, and the state didn't impose a legal barrier to their enjoyment of
conjugal bliss. The physical incapacity of a husband and wife to procreate jointly didn't mean they couldn't have children and raise a family
through artificial insemination, surrogacy, or adoption. In the Court's
mind, the state was legally obliged to ensure that gays and lesbians who
wanted to could do the same.

As a factual matter, the Court's conclusion was unassailable. Traditional marriage laws, by their terms, were prejudicial to lesbians and
gays. They were denied benefits the state made available to people who
marry someone of the opposite sex. Heterosexuals were free to marry,
homosexuals weren't. Even those opposed to the legalization of gay
marriage didn't fight the fact of inequality very hard. Instead, they took
the position that there were other sorts of reasons why the two groups
shouldn't be treated the same.

First, they advanced a couple of interpretive arguments. Nowhere, they
said, in a constitution otherwise overflowing with entitlements was there
any recognition of a right to marry. Like the approach favored by the US
Supreme Court, they argued that gays and lesbians were looking for

something in the Constitution that just wasn't there. Moreover, they said, if there were to be such a fundamental change in the traditional definition of marriage and family, it was for the people and their elected representatives to make, not eleven unelected judges.

The Court was unimpressed. It wasn't necessary, it said, for a right to marry to be specifically recognized in the Bill of Rights. The judges reminded heterosexuals their rights would be violated, even without any explicit reference to marriage in the Constitution if, for example, a law forced them to marry against their will or banned interracial marriages.[9] In the same way, the fact that the law did not allow gays and lesbians the same opportunity as heterosexuals meant that their rights to equality and dignity were engaged.

Opponents of gay marriage also urged the Court to decide the question on a simple linguistic analysis, but again the judges demurred. They acknowledged that marriage has always been defined as a conjugal relationship between a woman and a man and that it still is the dominant meaning in most parts of the world. But that didn't answer the legal question of whether the traditional definition of marriage violated people's rights to be treated with equal dignity and respect. Public opinion was not decisive on whether the death penalty was constitutional, and the same was true of the marital status of lesbians and gays. In both cases, determining the legitimacy of law was the Court's, not the people's, responsibility.

The last line of defense offered in support of traditional conceptions of marriage was that if gays and lesbians prevailed, it would give offense to the religious beliefs of millions of people. The traditionalists said the harm and the hurt to their values would be intense.

To respond to this line of argument, the Court adopted the same balancing model of judging it used to assess the legitimacy of capital punishment. It focused on the importance of the issue to each side and then made the comparison. And once again, with the scales of justice in hand, the answer seemed pretty obvious. For all eleven judges, the imbalance could hardly have been any greater.

On one side, the impact of exclusion on gays and lesbians was huge. On the most important relationship most people ever construct, they were being told they were outsiders – banished to a state of legal exile. They were not allowed to join in; their most intimate unions not worthy of the same respect as those of their heterosexual brothers and sisters.

No one doubted the psychological blow of being denied the equal protection of the state's marriage laws was very hurtful. The fullness of their humanity was ignored and they were reduced to one-dimensional characters. The only aspect of their being that mattered was their taste in sex. In the Court's words, they were defined by the law as "biological oddities, failed or lapsed human beings." To add material insult to their psychological injury, they were also denied all the benefits and support that the state provided to married couples.

On the other side of the balance there was nothing of equivalent weight. Indeed, in the Court's opinion there was practically nothing at all. As they saw it, preventing gays and lesbians from getting married was actually counterproductive. The purposes of marriage laws, of fostering stable and supportive families, would only be enhanced if gays and lesbians were allowed to join in.

The Court rejected the argument that inclusion of gays and lesbians would undermine the institution of marriage. It emphasized the fact that legalizing gay marriage did not interfere with anyone's freedom to marry according to their own set of values and beliefs. Believers in the traditional idea of marriage could still do their own thing. The right of heterosexuals to marry wouldn't be affected in any way.

For the judges, what was most important was the fact that there was nothing in the recognition of same-sex marriage that interfered with a person's ability to remain faithful to his or her own beliefs. To illustrate, the Court made the point that legalizing gay marriage didn't mean priests and pastors would have to perform marriage ceremonies for gay couples if it violated the central tenets of their faith. As the Court explained, religiously inspired people have the right to refuse to recognize gay marriages in their communities for the same reason that gays and lesbians have a right to have their conjugal relationships sanctioned by the state. Neither side is entitled to impose their ideas of what constitutes an ideal family and healthy sex on the other. Justice requires gay marriages be recognized in law but not in churches or mosques or temples in which same-sex relationships are considered a sin.

In working through the rights and wrongs of gay marriage, that simple idea of equality and fairness runs through the Court's judgment. The bottom line was that not allowing gays and lesbians to marry did immeasurably more harm than good. It never explicitly referred to the principle of proportionality, but the analysis it followed was the same. Denying gays and lesbians the opportunity to marry was unfair precisely because the harms they suffered were out of all proportion to the benefits that could be gained by hanging on to the popular definition.

At the end of the day, the only interest of traditionalists that was left on the balance was their strong aversion to the state treating gay and lesbian couples as their equals, but the Court was very clear that, on the scales of justice, harm of this kind carried no weight. Even though the Court had no doubt that their religious sensitivities were sincere and deeply felt, they conflicted with the commitment to equal human dignity that separated the new South Africa from the old. Their feelings were no different than those held by white Afrikaners who had objected to the equality of races and the end of the apartheid regime.

Both were cases of pure prejudice and prejudice, the Court insisted, could never justify the state treating some people as intrinsically inferior to others. On the scales of justice, no one can insist someone else be marked as lower class and count for less. In a rule of law state everyone, as a person, counts the same. Racists and misogynists and homophobes can't make an argument in favor of their biases because it fails to respect the intrinsic equality of people of different races, sexes, and sexual orientation.

The Court's ruling on gay marriage was certainly its most publicized decision, but as already noted, it was only one of eight. On each occasion that gays and lesbians petitioned the Court, the judges employed the same balancing approach. In every case in which the law treated gays and lesbians differently than heterosexuals, the imbalance was always the same. On marriage, adoption, inheritance, employment benefits, and making sodomy a crime, the scales of justice always tilted strongly in the same direction. The burden borne by lesbians and gays was always beyond anything the traditionalists would have to bear as a result of the state being ordered by the Court to treat gays and lesbians the same as everyone else.

The way the judges in Johannesburg righted the wrongs that had been done to gays and lesbians in South Africa was unprecedented. They defended the rule of law at a time when the great majority of politicians and the public were less sympathetic. Other courts, including the Supreme Courts of Canada, Israel and the United States, Germany's and Hungary's Constitutional Courts, and the European Court of Human Rights, have all handed down rulings in favor of lesbians and gays but never on the same scale nor with the same vigilance and consistency.[10] Only the South Africans were prepared to guarantee gays and lesbians the full benefit and protection of the rule of law every time they were asked.

The Sick and the Homeless

Insisting on the legal recognition of marriages between individuals of the same sex was perhaps the most controversial ruling the Court has made. But there have been others that were pretty close. Telling the South African government, which for a long time denied the findings of the scientific community on HIV/AIDS, it had to make an antiretroviral drug called nevirapine, which sharply reduces the chances of mothers transmitting HIV to their newborn children, more widely available was front-page news as well.[11] Indeed, the way the Court dealt with issues of social and economic rights in general is seen by some to be the most impressive and innovative jurisprudence it has written.

Social and economic rights have had almost as long and distinguished a history as political and civil rights, but the conventional wisdom has always been that they are not as powerful as traditional freedoms like religion and speech because they can't be legally enforced. The UN Covenant on Economic, Social and Cultural Rights, for example, has no means by which governments can be made to provide the benefits they guarantee.

The objection against judges enforcing rights to things like housing, education, and health care is that it would be hugely undemocratic and fundamentally inconsistent with the principle of separation of powers. If judges could order governments to provide housing, schools, and medical care, it would effectively give them control of taxation and power over the purse. It would run counter to Alexander Hamilton's famous dictum and transform the judiciary from the least to the most powerful branch of government.

The South Africans solved the problem of how to make social and economic rights legally enforceable without violating the separation of powers between the judiciary and the elected branches of government by employing the same method of reasoning they used to analyze the death penalty and gay rights. Once again, they focused on the ends and the means of the laws they were reviewing and on how they balanced the different interests they touched.

The South Africans were pioneers here as well. In choosing to adopt a balancing approach, they rejected the suggestion that they should define minimum, core entitlements for each of the guarantees recognized in the Constitution. Even though the definitional approach had a lot of support in the academic and human rights communities, the Court took the position that it was neither an appropriate nor effective way to ensure governments were taking care of the basic needs of their citizens. Once again, the judges signaled that balancing, not interpretation, was the right way to exercise their powers of constitutional review.

The Court explained its thinking in a case brought by a woman named Irene Grootboom and nine hundred of her neighbors, who had been evicted from the land on which they had been squatting. Homeless and without any protection against the forces of nature, they asked the Court to order the government to do something about it.[12]

As distressing as Grootboom and her neighbors' circumstances were, the judges proceeded cautiously. They conceded it was the politicians' responsibility to construct housing programs for the country and they acknowledged that there was more than one way that the guarantees in the Constitution might be met. It was not their job to instruct governments on how much money they had to spend putting a roof over everyone's head. Nor was it in their power to provide Grootboom or any of her neighbors with a house on demand.

What the Constitution required the Court to do, they said, was examine whatever program the government had put in place and determine whether, in terms of its own ambitions, it struck a reasonable balance. To do that, the judges once again looked at the ends and means of the government's policy and the way it calibrated the different interests it affected. And once more they relied on the scales of justice, rather than legal dictionaries or international standards of human health and well-being, to reveal who was right.

In Grootboom's case, the Court ruled that the government's housing program failed the test of reasonableness because it made no provision for those whose needs were the greatest and whose personal circumstances were most acute. Although the government had developed an elaborate program to build millions of low-cost homes, those who were in most urgent need had been ignored. There was nothing in the law to provide emergency shelter and relief to those living in the worst conditions. Like gays and lesbians, the poorest of the poor were left out in the cold.

Assessing laws in terms of the balance of the interests they effect was also the way the Court sorted out claims for medical care. When an essential health service or medication, like nevirapine, could be provided for little or no cost, the Court was prepared to intervene. It was a different story, however, when the scales were more evenly balanced or tipped the other way. So, for example, the judges would not say the government had acted unreasonably when it decided it could not afford to make dialysis units available to every person who needed one to survive.[13]

The difference in the two cases was in the balance. Even though lives were at stake in both cases, on the scales of justice, the relative weight of their claims was radically different. In the first case, making nevirapine universally available instead of restricting it to a small number of test centers was virtually costless. Resources were not an issue and distributing the drug as widely as possible did not compromise the government's ability to fund other parts of the health-care system.

In the case of dialysis units, the balance of interests was reversed. Even though the failure to make these machines available to everyone who needed one would result in the loss of life, the cost of making dialysis universally available was prohibitive. If every person with kidney failure had a right to such treatment, it would bankrupt the system; it would result in their getting more than their fair share of the available health care.

As a practical matter, the balancing approach the Court used to enforce social and economic rights allowed the judges to establish core entitlements on a case-by-case basis and in a way that respected the authority of the elected branches of government to retain control of their own spending. After *Grootboom*, homeless people couldn't be evicted from property on which they were squatting unless the government had a plan that could provide them with alternative shelter. After the Court's order to make nevirapine available to mothers infected with HIV, South Africans have a right to life-saving drugs that are within the state's means to provide.

When the Court's judgments on social and economic rights are placed alongside its rulings on punishment and gay rights, the composite is a stunning body of work. On its own, each of these cases was a big moment in the history of the rule of law. They meant no more executions, no more gay-bashing, and no more failing to rescue those most in need on the part of the state. As a volume of jurisprudence, they tell a story that is bigger than the sum of its parts. They are a testimonial to how judges can exercise their powers of review and enforce the rule of law impartially and without the influence of their personal biases.

Moreover, as noted at the beginning of this chapter, other cases could be added to the list. In addition to bringing discrimination against gays and lesbians to an end, the Court has also been a committed defender of women's rights. It has told South African politicians they must be proactive in protecting women from domestic and sexual violence.[14] It has also insisted that the customary laws of inheritance and leadership must conform to modern standards of gender equality. In one high-profile case, it found the balance struck by an Indigenous (tribal) law that tolerated traditional rules of inheritance that gave everything to the boys (primogeniture) so unequal that it ordered it removed from the books.[15]

As the list of injustices that South Africans have banned from their new republic is extended, the magnitude of their accomplishment is quite stunning. A dozen judges standing up for murderers, homosexuals, women, homeless people, and those infected with the HIV virus – none of whom had any friends in high places. They put a stop to politicians who would abuse their lawmaking powers when nobody else would. That this was done in the space of ten years makes the performance truly remarkable.

As dazzling as the South Africans have been, however, it must be said that they didn't advance the cause of justice in every judgment. Men who complained about arbitrary treatment by the state, for example, did not always receive a sympathetic hearing. On one occasion the Court found nothing wrong with Nelson Mandela announcing a general amnesty for mothers but not single fathers on the day he took office as the country's first democratically elected president.[16] On another, it did nothing to correct a law that defined forced anal penetration of a woman but not a man to be rape.[17] As heroic as the judges in Johannesburg have been, they are still human.

Even if the jurisprudence the Court wrote was not perfect, its rulings on punishment, discrimination, and social rights represent one of the great moments in law's four-thousand-year saga. Even though there have been occasions when they failed to live up to their own standards, in their big, high-profile judgments, this small group of self-effacing jurists took the rule of law and standard of good governance to a new level. In little more than a decade they managed to reestablish the four-thousand-year-old connection between law and justice, found a method to make it work, and insisted the elected representatives of the people respect it.

Democracy, Rights, and the Rule of Law

The way the South Africans thought about whether or not laws on punishment, marriage, housing, and health care were arbitrary and unjust did more than just put those issues (as important as they are) to rest. They also brought the full force of the rule of law back to life. All three dimensions were enhanced by the jurisprudence they wrote. Ruling by law, rulers bound by law, and promoting justice through law were all given new force and meaning. The South Africans found a way to bring the realty and idealism of the rule of law back together.

Rule by law. For the South Africans, the original idea of rule by law means more than just exercising power through rules that are general, clear, consistent, prospective, public, and capable of being followed by those they address. The form of law includes a dimension of balance and proportionality as well. Rule by law implies moderation and even-handedness in government. Alongside inconsistency, retroactivity, and secrecy, it condemns the injustice of extremism and excess.

Rulers bound by law. Putting ideas of balance and proportionality at the center of the rule of law binds all three branches of government in a way that is compatible with modern conceptions of democracy and popular sovereignty. Balance and proportionality mean laws must reflect a measure of fairness or reasonableness in pursuing their objectives without telling governments what those objectives must be. Exercising the powers of judicial review in this way respects the separation of powers between legislatures and courts. The only substantive restriction that the scales of justice and proportionality proscribe is that no one can be branded as second class. In the eyes of the law, the interests of gay and straights, the sick and the homeless, even convicted murderers, are all entitled to equal respect.

Making balance and proportionality the ultimate criterion of legality reinforces the sovereignty of the people in another way. In contrast with how law has been traditionally understood, proportionality isn't a rule or principle that can be manipulated and monopolized by legal elites. When it is built around a principle of proportionality, balancing distinguishes between just and unjust laws in a way ordinary people can understand. You don't have to be a jurist to figure out how it works. On the social issues that matter most, the scales of justice give everyone an equal voice. Proportionality revives and remains true to the original Greek idea of law and justice being the virtue of the common man.

As a measure of when governments get the balance right, proportionality is good for politics and it is also good for the law. Because it makes the weights that the parties to a dispute ascribe to their own interests the deciding factor in resolving conflicts, it has a measure of objectivity that the pluralist model that dominated Roman, medieval, and modern legal history lacks. Proportionality provides judges a metric with which they can maintain their impartiality and avoid the pull of their personal preferences. It binds judges as tightly as politicians and their officials. With proportionality, cases are settled on the basis of evidence that can be established empirically rather than by a language game about the meaning of words. Everything turns on the facts that the parties bring to court.

When cases are decided on the basis of findings of fact rather than the meaning of words, it is much more likely that judges can agree that there is one right answer in a case. The contrast with the US Supreme Court is striking. Even though the judges on the South African Court were a much more diverse group in terms of their racial, sexual, religious, and ethnic backgrounds, in all of the cases we have examined their rulings were unanimous. Regardless of their politics, the facts were the same.

In the death penalty case, the fact it was carried out so infrequently justified the conclusion that lawmakers in South Africa didn't value statistical lives as much as the real, flesh-and-blood person standing (or strapped down) in front of them valued his own. Similarly, in overturning the ban on gay marriage, the fact that gay couples can't procreate together was deemed irrelevant because the government didn't consider such capacity to be pertinent when it came to infertile and elderly couples. In accepting the force of Grootboom's claim, the comparative suffering of the homeless and other beneficiaries of the government's housing programs was an empirical, observable fact.

Justice through law. In their jurisprudence the South Africans also worked through a solution to the question of how law and justice are related, which, as we have seen, has been a seminal source of legitimacy for sovereign authority since Hammurabi and the Greeks. They reestablished the link between law and morality that is timeless and universal. They found a space where advocates of positivism and natural law, the two preeminent visions of law, can find common ground.

For some people, like Thrasymachus and Glaucon in Plato's Republic and modern positivists like Kelsen and Hart, law and morality have no necessary connection. Today, positivists say the validity of law depends entirely on its formal characteristics (its generality, clarity, consistency, stability, prospectivity, etc.) and its source or pedigree (enacted in the legislature or decreed by the king) and has nothing to do with justice or community standards of right and wrong. They take as their motto Ulpian's maxim that "what pleases the prince has the force of law." Laws that meet the formal structure of rules, and are brought into being through the proper procedures, qualify as law regardless of whether or not they are fair. On this theory, legislation enacted by the Nazis that persecuted Jews, Gypsies, and gays qualifies as valid law.

As we have seen, there have always been others who argued against the positivists and who insist that the legitimacy of law depends as much on its content as its formal attributes and the way it comes into force. Plato and Aristotle took this position and it was kept alive by the great natural lawyers we have met along the way, including Cicero, Aquinas, and Grotius.

The big advantage of theories that make morality a necessary attribute of legal validity is that they are able to handle cases of wicked laws like the Nazis' more convincingly than the positivists. The downside is that they are widely thought to suffer logical problems because they seem to derive their moral conclusions (an ought) from empirical observations (an is). Equally fatal, they have also failed to identify a set of moral values that everyone agrees are right.

What the South Africans managed to do was to embrace a conception of justice that contains no substantive moral imperatives and so has the potential to appeal to both sides. Positivists should find the standard of fairness and reasonableness the judges used attractive because it is purely formal. Like properties of generality, retroactivity, and clarity, proportionality is an empty idea; it is not attached to one set of moral values or vision of the good life. It provides an analytical framework, like the rules of grammar, of the law. Nothing turns on what goes onto the scales; it's all and only about the balance.

The principle of proportionality should also appeal to those who believe that law and morality are inseparable. Indeed, it is a test of legitimacy that is compatible with all of the ways that the idea of justice has traditionally been understood. Whatever your theory of justice, a principle of proportionality seems like an integral part.

Over the course of human history, three broad ideas have dominated our understanding of justice. The most basic, which was implicit in the earliest law codes, was the duty to obey. That was the message that was chiseled into Hammurabi's Code. It was also the meaning Socrates acted on when he accepted the verdict of his fellow citizens that he had corrupted the city's youth, even though he knew it to be wrong.

As we saw in chapter 2, the other two meanings that people usually associate with the idea of justice – equality and desert – were also known to the Greeks. For Plato and Aristotle, as for us, justice means that people who are similarly situated should be treated the same and that everyone should only and always be treated by the state in ways they deserve. Justice means treating equals equally, unequals differently, and (as a result) everyone receiving their just deserts.

Equality and desert are at the heart of our ideas about punishment. People who commit the same crime in similar circumstances should be punished with equal severity. Those whose behavior is most evil should face more serious consequences than those whose offenses are comparatively minor.

In just societies, honors and rewards and a community's largesse are distributed on the same metric. Gold medals are not awarded to people who finish second or third because they don't deserve them. The lesson of Grootboom is that it is also wrong for the state to distribute its wealth in a way that ignores those who are in greatest need. "Fair shares" as a principle of distributive justice is a matter of both equality and receiving what one deserves.

The early jurisprudence of the Constitutional Court shows how the traditional ideas of justice overlap; how duty, equality, and desert are all connected. Its judgments on punishment, discrimination, and homelessness all share a common conception of right and wrong. The death penalty, traditional definitions of marriage, and social programs that leave out those most in need of the services they provide are all unjust and unlawful because they are unbalanced and heavy-handed. Convicted murderers, gays and lesbians, the homeless, and HIV-infected mothers were all treated unequally, unfairly, and in ways they did not deserve because in each case the laws that adversely affected them were excessive. The harm they faced was out of all proportion to whatever good might be achieved.

The message the Court sent in its very first ruling was that, while obedience to the law is an essential element of a just society, so, too, is an offender's right to be treated as an equal. Proportionality requires a balance between the two. Punishment is unjust when it is too heavy or too light. It is just as wrong to imprison a person for his or her inability to repay a debt,[18] as it would be to punish a rapist with a fine, which was the state of the law for much of human history.

Balance was also central to the Court's thinking about equality and desert. Treating gays and lesbians worse than heterosexuals gave their erotic preferences more weight than what, from their own perspective, they warranted. So, too, when the state distributed more of its resources to those who were already comparatively well-off, and less to those who needed them most, the unfairness of such a regressive allocation was palpable.

The conception of justice on which the South African jurisprudence is built has a long and distinguished pedigree. As we have seen, making balance and proportionality the organizing principle of justice goes back at least twenty-five hundred years. Proportionality was an important principle for both Aristotle and Aquinas, and balancing scales have been the primary symbol of truth and harmony since the beginning of recorded history. They first appear in the Book of the Dead in Ancient Egypt, weighing the Goddess Ma'at's feather of truth against the purity of the dead person's soul, two thousand years before Athens declared itself to be a rule of law state. And they still command pride of place in the reliefs that are carved over courthouse doors all over the world.

When balancing scales are calibrated with the principle of proportionality, they have the capacity to bring competing conceptions of justice within a common analytical framework that is relevant in any society that aspires to harmonious relations among its people. Except for the requirement that everyone who is affected by a case must be treated as an equal, the idea of justice that runs through the South African Court's major decisions does not contain any substantive moral vision of what good societies look like or what their governments should and shouldn't do.

In the spirit of Montesquieu, proportionality authorizes local communities to balance competing values to reflect their cultural priorities. It respects the different weights societies ascribe to the most basic rules of social cooperation. Laws that tell people what they can say and wear, eat and drink, when they can shop, or how fast they can drive can be tailormade to suit different images of what good societies look like. Proportionality is a universal rule of law that allows multiple ideas of humanity to flourish.

In addition to revitalizing the scope and power of the rule of law, the early jurisprudence of the South African Court clarifies what it means when someone asserts he or she has a "human right." People have been debating the nature of rights for a very long time, and in the last hundred years rights have flourished as never before. In courts and classrooms and even in casual conversation, rights talk is the rage. The jurisprudence the South Africans wrote at the very beginning of their new constitutional democracy shows how rights and the rule of law are related.

Claiming a right is often described as something like playing the highest trump in a game of cards. In an argument, rights are supposed to be decisive. Not surprisingly, therefore, everyone defends the things they care about most by insisting they are human rights. The result, as we have seen, is that modern constitutions, like South Africa's, typically recognize as rights just about anything that improves the quality of people's lives. The judges on Germany's Constitutional Court once ruled that the scope of Germany's Basic Law was broad enough to include a person's right to feed pigeons in a park!

What the decisions of the judges in Johannesburg show is that the status of rights has been greatly exaggerated. In none of the judgments we have examined were rights the deciding factor. Proving a wrong was what counted. The fact that all the claims to life or equality or having a roof over one's head could be designated as rights was never conclusive. What was critical was a finding of wrongdoing by the state. Duties (of the rulers) not rights (of the individual) are what mattered most.

In their judgments on punishment, discrimination, and personal wellbeing, rights are defined in relation to wrongs committed by the state. Wrongs come before rights, not the other way around. In law, rights are what people have at the end of the analysis, not a priori assumptions or agreements at the beginning. Rights are guarantees that governments will not abuse the state's coercive powers by enacting laws that are biased and one-sided. Rights are simply particular examples of the larger principle that rulers are always bound to craft their laws in a balanced and evenhanded way.

In effect, the judges in Johannesburg turned the concept of rights on its head. Philosophers have argued for centuries whether rights come from God or nature or logic or some grand social contract. The lesson of the South African cases is that in the real world in which ordinary people live, these philosophical debates are irrelevant. In law, rights come from wrongs.[19] Rights to life, marriage, and shelter are all derived from the same overarching obligation on governments to pursue their objectives in ways that are balanced and evenhanded.

The South Africans built on the same conception of law that Plato, Aristotle, Cicero, and the Stoics talked about more than two thousand years ago. In the jurisprudence they wrote, "law" is more than a compendium of categories and a list of dos and don'ts.

At its core, it is a way of thinking. It is a form of reasoning that is different than the way philosophers or historians or linguists go about their work. It is a way of resolving conflict impartially, without allowing one's own personal preferences to influence the outcome of a case. Law is a discipline that frees the mind of personal biases. Reasoning by law makes it possible, even in the most acrimonious cases, to see both sides.

In the history of the rule of law, the record of decision making on Constitution Hill in Johannesburg in the ten years between 1995 and 2005 is one of its most impressive achievements. By 2009, all of the original judges had retired from the Court and the curtain had come down on what was by any measure a brilliant opening act. Even though their tenure was short, the judgments they wrote certainly matched the tectonic jurisprudence of the Marshall Court. How long they will provide the benchmark for conflict resolution in the future depends on the choices we make.

PART 4

Future History: The People

Chapter Ten

New France

Let's recap where we are. The rule of law is an idea that has been around in one form or another for at least four thousand years. Its quest – to settle conflict fairly and eliminate arbitrariness and abuse of power from government – is as old as recorded history. Rulers governing by law, being bound by the law, and doing justice through the law has been the mantra for at least the last twenty-five hundred years.

As we have seen in the first three parts of this book, notwithstanding its high ambition, for most of law's history there has been a gap between its aspirations and its achievements. There has been a disparity between theory and practice, between law in the books and law on the street. More often than not, in Athens, Rome, medieval Europe, North Africa, and the Middle East, rulers have fallen short of the ideal. On the authority of their lawyers, they insisted they were above the law. Although they conceded that, ultimately, they were accountable to a higher law, they said no earthly power had the authority to hold them to it.

Two hundred years ago the Americans tried to guarantee the supremacy of law by asking their best jurists to watch over the elected representatives of the people to ensure they didn't abuse their lawmaking powers. In light of lawyers' past performance, the American experiment – giving judges the final word on what governments could and couldn't do – was a bold initiative. As we saw in chapter 7, it didn't deliver. Like their classical, civilian, Catholic, and Islamic brothers, the American jurists who were entrusted with the responsibility of guarding the integrity of the law betrayed it almost from day one.

Again and again, in big, high-profile cases, the judges on the US Supreme Court gave law's seal of approval to assertions of state power that were arbitrary and unjust. The idea that law and justice are inextricably linked was sacrificed to the "power of the people" to discriminate against others because of their race or their sex or their physical disabilities. In America, Congress, the president, and each of the states were authorized to enact laws that were blatantly racist and sexist. As in Rome, medieval Europe, and the Arab world, the elite of the legal profession subverted the integrity of law to serve their own interests and those of their political masters.

In the last fifty years, law has rebounded from the disappointing performance of the Americans and is currently enjoying a surge of popularity worldwide. At the end of the Second World War, and again after the collapse of the Soviet Union, law's empire grew exponentially. By the new millennium, judges were enforcing the rule of law in Africa, Asia, Europe, the Americas, and the Middle East. Now, in most countries in the developed world, the use of force by a state is subject to review by a supreme or constitutional court.

As more and more judges have been given the power of overseeing the activities of the legislative and executive branches of government, a subtle shift has occurred in the way they have come to understand their work. The traditional view was (and in Washington still is) of judges interpreting a foundational text in order to determine whether or not it has been adhered to by the politicians and their officials. The judges read the constitution, settle on what it means, and determine whether the government has complied with its terms. Like civilian, sharia, and canon jurists in the past, American judges spend most of their time explaining definitions and drawing linguistic boundaries around what governments can and cannot do.

In the second half of the twentieth century that changed. As judicial review has become more common, a different conception of the job of the judge has taken hold. On this new understanding, while judges still look at the words of the constitution, an act of interpretation rarely settles a case. Whether a government acted legally or not has become more than a matter of words. As Barack Obama put it, the traditional sources of legal reasoning (texts, precedents, analogies, etc.) are like the first twenty-five miles of a marathon. They can carry the judges most of the way, but they can't determine the outcome of the case.

What happens, as we saw in South Africa, is that the majestic, sweeping phrases that are characteristic of modern constitutions throw up competing rights and entitlements that have to be reconciled in some way. At the end of most cases, courts are forced to strike a balance. In the cases we examined, the South Africans had to find an equilibrium between the life of the condemned man and the lives of future murder victims; the feelings of love and intimacy of gays and lesbians and the religious sensibilities of their Christian and Muslim neighbors; the well-being of the homeless and the welfare of those who already had a roof over their heads. Finding the right balance, rather than the correct definition, has become the most important thing judges now do.

Even in the United States, balancing has become a much more prominent part of the way the Supreme Court goes about its work – so much so that the last fifty years have been characterized by some legal scholars as an "age of balancing." In its famous ruling on the legitimacy of abortion laws, for example, the Court crafted a delicate balance in which the weight of the woman's and the fetus's interests were adjusted over time. On same-sex marriage, it overruled an earlier precedent and recognized its legitimacy because it meant more in the lives of lesbians and gays than it did to people of traditional religious beliefs.[1]

The judgments written by the South Africans highlight a shift in the legal analysis judges employ when they fix the limits of legitimate lawmaking, but they also reflect ideas about the rule of law that have been around since the beginning. In making the principle of proportionality the ultimate rule of law, the approach of the South Africans can trace its pedigree back to Classical Greece, where, as we saw in chapter 2, proportionality was at the center of Aristotle's theory of justice and was celebrated in every dimension of community life. It also employs the same casuistic style of reasoning favored by Hammurabi, in which prior cases are considered more as examples and teaching tools than binding precedents. And, it shares with the formulary procedure developed by the Roman praetors the preference for adjudication over formal amendment in maintaining the currency and relevance of a country's constitutional order.

Documenting South Africa's contribution to the rule of law brings us into the present. At the dawn of a new millennium, this is where we stand. Given our place in law's history we must switch our focus. Instead of looking back at the past, as we have so far, now we must look forward. We must decide what to make of the history we have read. What are the lessons learned?

One way to address that question is to ask how far the South African model of legal reasoning might be extended. Or, to put the question another way, to what extent can the principle of proportionality shape our future? Will it allow us to avoid the injustices and mistakes of the past? What other sorts of conflicts can it handle? How, for example, do balancing and proportionality resolve religious and ethnic conflict?

In the world in which we live, cultural clashes, both secular and spiritual, are surely the litmus test for whether a balancing approach can make a difference. In the last twenty-five years, faith and ethnicity have been the most virulent breeding grounds of conflict and confrontation at home and abroad. Almost a thousand years after the Crusades, the great fault line of global politics still runs between the worlds of Islam and the West. In the Middle East, Asia, and Africa, Islam and rival faiths are still at war. Samuel Huntington famously characterized it as a catastrophic clash of civilizations.[2]

Again and again, near and far, terrorist acts and culture wars exacerbate tensions and foster misunderstanding. Fights break out over the extent to which we have to accept their religious customs and they have to put up with our poking fun at them. More than jihad and targeted killings, disputes about the most routine dimensions of people's lives, like how to dress or what to say, repeatedly disrupt the peaceful patterns of communal life.

Conflicts between Muslims and secular authorities over what clothes a person can wear are pervasive. Women have been told they can't wear headscarves, face veils, athletic uniforms, and even bathing suits that are designed to reflect the virtues of their faith. More friction and resentment result when Muslim prisoners are made to shave their beards and workers are denied the opportunity to take time off to pray. Islamic laws governing family relations and the slaughter of animals provoke heated debates and numerous legal challenges. Occasionally, some of these clashes, like those triggered by a series of cartoons that mocked the Prophet Mohammad, have boiled over and turned violent, and innocent people have been killed.

Spiritual Highs

Contrary to what you might expect, it's not immediately obvious that adopting the balancing approach of the South Africans would make a difference. When you read the cases, it turns out that the results in Johannesburg and Washington are not that different. The truth is that, so far, religious minorities in neither country have had the unqualified support of the judges. That the Americans have been very erratic on when the state should accommodate the circumstances of religious communities will come as no surprise. That the South Africans have also struggled to strike a reasonable balance between church and state surely will.

Before we examine what the South Africans have done, a quick look at the American jurisprudence is in order. Even though it provides little guidance on how a country can best accommodate its religious minorities, it does give us another chance to see why searching for the meaning of words is not a good way of resolving disputes between people of different faiths.

Two cases illustrate the American approach. In one, the Court rejected the petition of a group of Native Americans who sought an exemption from the state's drug laws so they could use peyote in their religious ceremonies.[3] In the other, it validated an exemption in a state's antidiscrimination laws that allowed the Church of Jesus Christ of Latter Day Saints (Mormons) to fire a building engineer because he didn't believe the story of Joseph Smith and the Golden Plates and so wasn't a member of their church.[4]

In both cases, the Court spent most of its time in an interpretive mode looking for answers in its prior decisions. As a result, once again, its judgments missed the mark. In the peyote case, the Court refused to recognize an exception when one could easily have been given. In the case of the Mormons, it went to the other extreme. Because it did not take the time to measure the weights of the interests involved, it validated an exemption that was wider than it needed or ought to have been.

In the peyote case, the Court said making an exception for the religious ceremonies of Native Americans would lead to anarchy: it would amount to a private right to ignore public laws whenever it suited one's conscience. If your religious beliefs told you to beat your children but not pay your taxes, there would be nothing the state could do. It would put religion above the law and turn everyone into a personal theocracy.

In the mind of Antonin Scalia, who wrote the judgment, a legal order of that kind defied common sense. In his opinion, there was nothing in the text of the Constitution or the Court's precedents that required a state to behave that way, and so that was the end of the case. No effort was made to evaluate the substance of the claims being made.

Had Scalia stuck to the facts and done the balancing, he almost certainly would have shown more sympathy for the beliefs and practices of Native American religions. Four of his colleagues did, and for three of them providing a religious exception was a no-brainer. The fourth, Sandra Day O'Connor (the first woman appointed to the US Supreme Court), was a jurist known to elide the distinction between law and politics and evaluate the competing interests in a case through the lens of popular opinion.[5]

The evidence before the Court was clear and unequivocal, the imbalance impossible to miss. Peyote is an essential part of the spiritual ceremonies of some Native American religions and virtually irrelevant to the State of Oregon's war on drugs. If the government could make an exception for the sacramental use of wine in the Catholic Church during the crime-infested years of Prohibition, it should have been easy for the Court to tell the state to show the same measure of respect to Native Americans.

A religious exemption for peyote wouldn't have done any harm to the citizens of Oregon. The government had always tolerated its religious use and had made no effort to enforce the law against people who ingested it as part of a religious experience. The evidence was that it was not a drug widely used or trafficked in the general community, and most importantly, other states had legalized its use in religious ceremonies without any adverse effects.

In the peyote case a small, peripheral religious minority was denied an exemption to which, if the Court had used the scales of justice to evaluate their claim, it was entitled. In the case of the more established and politically powerful Mormons, the Court's failure to weigh the competing interests worked to their advantage.

In their case, the Court read the words in the First Amendment to mean that religious organizations could be authorized by a state to discriminate in all their hiring decisions against anyone who didn't share their faith. Even for a job like a building engineer, which was completely unrelated to any religious activity, the ruling of the Court was that nonbelievers could be shunned. In the view of all nine judges, governments could favor religious organizations with broad exemptions from antidiscrimination laws without giving any consideration to the people who were barred from and/or lost their jobs.

Had the Court attempted to balance the interests of the church and state fairly, it would have limited the exception to positions in which a person's faith was critical to the job. Preachers and church leaders are obvious examples.[6] In positions of authority, faith is a bone fide occupational qualification and people with different beliefs can be told not to apply. When it comes to choosing their clergy, religious groups have more at stake in maintaining control over the sovereignty of their communities than the state has in ensuring everyone has an equal opportunity to pursue a clerical career.

However, in more secular jobs like the building engineer's, where a person's religious beliefs have no bearing on his or her performance, the scales tip in the opposite direction. In these cases, the effect on religious organizations in having to comply with antidiscrimination laws must be minimal, by definition. Believers and nonbelievers are equally capable of doing the job. In the particular case before the Court, the employee had done the job satisfactorily for sixteen years even though he wasn't a Mormon. The fact he didn't belong to their church didn't affect his performance or prejudice their interests in any way.

The only cost to religious organizations of a more focused exemption would be the time and expense in having to explain why it characterized certain positions as religious rather than secular if any of its decisions were challenged. Whatever increase in its administrative costs resulted from having to defend such decisions would be trivial compared to the burden borne by workers whose religious beliefs cost them their jobs.

On the scales of justice, the Court got the balance wrong in both cases. After tracing the Supreme Court's performance on race and gender over the course of the first 150 years of its history and reviewing its thinking on capital punishment, you would expect that its treatment of religious minorities would also be a disappointment. If that's true, and the lesson of the American experience is to pay attention to past performance, you would think that the obvious place to find out how to balance the scales between church and state would be back in Johannesburg. But if you did, you would be in for a surprise.

It turns out that, in responding to the pleas of religious minorities, the South Africans have also struggled to get it right. When questions of faith were part of a case, the judges have not been able to reach a consensus and their rulings often seem at odds with what we read in the last chapter.[7] Despite their condemnation of corporal punishment, for example, they allowed that it could still be legitimate for parents to smack their children if it was done in the name of God.[8] As well, like the Americans, the South Africans refused to legalize the use of drugs as a religious sacrament.[9]

In deciding that the state had no obligation to make an exception in its drug laws that would allow for the ceremonial use of marijuana by members of the Rastafarian faith, the judges followed the same analysis they used in their decisions on the death penalty, gay rights, and homeless people. The case would be settled by comparing the interest of the state in pursuing its war on drugs and the freedom of Rastafarians to adhere to one of the basic tenets of their faith. For all of them, the task at hand was to get the balance right.

The South Africans were aware of the American approach but were unimpressed. None of them found Scalia's thinking very helpful. Once again, for the South Africans, the case couldn't be solved with a definition.

However, while the judges were agreed on the way to analyze the case, when it came to decide how the balance should be struck, they were badly divided. The problem was they couldn't agree on whether or not a religious exemption would substantially interfere with the state's war on drugs.

The sticking point was that, unlike peyote, cannabis was widely used in the general population and constituted a major part of a very large and illicit domestic and international trade in drugs. On the scales of justice, the state had a much more compelling interest in controlling marijuana than it did outlawing peyote.

For all the judges, the case came down to determining how badly the state's interest would be compromised if an exception were carved out for the Rastafarians. Would legalizing religious highs lead to more drug use and crime? The decision was close but in the end the Rastafarians lost by one vote.

The majority thought that because marijuana was so widely used for recreational purposes by the general public, any religious exemption would be liable to be abused and set back the government's war on drugs. The fact the regulations made an exception for the medical use of marijuana didn't persuade them something similar could be done for religious purposes. Nor were they open to the idea of an exemption that made marijuana available for some but not all of its religious uses. They thought that if there was an exemption it had to include every spiritual high. It couldn't go only part way. For them, it was all or nothing.

Albie Sachs took issue with his colleagues, and from a distance it looks like he had the stronger argument. The fact that the Rastafarians could not be given unlimited access to the drug was no reason to give them nothing. Half a loaf is better than going hungry. It is certainly a less drastic alternative. Moreover, as Sachs pointed out, if the government could craft a permit system that allowed cannabis to be used for medical purposes and for scientific research, it should not have been difficult to create a parallel set of procedures that would control its religious use.

To settle the difference of opinion on the Court, one would need to know all the facts. However, from what is reported in the judgment, the majority's ruling seems to leave the scales of justice out of balance. The fact it could make space for medical and research programs at least puts the onus on the government to explain why a similar exception for the religious use of marijuana would put the public interest in jeopardy. Again, if the Americans could create a religious exemption in the Prohibition laws for the Catholic Church in the gangland era of the 1920s, it's hard to think of a reason South Africans couldn't do something similar for the Rastafarians.

For anyone who roots for the little guy, the judges' failure to find any room of accommodation for such a disempowered and marginalized group is disappointing. For everyone who cares about the rule of law it is also ominous and disturbing. Until now, in all of the other rulings we have considered, the judgments of the South Africans have been unanimous. The lack of any dissent added an aura of integrity to their conclusions. The fact that the South Africans were unable to agree on how the balance should be struck when the Rastafarians pleaded for their protection suggests proportionality may not be as objective as it appeared to be in the last chapter. It may be just as vulnerable to judicial bias as the interpretive methods of the Americans.

At this point (if not long before), many legal scholars will be shaking their heads. Especially in the United States, there has always been a lot of opposition to the idea that balancing is a universal panacea. For sceptics, balancing is far from being an unalloyed and untarnished good. There is a widespread feeling that balancing lacks a clear, objective standard that can constrain the judges and allow them to retain their impartiality.

The critics say balancing is just as open to manipulation as any of the interpretive strategies judges use to analyze a case. For them, proportionality is just another legal doctrine that allows judges to impose their own ideas of right and wrong. Landmark cases, like *Brown v. Board of Education* and *Roe v. Wade*, which are cited as great victories of social justice, are often explained, even by their defenders, as judges imposing their own values and/or doing what they think is politically correct.

The sceptics say there is no common scale of values available to courts to balance the competing interests that are at the heart of every high-profile case. Weighing the divine inspiration marijuana provides to Rastafarians against the social harm it wrecks on the rest of the community, or comparing the lives of fetuses to the freedom of women, is like comparing apples and oranges.

Without any universal, neutral standards that can tell the judges whose interests should prevail, balancing is said to be doubly flawed. It is both highly undemocratic and an unreliable defender of people's rights. The sovereignty of the people and the rights of the individual are both vulnerable to the bias of the bench.

If proportionality does not provide an objective measuring device, there is no basis on which the ruling of a court can trump the decision of the elected representatives of the people. If the rights and wrongs of smoking marijuana and having an abortion are just matters of personal opinion, the sovereignty of the people takes precedence over the moral compass of the judge.

The argument resonates with lots of people. If the South Africans can't agree on where the balance should be struck, how objective and impartial can the scales of justice really be? To allay the suspicions of balancing's detractors, we need to find examples where the principle of proportionality points to solutions that religiously inspired people and secularists can all agree are fair. We need to find cases where judges are able to mark out the boundaries of religious tolerance using the scales of justice and come to a unanimous result.

Canadian Multiculturalism

When one goes out in search of such rulings, there are a number of places one might look. India's Supreme Court and the European Court of Human Rights are two obvious possibilities. Both have examined the rights of religious minorities on multiple occasions. Canada's Supreme Court is another. Canadians pride themselves on their accommodation of cultural diversity. They like to point out that when Sikhs were hired by the Royal Canadian Mounted Police, they were able to take off their Stetsons and put on their turbans without having to ask for help from a judge.

At first glance, the record of the Supreme Court of Canada reconciling the conflicting interests of church and state doesn't look any more promising than the Americans' or South Africans'. The jurisprudence it has written on the issue is decidedly mixed. Sometimes it has insisted on an exception being made, other times not, but in most of the cases what is most striking is how, like the Americans and South Africans, the Canadians were badly split.

On one occasion, when they were asked whether laws that outlawed Sunday shopping had to make an exception for Sabbatarians who closed their shops on their holy days, nine judges wrote four separate opinions.[10] On another, by a vote of 4–3, they denied a group of Hutterites an exemption to a law that required them to have their photos embossed on their drivers' licenses, even though it conflicted with the teaching of their church.[11] In both cases, the sharp division of opinion among the judges showed how difficult it was for them to agree on how the balance should be struck.

Initially, reading through the Canadian jurisprudence on religious freedom seems to lend more support to the critics' perception of how partial and subjective balancing can be. But in the middle of this jurisprudential potpourri there are two cases that seem to be what we are looking for. In both, the Court used the principle of proportionality to mark out the limits of a state's legal authority to control the practices and activities of religious groups in a way that appears to be unbiased and evenhanded. In one, the Court ruled that parents do not have a right to stop state officials from giving their child a medically prescribed blood transfusion even though, as Jehovah's Witnesses, it offends their religious beliefs.[12] In the other, it recognized the right of an orthodox Sikh student to wear his kirpan (a ceremonial dagger) at the public school he attended in a suburb of Montreal.[13] Significantly, no one dissented in either case.

In the first, the judges were asked to compare the rights of parents to ensure that the medical treatment practiced on their children is consistent with their religious beliefs against the lives of the children that could be put at risk by the parents' decisions. All of the judges were agreed that parental sovereignty over their children does not extend to the point of putting their lives in danger, although they came to their conclusion for different reasons. Half the judges adopted the interpretive style of the Americans and said religious freedom does not go that far as a matter of definition. The other half applied the proportionality principle and said the life of the child hung heaviest in the balance, as a matter of fact.

On the metric of proportionality, it is hard to quarrel with the judges' conclusion. If the parents' authority over the child is absolute and unconditional, the whole of the child's life may be lost. By comparison, only a small part of the parents' child-rearing authority and religious beliefs will be sacrificed if the state orders a transfusion to be performed. Putting the interests of the child ahead of the interests of the parents minimizes the harm in the case and evens the balance as much as possible.

The second case, of the Sikh student who wanted to wear his kirpan at school, also involved the state claiming the right to prohibit a particular religious practice because of the threat it posed to the safety and security of others. When law students (and even some law professors)[14] first encounter this case, many of them think the result should be the same and that the state's interest should prevail once again. Even recognizing that the kirpan looms large in Sikh symbolism, the danger it poses to the lives of others leads lots of people to the conclusion that the Board of Education was justified in refusing to allow them in its schools.

Not, however, the nine judges who heard the case. All of them were of the opinion that this was a bigger deal for the Sikhs than for the school. All of them thought that the psychological harm and financial penalty the student would suffer if he were not allowed to wear the kirpan was more substantial than the physical threat he posed to others. For all of them it was an easy case. Outlawing the kirpan imposed a restriction on his life that was out of all proportion to the good it could do.

The evidence in the case was unequivocal that safety and security in the school would not have been significantly improved by outlawing the kirpan. The student himself had never exhibited any behavioral problems and there had never been an incident involving a kirpan in a Canadian school in over a hundred years. The judges also noted that the kirpan was kept in a sheath that was sewn into the believer's clothing, so that it was actually less dangerous than other potentially violent instruments, like scissors and baseball bats, which were left lying about the school and could easily be weaponized.

The fact of the matter was that the threat posed by the kirpan was tiny and was of a kind that didn't concern the school authorities unduly. Allowing other potentially dangerous objects to be left unprotected showed the school was willing to tolerate some degree of risk. Its real interest was in being able to provide a reasonable measure, not an absolute guarantee, of safety, and the evidence showed that the threat posed by a kirpan was minimal to nonexistent.

By comparison, telling a Sikh he could not do what his religion prescribed was a big deal. The kirpan is one of the core symbols of Sikhism. It is central to Sikh identity. It is one of the religion's five *Ks*, along with *kesh* (uncut hair), *kanga* (wooden comb), *kara* (metal bracelet), and *kaccha* (cotton shorts). In the case of the particular student who questioned the school board's authority, his religious commitments were so central in his life that, rather than being stripped of his kirpan, he left the public school system altogether. He was, in effect, forced to attend a private school and pay for his religious beliefs.

Although the rulings of the Supreme Court of Canada on blood transfusions and religious daggers did not directly affect the lives of very many people, in jurisprudential terms they are big cases. Both prove judges can use the principle of proportionality to balance the competing interests of church and state in a way that is impartial and evenhanded. They show there is no need for an overarching consensus of common values that transcends the interests of the parties.

The value the people involved in a case place on their own interests is all that counts. In each case it is a purely factual question how important the threat to each of the parties really is. There is no general, abstract value to life that figures in how either case should be resolved. With the proportionality principle, it all depends on the particular facts before the Court.

In the case of blood transfusions, the evidence showed that the threat to the child's life posed by the parents' religious beliefs was more serious than the restriction on their religious freedom, and so in the end it prevailed. In the kirpan case, the weights were reversed. The school authorities had demonstrated, by their relaxed attitude toward other potentially dangerous objects, that these kinds of threats really didn't matter much, and so this time the state's interest in safety and security had to give way. Actions spoke more loudly than words.

The Supreme Court of Canada's decisions in the Jehovah's Witnesses and Sikh cases highlight once again what makes the balancing method of legal analysis so compelling. With the principle of proportionality as its pivot, balancing is simple, straightforward, and easy to do. Unlike so much law talk, it is a way of thinking that anyone, lawyer or layperson, can understand. It fits with Cicero's conception of law being part of everyone's general education.

To assess the two sides of a conflict, you place them on the scales of justice, opposite each other. The scales of justice are a balancing device that displays the comparative weights of different objects without making any judgment about the value or uses to which they may be put. Everyone – rich and poor; Black and white; men and women; even convicted murderers and innocent victims – counts the same. With balancing scales, apples and oranges can be compared.

In real cases, of course, judges don't measure physical weights. Conflicting interests and psychological states don't have any mass. On the scales of justice, it's all about measuring harm. What is the gravity of the claims that have been put on opposite sides of the scales? How do the different possible outcomes weigh, mentally and materially, on the lives of those whose interests are most directly affected? How heavy are the burdens that will be borne by the parties if the judges rule against them?

To compare the "weights," an assessment is made of the significance of the conflict in the lives of the relevant parties. The critical fact is the proportion of a person's life a case impacts. How central is the particular interest that is affected by the case to what the rest of their life is all about? The measurement calls for an objective, factual assessment of how a person ranks their subjective preferences.

Cases in which the life of one of the parties is at stake (as in the challenges to the legality of compulsory blood transfusions and capital punishment) provide the clearest examples of how the method works. For the child and the person who has been sentenced to death, the cases touch every aspect of their lives and threaten their very existence. By contrast, however aggrieved parents and the community at large might be by losing the case, life goes on.

After determining how seriously a conflict bears on the lives of the people involved, the principle of proportionality is applied. The principle provides that those who will be hurt most if they lose the case deserve to win. Sikhs should be accommodated when what are important religious symbols collide with comparatively minor interests of the state, but not, for example, in places like airplanes, where all potentially dangerous objects have been banned.

In assessing the impact of different possible outcomes, the two sides are judged independently. No ranking is made of the value or worthiness of the parties' interests. The judge focuses exclusively on the intensities of preferences and the significance of the issue for each side. The goal is to maximize the collective welfare of the parties by avoiding worst-case scenarios.

Although the principle of proportionality is based on the well-being of the people whose interests conflict, its method is not strictly utilitarian. In each case the weight that is given to the competing interests depends on their importance to the lives of which they are a part, not the number of people who are affected. The fact that there are very few people who are prejudiced by a rule banning knives from schools does not reduce the strength of their claim. Even if there is only one person on a plane who has an allergy to peanuts, telling the rest of the passengers they have to do without is still the right thing to do. Whenever the disparate impact is so extreme, proportionality requires the majority to recognize another exception to its rule.

One of my colleagues, Bruce Chapman, has a nice way of describing this way of thinking. He says that when judges exercise their powers of review through the lens of proportionality, they go about their job in a way that is similar to how people make up their minds deciding which dog is "best in show" or who should be chosen "athlete of the year."

In human and canine competitions, no judgment is made about the relative merits of the different breeds of dogs or types of sport. Chihuahuas and Great Danes are treated the same, as are football and basketball players. In all cases, the judgment is about how the individual (dog, athlete) ranks within his or her peer group, not about which breed or sport is better. The judgment is about how he or she measures up to the standards of his or her own kind. The winner is the one that comes closest to perfection in his or her class. The only difference between competitions and conflicts is that, whereas judges of dogs and athletes are looking for the best within each category, in law the winner is the person who is potentially the biggest loser.

Exceptions That Prove the Rule: Motorcycle Helmets, Female Priests, and Circumcised Children

Even with such clarification of how the principle of proportionality works, it has been my experience that some people still find the logic that leads to religious minorities being allowed to carry knives in school and smoke marijuana in church, counterintuitive, even slightly suspicious. To offer some reassurance, I remind them that there are exceptions to almost every rule.

As we saw in the last chapter, even the divine commandment "Thou shall not kill" does not proscribe the taking of another person's life as an act of self-defense. In a rule of law state, exceptions must be recognized whenever they satisfy the principle of proportionality. Whenever the harm an exception averts is significant, and does little to undermine the purpose of a prohibition, it is not only compatible with but mandated in societies that claim to be governed by the rule of law.

Making an exception for Sikhs is consistent with – it "proves" – the general rule outlawing knives in schools. In normal circumstances, the general prohibition against weapons in schools meets the requirements of proportionality. So does the exception for Sikhs. Their spiritual beliefs make knives more important in their lives and less dangerous than they are in the hands of the general student population.

To test your own comfort with this way of thinking, consider that, on the same logic, Sikhs are also entitled to an exemption from laws that require motorcyclists to wear safety helmets to protect them from the risk of serious head injuries. In some ways helmets are even an easier case.

For Sikh men turbans, like kirpans, are a big deal. The turban is a symbol of spirituality and piety, but unlike the kirpan, it is an article of their faith that should be visible, not covered or hidden. Moreover, the biggest risk of allowing Sikhs to follow their religious beliefs is not to others (as with blood transfusions and kirpans) but to themselves.

Risks of this kind are normally not matters of much concern to governments. People are allowed to engage in all kinds of activities that are dangerous and potentially life threatening (mountain climbing, skiing, sky diving, rafting) when no one else is directly affected. In a state governed by the rule of law, Sikhs are entitled to the same freedom to calculate what risks are right for them.

It is true that making an exception to the helmet law for Sikhs will lead to more deaths and cases of serious trauma, which in turn will result in the state having to provide more medical services than would be the case if everyone wore a helmet. These extra fatalities and injuries will also impose emotional and economic costs on the families and dependents of the victims. But on the scales of justice, these burdens do not carry a whole lot of weight. In fact, they are insignificant compared to the costs society is willing to bear by allowing people to ride motorcycles in the first place.

The accident rates and injuries suffered by motorcyclists in general are much, much greater than the additional loss that would be caused by those few motorcyclists who (like Sikhs) can provide a compelling reason for not wearing a helmet. If the state is willing to accept the very significant costs that motorcyclists as a group impose on their families and the wider society, it cannot consistently say the additional losses that would be caused by Sikhs riding without helmets outweigh the importance of their religious beliefs. If the economic and emotional losses caused by motorcycles are not serious enough to override the freedom of those who want to ride them, they cannot outweigh the freedom of Sikhs to take a slightly greater risk so that they can remain faithful to those religious beliefs that matter most to them. Once again, when judging how important a law is for those it affects, actions speak louder than words.

Making exceptions for Sikhs when it means a lot to them and when it can be done at comparatively little cost to the rest of us is just common sense. We see examples of the same logic all over the place. Even cases of blatant discrimination against women and physical mutilation of children may be justified when they cut to the core of a person's faith.

Few brave souls and no states question the authority of the pope to tell women they can't become priests. On the scales of justice, the imbalance is clear. As hurtful as all discrimination can be, losing control over the hiring of its clergy would be an even bigger blow for the church. State prohibition of discrimination cuts much deeper when it fixes the qualifications of clerics than building engineers.

As we saw in chapter 5, church fathers have been fighting to maintain control over clerical appointments for more than a thousand years. When he was pope, Benedict XVI declared the ordination of women to be a serious crime, on a par with abusing children. It's hard to imagine how the stakes for the church could be any higher.

To allow the state to impose its will on gender equality in the Catholic clergy would be a major breach in the sovereignty of the church. Forcing the Vatican to admit women into the priesthood would transform how it governs itself and how its dogma and doctrine are fixed. It would reverse two millennia of history and allow outsiders to dictate who had authority to administer its most solemn sacraments.

On the other side of the balance, tolerating a church rule against the ordination of women does not seem to do equivalent damage to the individuals affected or to the cause of gender equality. Though discrimination in the church does do harm, both to individual women and to females generally, the costs seem relatively contained.

Every other vocation remains open to women (including being part of the clergy in other churches) and there are other (admittedly less powerful) roles women can play in the Catholic Church. Even if one included the burden women bear as a result of church doctrine (for example on abortion) being formulated exclusively by men, the constraint on a woman's autonomy, of being excluded from the priesthood, doesn't affect her potential to realize the deepest values of her faith. Being barred from becoming a priest doesn't restrict a woman's opportunity to play the role of Mother Theresa.

An even more dramatic example of the compatibility of religious exemptions and secular laws is our toleration of some parents physically mutilating their children as part of the initiation rituals of their faith. No governments anywhere question the authority of Jewish parents to cut the foreskins from the penises of their sons. (Emperor Hadrian tried and failed in the second century CE.) In a reversal of roles, when a lower court judge in Germany ruled that ritual circumcisions violated the rights of the child, the government stepped in to ensure they could continue. Male genital mutilation is a textbook case of why religious exemptions, even to laws of assault and battery, may be compatible with the rule of law.

From the perspective of a Jewish parent, male circumcision, performed on the eighth day after the child is born, was God's first command. It marks the inclusion of the child in the covenant between God and Abraham and his descendants. The religious symbolism is massive: without the cutting, the child is not a member of the tribe.

On the other side of the balance, the costs to the child are mostly superficial. Unlike female genital mutilation, the procedure is not particularly invasive and the consequences for the infant's health and future sex life are not nearly as severe. The chances of complications are even lower than occur in other elective procedures routinely performed on children, like tonsillectomies. Indeed, male circumcision is now a medically recommended procedure to reduce the risk of urinary-tract infections and the transmission of HIV/AIDS.

Dress Codes

Cases that authorize occupational discrimination against women and physical mutilation of children are evocative examples of the range and power of the proportionality principle and the casuistic method on which it operates. Cases contesting the legitimacy of dress and speech codes are even better. They touch the lives of many more people and are even more revealing. In marking out the boundaries of government authority over what each of us can wear and say, the principle's subtlety and sensitivity to detail are on full display. On issues about which people care a great deal, they showcase its evenhandedness and commitment to the idea of justice as fairness to everyone who has a stake in a case.

Laws that tell people how they must dress have disfigured most of human history. Dress codes have been used by rulers to mark people by class and rank for a very long time. All over the world, disfavored groups have been forced to wear clothes of a designated fabric and/or color. Kings, popes, and caliphs have all ordered Jews to identify themselves with a yellow patch. For their part, Jews had rules against cross-dressing, and even in the land of liberty Puritan settlers had laws outlawing extravagant clothing.

Today, dress codes still sew discord and strife between Islam and the West but for a different reason. Unlike dress codes in the past, which for the most part forced people to identify their differences, now it is common to punish people who want to express their identities in distinctive religious clothing. All over Europe, governments tell their citizens what sorts of religious attire they can and cannot wear at work, in school, on the street, and even at the beach.[15] Headscarves and face veils have stirred up the most controversy and have generated lots of litigation.

Of all the countries where dress codes have been an issue, how Muslim women dress in public has proven to be especially troublesome in France. In 2004, the French passed a law that imposed an absolute ban on all conspicuous religious symbols, including headscarves, in schools, and six years later they were the first to make it unlawful for Muslim women to wear face veils anywhere in public. Across the political spectrum, from far left to extreme right, these laws had widespread support.[16] Even their cousins in Belgium and Quebec favored a hard line.

The French care so passionately about religious clothing because they put a lot of emphasis on the secular character of their republic. They call it *laïcité*. It goes back to the revolution of 1789 and calls for a strict separation of church and state. It requires that laws draw very bright lines between the two.

Muslim women and other religious minorities affected by these bans (including Sikh and Jewish boys) challenged them in court but with limited success. For the most part, judges have not been sympathetic. Once again, as we have witnessed all through history, there are times when the record of the professionals defending the rule of law is only half-hearted and lukewarm at best.

When Muslim women knocked on the doors of the European Court of Human Rights and the European Court of Justice, for example, both said there was next to nothing they could do. They insisted their hands were tied. Proportionality was replaced by legal doctrines that demanded courts respect a "margin of appreciation" and show due deference to the executive and legislative branches of government. In their opinion, it was up to the politicians, not the judges, to design the dos and don'ts of permissible fashion. As a result, the bans on headscarves in schools and at work and of face veils on the street were all certified as valid assertions of state authority.[17]

Some judges have done better. The German Constitutional Court has shown more sympathy for the sensitivities of religious minorities.[18] The US Supreme Court has also ruled in their favor.[19] Since deciding that the French could outlaw headscarves in schools, the judges in Strasbourg have affirmed an employee's right to wear a cross at work and a witness's right to wear a headscarf when giving evidence in court.[20] Even the Conseil d'État (France's highest administrative court) has said that banning full-body bathing suits ("burkinis") was antithetical to the rule of law and defied common sense.

The failure of European judges to rigorously apply proportionality as part of its assessment of the legitimacy of dress codes has been criticized by human rights advocates and international jurists who sit on the United Nations Human Rights Committee. The latter, who are drawn from a wide range of legal traditions, have issued multiple rulings in which they have said that attempts by the state to control what people can wear must strike the right balance and that neither of the French bans, on headscarves in schools or on face veils in the street, measured up.[21] Shamelessly, because the committee's rulings are not legally binding, the authorities paid no attention.

In the face of the overwhelming consensus of the experts, the government's refusal to make any accommodation for those who wanted to follow the teachings of their religion when they went about the business of daily living was disturbing. Especially for the students who were not allowed to wear their headscarves and turbans in class, the penalty they had to pay was steep. Like the school regulation in Montreal that outlawed the kirpan, the French government effectively compelled students who wanted to wear headscarves either to enroll in private schools and pay for their own education or follow their course of studies alone, online, from home. In either case, forcing a person to violate the laws of their faith in order to attend the neighborhood school was a steep price.

On the other side of the balance, the government had nothing of equivalent weight. In terms of protecting the secular character of the state, public order, and the rights of other students, the evidence suggested that if religious symbols like headscarves and turbans were allowed in schools, little or nothing would have been lost. As one commentator put it, the Fifth Republic wasn't going to collapse if a few students followed the rules of their religion in deciding what to wear to class. In fact, allowing everyone the choice of whether to cover their hair seems more consistent with the core French values of "liberty, equality, and fraternity" than telling everyone to dress "à la mode."

The government's assessment of the weight of its case was badly overstated. While it is true that the principle of laïcité is fundamental to the character of French society, the evidence showed that the government tolerated, even supported, a lot of religion in public life. Most of its school holidays, for example, celebrate important dates in the Christian calendar. In addition, Catholic schools receive massive subsidies from the state, as do churches in some départements and overseas territories. Moreover, Christian students were permitted to wear the symbol of the cross if it was suitably discreet.

Having shown its willingness to compromise the secular character of French schools for Christianity, the government could not consistently claim that allowing students of other religions to wear symbols of their faith would be a big deal. Once again, actions speak louder than words. Allowing Muslim women to wear headscarves in institutions of higher learning confirmed that there was room for religious symbols in the sphere of public education. The universities' experience taught that wearing religious symbols does not disqualify people from simultaneously embracing core values of French citizenship and being part of the "general will" of the school. If headscarves can be accommodated in universities, how could lycées be that different?

Nor could it be said that allowing headscarves in schools would have constituted a major threat to the public order and/or the rights of others. The facts were that from 1989, when the Conseil d'État ruled that wearing headscarves in schools did not violate the principle of *laïcité*, until 2004, when the ban was introduced, schools were able to operate normally and other students were not pressured to follow suit. Disputes that arose (like what clothing could be worn in a gym class or a science lab) were settled peacefully with the help of state mediators. During this period, France's experience was no different than any of the other countries in Europe that allowed headscarves to be worn in public schools without disruption to or interference in the lives of others.

At the time of its enactment, many supporters of the French law defended it as an appropriate and timely response by the state to sexism and the subordination of women. Too often, they said, students were pressured by males in their families to submit to Islam in the way they dressed. Secularists and feminists said that the freedom of young women who didn't want to cover their hair was just as important as the freedom of those who did. They defended schools as public spaces in which future citizens are given the means to free themselves of the religious and ethnic chains of their families.

Protecting people from being forced to wear religious clothing is a legitimate concern for any government. The issue was whether the French pursued it in a balanced and evenhanded way. To protect young girls from being coerced into wearing a headscarf against their will, was it necessary to override the freedom of other women whose decision to cover their hair was voluntary? Was an absolute ban that forced some girls to leave school a proportionate response?

The wide scope French law gives parents to impose their spiritual and moral values on their children suggests that it wasn't. If, as it did, French law allowed parents to indoctrinate their children into any of the established religions, what could be gained by excluding from their authority

the right to insist their children dress in a fashion their religion recom-
mends? Even in a culture that puts a lot of emphasis on appearances,
could clothes be that important? In a society that allowed parents to cir-
cumcise their male children in the name of religion, recognizing their
right to dress their offspring according to their faith seems like small
potatoes.

The French government was caught by the same kind of contradiction that undermined the position of the Montreal school authorities
who tried to keep the kirpan out of their schools. In both cases, the
state showed that its interest – in safety in one case and secularism in the
other – was not absolute and unyielding. Such significant concessions
had already been made that nothing much would be lost if a few students
were allowed to follow their faith in deciding how to dress for school.

Moreover, even if the government could establish that protecting the
freedom of children to override their parents' objections in choosing
their clothing was pressing and substantial, the law would still fail the
proportionality test because it wasn't focused precisely on that objective.
As we saw in the last chapter, proportionality requires not only that an
interest be sufficiently weighty, but also that it be pursued in a way that
does as little damage as possible to the interests it adversely affects. Even
if protecting the right of children to dress as they choose is the most
significant matter in the case, it must be achieved by means that burden
others as little as possible.

Rather than a law that banned all headscarves, the prohibition could
have been limited to the targeted group. To conform to the principle of
proportionality, the law could have made an exception for girls who were
of an age and maturity that they could show their choice to wear a headscarf was voluntary. For many (most?) "hijabis," headscarves and modest
clothing are assertions of both their spirituality and their autonomy to
control what parts of their body they want to expose.

Defending the right of Muslim students to wear headscarves in school
should have been an easy brief. It is even more straightforward than
defending the liberty of a Sikh student to wear his kirpan in class. Headscarves seem so inconsequential to everyone except the people wearing
them, it is hard to imagine venues where they are out of place. As just
noted, even the European Court of Human Rights has said it would be
wrong to outlaw them in court.

The fact that the French state has no legitimate authority to tell women
they can't cover their hair with a scarf doesn't mean its collective sense
of proper fashion can always be ignored. Change the article of clothing
or the venue where it's worn or the person wearing it, and the outcome
can be very different. Even a headscarf may be problematic if it's worn

by a judge. If you switch the headscarf for a face veil, the story changes even more.

Telling a woman she is not permitted to wear a face veil can be as arbitrary and unjust as banning headscarves from schools, but not always. On the question of where a woman is entitled to cover her face, rather than just the top of her head, proportionality tells a more nuanced story. In these cases, like those evaluating the legitimacy of abortion laws, the balance is struck along a sliding scale.

In some circumstances, the personal interest of the woman is clearly predominant. Choosing to wear a face veil while out for a walk would be one of them. Outlawing face veils any time a woman steps out of her home is as extreme as banning headscarves from schools; both are heavy-handed.

The critical fact that condemns the legitimacy of a law that fines women for wearing a face veil anywhere in public is that the cost to the community of allowing them in open spaces like sidewalks and parks ranges from negligible to nothing. Some people say niqabs and burqas weaken a community's sense of social solidarity by shielding the faces of people you pass on the street, but that is simply not credible in a world in which many people cover their face for a variety of different reasons. Already, helmets cover the faces of motorcyclists and scarves hide the faces of practically everyone on cold and snowy days. Indeed, as pollution levels and pandemics have become more threatening, face masks have come to be seen as smart accessories, with local authorities regularly encouraging and sometimes ordering people to cover their faces to protect their own and other people's health.

To respect the core values of the rule of law, the French authorities would have to show that wearing a burqa or niqab posed a real threat to the security and well-being of others. It would have to be linked to some wrongdoing or real harm. If, for example, suicide bombings had been carried out by assassins hiding beneath a burqa or niqab (as happened in Cameroon, Chad, and Tunisia), a total ban might be defended as a proportionate response, as it was in those countries.

On the other hand, even if there were a rash of robberies by burglars wearing burqas, forcing all women to uncover their faces when they went for a walk would be too much. The obvious, less drastic solution would be to require women to show their faces only if and when they entered a bank or other commercial establishment. So long as they stayed on the sidewalk, there would be no reason why they shouldn't be able to follow the precepts of their religion in choosing how much of their body to expose.

In other settings, the consequences of wearing a face veil may matter more and the state may be able to justify more targeted regulations. For example, in courtrooms and at school niqabs and burqas may be out of place at least some of the time and for some people. In legal proceedings and educational institutions, covering one's face can conflict with basic community values in a way that headscarves rarely do. In courtrooms and classrooms, the religious pieties of conservative Muslim women may have to give way to the secular values of their neighbors.

The community's right to insist everyone show his or her face seems strongest when the force of the law is in play. A legal system that lacks openness and transparency fails the most basic precepts of justice. The requirement that justice must not only be done, but be *seen* to be done, is an essential characteristic of a rule of law state. Being questioned or accused by someone wearing a mask constitutes a flagrant violation of that ideal. At a minimum, a person who is charged with sexual assault is entitled to see the face of his accuser and the judge who will decide his fate.[22]

On the other side of the scales, the sacrifice of religious beliefs that would result from requiring judges and accusers to show their faces in court would be considerably less severe. Dress codes are not one of the five pillars of Islam and the Qur'an's injunction to dress modestly is generic. It does not specifically direct women to cover their face or their hair. Each of the schools of Islamic law interprets the relevant passages of the Qur'an differently. The fact that most Muslim women believe that they can satisfy the Qur'an's requirements by wearing a headscarf shows it would not constitute a major compromise of a person's faith if, instead of hiding her face, she only covered the top and back of her head.

The balance tips in the same direction in the cases of teachers and students who want to cover their faces in school. Here again, the constraint on a woman's freedom to practice her religion seems pretty contained. Because of the headscarf alternative, women who are not allowed to wear a face veil are not forced to violate any laws or values of their religion. Indeed, as Egypt's Supreme Constitutional Court pointed out when it considered the issue, not only do headscarves fully satisfy the Qur'an's command to women to dress modestly, they also allow females to interact more effectively at work and in society at large.[23]

By contrast, the cost of allowing face veils in the classroom, in terms of compromising community values, would be substantial. Facial expression is of a similar order of importance in teaching and learning as it is in interrogations in the police station and cross-examination in the courts. Looking at a student's face helps a teacher see whether she is engaged. Veils make it harder to know if the message is getting through. Their purpose, after all, is to impede communication. Even in Islamic countries, teachers talk to their students face-to-face.

If veils were allowed in schools, they would take away some of the familiarity and personal connection that is an important part of learning. There would be a barrier in communication, a rejection of a certain level of reciprocity and trust between teachers and their students and among teachers themselves.

Face veils are fundamentally inconsistent with the idea that public schools are communities in which teachers and students can look at and treat each other in a respectful, nonthreatening way. They are based on assumptions about relations between the sexes that stereotype and are demeaning to men. They are at odds with our commitment to a culture of employment equity in which men and women are expected to work together in an environment of mutual respect.

When dress codes are tested against the principle of proportionality, religiously inspired women and their secular sisters end up being treated the same. Laws that prohibit veiling and clothing that is too revealing outlaw opposing extremes. In fashion as in law, time, place, and manner determine what is acceptable and what fails the grade. Just as Norma the Nudist cannot show up topless, Mariyah the Muslim cannot cover her face when either performs the duties of a teacher or judge.

But remember, in a world in which proportionality is the ultimate rule of law, there are no absolutes. Change one fact, like COVID-19, and the rights and wrongs of face masks can shift 180 degrees. During a pandemic, not only do religiously inspired women have a right to cover their faces in public – the rest of us have a civic duty to follow their example.

Speech Codes

When the question of what Muslim women wear in public is approached using a case-by-case, casuistic method, proportionality has the capacity to settle seemingly intractable conflicts between incommensurable values while remaining value-free itself. In some cases of multicultural conflict, it may do much more. Where one or both sides are fanatical about an issue, it may even save lives.

Consider the collision of Western freedoms and Muslim devotion that was triggered by newspapers, books, and films that poked fun at the Prophet Mohammad and the message he recited in the Qur'an. The conflict was ignited in 2005 when a Danish paper published a series of cartoons that included disrespectful images of the Prophet. Some, but not all, included a drawing of his physical person. In a couple, he was depicted as a warrior or terrorist. One had him naked with his genitals showing; another had him wearing a turban in the shape of a bomb.

Muslims everywhere were offended. Many were really upset. In some countries the cartoons provoked violent demonstrations. Danish embassies were attacked and set on fire. Property was destroyed. People were killed.

The Danish authorities didn't think the cartoons were that serious. They recognized that publication of these images could be insulting and hurtful, but they defended them as being in the nature of political satire. There was no intention to offend, they said, and so the intervention of the state wasn't warranted. For Danes, poking fun can't be compared to a poke in the eye. Like many people, they draw a bright line between being offensive or obscene and inciting hate.[24]

The government insisted that people in Denmark have a right to express themselves in whatever way they want, no matter how much it hurts other people, so long as there is no intention to threaten or vilify another person. They said that in their corner of the world, no one has a right not to be insulted or offended. As they saw it, sticks and stones can break your bones but names can never hurt you – at least not in a legally significant way.

At no stage of the conflict did the politicians on either side provide effective leadership. For the most part, they relied on political posturing and traditional diplomacy. Both proved to be dead-ends. Hamid Karzai, the president of Afghanistan, demanded an apology that Anders Fogh Rasmussen, the prime minister of Denmark, refused to give. There never was a resolution that satisfied both sides.

Each thought the other behaved badly. A residue of mutual mistrust remained. Despite the benign intentions of the journalists, Muslims said they felt as though their religion had been attacked. The Western press claimed the Enlightenment project of challenging religious pretensions was under siege.

The embers of the argument continued to smolder. Seven years after the cartoons were published, an American film mocking the Prophet Muhammad set off another round of violent demonstrations, although in this case, America's political leaders condemned its release. Then, on 7 January 2015, two Islamic militants attacked the offices of *Charlie Hebdo*, a satirical French magazine that had reprinted the Danish cartoons along with some of its own, and murdered twelve of its staff.

The *Charlie Hebdo* killings polarized the world. While virtually everyone condemned the violence of the extremists, people were sharply divided on whether Western laws, like those in Denmark and France, should permit journalists to mock the religious beliefs of their fellow citizens. Some thought the example of the cartoonists so heroic they honored them with awards. Others deplored their "punching down" on religious minorities who were already disadvantaged and pushed to the margins of the countries in which they lived. Again, both sides talked past each other and neither could hear what the other said.

Incredibly, five years later, when *Charlie Hebdo* republished the cartoons to focus attention on the trial of some of the terrorists, more innocent people were murdered. Again political leaders, this time the presidents of Turkey and France, doubled down on the rhetoric and raised the stakes.

The cartoon controversy, like the world of French fashion, is an ugly story. If France were fully committed to the rule of law, it would have handled the case very differently. If it recognized proportionality as the highest expression of the rule of law, it would have seen the cartoons in a very different light and innocent lives might have been saved.

On the scales of justice, the difference in the burdens faced by Muslims and the cartoonists is plain to see. There is no comparison in the gravity of the interests at stake: On one side is a religious community asking that it be treated politely and with respect. On the other are a bunch of guys insisting on the right to insult the spiritual leader of their neighbors' faith for the sake of a laugh. We cannot claim to have moved much beyond the mind-set that launched the Crusades if we can't get this balance right.

For Muslims, there is no doubt about the gravity of the offence. Their holiest icon is being defamed. On this, the whole Muslim community, Sunni and Shia, modern and traditional, are agreed. All physical depictions of the Prophet, even those that are pious, are forbidden. They are considered blasphemous and sacrilegious. Among the faithful, they are universally considered a mark of disrespect.

It is not just religious fanatics who regard the cartoons as an affront to one of the central rules of their faith. As Hamid Karzai told the Western press, for anyone who believes in the Prophet, God is no laughing matter. As an art show organized by the Iranian government was intended to illustrate, mocking the Prophet is as offensive for Muslims as Holocaust denial is for Jews. Even though making a bad joke and denying the truth of a historical event are two different types of expression, the hurt they cause can be equally painful.

For many Muslims, maligning their Prophet is that upsetting, and when the principle of proportionality is being applied, it is their feelings, not those of more "enlightened" Danes or French, that count. Telling them that Christians have learned to accept jokes about Jesus is the same as the judges in Washington telling Homer Plessy he should think like a white. That the French and Danes consider historical truth to be supremely important doesn't change the fact or answer the claim of Muslims that for them Mohammad's reputation is what matters most.

On the other side of the balance, the restraint that is entailed in banning drawings of Mohammad is a small restriction of freedom of speech. It adds hardly anything to the limitations that already exist. No country in the world, including the United States, allows people absolute freedom to say or write or draw whatever they want.

Indeed, many kinds of harmful speech are already banned. You can't falsely shout "Fire!" in a crowded theatre, as Oliver Wendell Holmes famously said in another of his punchy one-liners. Likewise, inciting violence is beyond the pale. Broadcast regulations condemn the most obscene forms of speech and defamation laws proscribe false and misleading assertions that injure another person's reputation.

There are also laws in most Western countries, including Denmark and France, prohibiting messages that promote hatred toward people on the basis of their religion or sex or race. Holocaust denial is outlawed in many countries and child pornography is a subject that is recognized all over the world as being beyond the bounds of permissible speech. Most telling of all, even a simple insult, if it is directed at a judge, constitutes contempt of court and can land you in jail. In a rule of law state, no right is absolute, including freedom of speech.

Within the existing restrictions on what a person can say publicly, adding religious slurs to the list of things that are already censured would compromise freedom of expression very little. Gratuitous insults and fighting words would be eliminated from public conversation. That's hardly a big deal. Cartoonists would lose the liberty to depict their ideas through images that are over the top, but they would still be able to get their message across in ways that were less biting. Cartoons that respected Islam's strong aversion to physical representations of the Prophet (which was true of a couple of those that were originally published) and refrained from humiliation and ridicule would pass the test. What was problematic about the cartoons wasn't so much what they were saying as the way they said it.[25]

Proportionality calibrates the scales of justice in the case of the cartoons in exactly the same way it addresses the question of what Hindu men and Muslim women should be allowed to wear. It is highly sensitive to context. Each case (cartoon) must be judged on its own – like screening movies to protect children from scenes of torture and mass killing. In every case, its purpose is the same: to minimize the harmful fallout of collisions between cultures that understand the world in radically different ways. If conflict is unavoidable, proportionality ensures the damage is kept to a minimum.

In a more perfect world, all conflict between cultures would be settled by impartial judges applying the principle of proportionality, one case at a time. If all communication across cultures were carried on in a tone of moderation and respect, there would be reason to hope future conflicts could be settled peacefully and without further violence. No one could expect to prevail in every case, but when they lost they would understand why. Even if they didn't like the result, they could not deny the justice of the principle on which it was based.

Of course, in the imperfect world in which we live, such a prospect is pure fantasy. As we shall see in the next chapter, some conflicts defy rationality and can only be settled by physical force. Sometimes the need to resist aggression is unavoidable. When that happens – when we are forced to fight – our only consolation is that proportionality can still help us control our hormones and stop us from giving in to excess and the urge to fight dirty.

Chapter Eleven

New World

The murder of *Charlie Hebdo*'s staff was a bleak day for the rule of law. Lives were lost because neither side was willing to submit to the sovereignty of law and embrace the principle of proportionality to solve their differences. The cartoonists insisted their interest in freedom of speech was more important than showing respect for their neighbors' religious sensibilities. They were willing to balance the competing interests in the case but only if they were allowed to keep their thumbs on the scales.

If the cartoonists were guilty of arrogance and narcissism, the killers' behavior was exponentially more depraved. They rejected the idea of balance and proportionality altogether. Like the medieval Muslim scholars whom we met in chapter 4, they say reason and rationality have no place in deciding what is just and right. Their interpretation of the Qur'an and sharia law is definitive. It is the only thing that counts. Anyone who refuses to see things their way is liable to be labeled an infidel and killed. On their law, anyone who disrespects the Prophet Mohammad deserves to die.

The devotion of Islamic extremists to a medieval reading of sharia law puts defenders of the rule of law in a place they would prefer not be. The hard reality they confront is that force is the only way some of the most difficult and threatening conflicts in today's world can be solved. For Islamic purists, that is the only basis on which they will engage. Faced with jihadists who refuse to settle their differences in court, on some occasions, those who put their faith in the law have no alternative but to fight.

Having to decide whether to commit their countries to military action is one of the heaviest responsibilities government leaders have to shoulder. Choosing to do battle with an enemy amounts to a death sentence for lots of people. To lighten (but not eliminate) the burden of their decision, presidents and prime ministers can count on the principles of proportionality and necessity to tell them when it's right to fight and how to avoid fighting dirty.

Adherence to the principles of proportionality and necessity guarantees that political leaders will act legally. Each of the detailed rules of armed conflict that are recognized in international law are just specific illustrations of the way proportionality and necessity work. None of the major doctrines that one finds in the jurisprudence of the International Court of Justice adds anything beyond the requirements that states can only use force as a last resort to defend themselves (necessity) and with a measure of ferocity that roughly compares to the hostile acts they are trying to repel (proportionality).[1]

Proportionality is embedded in all the basic rules of international humanitarian law. Weapons are outlawed in The Hague Conventions that cause "unnecessary" suffering and "excessive" loss of life. Civilians (as well as sick and wounded combatants and prisoners of war) merit special protection in the Geneva Conventions because attacking them inflicts pain and suffering that bears no relation to the military threat they pose. Except in the kind of extreme circumstances the Court contemplated in the nuclear weapons case, strategies that result in extensive death and destruction of civilian populations are not proportional in any conventional sense of the word.

Even the concept of a war crime is essentially a matter of proportionality and a question of degree. War crimes are defined as violations of international law that are especially flagrant. Under the Statute of Rome, individuals can be held personally accountable for breaches of international law that are "serious" and "grave." It makes attacks that cause death and devastation among the civilian population a crime when their magnitude is "clearly excessive."

When political and military leaders adopt necessity and proportionality as the litmus tests of when and how much force is a legitimate option for a state to defend its interests, they can be certain they are living up to all the requirements of the international laws of war. They can also take some consolation from the fact that they will be doing everything they legally can to minimize the loss of life. Proportionality instructs the commander in chief to deploy every strategy and weapon that can reasonably be expected to reduce the death toll.

To guarantee a secure and peaceful life for as many people as possible, proportionality encourages governments to fight smart as well as fair. It allows for more robust use of force than you might expect. Law-abiding leaders don't have to fight with one hand behind their backs. Indeed, in extreme circumstances, when everything else has failed, torture, killing civilians, and even armed intervention to stop wholesale violence in another country may all be justified in order to minimize loss of life.

Torture

Consider the question of torture. Today it is considered one of the most vile and odious of all human behaviors. The deliberate infliction of excruciating pain against any sentient creature is universally condemned. It is considered by just about everybody to be completely antithetical to every dimension of the rule of law. The UN Convention against Torture and Other Cruel, Inhuman or Degrading Acts imposes an absolute ban on its practice. It allows for no exceptions, not even in times of war. Torture is always and everywhere against the law.

After following the history of the rule of law in the first three parts of this book, readers will know that the abolition of all forms of torture has only happened in the last hundred years. Prior to that, lawmakers in imperial Rome and medieval Europe made it an integral part of their legal systems. The Romans routinely tortured slaves to elicit evidence (often to get the goods on their masters), and as recently as the early eighteenth century, it was a standard tool used by both secular and religious courts all over Europe to draw confessions from witches and heretics.

When torture is examined through the lens of proportionality, both current and past perceptions appear wide of the mark. Neither total abolition nor wholesale legalization pass the test. On the scales of justice, the first is too little and the second too much. Today no one advocates making torture a routine part of the legal process and only the most dogmatic deny there are some circumstances in which torturing a person is the right thing to do.

To test yourself, consider the case of the terrorist who has hidden a ticking bomb somewhere in the center of a crowded city. As the commander in chief, you have to make the final decision. You have had the most professional interrogators try to reason with him to reveal its location but the only laws he respects are the rules and injunctions given by the Archangel Gabriel to the Prophet Mohammad. Every less drastic alternative has been tried and failed. Unless you can force him to tell you where the bomb is, lots of people will die. You must decide whether to authorize the use of whatever forms of nonlethal torture it will take to persuade him to call off the attack.

Unless you are a religious (e.g., a Quaker) or philosophical (e.g., a Kantian) fundamentalist,[2] it's hard to argue that, even when torturing a person can save a lot of lives, and without taking the terrorist's, it is the wrong thing to do. Especially when the person who is to be tortured is complicit in the commission of a crime, this seems an easy case. If it is legal to kill a person with whom you are in armed combat in order to save lives, then surely torture, as a less drastic alternative, must be legal as well.

On one side of the balance, the lives of innocent people are on the line. On the other, the suffering of terrible physical and mental pain by a person who is unlawfully threatening the lives of innocent civilians and who will survive the ordeal. On any measure, saving *their* lives counts more than relieving *his* pain. As in every case of lawful self-defense, the lives of those under attack weigh more heavily in the balance.

In the case of the ticking bomb, nonlethal torture is a proportionate response to the bomber's attack. It is a less violent and less drastic way of exercising the right of self-defense than killing him. To satisfy the principles of necessity and proportionality, torture can only be applied after all other noncoercive methods of persuasion have been found wanting. Injections of sodium pentothal (colloquially known as "truth serum") and other less coercive techniques of persuasion like stress positions or sleep deprivation must come before more extreme measures like "waterboarding" (simulated drowning). Like all government decisions, torture is only legal when it is the least inhumane means of obtaining the information it seeks.

The ticking bomb case has been the subject of lots of lively debates, especially among philosophers and lawyers. For some, it is another powerful reminder that even a rule as basic as outlawing torture has exceptions. Others, who are opposed to all forms of torture, disagree. They say it is a purely hypothetical exception without any relevance in the real world.[3] In their opinion, the lesson it teaches has no practical value; it's just another mind game played by cloistered academics. Although they are willing to concede the propriety of applying torture hypothetically, they deny that it can or should be used as a precedent in the sorts of cases political leaders actually have to face.

They make the point that the ticking bomb case is as compelling as it is because it is based on a set of assumptions – a bomb is about to explode; the person being questioned knows its location and will betray his principles if subjected to enough pain – that only happen in novels. In reality, these people say, it is almost always the case that it is uncertain if the person being tortured has the sought-after information, whether he will succumb to the pain, or even if he will tell the truth. In effect they say, even if torture is the right thing to do in the ticking bomb case, that doesn't mean it's justified in the cases that politicians and security forces have to deal with.

In one respect, the abolitionists are right. The ticking bomb case can't serve as a precedent for other threats we may face in the future. Each attack must be analyzed on its own set of facts. Like each of the laws Hammurabi had chipped in stone, the ticking bomb case is meant to illustrate how the balance in these sorts of cases should be struck. It presents a picture of what justice looks like. As we have seen in its assessment of dress and speech codes, proportionality works as a meta principle that structures a (casuistic) way of thinking, in which the facts of each case are decisive.

In almost all cases, torture will be unnecessary and/or excessive. However, that does not mean it can never be the right thing to do. Even in the real world, there are exceptions when torture can be justified as a lifesaving strategy. The case of Khalid Sheikh Mohammed, a senior member of al-Qaeda and the mastermind behind the attacks on the United States on 11 September 2001, is one and Zakaria Mohammed, a high-ranking member of Boko Haram who was involved in the kidnapping of the two hundred Chibok schoolgirls on 14 April 2014, is another. Both were captured and held in custody. Both were in possession of valuable information but refused to talk.

Khalid Sheik Mohammed was tortured to encourage him to tell everything he knew about the 9/11 attacks as well as the identities of other leaders of al-Qaeda and other plots that were being planned. There is no hard evidence as to how Zakaria Mohammed was treated by the Nigerian authorities but it is difficult to believe he wasn't also subjected to coercive interrogation techniques in the hope that he would divulge information that would help rescue the girls.

On the scales of justice, torture was lawful in both cases. Even though there was no guarantee that aggressive interrogation would result in success, torturing both Mohammeds was a legitimate means of self-defense. When the stakes are high enough – to liberate young girls from a brutal regime of sexual violence and enslavement or to defend against almost certain attacks in the future – nonlethal forms of torture may be applied. Where there are reasonable grounds for believing it may save lives, it is the right thing to do.

Even a small chance of avoiding a major catastrophe or ending a terrible ordeal may justify forcing enemy combatants to endure a lot of pain and suffering to persuade them to talk. The fact that people who are tortured sometimes lie doesn't alter the reality that other times they tell the truth. The chance to avert future terrorist attacks and free the Chibok girls weighs more than the suffering of two people forced to endure a finite period of excruciating pain.

Making the terrorist feel the sort of intense pain he inflicts on others strikes the right balance. It works on the same logic as the Golden

Rule: it does to him what he has done to others. It is an example of an exceptional case when *lex talionis* gets it right.

Moreover, because cases like Khalid Sheik Mohammed's and Zakaria Mohammed's don't include the urgency of a ticking bomb, it is possible to ask the courts to pass judgment on the government's claim that the interrogation techniques they propose really do pass the proportionality test. In the same way the police must get permission from a court before they can come in and search your home, it makes sense to require the government to persuade a court to give it a warrant to torture.[4] In each case, the government would have to prove that the magnitude of the threat it was facing justified the coercive measures it proposed.

Even though they are meant to limit the number of cases in which torture will be allowed, some people reject the idea of torture warrants categorically. They regard them as an anathema, a perversion of the legal process. As a practical matter, they say judicial review is likely to slide down a slippery slope, become a rubber stamp, and result in torture becoming a common rather than an exceptional event. They worry it will give legitimacy to the practice through a process that almost certainly would be neither transparent nor accessible to the general public.

To ensure torture warrants do not replicate the injustice that compromised the integrity of the legal systems in Rome and medieval Europe, the independence and transparency of the process would need to be designed with great care. However, in principle and when time permits, it must always be preferable to have an independent, impartial adjudicator evaluate the circumstances of a case before a person is tortured. Torture warrants ensure those responsible for making the final decision are held accountable for the choices they make. Where the independence of the judges can be guaranteed, they will have an impartiality and objectivity in assessing the balance that neither of the elected branches of government can match.

In modern wars involving insurgents, militias, and other nonstate actors, the chances that political leaders will have to decide whether to torture an enemy combatant are not insignificant. By some estimates, the number of governments that make use of coercive interrogation techniques is almost the same as the number who have signed the UN Convention against Torture. To make matters worse, such is the nature of our "wars on terror" that, in addition to having to twist the arms of a few nasty characters, some presidents and prime Ministers are almost certainly going to have to decide whether to take military action that they know will result in the deaths of innocent civilians.

Killing Civilians

Killing civilians is a lot like torture and nuclear weapons: it is almost always unlawful and the wrong thing to do.[5] In the list of customary rules of international law compiled by the Red Cross, it is rule number one. And for good reason, since killing noncombatants adds little or nothing to the purposes for which wars may legitimately be fought. It doesn't weaken the military strength of the enemy. Civilians are by definition not part of the threats and acts of aggression that just wars are aimed at stopping. Killing them doesn't improve the killer's security.

But again, there are exceptions. Like all of the rules we have considered so far, the rule against killing civilians isn't absolute. Accidental, collateral, sometimes even intentional killings will be lawful if they pass the proportionality test. Like the torture of the terrorist who has information concerning the next attack, sometimes they are the lesser evil.[6] Grotius offered the example of women and children trapped in a house of bandits or on a pirate ship to demonstrate that there may be cases when killing a small number of civilians is not only proportional but may be necessary to prevent even greater loss of life.

It's not hard to put Grotius's case in a modern context. Al-Qaeda insurgents hide out in the homes of innocent civilians. Can a military commander order a drone attack knowing that for every hundred enemy combatants killed, four or five innocent people will also lose their lives? Or, think about what you would do if you were president or prime minister and were told that a group of terrorists had captured a commercial airplane and were intending to crash it in the center of a crowded city. What should you do?

Using remote-controlled drones to attack enemies in the distant, isolated places they usually live, knowing innocent people will also be killed, seems as easy a call as torturing the two Mohammeds.[7] If the answer Grotius gave was right four hundred years ago, it must be no less true today. So long as all other alternatives have been exhausted and the number of lives lost is not excessive, killing civilians along with the enemy always was and still is the right thing to do.

Despite the history and logic that supports the use of drone warfare, its optics are not inspiring. Compared to the courage of the Spartan warriors at Thermopylae, the image of a weapons expert in a remote location running through a checklist before firing a lethal missile doesn't look very heroic.

Viewed through the lens of necessity and proportionality, however, drone warfare is unambiguously a good thing. Above and beyond everything else, using drones rather than troops to disarm an aggressor saves lives. Drones have the advantage of being able to monitor a target for days and weeks before an attack is launched and to strike with a precision that cannot be matched. While bombs had a 50 percent chance of landing within half a mile of their targets in the Second World War, they are now accurate to within a couple of meters. In addition, using unmanned weapons reduces the number of people who have to put their lives at risk defending their country.

Drone attacks, like torture warrants, also lend themselves to being double checked in the courts. In most cases, decisions to defend a country's security using remote-controlled weapons can be reviewed by judges before they are fired to ensure the principles of necessity and proportionality have been met. If, for example, the target of an attack could just as easily be captured as killed, or killed at another location where fewer civilians were at risk, authorization could be refused.

In cases where time is of the essence, judicial review could still be carried out after the fact. The police have to prove their use of deadly force was necessary if they are to avoid criminal liability and military officials should have to as well. Even if a review can only be conducted after the damage has been done, it can ensure that anyone responsible for the use of excessive force be held accountable. While clearly a second-best solution in terms of minimizing the loss of life, by setting an example for future cases, judicial oversight, whenever it happens, must be a good thing. Forcing governments to account for the decisions they make is always better late than never.

Compared to launching an unmanned drone against enemy combatants, the decision to shoot down a hijacked airliner is much more dramatic and gut-wrenching but the principles of necessity and proportionality are no less applicable and the analysis is exactly the same. Once it is accepted that there is an intrinsic equality between all of the people who are caught up in the crisis, the result is a foregone conclusion. If more innocent lives will be saved than lost by shooting down the plane, then it is a matter of common sense and collective self-defense that the state is legally obliged to open fire.

Had the American government been able to mobilize its air force more quickly on 9/11, it could not have been said to have acted unjustly or unlawfully if it had shot down the planes before they hit the Pentagon and the twin towers. Once it was clear there was no other alternative, and the planes could not be diverted, George W. Bush's obligation to each innocent victim was the same whether they were on the ground or in the air. When, as president, you can save three thousand people by killing three hundred, majorities rule and you have a constitutional duty to ensure as many people as possible survive.

Although Germany's Constitutional Court handed down a judgment in which it said that the German government could not pass a law authorizing such an attack in advance, it did not rule out the possibility that the chancellor or one of her ministers could justify such a decision, after the fact, as a matter of necessity and self-defense.[8] Deliberately killing 300 people on a plane who face certain death, even if the state does nothing, to save ten times that many, is a proportional and therefore legitimate use of force.

Shooting down an airplane that has been hijacked by a suicide bomber is an all too realistic example of a genre of moral dilemmas that are collectively known as the "the trolley problem." The brainchild of Philippa Foot, a British philosopher, the original trolley problem asked how the conductor of a runaway train should respond if she were faced with the choice of doing nothing and watching the train run over five people who were trapped on the tracks or pulling a lever and moving the train onto another track where only one person would be run over. The vast majority of people who have been asked this question (and thousands of college students have) tell the conductor to hit the switch.

Foot's question spawned a cottage industry of philosophers, psychologists, and neuroscientists who have devised a series of more complicated and subtle cases that are meant to raise doubts in the minds of those who would flip the switch. So, for example, Judith Jarvis Thomson asked whether the same logic would apply if the only way to stop the train from killing the five people was to shove a fat man onto the tracks. Even though the numbers are the same, in survey after survey most of the people who would divert the train onto a different track recoil at the idea of pushing anyone to his death.

In the academic world, there is a lively literature that tries to make sense of the different reactions people have to these two very similar cases.[9] For modern casuists, it's perfect beach reading. However, whatever you think of the problems posed by Foot and Thomson, the case of the hijacked airplane that has been converted into a guided missile should seem much simpler and more straightforward.

What makes the case of the hijacked airliner easier than any of the different versions of the trolley problem is that the people on the plane who will be killed if the commander orders the plane to be shot down will die even if she doesn't. As on 9/11, if she does nothing, they still perish; her decision only concerns how many lives will be saved. In that sense, she is like a pilot of a plane whose engines have failed and is looking for the least populated area to attempt a crash landing.

Shooting down a hijacked airliner is yet another striking example of an exception that proves the rule. Both the exception and the rule promote the value of human life. Like torture and nuclear weapons, however, it is important to repeat that in almost every other case, killing civilians will be wrong. As the International Court of Justice has made clear, even when a country is acting in self-defense, it can only use force that is proportional to the attack it is facing and necessary to repel it.

On the standard fixed by the judges in the Nicaragua case, there must always be a rough balance between opposing forces – between the military power a state uses to defend itself and the death and destruction it has or is likely to suffer. Whenever the number of innocent victims who are killed in a military operation significantly exceeds the lives saved by the attack, it is likely there has been a violation of international law. If the imbalance is severe, there is a good chance someone has committed a war crime.

Israel's conflicts with Hamas in Gaza in 2008–9 and again in the summer of 2014 are glaring examples of a defender going overboard and giving in to excess. The disparity in the number of casualties suffered by the two sides was appalling. In 2008–9, in order to stop rocket attacks that had resulted in the deaths of 16 of its citizens over the preceding four years, the Israeli government invaded and occupied Gaza for three weeks, killing almost 1,500 Palestinians, most of them civilians. In 2014, almost 2,200 Palestinians were killed in "Operation Protective Edge," of whom more than 70 percent were civilians. On the other side, 70 Israelis (and 1 Thai) lost their lives, all but 5 of whom were armed soldiers. Nor were the huge imbalances in fatalities accidental. A principle of "disproportionate force" has been part of Israel's military strategy even before the country's founding. Its invasion of Lebanon in 2006 produced death tolls of similar proportions.

On the arithmetic of proportionality, the Israeli response to Hamas's rockets cannot be justified as a legitimate act of self-defense: the difference in lives lost is too great. The traditional accounting of *lex talionis* looks soft by comparison. In effect, the Israelis exacted a hundred eyes for one of their own and whole jaws for a single tooth. Especially when innocent civilian lives are at stake, a ratio of 100 to 1 is overkill of criminal proportions.

The psychological trauma that thousands of Israelis suffered from the steady barrage of rockets fired by Hamas was a terrible burden to have to bear, but it can't even the balance – the number of innocent Palestinians who died is just too great. As Grotius explained almost four hundred years ago, even those fighting a just war are bound to abide by the rules.

Rescuing Women and Children

Torturing terrorists and killing innocent civilians are actions that can be justified in exceptional circumstances by states that are under attack.

Proportionality authorizes both when they can be shown to minimize loss of life. Even more dramatically, to stop a bloodbath, proportionality may legitimate the invasion of another state.

In addition to authorizing the use of force in self-defense, proportionality may call for a proactive intervention in the affairs of another country in order to prevent a humanitarian disaster. Genocide is the paradigm case. In an international order that swears allegiance to the rule of law, proportionality imposes a legal duty on states to do what they can to stop mass murder whenever and wherever it occurs. Today, that duty goes by the name of R2P: the responsibility to protect.

For many people, an irrefutable case, in which an armed invasion would be justified, is if another Hitler came along and ordered a second Holocaust. Even if he never attacked another country, they would say his victims have the right to call on the rest of us for help. Assuming we have the capacity to pull it off, they would insist we are under a legal obligation to mount a rescue mission, even if it violated the sovereignty of the country he ruled. Humanitarian interventions safeguard those who are not in a position to protect themselves from being brutalized and beaten up.

To bring the moral imperative of rescuing others when you can closer to home, think of what you would do if you heard a child screaming for help in the apartment next door and you were unable to contact the police or they were unable to respond. If you decided to break down the door and save the child, the criminal law in many countries would acquit you of any wrongdoing. On the principle of necessity, the law would say you did the right thing. Even though you technically committed a trespass when you broke into your neighbor's apartment, Good Samaritan laws (as they are known in some places) say you should incur no criminal or civil liability for what you did.

The moral authority of the person who breaks into another person's home when it is the only way a child can be saved is so compelling that nonlawyers naturally assume that the logic of domestic criminal law will be replicated in the international law regulating relations between states. It comes as something of a surprise, therefore, when they learn that this isn't the case. In fact, ever since the Treaty of Westphalia in 1648 the prevailing view among international lawyers has been that states can never legally violate the sovereignty of another country, even when its government is committing mass atrocities against its own people. Even in the case of a future Hitler, when they agree that an armed invasion would be morally required, most lawyers still say it's against the law.[10]

The way the lawyers tell the story, the fundamental lesson that those who lived through the horrors of the Second World War drew from their experience was that no state must ever again be allowed to intervene in the affairs of other countries. As we read in chapter 8, in article 51 of the UN Charter, the international community laid down the law that the only occasion a state may legally deploy military force is when it is defending itself against an armed attack. Too often in the past, countries with imperial ambitions, including the Nazis, crossed their neighbors' borders claiming they were protecting vulnerable minorities from persecution. We have already seen that humanitarian intervention was part of the cover story for the Crusades and the Spanish conquest of the Americas.

The claim that the UN Charter and international law render all armed intervention illegal resonates in lots of countries, including Russia and China and many smaller states in Africa, Asia, and South America. They fear that any exception will be exploited by powerful states to dominate the affairs of their weaker neighbors. It is endorsed by the vast majority of international lawyers and the judges in The Hague seem to be of the same opinion. In its ruling in the Nicaragua case, the International Court of Justice told the Americans that force could not be used to ensure human rights were being respected in other member states (paragraph 268).

The widespread suspicion of humanitarian interventions has undoubtedly reduced the incidence of armed conflict, but the price that has been paid for peace is unconscionable. Since the UN system has been in place, millions of people have been slaughtered by an endless line of dictators and despots, in large part because the international community has insisted there was no legal way to stop them. Opting for peace regardless of the cost has meant that the international community's record of helping those in distress over the course of the last seventy-five years has ranged from spotty to deplorable.

The massacres of innocent civilians in the last half of the twentieth century in Indonesia, Guatemala, Cambodia, Zimbabwe, Rwanda, Sudan, Syria, and the former Yugoslavia by their own governments is the price that has been paid for maintaining that all member states have absolute sovereignty over the territories they govern. Characterizing the rule of nonintervention as absolute and inviolable has empowered rulers to subject their rivals to the most barbaric acts of violence and repression. The reluctance of the international community to get involved has helped ensure that governments that are inclined to abuse those who oppose their rule can act without fear they will ever be held responsible for their crimes. Even when the body count numbered in the tens and hundreds of thousands, the international community has insisted it couldn't fight for the victims and stop the killing.[11]

No one did anything to help the roughly 1 million Indonesians who were butchered by Suharto and his military colleagues nor the 200,000

Guatemalans who lost their lives at the hands of government death squads. None of his neighbors (including South Africa) tried to stop Robert Mugabe carrying out the mass murder of an estimated 20,000 political opponents who came from a rival (Ndebele) tribe. The whole world stood by and watched the Cambodian genocide in which over 1.5 million people lost their lives and the country lost 20 percent of its population. The failure to prevent the murder of 800,000 people in Rwanda is widely regarded as one of the worst moral lapses in the history of the UN. More recently, more than 70,000 civilians have been slaughtered in Darfur. In the last ten years, diplomats have dithered and dined while almost 500,000 Syrians, mostly innocent civilians, have been massacred.

By any measure these are death tolls of staggering proportions. For any sentient being, the unleashing of such epidemic death and destruction by repressive governments behind their legally sealed borders "shocks the moral conscience of mankind." When one looks for answers as to how such horrific mass murders could be allowed to happen, lawyers once again bear some responsibility. They obviously didn't do the killing, but they helped construct a legal regime that made it easier for despots and dictators to get away with mass murder. Like the Roman and medieval lawyers we met in parts 1 and 2, international judges and jurists have created spaces where political leaders can act above and unconstrained by the law.

International lawyers have deliberately chosen to construct an international law of humanitarian intervention that ignores what the scales of justice require. They have fashioned a set of rules that favor international peace over local justice even when it has meant millions of innocent people would be killed. In effect, they rejected the logic of Good Samaritan laws that even criminal behavior, if it is essential to avert a more monstrous evil, becomes a legal imperative by necessity.

Like the judges who told Dred Scott he was not a citizen of the United States, international lawyers who favor an absolute rule of nonintervention will insist the current state of the law isn't their doing. They will say the meaning of the UN Charter and other relevant texts is plain and free of ambiguity. But the fact is, there were other ways the postwar history of international law could have been written.

Not all jurists are comfortable with the complete separation of international law from the natural law principles of reason and balance that have dominated the discussion on the use of armed force from Cicero to Grotius.[12] Some say the relevant treaties and protocols can be interpreted to maintain the connection between law and justice that has been part of the story of the rule of law from the beginning. They reject the idea that those responsible for drafting the UN Charter intended to construct an international legal order in which the rules governing the use of force would help a future Hitler liquidate the people he hated.[13]

The most important link between the international law governing the use of force and basic precepts of justice (like Good Samaritan laws) is the Marten's clause that we encountered in chapter 8. As we have seen, its pedigree is long and distinguished. It was included in the preamble of the first Hague Convention in 1899, was reaffirmed in 1949 and again in 1977 in protocols added to the Geneva Conventions, and continues to be recognized as one of the formative principles of international customary law to this day. For more than a hundred years, it has guaranteed civilian populations are "under the protection and empire of the principles of international law as they result from ... the laws of humanity and the requirements of the public conscience."

Although the "laws of humanity and requirements of the public conscience" mean different things to different people, the moral force of Good Samaritan laws resonates with just about everyone. When the life of the child is compared to the violation of the neighbor's property rights, the imbalance is plain to see. When Augustine, Aquinas, and Grotius thought about using force to defend innocent people against rulers bent on mass murder, they made the same calculation. A humanitarian disaster that can be averted by a relatively small restriction of a ruler's sovereignty is, in terms of the Martens clause, a requirement of the public conscience.

To insist on the absolute inviolability of state sovereignty makes the mistake of claiming to be a categorical rule that allows for no exceptions. We have yet to encounter a legal rule that does not recognize special cases, and the rule of state sovereignty can be no different. For the same reason the law allows you to break into the neighbor's apartment to save the life of the child, it cannot be a violation of international law to invade a country whose government is about to unleash a second Holocaust.

More broadly, in any case in which large numbers of innocent people are losing their lives and peaceful means have been ineffective at stopping the killing, the case for military interventions that are likely to succeed will be mandatory. Even when the Security Council refuses to intervene, individual states with the requisite military power have a moral duty and the legal right to act. Just because the police are unable to come to the aid of the child who is being beaten in the apartment next door doesn't relieve the rest of us of our responsibility to do what we can.

On the scales of justice, India's invasion of East Pakistan in 1971 and NATO's bombing of Kosovo in 1999 are modern interventions that got the balance right. Tested against the principles of necessity and proportionality, both put a halt to unfolding massacres. In both cases, the opportunity to save thousands of innocent men, women, and children outweighed the marginal loss of sovereignty (of being able to slaughter one's own citizens) that these armed interventions entailed.

When the balance argues in favor of invading the territory of another state, necessity and proportionality provide the framework for when and how such operations should be conducted. First and foremost, using force to protect people from abusive rulers is only legal as a last resort when all other (peaceful) methods have failed. As well, and like every other instance when force may be used, humanitarian interventions can only flex as much military muscle as is proportionate to the circumstances of the case. Finally, as Grotius insisted four hundred years ago, to constitute a legitimate use of force, it must have a reasonable prospect of success. Armed interventions that cannot solve the problem and/or lead to more death and destruction do not pass the test.

If would-be rescuers were required to prove that their interventions were both necessary and proportionate, fears that humanitarian interventions will become a cover for illicit purposes should be allayed. Because these are principles of casuistry that only apply on a case-by-case basis, there is no danger that one intervention will lead down a slippery slope and justify more armed attacks in the future. Each case would be decided on its own set of facts.[14] Every time a claim of humanitarian intervention is made, the balance between peace and justice must be assessed. Just because armed intervention would have been the right thing to do to stop the genocide in Rwanda doesn't mean the invasion of Iraq to topple the regime of Saddam Hussein was either a necessary or a proportionate attack.

The conflicts in East Pakistan, Kosovo, and Rwanda demonstrate how putting proportionality at the center of the world's legal order would make the planet a more just and safer place. In the state of the world in which we live, however, this is not going to happen in the foreseeable future. The history of international law is marked by the same gap between aspiration and achievement that has plagued the story of the rule of law from its beginning, and there is no reason to think that will change soon.

As a matter of both "legal realism" and "realpolitik" there is no more chance the judges in The Hague will forsake their national allegiances than their brethren in Washington or the scholars of Islamic law will betray their political stripes. International jurists are just as prone to bend the law to suit their own purposes as their ancestors in Baghdad and Bologna, London and Rome.

Given the frailty of the politicians' and the professionals' fidelity to the sovereignty of law, the hard truth is that the rule of law will only prevail when each of us personally submits to the force of reason and refuses to flex our own muscles. Politically, this means every citizen has an obligation to make his or her voice heard whenever the drums of war start to beat. There is no excuse for staying silent. Proportionality allows civilians to speak as authoritatively about the rights and wrongs of armed conflict as the politicians and the generals.

Political engagement by every citizen is a necessary condition for the sovereignty of law to prevail globally, but it is not sufficient. If its supremacy is to be truly universal, proportionality must also "govern" how each of us interacts with each other. We cannot reasonably insist our leaders follow principles we ignore. It will only be when each of us personally "governs" our own behavior with the rule of law that right will triumph over might and we can bequeath our children a world in which everyone respects each other's right to pursue their own destiny and live in peace.

Chapter Twelve

New Person

Law and Justice

The story of the rule of law that we have been following has the feel of a roller coaster ride: highs, lows, ups and downs, ending on a flat. It is a story of great expectations and repeated rejections from Hammurabi till today. Flashes of brilliant insight and inspiration set against a landscape of pervasive injustice and deadening repression. As I write, the prosecution of international war crimes is juxtaposed with the daily slaughter of innocent Afghans, Syrians and Yemenis. The climax, if there is one, is still to be written.

The Athenians made the connection between proportionality and the rule of law and then broke it by discriminating between people on the basis of their sex, birth, and wealth. The Roman jurists produced the Corpus Juris Civilis but insisted that the emperor was above it. Islamic scholars said sharia law was universal and eternal and then wrote it to suit the convenience of the guys. Medieval lawyers teamed up with absolute monarchs to persecute heretics, dominate women, conquer the New World and discriminate against Jews in the name of God and the natural order of things. The Americans put guarantees of liberty and equality into the heart of their constitution and then read them in a way that certified laws that were racist and sexist and tolerated a lot of physical abuse. The United Nations opted for judges over generals to settle international conflicts but the jurists they chose played politics and ignored the law.

In the future, when the history of our time is written, there will be an answer to the question of whether our generation was doomed to repeat the cycle of boom and bust that is the only pattern the law has known, or whether we were able to find a way that guaranteed law's place on top. We are part of a conversation about what is the best way to solve disagreements and settle differences that has been going on for thousands of years. Collectively, we can't avoid taking a position on how strong our commitment to the law will be. Whatever we do, history will pass judgment on the choices we make.

In the broad sweep of legal history, here's the challenge: How can we turn a great idea of justice and conflict resolution into an everyday fact of life? In our present circumstances, of unending cultural and civilizational conflict, the task is to find a way that will ensure law can provide an effective check against the forces of extremism and excess. What can we do, to invoke Thomas Paine one last time, to make law the king?

So far, advocates for the rule of law have come mostly from the top. The elites – philosophers, political leaders, and jurists – have been its greatest champions. Plato and Aristotle, Cicero and Ulpian, Bracton and Coke, Aquinas and Grotius, Madison and Marshall – all are legends in law's pantheon.

The problem has been that despite their many accomplishments, too often our political leaders, philosophers, and jurists have let us down. Even the greats have found it hard to measure up all the time. As we have seen, Cicero was inclined to jettison the law in moments of crisis when it suited his interests. Coke equated the common law with "right reason" but insisted only a professional elite were competent to master its "artificial" way of thinking. Marshall turned the American Constitution into a "government of laws" and then denied enslaved people and Native Americans its protection.

One of the lessons of the history we have followed is that we can't rely on others to establish an international order based on the rule of law. In a world of fundamentalists and extremists, a rule of law state is something we have to build for ourselves. To make law supreme, we need to take it out of the guilds and ivory towers of the professionals and put it into the hands of "we the people." Not until everyone makes a personal commitment will law rule the world.

The suggestion that the rule of law binds each of us, as much as our rulers, may strike some readers as more than a little odd. How can a concept that is intended to resolve conflict and limit abuse of power in government be relevant to how you and I live our lives? The answer, of course, is that to a large extent each of us is our own sovereign. In the day-to-day, nitty-gritty details of getting out of bed, getting the kids off to school, and getting ourselves to work, we set a lot of the rules we live by.

In everyday conversation we talk about "governing" our behavior in various ways, so why not by law? If proportionality is the ultimate rule of law, why not use it to solve all the moral dilemmas and personal conflicts we encounter every day of our lives? Moderation (read "proportion") in all things, excess in none, sets a standard of good behavior that is as pertinent in our private lives as it is on the public stage. A balanced, harmonious life is a way of defeating law's enemies from within.

The idea would be to build the rule of law into the fabric of society from the bottom up. As we have seen, this was the approach favoured by the Greeks. Plato adopted it when he wrote the *Republic*. His purpose in examining what it takes to create an ideal city-state was to discover at a personal level how to lead a just life. The book begins with Socrates defending the position that justice is one of the cardinal virtues along with wisdom, courage, and temperance (self-control). Indeed, he thought justice was the preeminent virtue because it kept the other three in a state of harmony and balance. Moreover, unlike wisdom and courage, which were more accessible for some people than others, justice was the virtue of the common man.

Plato thought a just life and a just society were based on the same principles. In writing the *Republic*, his thinking was that it would be easier to discover the meaning of justice if we looked at the legal structure of the communities in which we lived than if we obsessed about ourselves. We are more likely to be objective and impartial in deciding what it takes to live a just life if we are not distracted by the bias of our personal circumstances.

In following the history of the rule of law, we have, in effect, applied Plato's method and we have discovered a principle that offers impartial solutions to all kinds of social conflicts – from what people can wear and say out loud, to whom we can marry and what sorts of services we are entitled to expect from the state. We have found a legal principle that organizes relations within and between states that seems tailor-made for life on the street.

Proportionality is based on a concept of law that is easy for ordinary people to comprehend. You don't have to be trained in the law to know how the scales of justice work. Unlike the jurisprudence written in Washington, The Hague, and the mosque, this is a kind of law ordinary people can apply themselves. Just as in Thomas More's Utopia, everyone can be their own lawyer and resolve their personal conflicts on their own; all you need is the integrity and discipline to be able to look at a dispute from your adversary's point of view.

From our quick tour of legal history, we know the principle has a long and distinguished pedigree. Equating law and justice with harmony and balance, Plato prepared the ground. Although a distinct principle of proportionality did not stand out to him as one of the golden rules of justice, it certainly did to his most famous student. For Aristotle, like Plato, justice was first and foremost a matter of personal character, of being concerned with making sound judgments and knowing what is fair. The just man, he said, sought out intermediate positions between extremes; he avoided both doing too little and demanding too much.

Aristotle thought that proportionality was one of the fundamental principles of justice because it guarantees everyone gets what they deserve. Rewards and punishments should be based on the nature of the accomplishment and wrongdoing. Great honors should be reserved for outstanding achievements and punishments should fit the crime. What is proportionate is just; too much and too little are not.

Because of the time and place in which he lived, Aristotle didn't apply the principle of proportionality the way we do today. His big blind spot was in believing that some people (men in particular) were more equal than others and that slavery was part of the natural order of things. Applying the principle of proportionality in his world meant the shares and punishments that people got depended on their sex and whether or not they were free. By virtue of their inferior, servile status, slaves could not claim equal shares with their masters and women did the bidding of their fathers and husbands.

As we have seen in the last two chapters and in the example of South Africa's Constitutional Court, when caste and class are not allowed to diminish the value of a person's life, the idea of proportionality leads to very different results. When it is applied impartially, it treats the least powerful and least advantaged the same as those who are materially better-off and politically connected. Conflicts are settled so that losses are kept to a minimum. Judgments are rendered in favor of those who stand to lose the most if a ruling goes against them, not those whose politics align with the court.

Proportionality is a principle of justice that runs through recorded history from start to finish. Its roots go back to law's earliest moments and it still resonates with people who think about justice and fairness today. John Rawls, considered by many to be the preeminent political philosopher of the twentieth century, wrote a big book explaining why a principle like proportionality would be embedded in the basic structure of any society that treated all of its members as equals.[1] Rawls called his principle "maximin" (as in, "*maxi*mize the well-being of those with the *mini*mum"), but it operates on exactly the same logic as proportionality. It is just another way of saying "choose the least worst solution," which, as we have seen, is what proportionality purports to do. For Rawls, as for the first judges appointed to South Africa's Constitutional Court, doing justice means solving conflicts by ensuring the most vulnerable suffer least.

Stop Hitting

Now that we understand the way proportionality works in societies governed by the rule of law, we are in a position to return to Plato's and Aristotle's respective projects of clarifying what it takes to live a just life. Switching the focus from the public to the private will allow us to test their assumption that the principles that define a just society and a just life are the same. To see whether the principle of proportionality is as pertinent to our private lives as our public careers, we might begin by returning to the discussion we had in the previous chapter on the rights and wrongs of resolving disputes by physical force.

In international law, we saw that the basic rule is that force can only be used as a matter of self-defense and, occasionally, when it's a matter of life and death, in defense of others. Moving from the battlefield to the backyard, every parent faces an analogous question: When, if ever, is it right to spank or, as the English say, smack a child? Another is: What is our individual responsibility to come to the aid of people who will surely die unless we offer our help? What is the personal equivalent to R2P?

Spanking may seem like a trivial issue compared to questions like the legality of nuclear weapons and security walls or the force that can be directed against insurgent groups, but it is a topic that still sparks lively debates. When Adrian Peterson, the star running back for the Minnesota Vikings, was suspended by the National Football League for hitting his son with a stick, it was front-page news. The Council of Europe has criticized member states for not doing enough to stop parents from hitting their children. In Canada, lawyers for children's rights thought it important enough to ask the Supreme Court to outlaw spanking completely. (In another act of betrayal, the judges in Ottawa demurred.)[2]

One reason why spanking is still controversial is that, over the course of the last twenty-five years, the law and popular opinion seem to have moved in opposite directions. On the one hand, since Sweden set the standard in 1979, governments in forty-four countries have passed laws outlawing physical punishment of children by parents and teachers. Over the course of the last quarter century, the law has become much less tolerant of permitting force to be used as a method of instruction and correction. On the other hand, public opinion polls consistently report that a large majority of parents still believe that, as part of a balanced approach to discipline and punishment, spanking can be a good thing. In 2009, two years after New Zealand adopted a no-spanking law, almost 90 percent of parents voting in a nonbinding referendum said they still thought mild forms of physical discipline should be legal. The will of the Kiwi people favored tough love.

So far, the debate between spanking's supporters and detractors has mostly been a battle of numbers. Each side cites reports on the pros and cons of reinforcing messages of parental guidance with a physical reminder. Opponents of spanking argue it breeds a culture of violence and child abuse and amounts to a serious affront to the dignity of the child. Its defenders counter that studies show that, at the right time and place, it works. They point to Sweden, where, they say, after spanking was banned there was a rise of delinquent and antisocial behavior among youths who had never been disciplined physically. And they warn that outlawing spanking threatens the family by turning conscientious parents who believe in a traditional way of raising children into potential criminals.

The disagreement remains locked in a stalemate, with little prospect the two camps will find common ground. Like debates on the deterrent effects of capital punishment, both sides spend most of their time talking about the studies they claim prove they're right. As in so much of social science research, statistics can be cited by both groups to support their positions, but so far none have been found on which they could forge a consensus. The problem is there is some truth in what both say, so that more research is unlikely to provide an answer that everyone will find convincing.

Proportionality provides a way to break the deadlock. It sets up an analytical framework in which the good and the bad of spanking that we already know about can be weighed and compared. It allows us to assess the advantages and disadvantages of physical discipline in a way that treats the competing philosophies of parenting as equals.

Proportionality answers the question of whether spanking should be outlawed in a way that is fair to both sides. As we have seen in the last two chapters, the idea is to look for evidence of the parties' own behavior to establish how intensely those involved feel about the issue at stake. To settle the rights and wrongs of spanking, one needs to compare its importance for those doing the hitting and those being hit. Just as on conflicts over what people can wear and say, proportionality demands that the law rule in favor of those who will suffer the most if they lose the case.

So picture the scales of justice. On one side of the balance sits the child. From her perspective, spanking is obviously not something she would choose. No one wants to be hit – it hurts. The point, after all, is to cause pain. That's the logic on which this method of teaching is based. Hit the kid hard enough, and often enough, and sooner or later she'll get the message.

Moreover, the evidence on how hitting is treated in society at large shows that the harm the child suffers can't be dismissed as some trifling and transitory violation of their person. Even if, in the end, it can be shown that the child will benefit from being struck, in any other place than in the home and against any other person than a child, being hit with the force of even a moderate smack would constitute an assault. In all cultures and in every community, touching another person without their consent is regarded as a serious wrong. If you hit someone you can be sued, and in most places anything except the most trivial, inconsequential contact is a crime.

This universal condemnation of hitting is based on the belief that, in normal circumstances, each of us has virtually absolute sovereignty over our own physical being. Our bodies are private property. They mark the most basic boundary of our sovereignty over ourselves. In extreme circumstances, exceptions may be allowed. As we saw in chapter 7, vaccinations are an example of a justified assault that proves the rule. So, we now know, is torturing some terrorists.

Exceptional circumstances aside, laws against assaulting another person are typically clear and emphatic and admit of zero tolerance. Indeed, even those who argue that moderate forms of physical discipline can be an effective instrument of correction usually concede that spanking only works for a relatively brief period of a person's life. Smacking infants before they are capable of understanding the difference between right and wrong is obviously counterproductive, and hitting teenagers is widely understood as sending the wrong message.

On the other side of the scales, the limitation on parents' freedom to decide how their children should be raised seems to weigh a whole lot less. Parents do not have anything like the same sovereignty over their children that each of us has over our bodies. A parent's authority to do what he or she thinks is in the best interest of their children is already subject to extensive regulation by the state. Governments tell parents they must provide a safe and healthy home environment and a proper education for their children, and if they don't the state will take over custody to ensure that they do.

Even when they are going about their daily routines, laws impose all kinds of very strict legal obligations on parents, like restraining their children in car seats that meet rigorous safety standards. In many places, driving under the influence of alcohol is treated as a more serious crime if there are children in the vehicle. Even in states where spanking is allowed, parents can't use excessive force on their children and those that do can be prosecuted.

In a world in which governments already set basic standards of health, safety, and education for children, a law that outlaws spanking is hardly a significant restriction of a parent's authority to raise their family the way they think best. It leaves parents free to teach their children the values and lessons they think are essential to living a good life. Anti-spanking laws are all and only about the means, not the ends, of raising a family. Even as a restriction on methods of good parenting, it only outlaws one weapon from the large arsenal of disciplinary powers from which parents can still choose. Every other soft, nonphysical strategy of behavior modification remains an option.

As a matter of limiting the power of parents to raise their children, anti-spanking laws are small potatoes. The experience of countries, like Sweden and New Zealand, that have outlawed spanking shows that fears that making all physical discipline illegal will pose a serious threat to the autonomy and integrity of the family are unfounded. Where they have been passed, these laws have not led to a culture of nosey neighbors reporting every slap, let alone a wave of criminal prosecutions. In Sweden, when offences do occur they are handled by child welfare authorities, not the criminal justice system. In the end, the New Zealand government was not swayed by the strong expression of popular support for spanking because there was no evidence that its anti-spanking law had resulted in the state forcing its way into people's homes.

As straightforward and compelling as anti-spanking laws appear to be, it is important not to forget one of the most basic lessons law's history has taught: no rule is absolute. Legislation that limits the authority of parents to hit their children will almost certainly have to accommodate exceptional cases. Consider the child reaching to touch the red glow of a burner on the stove. How do you respond to the mother who says slapping may be the best way to convey the lesson (feel the pain) the child needs to learn?

Start Sharing

As a first step in bringing our personal lives in line with the rule of law, stopping spanking shouldn't be a big challenge. Spanking doesn't feature prominently in most people's lives. Even though King Solomon recommended it in his list of proverbs, no religion considers it one of the cornerstones of their faith. Even if you are an advocate of tough love, it is unlikely to be a great hardship if you had to give it up and make do with your next favorite mode of behavior modification. You lose the opportunity to hit your kids once or twice or even twenty times and then you get on with your life.

The next step, however, is likely to require more resolve. We will have to show a more serious commitment to the rule of law if we're to meet the personal equivalent of states' responsibility to protect those who are victims

of criminal repression by their own governments. It need not be too oner-
ous, but it will mean that most of us will have to hand over some cash.

The idea that states have a responsibility to protect victims of genocides and crimes against humanity, when it can be done without having
to make a huge sacrifice of their own and other people's interests, is an
example of what philosophers call the duty of an easy rescue. A personal
analog that Peter Singer, the Australian philosopher, has made famous is
the child drowning in a municipal wading pool.[3] Like the international
community's responsibility to prevent avoidable catastrophes, people
passing by the pool have a duty to rescue the infant even if it means ruin-
ing a new pair of shoes. Both governments and ordinary people have an
obligation to act if they are to do the right thing. In both instances, the
balance of interests is so one-sided, so disproportional, that it would be
wrong to do nothing and just watch a fellow human take her last breath.

Most of us will never face the sight of a child floundering in a wading pool. We do, however, see on our telephones and television screens
children dying every day from malnutrition and diseases that could easily
be cured with food and medicine that are beyond their financial means.
In fact, all of us have the chance to save the life of a child who is sure to
die for about the same price that we would pay for a new pair of shoes.[4]

The truth is, many of us could easily save more than one child, and if
we really believed in the rule of law we would. The number of kids who
are "drowning" is huge. More than twenty-five thousand children die
every day from causes that could easily be avoided. That's almost one
every three seconds! The World Food Organization has reported that
a child dies every six seconds from malnutrition and related causes. It
has been estimated that over half of all deaths of children under five are
related to inadequate nutrition. Another three million die every year
from malaria.

The numbers are numbing. UNICEF estimates nearly ten million
children under five die every year from poverty related causes. If you
add older children and their parents, the number nearly doubles. More
people die annually from poverty-related causes than were killed in any
year in the Second World War. By any measure, poverty is a force of mass
destruction.

In 2010, the World Bank put the number who live in extreme poverty
at 1.2 billion people. That's roughly 20 percent of the planet's population. All of these people live on less than $1.25 a day – what you and
I spend on a bottle of water or cup of tea. They lack access to clean water,
sanitation, schools, and health care. Their poverty puts them in the line
of fire of diseases that kill. At best, they face a life of extreme deprivation
and degradation; at worst, they die very young.

To compound the desperation of their situation, there is nothing most of the billion people who live in extreme poverty can do about it. The "bottom billion" of the earth's population are caught in what economists call a "poverty trap" from which they can't escape without our help. They are so destitute they need everything they can put their hands on just to survive. Neither they, nor their governments, have money to buy the medicines, dig the wells, build the schools, fertilize the soil that are needed if they are to lift themselves out of poverty and lead healthy, productive lives. Like the infant in the municipal wading pool, if we don't step in, they will drown.[5]

The facts of extreme poverty speak for themselves. So do the excesses of extreme affluence. Standing opposite the poorest of the poor are roughly the same number of people who live in the so-called First World, who can be called the richest of the rich. These are the billion people who, far from drowning in poverty, are swimming in wealth.

The statistics tell a story of greed and gluttony never before witnessed in human history. The billion wealthiest people on the planet consume roughly thirty times more than their opposite numbers who live at the bottom. It has been estimated that each person living in the developed world uses twenty times more of the earth's resources to sustain their style of living (the equivalent of almost twenty football fields) than those condemned to eke out an existence in the poorest parts of the world. United Nations' figures show that the income earned by the top 10 percent in the United States is greater than the combined income of the poorest 40 percent of the world's population. The per capita GNP (gross national product) in the richest countries in the world is an astounding two to three hundred times what it is in the poorest. In 2017, the charity Oxfam reported that the eight richest people on earth had as much wealth as the bottom half of the world's population (more than 3.5 billion people)!

There is so much wealth in the developed world that huge quantities of it go to waste.[6] Studies show that between 25 and 30 percent of all the food produced in the world (enough to feed everyone who goes to bed hungry) is thrown out. In the United States, it has been estimated that Americans pitch between 35 and 60 million tons of food every year. Studies put the price at between $100 and $150 billion annually. Just in terms of meat, fruits, vegetables, and grains, the value of what ends up in the garbage is almost $600 per person per year. In the hands of anyone living in extreme poverty, $600 would more than double their income.

Not only are most of the people in the developed world so rich they can afford to buy things they never use, their affluence allows them to spend billions of dollars on things, like water, that are available for virtually nothing. Even though most people in the developed world can get all the water they want from their kitchen taps for pennies a day, collectively we spend over $80 billion on bottled water every year. The average American spends $100 on bottled water annually.

By comparison, the price of one case of bottled water could supply a person in Africa with clean drinking water for five years. Giving up bottled water can save lives. Drinking from the tap, like resoling an old pair of shoes, is an easy rescue.

On any standard of justice, the gluttony and indulgence of people living in the industrialized world is a serious failing but, to concede a point that is often made, it is certainly not the worst. It is obviously not the equivalent of mass murder. No one in the developed world *wants* anyone living in extreme poverty to die. No one is actively plotting another person's death.

But while it is true that neglecting the welfare of the poorest of the poor is not as malevolent as homicide, we should not be distracted from the fact that it still is a terrible wrong. It seems worse, for example, than causing loss of civilian life in a military operation like those we considered in the last chapter. It is certainly no less of a crime. In war, as we have seen, some civilian casualties can be justified when they occur as part of a legitimate act of self-defense. No comparable purpose is served when some people die of causes related to their living in extreme poverty while others spend billions on their appearance and throw away much of what they buy.

The injustice of squandering so much wealth in the face of such extreme deprivation is compounded by the fact that most of what people earn in developed countries is the product of "social capital" like schools, hospitals, law enforcement, infrastructure (roads, communication networks, power supplies) that allow us to earn the wealth we do but which none of us "deserve." Those who live in the wealthiest countries in the world just won the birth lottery. It is estimated that 60 percent of a person's income is determined by where they were born and a further 20 percent by how rich their parents were. As Warren Buffett, one of the world's richest men, once said of his own good fortune, "If you stick me down in the middle of Bangladesh or Peru, you'll find out how much this talent is going to produce in the wrong kind of soil."

Historically, the world's wealth was more evenly distributed in the past than it is today. For most of human history, except for the few born to nobility, almost everyone was poor. In the early 1800s, the difference in per capita income between the richest and poorest countries was a factor of four or five to one. That, it will be recalled, was about what Plato thought was the limit of what a just society would allow. Today, thanks to the industrial and digital revolutions that have taken place in the developed world, the ratio is twenty to one and growing.

The billion richest people in the world are all beneficiaries of a global wealth the likes of which has never been seen before. Because of our inheritance, we are uniquely placed to eradicate poverty on the planet. All we have to do is establish a better balance in how we spend it. We must acknowledge the fact that wasting resources on ourselves that could keep others alive is an act of excess and injustice of appalling proportions.

Our circumstances are not that different from those of our ancestors who brought an end to the slave trade at the beginning of the nineteenth century. We, like them, have profited from a political and economic world order that is manifestly unjust. Ordinary people in both generations faced a choice: Should we be actively involved helping eradicate evil, or should we live in denial and passively reap the benefits (for us) of continuing to do business as usual?

The example of a small group of religiously inspired Englishmen with a keen sense of right and wrong sets the standard. Once they set their minds to it, it took the abolition movement less than fifty years to outlaw the slave trade in Great Britain and its colonies.[7] We have an opportunity to do even more. We can rescue a billion people from the chains of extreme poverty just by giving them what we pitch in the garbage.

So far, the position of most people in the world has been that even that is too much. Over the last fifty years, the developed world has shown little interest in bringing one of the great evils of our time to an end. During the last half of the twentieth century, the amount of foreign aid the developed world sent to the world's poorest countries added up to $60 per person per year.

Such callous stinginess is impossible to justify or excuse. If everyone were to give a few hundred dollars a year, the number of people living in extreme poverty could be halved in ten years. If we fixed each person's contribution on a progressive scale, like our income tax, no one would have to endure any hardship to meet his or her fair share. Living a just life would not demand sacrificing the well-being of one's family and children. It wouldn't mean having to live like a saint.

The top 10 percent of American families could do it on their own. Peter Singer has estimated that if those earning between $100,000 and $400,000 year contributed 5 percent of their income, and those earning over half a million contributed between 10 and 33 percent, more than twice what is needed to reach the UN's Millennium Development Goals could be raised. If the top 10 percent in the rest of the developed world did the same, there would be eight times what the UN estimates would be needed to reach its targets in the next five years!

Some people try to defend their way of life by saying they didn't cause the problems of the bottom billion, so they shouldn't have to do anything about it. On this logic, a person is only accountable for harm they cause, not for omissions and failures to act. They recognize it may be the proper thing to do morally, but they insist there is no legal obligation to contribute to the eradication of poverty because no one is responsible for the well-being of someone who lives thousands of miles away.

In academic circles, the distinction between acts and omissions has a lot of supporters. One of its greatest champions was Immanuel Kant. In the world in which most people live, however, the line tends to blur. Moreover, on the question of our complicity in the plight of the bottom billion, the claim is not true, and even if it were it wouldn't change what we must do to answer those who say our lifestyles are unjust.

As a matter of fact, the developed world does bear a lot of responsibility for the way the world's resources are distributed and for the inability of the poor to lift their heads above water. We pay huge subsidies to our own farmers and favor our own industries in ways that make it difficult for those in the developing world to compete. We also support and provide aid to corrupt governments that serve our interests but ignore the needs of their own citizens. Flawed rules of international trade and bad local government are major reasons why the world's bottom billion have been unable to escape the disease, destitution, and death that stalks everyone who is forced to live in conditions of extreme poverty.

Moreover, even if we were wholly innocent of any involvement in the circumstances in which the world's poorest must grind out their daily existence, we would still have a duty to come to their aid. The passerby must rescue the child who is drowning in the wading pool even if she wasn't responsible for the emergency or there were other bystanders nearby. Anyone who aspires to live the just life must do the same. The obligation is a simple matter of helping out others in desperate circumstances when there is no hardship to us. When lives can be saved for little or no cost, the principle of proportionality says everybody has a duty to act.

In setting the rules of daily living, the scales of justice insist on a measure of moderation and balance. Spending resources on things that we already have, like water, and throwing out a lot that we never use, is an obsessive-compulsive behavior that contributes to one of the worst inequities of human history. Refusing to give a little to correct a huge injustice is a serious wrong. It has no place in a life that professes fidelity to the rule of law.

History will surely condemn us for gorging and primping ourselves instead of giving what it takes to save children who are dying in circumstances that could easily be prevented. It displays an indifference to pain and suffering that will tarnish the legacy of our generation. Rather than balance and proportion setting the standard of the just life, our ideal will be remembered as one that exalts an infatuation and indulgence of the self.

Some people acknowledge that everyone in the developed world has an obligation to come to the assistance of those drowning in poverty but argue that this is a matter of collective not individual responsibility. Foreign aid, they say, should be provided by governments, not personal donations. Using tax dollars to rescue the poor ensures there are no "free riders" and everyone pays their fair share.

The problem with relying on governments to come up with the resources necessary to rescue people struggling against extreme poverty is that we know they won't do it. For forty years the United Nations has had a standard that governments should commit 0.7 percent of their GNP to foreign aid, but only a handful of counties have ever met it – Norway, Sweden, Denmark, the Netherlands, and Luxembourg. That's it. Even though it is widely agreed the number is fair, no one else has shown the resolve to make it happen. In fact, many industrialized countries give less than half of that and in some (including the United States and Japan) it's less than a third.

One way of combining the force of collective action with the logic of personal responsibility, while avoiding the inertia and mixed motives of government, would be to raise the funds at the office. The UN standard of 0.7 percent of GNP could be applied to corporate profits and individuals could give where they work. Unions, works councils, and employee associations could participate in fixing contribution rates for different income levels and in deciding where their money would be spent.

Not only would "giving at the office" ensure each of us takes personal responsibility for contributing our fair share to rescuing the poorest of the world's poor, it would also make it less likely that the aid that is given is diverted by corrupt political leaders and siphoned off to their families and friends. Aid could be directed to NGOs and community groups with records of proven results. Without being compromised by foreign policy objectives, the private sector is more likely to ensure aid ends up where it can do the most good.

Switch to a Balanced Diet

More sharing and no hitting are critical parts of a life lived under the sovereignty of law. Together they expand the space in which mental force replaces physical power in solving conflict and bring one of the worst injustices in the world to an end. As positive as such developments would undoubtedly be, there still would be something missing if this were all the principle of proportionality demanded.

If a just life only required us to stop hitting and being wasteful, it wouldn't warrant its status as one of our highest ideals. Neither calls for the discipline and effort that we usually associate with always trying to do the right thing. Just avoid a behavior that for most people is a rare event and contribute a little more at the office.

When thinking about what it takes to lead a just life, we typically imagine something more demanding and heroic. We picture someone who is able to weigh her own interests against the interests of others without putting her thumbs on the scales, even when something she cares about a lot is hanging in the balance. If proportionality is to define what a just life is all about it must hold us to account, especially when real concentration and commitment are required. It must force us to give up even our most familiar habits and creature comforts when they become excessive and over the top.

If a just life is organized around a principle of balance and moderation and an impartial regard for the interests of others, we can all think of times in which we have fallen short of the mark. When push comes to shove, it is hard not to be partial to oneself and subconsciously undervalue the interests of others. Especially when it's a regular part of our daily routine, it's easy to inflate the importance of our own circumstances and ignore evidence of excess.

Too easy, in fact. The truth is that for the vast majority of people who live in the developed world, denial of their extremism is a ritual event every time they sit down at the dining room table. In its eating habits, the developed world is on a binge of gargantuan proportions. It turns out that just about everyone who is not a vegetarian or vegan gorges themselves on a staggering amount of the earth's resources every time they dig into the next meal. And that's a lot of people. In the developed world, carnivores represent over 95 percent of the population.

Eating the flesh of other animals consumes stupefying quantities of food. To fatten animals to their desired weight requires mountains of grain (mostly corn) and legumes (mostly soya beans). Even a modest portion of the standard, all-American meal of meat and potatoes displays a measure of greed and gluttony that is hard to swallow. Sadly, almost no one is ashamed. Not even Pope Benedict XVI, who was reported to love cutting into a Bavarian *weisswurst* (veal and pork sausage) either unaware or unconcerned that such behavior violated two of his faith's seven deadliest sins.

Measured against the principle of proportionality, eating animals is immoderate and indulgent in the extreme. Eating meat means eating

(1) more than is necessary, (2) more than a fair share, and (3) more than can ever be justified given the destruction and devastation it leaves in its wake. Even modest portions are pretty gross.[8]

More than necessary: because eating meat essentially means turning a whole lot of artificially cheap (government-subsidized) corn and soya beans, which are fed to animals, into a very small amount of what is comparatively very expensive flesh.

It takes about 13 kilograms of grain to produce 1 kilogram (2.2 pounds) of beef. For pork, the conversion rate is about 6 to 1. Chickens are more efficient. They turn the grain they are fed into a delicious wing or drum stick at a rate of 2 or 3 to 1. Farmed fish are fed a diet of marine life that is also roughly three times their weight.

As a means of providing for our physical needs, eating meat is inexcusably inefficient. It would be much more responsible if we ate the grain and vegetables directly instead of feeding them to animals and then eating them. As a rule of thumb, an acre of land planted with cereals and vegetables for human consumption can produce ten times more protein than if it is used to grow food for animals. The ratios are similar for calories and the other vitamins and minerals we need to survive. On one estimate, thirty acres of grazing land that can produce five hundred pounds of beef can also yield close to two million pounds of lettuce!

In the jargon of proportionality, eating meat is not the "least drastic means" of putting a healthy and well-balanced diet on the table. (Unless of course, like the Inuit, you live in an environment where plant life cannot grow.) As a matter of social justice, the life of the carnivore can not be defended on the principle of providing "to each according to his need." Nor can it be justified on the basis that it is something we deserve.

More than our fair share: because the earth simply can't sustain the world's current population on the eating habits of the developed world.

Americans are the worst offenders. Collectively, they kill over a hundred million cows, pigs, and sheep every year. For poultry the number is a staggering five billion! On average, Americans eat over two hundred pounds of meat every year. Now consumers in emerging economies like China and India, with a third of the world's population, want their slice. The result is that meat consumption worldwide is skyrocketing. Per capita consumption has more than doubled in the last fifty years. It is expected to double again by 2050. The war against the animal kingdom has reached proportions of a global crusade.

It can't continue. The amount of grain and legumes it would take to put steak on everyone's plate is just not sustainable. Americans represent less than 5 percent of the world's population. If everyone ate like an American, the planet could only support 2.5 billion people (we are now over 7 billion). To sustain current levels of seafood consumption, the size of our oceans would have to double. Americans and others in the developed world are only able to gorge themselves on flesh that has been fattened on gigantic quantities of animal feed because everyone else has been eating a whole lot less, and a huge number – the bottom billion – are barely eating at all.

We are using more and more of our land for growing crops for animals that could be fed to people in the developing world who are hungry and malnourished. Our excessive eating habits contribute directly to the starvation and misery that stalks the world. Half of the land used for growing crops in the United States is planted for animal feed. Of all the corn grown in American soil, 60 percent ends up in feedlots and factory farms. Over 90 percent of soya beans are processed for animals. It has been estimated that the amount of grain that is fed to livestock in the United States could feed 840 million people on a vegetarian or vegan diet. That's almost the entire bottom billion of the world's population.

More than they need and more than their fair share, carnivores are guilty on both counts. On two of the most basic measures of justice – need and desert – they come up short. The proportion of the earth's resources they dedicate to their palates is impossible to defend. Only by switching to a vegetarian or vegan diet can a measure of balance be restored.

More than can be justified: because, no matter how deep the denial, the bad of eating the flesh of another being massively outweighs the tiny good it can do.

Meat eaters defend their habit by embedding it in our DNA. For them, even if eating meat is not necessary for our survival, it is part of the human condition. They like to point out that our teeth, digestive tracts, and even salivary glands are all designed, by divine will and/or natural evolution, to encourage us to devour the legs and loins of the creatures with whom we share the planet. Some even claim eating meat has contributed to the development of our brains and the evolution of human intelligence.

Meat eaters make celebrities out of their favorite chefs. (This may seem like a relatively harmless behavior but it should be remembered that the historian Livy thought the decline of the Roman Empire coincided with cooks achieving the status of stars.) They talk movingly about the important connection between animal sacrifice and our traditional religious and cultural festivals. Vegans and vegetarians, they say, would deny Americans their turkey at Thanksgiving, the French their foie gras at Christmas, and the Lebanese their lamb at Eid. Carnivores paint pictures of comradeship, communion, and conviviality with the calf and the capon at the center of the celebration. (Legend has it that the Romans created the capon – a castrated male chicken – as a response to a law that conserved grain stocks by prohibiting their being fed to hens.)

What's wrong with these images of divine inspiration and natural selection is that they are fatally myopic. Like Aristotle's claim that it was natural to keep slaves, they tell only half of the story. They hide the full picture in which these occasions of domestic bliss are set. They only look at one side of the balance.

Focusing on the joys and camaraderie of gastronomy and pleasures of the palate hides all the death and destruction that goes into putting this kind of fare on the table. Viewers are not allowed to see the extent to which the fetish and fanaticism of their culinary instincts degrades the planet and abuses billions of animals for the sake of an exceedingly transitory sensation of great taste. (There is a saying among food lovers that the banquet is in the first bite.)

To sustain the meat-eating habits of the developed world, the planet and all the animals on it have paid a huge price. Most of the meat that is eaten in the world comes from gigantic factory farms and feedlots housing tens and hundreds of thousands of animals, that have proven to be an environmental disaster.

In addition to all the corn and soya beans it takes to produce a pound of meat, to satiate the craving of the carnivore requires massive quantities of water and energy, results in staggering amounts of animal waste and greenhouse gases being spewed all over the planet, and huge tracts of forests falling to the chain saw. The industry that is necessary to support our meat-eating habits is a major contributor to global warming and a potential catalyst to the creation of new viruses and the outbreak of new pandemics, to say nothing of the degradation and destruction it visits on the animals who spend most of their lives crammed in cages in which they can barely move before they are shipped to slaughter.

The facts are a matter of record. Producing animal protein uses roughly ten times more energy than it takes to grow an equivalent amount of plant protein. It turns out that to grow all the corn that is fed to the animals people eat requires huge amounts of chemical fertilizers, which in turn use massive amounts of fossil fuels in their manufacture. To grow a bushel of corn uses the equivalent of a liter of oil; that's about 50 gallons of oil per acre of corn. Scientists have estimated that almost 300 gallons (1,100 liters) of oil go into fattening your average steer. The result is that feedlot beef uses between ten and thirty calories of fuel for every food calorie it yields. Even cattle raised on the range consume three times the calories they produce. No wonder even self-styled "conscientious carnivores" refer to these animals as "fossil-fuel machines."

The amount of water it takes to put a steak on your plate is even more shocking. Conservative estimates put the figure at about 1,500 gallons of water per pound of beef. (Others say the number is closer to 2,500.) Whatever the quantity, it's excessive. Producing a kilogram of animal protein requires between fifty and a hundred times more water than it takes to grow a kilogram of grain protein. A pound of beef requires fifty times more water than it takes to grow the same amount of wheat. More than half of the water consumed in the United States goes to livestock. It is on the basis of numbers like these that environmentalists are fond of pointing out that the amount of water that goes into raising a 1,000-pound steer could float a destroyer.

Not only does eating meat consume unconscionable amounts of the earth's natural resources, it leads directly to the dumping of unimaginable amounts of waste and pollutants on the planet. It is estimated that animals in factory farms in the United States produce a billion tons of excrement annually. That's five times more than Americans produce as a country. It's the equivalent of three tons (6,000 pounds) of manure for every American every year. A commonly cited (and more conservative) estimate puts the figure at 85,000 pounds of shit per second, most of which goes untreated and ends up in our lakes and rivers. According to the US government's own Environmental Protection Agency, factory farming is a greater source of water pollution than all other industrial sources combined.

And it doesn't stop there. Eating meat not only pollutes our water supplies, it is a major contributor to the destruction of the earth's atmosphere as well. In 2006, the UN Food and Agriculture Organization issued a report showing that farmed animals contribute more to global warming than the entire transportation sector. It is estimated that the livestock industry is responsible for almost 20 percent of all greenhouse gas emissions. Half of that comes from people's consumption of red meat. Dropping meat from your diet would do more to reduce the size of your ecological footprint than trading in your old car for one that is powered electrically.

The main villain is the methane gas produced from the digestive systems of the animals we eat. Methane is a very powerful greenhouse gas, 20 percent more destructive than carbon dioxide, and the number one source of methane in the world is animal agriculture. You begin to get a sense of the size of the problem when you realize that for every liter of milk each dairy cow delivers to your kitchen, she also burps almost a kilogram (2.2 pounds) of greenhouse gases into the atmosphere. The methane expelled in the production of each McDonald's quarter pounder (110 grams) creates the equivalent of 2 kilograms (4.4 pounds) of carbon dioxide.

The bottom line is brutal. It is estimated that carnivores are responsible for seven times the volume of greenhouse gases as vegans; that the average carnivore puts 1.5 tons more carbon dioxide into the atmosphere than a person who eats no animal or dairy products; and that Americans produce half as much greenhouse gas emissions from eating cheeseburgers as they do driving around in their SUVs.

As you add more greenhouse gases to more energy, more water, and more fecal waste, the scales of justice will eventually topple over. No matter how delicious, the fleeting taste of a ballpark hotdog or a veal parmigiana just can't offset the cumulative, long-term damage that is done to the rest of the world by sustaining ourselves on a regular diet of meat. The imbalance is simply too great.

For anyone, like the self-styled "shameless carnivore," who would like more proof before conceding the injustice and imbalance of his life, there is lots more evidence of other ways that meat-based diets do damage to the planet.[9] Deforestation and increasing the risk of pandemics are two additional costs of the carnivore's diet. Again, the science on both is undisputed.

Deforestation is the second-biggest source of carbon emissions after power generation. Cutting trees is like attacking the lungs of the planet. Trees are 50 percent carbon; cutting them releases all the carbon dioxide they stored when they were alive. The Smithsonian Institute estimates that land the size of seven football fields is being cleared every minute for raising animals and growing the crops that are needed to feed them. To sustain our habit, twenty-five thousand square kilometers of the Amazon rainforest is being cut down every year.

The link between pandemics and factory farms is also well established. Not surprisingly, feeding thousands of animals in overcrowded, feces-infested factories massive amounts of antibiotics to keep them alive creates a breeding ground for new drug-resistant pathogens. The World Health Organization has warned that modern methods of intense animal production increase the risk of super viruses like avian and swine flu. The flu pandemic of 2009, for example, was traced back to a specific pig factory in Mexico.

At some point, as the evidence keeps piling up, the only conclusion that can be drawn from balancing all of the harmful effects that meat eating has on public health and the environment is that every person who makes meat a regular part of their diet is leading a myopic and unexamined life. Despite their denials, they are extremists. The choices they are making do a great deal of harm and very little good. When you consider all the delicious tastes and smells coming from the vegetarian kitchens that feature Asian and Middle Eastern cuisine, the fleeting pleasure in chewing on the flesh of another animal can't count for very much.

So, unlike its effect on our styles of parenting and our relations with those in great need, if we take the principle of proportionality and the rule of law seriously it will have a big impact on the way we live day-to-day. In fact, it will challenge most of us three times a day. Every day. No more eggs and bacon. No more barbeque ribs.

Nor, it must be added, industrially farmed or commercially caught fish. Similar stories of gluttony and waste can and have been told about both. Fish farms suffer similar waste problems as feedlots and factories and contaminate the water around them. The World Wildlife Association estimates that Scottish salmon farms discharge twice as much waste as the entire population of Scotland. Antibiotics administered in intense dosages are also part of the production process and are recognized as major polluters and threats to wild stocks. To make matters worse, farmed fish are fattened on fish meal that has to be caught and that costs between one and two liters of diesel fuel for every pound of fish that we eat.

Catching wild fish using industrial trawlers is not much better. Over-fishing and waste are universal and endemic to the industry. In the last fifty years, populations of large fish – including sharks, tuna, and swordfish – are down by as much as 90 percent. By the end of the last century, North Atlantic cod had been practically wiped out. The magnitude of the slaughter is compounded by the practice of throwing overboard almost a quarter of the catch (of unwanted species) that is caught with the targeted fish. Commercial trawling is also a big user of fossil fuels. It has been estimated that it takes fourteen times more energy to catch fish than it takes to grow an equivalent amount of plant protein.

So it turns out that in a world that is governed by the rule of law there are no more steaks of any kind, beef or salmon – at least on a regular basis. Indeed, if truth be told, yogurt and cheese are off the menu as well. When it comes to global warming, dairy products are just as destructive as meat. On some estimates, together they account for more than 50 percent of the greenhouse gases caused by humans.

As spartan as the new regime appears, the good news is it can be relaxed on special occasions. There will be circumstances when dedicated carnivores can still savor the liver or leg of their favorite animal. At this point in the story, it is understood that, apart from its own authority, the rule of law knows no absolutes. All rules, including those regulating the consumption of meat, have exceptions. As we have seen, even killing is OK if it is a proportionate response of self-defense.

In the case of carnivores, we have already noted one legitimate exception. If you live in a part of the world, like the Arctic, where plant protein is not available, it may be necessary to kill and eat the flesh of other animals to survive. On a test of proportionality, it would be difficult to say the eating habits of the Inuit and Sami are excessive and unjust. In their part of the world, the natural laws of survival and a well-ordered life coincide.

The same goes for anyone willing to pick up their food after its expiry date from the dumpsters where supermarkets throw it out as garbage. They can give an account of their lives that is worthy of our respect. Freegans, as they are known, are simply recycling food that would otherwise go to waste. For the same reason, justice as proportionality comes down on the side of people who dine out on roadkill.

More appealing, perhaps, is the surprisingly strong case that can be made by connoisseurs of lamb raised on land that is unsuitable for anything but pasture, as is famously the case in parts of Wales. Not only is no harm done to the environment, the grass the animal eats would otherwise go to waste because we humans can't digest it. On the scales of justice, a juicy lamb chop in downtown Cardiff looks like a nice balancing act. For everyone except the animal in the pot, lamb stew looks like an unambiguous and unconditional good.

The animal in the pot!

The ghost in the plot finally makes its appearance. All this time we have been considering the justice of eating meat with hardly a word about the interests of those being eaten. Their stake in the discussion is obviously huge. The horrible lives of pain and confinement they are forced to endure in gigantic factory farms and feedlots have been well documented.[10] Their only consolation is that they don't have to endure it for long. Most are slaughtered when they are still very young so we can enjoy the softness of their flesh and the delicacy of the taste.

The lives of animals raised for human consumption are indecently short. Cattle that have a natural lifespan of fifteen to twenty years are slaughtered as adolescents at fourteen to sixteen months. Pigs live for six months and lambs one year instead of ten to twelve. Male dairy cows that are raised for veal are killed sixteen to twenty weeks after they are born.

The question of what weight we ought to give the lives of the animals that are extinguished long before the end of their natural cycle has no single right answer that holds true for everyone in all times and places. Some people will object that proportionality can't be applied when the interests of chickens and pigs are involved. In all the cases we have considered so far, proportionality assumed everyone involved was each other's equal. No one's interests were discounted or devalued because they were inferior on some moral basis or they came from a lower class.

However, when one set of interests belongs to creatures of other species, that assumption no longer holds. Even though animals have much of the same genetic makeup as humans, for lots of people, our human nature sets us apart, physically and spiritually, from every other living thing on the planet. Carnivores cite scripture and sages to support their plea that their appetites are only for "lesser beings" whose interests cannot be considered equal to our own. Even the South Africans, who debated the pros and cons, didn't think animals deserved the protection of their constitution.

Deciding how much weight should be given to the interests of those we want to eat is the same question that Plato and Aristotle faced in determining the legal status of women and slaves. It is at the heart of our own debates about the life of a fetus. Religious, scientific, and philosophical considerations are valued differently by different people. The results are not always what you might expect.

Peter Singer, the iconic philosopher of animal rights, for example, has only praise for conscientious carnivores who dine out on animals like Welsh lamb that are environmentally friendly and nutritionally efficient and that live their lives in a way that comports with their nature. Because he is a utilitarian, Singer isn't bothered by the fact that these animals will be slaughtered while they are still very young.

Singer thinks of the lives of lambs as a species, not as individual animals. For him, if a slaughtered sheep is replaced by a newborn lamb who would not have been conceived unless the first were killed (and who will be slaughtered and replaced on its first birthday), the total amount of "good sheep life" will be the same as if the first sheep had lived till it was ten and the new spring lambs were never born.

Not everyone will be comfortable with Singer's logic. For those who are concerned with the life of each individual animal, the lives of the ten lambs that were led to slaughter on their first birthday don't count the same as a ten-year-old ewe who dies of old age. They will say that eating meat is a blind spot as egregious as Plato's and Aristotle's excuses for slavery.

Proportionality can't answer the existential question of whether the value of human life and animal life are equivalent. It is a purely formal principle; a measuring device without any substantive moral content of its own. Like a set of balancing scales, it can only tell you whether a bag of feathers and a gold coin weigh the same, not what each is worth.

If you think like a lawyer, and reason the way the rule of law says you should, all you can do is to try to be consistent and avoid arbitrary distinctions. If, for example, you don't think it is right to eat a dog or a horse, then you probably should give a rack of bacon and a slice of Parma a pass. If the lives of the former count for more than the fleeting sensations of your taste buds, then so should the lives of pigs. To kill one and not the other is the kind of arbitrary behavior the rule of law is meant to suppress.

It's not hard to imagine other exceptions like Singer's. Meat eaten in celebration of important religious traditions involves a different calculus than wolfing down a Big Mac. If our drug laws and dress codes can recognize exceptions for important religious practices, eating meat as part of religious and cultural celebrations can't be all bad. Indeed, as Lon Fuller's case of the speluncean explorers is meant to teach (among other things), in extreme circumstances (trapped in a cave, facing death by starvation), it may even be lawful to eat the flesh of another human being.[11] Drawing straws to see who will sacrifice their life so the rest can survive can be defended on the same principle that justifies shooting down an airliner that has been hijacked by terrorists.

In the end, we are what we eat in more than just a biological sense. What we eat also defines us existentially. Even if we will never have to face the horror of cannibalism, three times a day, every day, we choose whether our sovereignty over ourselves will be exercised arbitrarily and unfairly to the detriment of others, or whether reason and justice will determine how we feed the beast.

Law and Utopia

The day when the rule of law governs life in all the dining rooms of the world, its odyssey will have come to its "hour of triumph." If law's authority knew no limit, its story would rank as one of the greatest epics of human history. Starting from 282 individual judgments, certified by Hammurabi, four thousand years later the rule of law would come to mean a way of reasoning that speaks to everyone; rulers in their positions of power and the ruled in their homes.

Along the way, we have seen law rid the world of a lot of injustice. The arbitrary and abusive treatment of women, gays, religious, and ethnic minorities has been arrested in many parts of the world, if not eradicated completely. People who are caught up in the criminal justice system are treated with more respect than ever before and the most vulnerable and desperate can claim access to the food and shelter they need to survive.

That's the heroic version of law's story, but, as we now know, it's only one part. In addition to our bad behavior in our dining rooms, we tolerate too many injustices. Too many rulers remain beyond law's reach. In many parts of the world, law provides only the thinnest veneer. Even in South Africa, the rule of law is back on its heels.

Despite all of its past successes, the violence that is the scourge of so much of our world makes it plain that law is still a long way from fulfilling its earliest ambitions. The inescapable lesson of law's pursuit of justice and universal sovereignty is that we can't rely on others to do the job. Law's history teaches that the elites of law and politics can't always be trusted. Even with judges as dedicated as those in Johannesburg, there is a limit on what they can do. If the rule of law is to realize its highest ambition, each of us has to sign up. Arbitrary treatment and abuse of others will disappear only when each of us stops ignoring the impact of our behavior on the world around us.

Thinking about what this means just in the narrow confines of our homes shows this will take effort. Making a personal commitment to the sovereignty of law is not a trivial decision. Doing justice, like all virtues, can be hard work. Governing our own lives by a principle of proportionality requires taking responsibility for how our behavior affects other people. As populations grow and the habitable part of the planet gets more crowded, living a just life means rethinking and recalibrating our relations with others. It means recognizing that, as lawyers are fond of saying, there are two sides in every case.

In our everyday lives, the rule of law requires everything be done in moderation and nothing to excess. "Defer to others when it means more to them than it does to you," would be the Golden Rule's new mantra. The current egotistical, self-centered rhetoric of rights would be replaced by a more balanced, less partisan mode of speech.

The scales of justice are the perfect symbol for law because they operate on a logic and method of reasoning that is easy to use and provides an infallible guide for doing the right thing. If justice is the virtue of the common man, proportionality is the principle to make it happen.

A world in which the rule of law governed both the public and private spheres would bring the curtain down on an era of violence, greed, and callous indifference to the suffering of others. It would turn the page on a period of our past that has been scarred by excess and hate. An Age of Justice could emerge from the ashes of a century that saw two world wars, unremitting local violence, and multiple genocides. Intolerance and extremism would become a spent force.

By acknowledging law's dominion over our own assertions of sovereign authority, we can write the climax of its heroic, four-thousand-year journey. Everyone claiming the right to do anything would be subject to its rule. No jurisdiction would be exempt. Every ruler, every king in his castle, would be bound. Both the personal and the political would be governed by the same overarching logic of fairness and balance. The scales of justice would come to rest in a state of perfect equilibrium.

If you think of law's history unfolding in the style of a chain novel, it is within our power to give it a Hollywood ending. The gap between the real and the ideal that has marked most of its existence doesn't have to persist forever. It could be bridged if everyone embraced the scales of justice and the principle of proportionality as the only way to settle their differences. When that day dawns, a just world order can become something more than just Utopia, an imaginary paradise that has no place on earth.

Equating the universalization and personalization of law with the perfect social order that the word "utopia" has come to represent will make some readers want to gag. Creating fair, harmonious societies by empowering ordinary people to master the method of legal reasoning will seem to some distinctly *dystopian*. And yet, this is precisely the way its creator, Thomas More, imagined it.

There were no lawyers in More's Utopia. When conflicts occurred, each person was expected to plead their own case. Without the involvement of paid advocates, judges concentrated all their efforts on the stories they were told, "weighing the facts of the case, and protecting simple-minded characters against the unscrupulous attacks of clever ones." In making up their minds, judges were not distracted by partisan lawyers doing whatever they could to advance their cause.

That More thought the world would be better-off without lawyers interfering in the resolution of disputes is quite extraordinary. After all, More wasn't just another rebel like Jack Cade or the butcher in Shakespeare's *Henry VI*. His whole life was immersed in the law. Like Socrates, he counts as one of law's true believers, willing to sacrifice his life to avoid betraying it.

More was raised by a father who was one of London's leading barristers and who, at the end of his career, was a judge on the Court of King's Bench. His own life in the law was even more decorated. When he wrote *Utopia*, More had already risen to the top of the legal profession. Eventually he became the lord chancellor, "the king's conscience," the highest-ranking legal officer in the realm. For More to paint the ideal world as one without lawyers was as much an act of professional treason as a validation of the people and the power of law.

It is possible, of course, that More didn't really think a perfect society would have no need of a lawyer class. It would not have been lost on his contemporaries that the word "utopia," which he coined, meant "nowhere" or "no place" in classical Greek. Scholars still debate how much More actually believed what he wrote. How, they ask, could someone who was very rich and owned lots of property, who reached the very pinnacle of the legal profession and became known for his fanatical persecution of heretics, advocate for the abolition of private property, the elimination of the legal profession, and the virtues of religious toleration?

Whether or not More was a crypto-communist or an early ecumenicist, there is good reason to believe that at least in describing how Utopians settled their differences, he meant what he said. As much as anyone we have met in this book, More had firsthand experience with the strengths and weaknesses of a functioning legal system. Settling routine, everyday conflicts between neighbors, merchants, workers and employers, debtors and creditors, and siblings fighting over their share of family property is what he did for a living.

At the end of his career, as lord chancellor, More listened, on average, to two or three cases a day that involved ordinary people looking to him to remedy injustices they had suffered at the hands of the legal system. The way cases came to his court would have reinforced whatever intuitive misgivings he may have had for a legal system controlled by lawyers. The mandate of the chancellor was to right the wrongs that had been done in the name of the law with the participation and collusion of the professionals. Moreover, by his own account, in rendering his judgments his only tools to soften the edges and eliminate the abuses in the legal system were the laws of reason and the commandments of God.

Having such intense, firsthand experience with solving conflict on the basis of fundamental principles of equity and fairness, it would have been natural for More to think that a world without lawyers doesn't have to be an idle fantasy. More knew his Roman law and would have been sympathetic to Cicero's idea of treating law as a subject everyone should learn as part of his or her general education. He took a strong interest in how the next generation, including his children and grandchildren, should be taught. In his own household, the children (including his daughters) were expected to master classical texts on logic, philosophy, and the "art of disputation." It seems certain More would have been delighted if he had been told that law was destined to become a standard part of the curriculum of the modern civics class.

In the end, of course, we will never know whether More really thought a perfect world would have no lawyers. What we can say for sure is that in the very near future people will be able to become as knowledgeable about the law as the Utopians, and so almost certainly will have less need for the services of professionals. With the advent of information technology and cognitive computing, the law that regulates people's ordinary, everyday interactions at work and play, with their families and friends, will become instantly accessible. With a touch of one's phone, it will soon be possible to find out what the law says to a parent who wants to disinherit a child, or to a neighbor who objects to a renovation next door, or to an employee who is bullied or harassed by colleagues at work. At a fraction of the cost it would take to ask a court to resolve a dispute, people will soon have the tools to solve most of their problems on their own.

In an age of machine learning and artificial intelligence, everyone will be able to find out what the law says about how the conflicts and disputes that are a part of their lives are likely to be resolved. Algorithms are now being written that can gather all the relevant cases and predict how the next one is likely to be decided. Like the ancient Greeks and Babylonians, ordinary people will be able to read the law for themselves. Where Hammurabi's subjects went to the city square to learn the law, soon we will be able to read whatever law we need to know at home on our electronic devices.

Although legitimate concerns have been raised about the transparency and due process associated with legal systems manned by artificial lawyers, there is much to be said in their favor. They give the casuistic method that runs through the whole history of law a quantitative dimension and a measure of impartiality that human systems have a hard time matching.

Rather than relying on a few paradigm cases to state the law, in the style of Hammurabi, information technology instructs the machine to consider every relevant precedent in determining how the next case should be settled. Due weight is given to all prior cases that have considered an issue, not just the ones favored by a particular judge. Outcomes are no longer influenced by whether the person hearing the case is a Roman Catholic or Sunni Muslim.

With universal access and understanding of the law becoming the new normal, a vital part of More's Utopia is the impending reality. It will not be long before we have the tools to extend law's sovereignty over every conflict that threatens peaceful and harmonious relations, whether it involves hostilities between rival states on the global stage or disputes with noisy neighbors in the backyard.

Although much work remains to be done, we are in a position to bring the rule of law to its "hour of triumph," just as Cardozo anticipated almost a hundred years ago. Anchored by the principle of proportionality, our legacy would be the realization of the highest ideals of Classical Greece: a rule of law that is of, by, and for "the people," living harmoniously in a world in which all souls weighed less than a feather.

Notes

1 Babylon and Jerusalem

1 Cynthia Brown, *Big History: From the Big Bang to the Present* (New Press, 2008); Robin Dunbar, *Human Evolution* (Penguin, 2014).

2 Marc Van De Mieroop, *A History of the Ancient Near East, ca. 3000–323 BC, Third Edition* (Wiley, 2015).

3 Raymond Westbrook, *A History of Ancient Near Eastern Law* (Brill, 2003); Russ VerSteeg, *Early Mesopotamian Law* (Carolina Academic Press, 2000).

4 Marc Van De Mieroop, *King Hammurabi of Babylon: A Biography* (Blackwell, 2005).

5 All of the important historical legal texts, including Hammurabi's Code, can now be accessed online. Two of the most extensive collections are Yale Law School's Avalon Project (https://avalon.law.yale.edu/) and Fordham University's Internet History Sourcebooks (https://sourcebooks.fordham .edu/). The leading academic commentary is G.R. Driver and John C. Miles, *The Babylonian Laws* (Oxford University Press, 1952).

6 More modern descriptions include Trevor Bryce, *Babylonia: A Very Short Introduction* (Oxford University Press, 2016), and Paul Kriwaczek, *Babylon: Mesopotamia and the Birth of Civilization* (St. Martin's, 2012).

7 Michael Coogan, *The Old Testament: A Very Short Introduction* (Oxford University Press, 2016).

8 Russ VerSteeg, *Law in Ancient Egypt* (Carolina Academic Press, 2002).

9 David P. Wright, *Inventing God's Law: How the Covenant Code of the Bible Used and Revised the Laws of Hammurabi* (Oxford University Press, 2009); N.S. Hecht, B.S. Jackson, S.M. Passamaneck, D. Piatelli, and A.M. Rabello, eds., *An Introduction to the History and Sources of Jewish Law* (Clarendon Press, 1996).

10 Robert Lingat, *The Classical Law of India* (University of California Press, 1973).

2 Athens and Sparta

1 Michael Gagarin, *Early Greek Law* (University of California Press, 1989).
2 H.D.F. Kitto, *The Greeks* (Penguin, 1951); Robin Lane Fox, *The Classical World: An Epic History from Homer to Hadrian* (Penguin, 2006); Charles Freeman, *The Greek Achievement: The Foundation of the Western World* (Penguin, 1999).
3 Douglas Maurice MacDowell, *Spartan Law* (Scottish Academic Press, 1986).
4 Paul Cartledge, *The Spartans: The World of the Warrior-Heroes of Ancient Greece* (Vintage, 2004).
5 Douglas M. MacDowell, *The Law in Classical Athens* (Cornell University Press, 1986).
6 Paul Woodruff, *First Democracy: The Challenge of an Ancient Idea* (Oxford University Press, 2006).
7 Russ VerSteeg, *The Essentials of Greek and Roman Law* (Carolina Academic Press, 2009).
8 Martin Ostwald, *From Popular Sovereignty to the Sovereignty of Law: Law, Society, and Politics in Fifth-Century Athens* (University of California Press, 1986); Mogens Herman Hansen, *The Sovereignty of the People's Court in Athens in the Fourth Century B.C. and the Public Action against Unconstitutional Proposals* (Odense University Press, 1974).
9 Adriaan Lanni, *Law and Justice in the Courts of Classical Athens* (Cambridge University Press, 2006).
10 Robert Johnson Bonner, *Lawyers and Litigants in Ancient Athens: The Genesis of the Legal Profession* (University of Chicago Press, 1927).
11 Paul Johnson, *Socrates: A Man of Our Times* (Penguin, 2012); Robin Waterfield, *Why Socrates Died: Dispelling the Myths* (Faber, 2009).
12 J. Walter Jones, *The Law and Legal Theory of the Greeks: An Introduction* (Clarendon Press, 1956).
13 Plato, *The Laws* (Penguin, 2004), 128.
14 Aristotle, *The Politics* (Oxford University Press, 1995), 124–7.
15 Aristotle, *The Nicomachaen Ethics* (Oxford University Press, 2009), book 5.
16 Karen Armstrong, *The Great Transformation: The Beginning of Our Religious Traditions* (Vintage, 2006).
17 Randall Peerenboom, *China's Long March toward the Rule of Law* (Cambridge University Press, 2002).

3 Rome

1 Anthony Everitt, *Cicero: The Life and Times of Rome's Greatest Politician* (Random House, 2003).
2 Cicero, *The Republic*, book 3.32.

3 Cicero, *The Laws*, book 1.19.

4 Francis Fukuyama, *The Origins of Political Order: From Prehuman Times to the French Revolution* (Farrar, Straus and Giroux, 2011); Ian Morris, *Why the West Rules – For Now: The Patterns of History, and What They Reveal about the Future* (Picador, 2011).

5 Christopher S. Mackay, *Ancient Rome: A Military and Political History* (Cambridge University Press, 2004).

6 Richard Alston, *Rome's Revolution: Death of the Republic and Birth of the Empire* (Oxford University Press, 2015).

7 Polybius, *The Histories*, 10.15, 4–6.

8 Tacitus, *The Agricola*, chapters 30–2.

9 Guy De la Bédoyère, *Praetorian: The Rise and Fall of Rome's Imperial Guard* (Yale University Press, 2017).

10 Hans Julius Wolff, *Roman Law: An Historical Introduction* (University of Oklahoma Press, 1951), chapter 2.

11 Russ VerSteeg, *The Essentials of Greek and Roman Law* (Carolina Academic Press, 2010), chapter 1; Wolff, *Roman Law*, chapter 3.

12 Fritz Schulz, *History of Roman Legal Science* (Clarendon Press, 1946).

13 Tony Honoré, *Ulpian: Pioneer of Human Rights* (Oxford University Press, 2002).

14 Jill Harries, "Legal Education and Training of Lawyers," chapter 12 in *The Oxford Handbook of Roman Law and Society*, ed. Paul J. du Plessis, Clifford Ando, and Kaius Tuori (Oxford University Press, 2016).

15 Wolff, *Roman Law*, chapter 6.

16 Gaius, *Institutes of Roman Law*, book 1.1.

17 Jill Harries, *Cicero and the Jurists: From Citizens' Law to the Lawful State* (Bristol Classical Press, 2012).

18 James Gordley, *The Jurists: A Critical History* (Oxford University Press, 2013).

4 Damascus and Baghdad

1 N.J. Coulson, *A History of Islamic Law* (Edinburgh University Press, 1964); Wael B. Hallaq, *The Origins and Evolution of Islamic Law* (Cambridge University Press, 2005).

2 Bernard Lewis, *What Went Wrong? The Clash between Islam and Modernity in the Middle East* (HarperCollins, 2002).

3 Among the best are Ibn Khaldun, *The Muqaddimah* (Princeton University Press, 1967); Albert Hourani, *A History of the Arab Peoples* (Faber, 1991); William L. Cleveland and Martin Bunton, *A History of the Modern Middle East*, 4th ed. (Westview Press, 2009); Bernard Lewis, *The Arabs in History* (Oxford University Press, 1950).

4 Patricia Crone, *God's Rule: Government and Islam* (Columbia University Press, 2004); Sami Zubaida, *Law and Power in Islamic Society* (I.B. Tauris, 2005).

5 The story is told in Noah Feldman, *The Rise and Fall of the Islamic State* (Princeton University Press, 2005).

6 George Antonius, *The Arab Awakening* (Simon, 1938), 64.

7 "Hama rules" refers to the killing in 1982 of thousands of civilians in the city of Hama by the Syrian dictator Hafez al-Assad. See Thomas L. Friedman, *From Beirut to Jerusalem* (Random House, 1989).

8 Mustafa Akyol, *Islam without Extremes: A Muslim Case for Liberty* (W.W. Norton, 2011), 69n15.

9 Popular, nontechnical introductions to Islamic law include Coulson, *A History of Islamic Law*, Knut S. Vikor, *Between God and the Sultan: A History of Islamic Law* (Oxford University Press, 2005); John L. Esposito, *Islam: The Straight Path* (Oxford University Press, 2005); and Hallaq, *The Origins and Evolution of Islamic Law*.

10 Shia jurists have traditionally put less emphasis on the duty to obey and some, especially in Iran, insist there is a right to revolt against tyrants and despots. For a short history of the role of Iranian jurists in challenging the secular state, see Roy Mottahedeh, *The Mantle of the Prophet: Religion and Politics in Iran* (Oneworld Publications, 1985).

11 For a very readable account of the method and structure of Islamic law, see Bernard G. Weiss, *The Spirit of Islamic Law* (University of Georgia Press, 1998).

12 Today there are many jurists who advocate a broader, purposeful approach. See Abdullahi Ahmed An-Na'im, *Islam and the Secular State: Negotiating the Future of Shi'a* (Harvard University Press, 2008); Abdullah Saaed, *The Qur'an: An Introduction* (Routledge, 2008); Akyol, *Islam without Extremes*; and Scott Siraj al-Haqq Kugle, *Homosexuality in Islam: Critical Reflection on Gay, Lesbian, and Transgender Muslims* (Oneworld Publications, 2010).

13 Fatima Mernissi, *The Veil and the Male Elite: A Feminist Interpretation of Women's Rights in Islam* (Basic Books, 1991), ix.

5 Bologna and Rome (Again)

1 Christopher Wickham, *The Inheritance of Rome: Illuminating the Dark Ages, 400–1000* (Penguin, 2010); Norman F. Cantor, *The Civilization of the Middle Ages* (HarperCollins, 1993).

2 R.H.C. Davis, *A History of Medieval Europe: From Constantine to Saint Louis* (Pearson, 1988).

3 Warren C. Brown, *Violence in Medieval Europe* (Routledge, 2011); Sean McGlynn, *By Sword and Fire: Cruelty and Atrocity in Medieval Warfare* (Phoenix, 2009).

4 Rosamond McKitterick, *Charlemagne: The Formation of a European Identity* (Cambridge University Press, 2008); Marios Costambeys, Matthew Innes,

and Simon MacLean, eds., *The Carolingian World* (Cambridge University Press, 2011).

5 James A. Brundage, *Medieval Canon Law* (Pearson, 1995).

6 Harold J. Berman, *Law and Revolution: The Formation of the Western Legal Tradition* (Harvard University Press, 1983).

7 James A. Brundage, *The Medieval Origins of the Legal Profession: Canonists, Civilians and Courts* (University of Chicago Press, 2008).

8 James Gordley, *The Jurists: A Critical History* (Oxford University Press, 2013).

9 Thomas Aquinas, *On Law, Morality and Politics* (Hatchett, 2002).

10 Albert R. Jonsen and Stephen Toulmin, *The Abuse of Casuistry: A History of Moral Reasoning* (University of California Press, 1988).

11 Kenneth Pennington, *The Prince and the Law, 1200–1600: Sovereignty and Rights in the Western Legal Tradition* (University of California Press, 1993).

12 Richard S. Dunn, *The Age of Religious Wars, 1559–1715* (W.W. Norton, 1979).

13 Paul Friedland, *Seeing Justice Done: The Age of Spectacular Capital Punishment in France* (Oxford University Press, 2012).

14 Stephen C. Neff, *War and the Law of Nations: A General History* (Cambridge University Press, 2005).

15 Judith M. Bennett and Ruth Mazo Karras, eds., *The Oxford Handbook of Women and Gender in Medieval Europe* (Oxford University Press, 2013).

16 Jeremy Cohen, *The Friars and the Jews: The Evolution of Medieval Anti-Judaism* (Cornell University Press, 1982).

6 London

1 Robin Fleming, *Britain after Rome: The Fall and Rise, 400–1070* (Penguin, 2011); Christopher Wickham, *The Inheritance of Rome: Illuminating the Dark Ages, 400–1000* (Penguin, 2010).

2 J.R. Maddicott, *The Origins of the English Parliament, 924–1327* (Oxford University Press, 2010).

3 Among the great histories of English law are Sir Frederick Pollock and Frederic William Maitland, *The History of English Law before the Time of Edward I*; Maitland, *The Constitutional History of England*; and Theodore F.T. Plucknett, *A Concise History of the Common Law*. All are available online.

4 W.L. Warren, *The Governance of Norman and Angevin England, 1086–1272* (Arnold, 1987).

5 W.L. Warren, *Henry II* (Yale University Press, 1977).

6 Geoffrey Hindley, *The Magna Carta* (Constable and Robinson, 2008).

7 Allen D. Boyer, *Sir Edward Coke and the Elizabethan Age* (Stanford University Press, 2004); Catherine Drinker Bowen, *The Lion and the Throne: The Life and Times of Sir Edward Coke* (Hamish Hamilton, 1957).

8 Carl Joachim Friedrich, *The Philosophy of Law in Historical Perspective* (University of Chicago Press, 1963).
9 1610, 8 Co. Rep 116, 77 E.R. 646.
10 Jeffrey Goldsworthy, *The Sovereignty of Parliament: History and Philosophy* (Oxford University Press, 1999).
11 *Entick v. Carrington* (1765) 95 E.R. 807, (Cantor 340).
12 *Somersett v. Stewart* (1772) 98 E.R. 499.

7 Washington

1 G. Edward White, *Law in American History* (Oxford University Press, 2012).
2 Bernard Bailyn, *The Ideological Origins of the American Revolution* (Harvard University Press, 1976).
3 Richard Labunski, *James Madison and the Struggle for the Bill of Rights* (Oxford University Press, 2006).
4 5 U.S. 137 (1803).
5 Jean Edward Smith, *John Marshall: Definer of a Nation* (Henry Holt, 1996); Joel Richard Paul, *Without Precedent: Chief Justice John Marshall and His Times* (Riverhead, 2018).
6 All of the Court's major rulings are analyzed chronologically in Laurence Tribe, *American Constitutional Law* (Foundation Press, 1999). A "people's history" of leading constitutional cases is presented in Peter Irons, *A People's History of the Supreme Court* (Penguin, 1999). For two general studies of the Court's role in American politics, see Robert G. McCloskey, *The American Supreme Court* (University of Chicago Press, 1960), and Lucas A. Powe Jr., *The Supreme Court and the American Elite, 1789–2008* (Harvard University Press, 2009).
7 *Dred Scott v. Sandford*, 60 U.S. 393 (1857).
8 *Bradwell v. Illinois*, 83 U.S. 130 (1873).
9 *Plessy v. Ferguson*, 163 U.S. 537 (1896).
10 *Buck v. Bell*, 274 U.S. 200 (1927); Adam Cohen, *Imbeciles: The Supreme Court, American Eugenics, and the Sterilization of Carrie Buck* (Penguin, 2015).
11 *Korematsu v. United States*, 323 U.S. 214 (1944).
12 *Adkins v. Children's Hospital*, 261 U.S. 525 (1923); *Lochner v. New York*, 198 U.S. 45 (1905).
13 James MacGregor Burns, *Packing the Court: The Rise of Judicial Power and the Coming Crisis of the Supreme Court* (Penguin, 2009).
14 347 U.S. 483.
15 Richard A. Posner, "Foreword: A Political Court," 119 *Harvard Law Review* (2005): 31–102.
16 Frankfurter and Black's hostile relationship is described in Noah Feldman, *Scorpions: The Battles and Triumphs of FDR's Great Supreme Court Justices* (Hatchett, 2010).

17 *Roe v. Wade*, 410 U.S. 113 (1973).
18 See, e.g., *Fisher v. University of Texas*, 579 U.S. (2016); *Obergefell v. Hodges*, 576 U.S. (2015).
19 428 U.S. 153 (1976).

8 The Hague

1 Stephen C. Neff, *War and the Law of Nations: A General History* (Cambridge University Press, 2005).
2 Cicero, *De Officiis*, book 11.34.
3 Cicero, *De Re Publica*, book 3.24.
4 John Kelsay, *Arguing the Just War in Islam* (Harvard University Press, 2009).
5 Arthur Nussbaum, *A Concise History of the Law of Nations* (Macmillan, 1954).
6 Edward Dumbauld, *The Life and Writings of Hugo Grotius* (University of Oklahoma Press, 1969).
7 Phillipe Sands, *East West Street: On the Origins of "Genocide" and "Crimes against Humanity"* (Vintage, 2017).
8 Telford Taylor, *The Anatomy of the Nuremberg Trials: A Personal Memoir* (Little, Brown, 1992).
9 *Military and Paramilitary Activities in and Against Nicaragua (Nicaragua v. U.S.)*, 1986 I.C.J. 14 (27 June).
10 *Legality of the Threat or Use of Nuclear Weapons*, 1996 I.C.J. 226 (8 July).
11 *Oil Platforms (Islamic Republic of Iran v. U.S.)*, 2003 I.C.J. 4 (6 November).
12 *Legal Consequences of the Construction of a Wall in the Occupied Palestinian Territory*, 2004 I.C.J. 136 (9 July).
13 *Armed Activities on the Territory of the Congo (Democratic Republic of the Congo v. Uganda)*, 2005 I.C.J. 168 (19 December).

9 Johannesburg

1 For a snapshot of how the most established and reputable courts have exercised their powers of review, see David M. Beatty, *The Ultimate Rule of Law* (Oxford University Press, 2004). For a collection of cases and commentary, see Norman Dorsen, Michel Rosenfeld, András Sajó, and Susanne Baer, *Comparative Constitutionalism: Cases and Materials* (West, 2010).
2 428 U.S. 153 (1976).
3 The case *S. v. Makwanyane*, 1995 (3) S.A. 391, is available on the Internet as part of the South African Legal Information Institute's collection of the Court's decisions.
4 *S. v. Williams*, 1995 (3) S.A. 632.
5 *Christian Education South Africa v. Minister of Education*, 2000 (4) S.A. 757.
6 *National Coalition for Gay and Lesbian Equality v. Minister of Justice*, 1999 (1) S.A.

7 These were *Satchwell v. President of Republic of South Africa*, 2002 (6) S.A. 1, and *Du Toit v. Minister of Social Welfare*, 2003 (2) S.A. 198, respectively.

8 *Minister of Home Affairs v. Fourie*, 2006 (1) S.A. 524.

9 The U.S. Supreme Court outlawed the latter in its celebrated decision in *Loving v. Virginia*, 388 U.S. 1 (1967).

10 The judges in Strasbourg have ruled that European states are under no obligation to recognize same-sex marriages (*Schalk and Kopf v. Austria*, 2010) and their brothers and sisters in Ottawa refused to give their opinion even when they were specifically asked for it (*Reference re. Same Sex Marriage*, 2004). France's Conseil Constitutionnel has upheld laws outlawing (2011) and legalizing (2013) gay marriage on the basis that this was an issue for Parliament to decide.

11 *Minister of Health v. Treatment Action Campaign*, 2002 (5) S.A. 721.

12 *Government of the Republic of South Africa v. Grootboom*, 2001 (1) S.A. 46.

13 *Soobramoney v. Minister of Health*, 1998 (1) S.A. 765.

14 *State v. Baloyi*, 2000 (2) S.A. 425; *Carmichele v. Minister of Safety and Security*, 2001 (4) S.A. 938.

15 *Bhe v. Khayelitsha Magistrate*, 2005 (1) S.A. 580.

16 *President of the Republic of South Africa v. Hugo*, 1997 (4) S.A. 1.

17 *Masiya v. Director of Public Prosecutions*, 2007 (5) S.A. 30.

18 As the Court explained in another of its rulings, *Coetzee v. Government of the Republic of South Africa*, 1995 (4) S.A. 631.

19 Alan Dershowitz, *Rights from Wrongs: A Secular Theory of the Origins of Rights* (Basic Books, 2009).

10 New France

1 *Roe v. Wade*, 410 U.S. 113 (1973); *Obergefell v. Hodges*, 576 U.S. (2015).

2 Samuel P. Huntington, *The Clash of Civilizations and the Remaking of World Order* (Simon and Shuster, 1996).

3 *Oregon v. Smith*, 494 U.S. 872 (1990).

4 *Corporation of the Presiding Bishop of the Church of Jesus Christ of Latter Day Saints v. Bishop*, 483 U.S. 327 (1987).

5 O'Connor's pivotal role on the Court is described in Jeffrey Toobin, *The Nine: Inside the Secret World of the Supreme Court* (Anchor Books, 2008).

6 In *Hosanna-Tabor Evangelical Lutheran Church v. Equal Employment Opportunity Commission*, 565 U.S. 1 (2012), the Court unanimously held that the Constitution guarantees religious organizations the freedom to choose their leaders without any interference by the government.

7 See, e.g., *Lawrence, Negal, and Solberg v. State*, 1997 (4) S.A. 1176

8 *Christian Education Association v. Minister of Education*, 2000 (4) S.A. 757, para. 51.

9 *Prince v. President of Cape Law Society*, 2001 (2) S.A. 388.

10 *Edwards Books and Art v. The Queen*, (1986) 2 S.C.R. 713.
11 *Alberta v. Hutterite Brethren*, (2009) 2 S.C.R. 567.
12 *B. (R) v. Children's Aid Society*, (1995) 1 S.C.R. 315.
13 *Multani v. Commission Scolaire Marguerite Bourgeoys*, (2006) 1 S.C.R. 256.
14 Brian Leiter, *Why Tolerate Religion?* (Princeton University Press, 2012); see also Marci A. Hamilton, *God vs. The Gavel: Religion and the Rule of Law* (Cambridge University Press, 2005).
15 A catalog of these restrictions has been compiled by the BBC in "The Islamic veil across Europe," available at https://www.bbc.com/news/world-europe-13038095.
16 John R. Bowen, *Why the French Don't Like Headscarves: Islam, the State, and Public Space* (Princeton University Press, 2007).
17 The European Court of Human Rights issued a useful summary of its major decisions as of October 2018 entitled "Religious Symbols and Clothing," including on headscarves in schools – *Sahin vs. Turkey* (no. 44774/98), 10 November 2005; *Dogru v. France* (no. 27058/05), 4 December 2008; and *Aktas v. France* (no. 43563/08), 30 June 2009 – and on face veils – *SAS v. France* (no. 43835/11), 26 June 14; *Belcacemi and Oussar v. Belgium* (no. 37798/13), 11 July 2017; and *Dakir v. Belgium* (no. 4619/12), 11 July 2017. See also *Achbita v. Belgium* (C-157/15), 14 March 2017, and *Bougnaoui v. Micropole Univers* (C-188/15), 14 March 2017, in which the European Court of Justice upheld the right of employers to ban all religious symbols, including headscarves, from the workplace.
18 Federal Constitutional Court (Bundesverfassungsgericht) Press Release No. 14/2015 (available online), a general ban on headscarves for teachers at state schools, is not compatible with the constitution; 1 BvR 471/10, 1 BvR 1181/10 concrete and not abstract danger to peaceful functioning of school is necessary before teacher can be prohibited from wearing headscarf.
19 *Abercrombie and Fitch*, 135 S. Ct. 2028 (2015) (in which it was ruled that the employee was not obliged to ask employer's permission to wear a headscarf); but see *Goldman v. Weinberger*, 475 U.S. 503 (1986) (in which it was ruled the air force officer had no right to wear his yarmulke when doing his job, as a clinical psychologist, in uniform).
20 *Eweida and Others v. UK* (ECHR nos. 48420/10, 59842/10, 51671/10, and 36516/10), 15 January 2013 (right to wear cross); *Hamidovic v. Bosnia* (ECHR no. 57792/15), 5 December 2017; *Lachiri v. Belgium* (ECHR no. 3413/09), 18 September 18 (right to wear headscarf in court).
21 See *Bikramjit Singh v. France* (UNHRC no. 1852/2008) (headscarves in school); and *Yaker, Hebbadj v. France* (CCPR no. 2747/2016), 14 November 2018); *Belcacemi and Oussar v. Belgium* (ECHR no. 37798/13), 11 July 2017; *Dakir v. Belgium* (ECHR no. 4619/12), 11 July 2017 (face veils on the street).

22 *R. v. N.S.*, (2012) S.C.C. 72.
23 Clark B. Lombardi and Nathan J. Brown, "Do Constitutions Requiring Adherence to Shari'a Threaten Human Rights? How Egypt's Constitutional Court Reconciles Islamic Law with the Liberal Rule of Law," *American University International Law Review* 21, no. 3 (2006).
24 See Timothy Garton Ash, *Free Speech: Ten Principles for a Connected World* (Yale University Press, 2016); Jeremy Waldron, *The Harm in Hate Speech* (Harvard University Press, 2012); Ivan Hare and James Weinstein, eds., *Extreme Speech and Democracy* (Oxford University Press, 2009).
25 Yale University Press was able to publish a thoughtful account of the whole controversy without reproducing any of the cartoons or other historical depictions of the Prophet Muhammad and without losing anything in the telling. See Jyte Klausen, *The Cartoons That Shook the World* (Yale University Press, 2009).

11 New World

1 Judith Gardam, *Necessity, Proportionality and the Use of Force by States* (Cambridge University Press, 2009); Michael Newton and Larry May, *Proportionality in International Law* (Oxford University Press, 2014).
2 Jeremy Waldron, *Torture, Terror, and Trade-Offs: Philosophy for the White House* (Oxford University Press, 2010); Yuval Ginbar, *Why Not Torture Terrorists? Moral, Practical, and Legal Aspects of the "Ticking Bomb" Justification of Torture* (Oxford University Press, 2010)
3 Elaine Scarry, "Five Errors in the Reasoning of Alan Dershowitz," in *Torture: A Collection*, ed. Sanford Levinsn (Oxford University Press, 2004); see also Kim Lane Schepple, "Hypothetical Torture in the 'War on Terrorism'" *Journal of National Security Law and Policy* 285 (2005).
4 Alan Dershowitz, *Why Terrorism Works: Understanding the Threat, Responding to the Challenge* (Yale University Press, 2002).
5 Igor Primoratz, ed., *Civilian Immunity in War* (Oxford University Press, 2007); Colm McKeogh, *Innocent Civilians: The Morality of Killing in War* (Palgrave Macmillan, 2003).
6 Michael Ignatieff, *The Lesser Evil: Political Ethics in an Age of Terror* (Princeton University Press, 2005).
7 Bradley Jay Strawser, *Killing by Remote Control: The Ethics of an Unmanned Military* (Oxford University Press, 2013).
8 An English translation of the Court's decision is available at https://www .bundesverfassungsgericht.de/SharedDocs/Entscheidungen/EN/2006 /02/rs20060215_1bvr035705en.html.
9 Thomas Cathcart, *The Trolley Problem, or Would You Throw the Fat Guy Off the Bridge? A Philosophical Conundrum* (Workman, 2013); David Edmonds, *Would*

You Kill the Fat Man? The Trolley Problem and What Your Answer Tells Us about Right and Wrong (Princeton University Press, 2014).

10 Thomas M. Franck and Nigel S. Rodley, "After Bangladesh: The Law of Humanitarian Intervention by Military Force," 67 *American Journal of International Law* 275 (1973); Martti Koskenniemi, " 'The Lady Doth Protest Too Much': Kosovo and the Turn to Ethics in International Law," *Modern Law Review* 65, no. 2 (2002): 159; Gareth Evans, *The Responsibility to Protect: Ending Mass Atrocity Crimes Once and For All* (Brookings Institution, 2008), 146–7.

11 The carnage is documented in Samantha Power, *"A Problem from Hell": America and the Age of Genocide* (Basic Books, 2003).

12 Luke Glanville, *Sovereignty and the Responsibility to Protect: A New History* (University of Chicago Press, 2014); Nigel Biggar, *In Defence of War* (Oxford University Press, 2013); James Pattison, *Humanitarian Intervention and the Responsibility to Protect: Who Should Intervene?* (Oxford University Press, 2010).

13 George P. Fletcher and Jens David Ohlin, *Defending Humanity: When Force Is Justified and Why* (Oxford University Press, 2008), 146.

14 Michael Walzer, *Just and Unjust Wars: A Moral Argument with Historical Illustrations* (Basic Books, 1977).

12 New Person

1 John Rawls, *A Theory of Justice* (Harvard University Press, 1971).

2 *Canadian Foundation for Children v. Canada*, (2004) 1 S.C.R. 76.

3 Peter Singer, *The Life You Can Save: Acting Now to End World Poverty* (Random House, 2009).

4 Jeffrey D. Sachs, *The End of Poverty: Economic Possibility for Our Time* (Penguin, 2005).

5 Paul Collier, *The Bottom Billion: Why the Poorest Countries Are Failing and What Can Be Done about It* (Oxford University Press, 2007).

6 Tristram Stuart, *Waste: Uncovering the Global Food Scandal* (W.W. Norton, 2009).

7 Adam Hochschild, *Bury the Chains: Prophets and Rebels in the Fight to Free an Empire's Slaves* (Houghton Mifflin Harcourt, 2005).

8 The subject of our eating habits has attracted a lot of attention in recent years. Among the most informative and entertaining discussions are Peter Singer and Jim Mason, *The Way We Eat: Why Our Food Choices Matter* (Rodale Books, 2006); Michael Pollan, *The Omnivore's Dilemma: A Natural History of Four Meals* (Bloomsbury, 2006); Jonathan Safran Foer, *Eating Animals* (Little, Brown, 2009); Jeffrey Moussaieff Masson, *The Face on Your Plate: The Truth about Food* (Norton, 2009).

9 Scott Gold, *The Shameless Carnivore: A Manifesto for Meat Lovers* (Broadway Books, 2008).

10 The animal rights literature is huge. Two of the classics are Peter Singer, *Animal Liberation: A New Ethics for Our Treatment of Animals* (HarperCollins, 1975), and Tom Regan, *Empty Cages: Facing the Challenge of Animal Rights* (Rowman and Littlefield, 2004).

11 Lon L. Fuller, "The Case of the Speluncean Explorers," *Harvard Law Review* 62, no. 4 (1949): 616. See also Peter Suber, *The Case of the Speluncean Explorers: Nine New Opinions* (Routledge, 1998).

Index